Using SCO™ UNIX®

Using SCO™ UNIX®

The LeBlond Group -
Geoffrey T. LeBlond
William B. LeBlond
Sheila R. Blust
Wes Modes
Ross Oliver

Osborne **McGraw-Hill**

Berkeley New York St. Louis San Francisco
Auckland Bogotá Hamburg London Madrid
Mexico City Milan Montreal New Delhi Panama City
Paris São Paulo Singapore Sydney
Tokyo Toronto

Osborne **McGraw-Hill**
2600 Tenth Street
Berkeley, California 94710
U.S.A.

Osborne **McGraw-Hill** offers software for sale. For information on software, translations, or book distributors outside of the U.S.A., please write to Osborne **McGraw-Hill** at the above address.

This book is printed on recycled paper.

Using SCO™ UNIX®

234567890 DOC 99876543210

ISBN 0-07-881641-6

To our mother, Patricia M. LeBlond.

—G.T.L. and W.B.L.

To my good friends, Dixie, whose unflagging interest in the project offered me encouragement, and the Ponkey, who was always willing to lend an objective ear.

—S.R.B.

To my father, Ron Modes, who let me dink around on his UNIX account so many years ago, and to my family, Karri and Sebastian, who made the whole thing worth it.

—W.M.

Contents at a Glance

Contents

Acknowledgments

The authors would like to thank the following people and organizations: Gwen Goss, who injected a friendly note into the publication process; Liz Fisher, for her understanding when we were running behind; Ilene Shapera; Madhu Prasher; Erica Spaberg; Lyn Cordell; Jeff Lieberman, for his diplomacy, his thorough technical edit, and his generosity with his time; The Santa Cruz Operation, and Brigid Fuller, for providing the SCO XENIX System V and UNIX System V used to produce this book; and DigiBoard, for providing the DigiCHANNEL multiport board that strung the office together.

Introduction

SCO (The Santa Cruz Operation) develops and markets UNIX System software for the PC. The Company has experienced phenomenal growth over the past ten years. In fact, since its inception in 1981, SCO has become the world leader in UNIX-based systems for microcomputers.

Perhaps one key to SCO's success has been their total-solution approach to the UNIX market. That is, in addition to a powerful operating system (XENIX/UNIX), SCO also sells and supports a wide variety of business-applications software and other software peripherals. Among others, SCO sells word processing, spreadsheet, database, and graphics software packages. Thus, SCO provides not only the core operating system, but also the applications that run on that system and take full advantage of its power.

About This Book

This book is intended for the beginning to intermediate UNIX system user. It contains numerous tutorial examples that are carefully structured to guide you through the process of learning to use SCO UNIX. For people who have some computer experience but little or no experience with SCO UNIX, the early chapters explain how to log on to the system, work with files and directories, and enter basic commands. The later chapters address more advanced topics such as using filters, text processing, electronic mail, writing complex shell programs, communications, and using MS-DOS within UNIX. Further, Appendix A provides both the beginning and inter-mediate user with a handy quick-reference guide to the more commonly used commands in SCO UNIX.

This book also addresses the needs of the system administrator. For example, Chapter 2 shows you how to install the basic system, and Chapter 12 shows you how to perform routine system administration tasks. Whether or not you happen to be the system administrator, you may want to read these chapters. They will give you a better understanding of how the system works and show you exactly what is going on behind the scenes.

Chapter 15 is a review of popular business software available from SCO. We have carefully selected a series of products that appeal primarily to the business user, and we take you on a guided tour of the features available in those products.

When you are finished reading this book, you will have a good basic understanding of how to install, use, and maintain the SCO XENIX/UNIX operating system. You will also know about the business related software applications SCO has to offer.

The Scope of This Book

This book covers two major versions of SCO UNIX: SCO XENIX System V (2.3 and earlier) and SCO UNIX System V/386 3.2. The first of these,

SCO XENIX System V, has traditionally been SCO's flagship product. Indications are that SCO will continue to offer XENIX as long as there is market demand for it. However, SCO has recently started shipping SCO UNIX System V/386. This new operating system represents SCO's platform for the future. Fully compatible with AT&T's System V 3.2, it offers unique enhancements from SCO. Of course, UNIX System V/386 is also fully compatible with its XENIX System V predecessor.

The similarities between XENIX System V and UNIX System V/386 are striking. However, because of the implications for the future, all of the discussion in this book is presented from the standpoint of UNIX System V/386. When a command or feature is unique to XENIX, it is so marked.

The primary user interface in UNIX is the *shell.* The two most common shells in UNIX are the Bourne Shell and the C Shell. Both are available in SCO UNIX. Although this book explores both of these shells, the Bourne Shell is emphasized as the primary command interpreter, except in Chapter 11, which focuses on the C Shell.

How This Book Is Organized

Using SCO UNIX is divided into 15 chapters and 2 appendixes. In general, Chapters 1 through 5 present introductory material, whereas Chapters 6 through 14 discuss more advanced topics. As mentioned earlier, Chapter 15 is a review of popular business software available from SCO.

Regardless of your skill level, you'll want to read Chapter 1. It presents an overview of the SCO UNIX system and provides a great deal of useful information. Chapter 2, on the other hand, tells you how to install SCO UNIX. If your SCO UNIX system is already up and running, you may want to skip this chapter.

For those who are new to SCO UNIX, Chapters 3 through 5 are designed to give you the basics. These chapters should be read in sequence. In addition, a thorough understanding of their contents is an important prerequisite for getting the most out of the rest of this book.

If you are an experienced SCO UNIX user, Chapters 6 through 14 will help you to further build your knowledge. These chapters deal with such topics as filters, text processing, printing, electronic mail, shell programming, system administration, communications, and using MS-DOS within SCO UNIX.

Chapter Summary

What follows is a brief description of each chapter in this book.

Chapter 1, "An Overview of SCO UNIX," presents the history of SCO UNIX and discusses the various components that make up the SCO UNIX and XENIX system software and documentation.

Chapter 2, "Installing the System," explains some of the concepts you should understand before installing an SCO UNIX or XENIX system. Together with the *SCO UNIX Installation Guide,* this chapter guides you through the installation procedure.

Chapter 3, "Using Your Account," is designed to acquaint you with your UNIX account and the basic structure of UNIX commands. You will learn about and have the opportunity to try some useful commands that allow you to get information about yourself and the system, control your working environment, communicate with other users, and more.

Chapter 4, "Files and Directories," explains the concepts of UNIX files and directories and demonstrates a number of commands with which you can create and manipulate them.

Chapter 5, "Command Line Fundamentals," introduces special UNIX symbols such as the pipe (I), which allows you to send the output of one command to another, and the ampersand (&), which lets you run programs in the background. These and other symbols greatly increase the power and flexibility of the UNIX command line.

Chapter 6, "Filters," discusses a number of UNIX utilities that perform useful and time saving tasks. A unique feature of these utilities is that their functions can be combined using the special symbols discussed in Chapter 5, so you can use them to manipulate data in numberless ways.

Chapter 7, "Editing and Text Processing," explains in detail how to use the visual text editor, **vi** and the UNIX text formatter, **nroff**. The **vi** editor is useful not only for creating ordinary text files, but also for creating programs and other special files. When you use the **nroff** utility to format a text file created with **vi,** you can produce professional, formatted documents.

Chapter 8, "Printing," explains how to print from within UNIX. Specifically, you'll learn how to use the printer spooling system to send a print request, cancel a print request, and check the status of the printer.

Chapter 9, "Sending and Receiving Mail," covers the UNIX mail utility in detail. This chapter tells you how to send mail to other users and other systems, and how to read and manage the mail you receive.

Chapter 10, "The Bourne Shell," introduces you to shell programming in the UNIX Bourne shell. It covers variables, programming, and modifying your Bourne shell environment.

Chapter 11, "The C Shell," introduces the many features of the UNIX C shell. It covers the history feature, aliases, and C shell programming, including variables and modifying your C shell environment.

Chapter 12, "System Administration," is designed to give new system administrators some insight into the various tasks involved in setting up a system and keeping it running smoothly. This chapter will also be of interest to ordinary users who want to know what goes on "behind the scenes."

Chapter 13, "Communicating Using the UUCP System," explains the many components of the UUCP System, which connects UNIX systems via phone lines. Using the UUCP System, users can transfer files between systems, execute commands on remote systems, and communicate with other systems.

Chapter 14, "Using MS-DOS Under UNIX," explains how to use the VP/ix package, which allows you to run MS-DOS programs from your UNIX account. You will learn how to execute MS-DOS commands and transfer files between MS-DOS and UNIX filesystems and diskettes.

Chapter 15, "An Overview of SCO Business Software," provides in-depth overviews of many business software products offered by SCO.

Appendix A, "Command Reference," provides descriptions and examples of the utilities discussed in earlier chapters, and of many additional utilities.

Appendix B, "Software Reference," lists the sizes of all SCO UNIX and XENIX operating system software and other major applications. If you are considering purchasing an SCO UNIX or XENIX system, you can use this table to determine what size hard disk you will need.

Conventions Used in This Book

Throughout this book, certain conventions are used to make the text easier to read and understand.

The Text

Within the text, when a term is first defined, it appears in italics. For example, "*User variables* are created and assigned values by the user."

Whenever commands, file names, directories, account or system names appear in the text, they are printed in boldface type. For example, "Backups can be done automatically with the **cron** command."

UNIX is *case sensitive*. Most file names, directory names, and commands in SCO UNIX are typed in lowercase. If all or part of a name or command appears in uppercase, there is a specific reason, and the name should be typed as it appears. For example, the file **Report** is not the same as the file **report**.

The Examples

In the examples used throughout this book, a typewriter typeface represents examples of interaction with the computer. Computer output is in a regular typewriter typeface, while user input—what the user types—is in bold typewriter typeface. For example,

```
$ lp average
request id is laserjet-534 (1 file)
```

In many examples a prompt symbol (usually $, %, # or ?) appears before a line of user input. UNIX displays the prompt to tell you that it is waiting for you to type a command. When you are typing input from examples, do not type the prompt character.

Some of the examples in Chapters 5, 10, and 11 use a character called a *backquote* (`). It is not to be confused with a *forward quote* or *prime* ('). The backquote is used for command substitution, while the forward quote is used to indicate text.

Notes and Tips

There are many notes, tips, cautions, and things to remember in this book. Notes point out things that are important and that might be otherwise overlooked. For example:

NOTE   If you type only one number as an argument to the **cal** command, it will be interpreted as a year, not as a month.

Tips point out shortcuts and provide insights into using SCO UNIX. For example:

TIP   Although a file name can have up to 14 characters in SCO UNIX, long file names can be tedious to use if you have to type them frequently.

Things to remember point out information that was mentioned earlier, but is also important in the current context. For example,

REMEMBER   If you make a serious mistake but don't know how to use a text editor to correct it, you can always kill the message and start again.

Cautions point out possible missteps that could harm the user or the system. For example,

CAUTION   Once a letter is sent there is no way to "unsend" it, so be careful what you send.

Differences between UNIX and XENIX

Differences between SCO UNIX and SCO XENIX are noted as follows:

XENIX   XENIX does not have forms. You must load different types of paper manually before you begin printing.

Keys

Key names, such as DEL or TAB, appear in small capital letters. When two keys must be pressed simultaneously, those keys are joined by a hyphen, like this: CTRL-d.

Throughout this book, we use the RETURN key. This key may be labeled either ENTER or ⏎ on your keyboard.

Some terminals may not have a BACKSPACE key. This key is often simulated by pressing CTRL-h, although it may be assigned to any key on your keyboard.

Learn More About UNIX

Here is an excellent selection of other Osborne/McGraw-Hill books on UNIX that will help you build your skills and maximize the power of this widely used operating system.

If you are just starting out with UNIX, look for *UNIX Made Easy* by LURNIX. This step-by-step, in-depth introduction covers all versions of UNIX and includes plenty of hands-on exercises and examples.

If you're looking for an intermediate-level book, see *Using UNIX System V Release 3*, by The LeBlond Group, a fast-paced, hands-on guide that quickly covers basics, before discussing intermediate techniques and some advanced topics. If you're using UNIX System V Release 2, see *A User Guide to the UNIX System, Second Edition* by Rebecca Thomas, Ph.D. and Jean L. Yates.

For all UNIX users with System V Release 4, from beginners who are somewhat familiar with the operating system to veteran users, see *UNIX System V Release 4: The Complete Reference* by Stephen Coffin. This handy desktop encyclopedia covers all UNIX commands, text processing, editing, programming, communications, the shell, the UNIX filesystem, the X Window user interface, and more. If you're using UNIX System V Release 3.1, see *UNIX: The Complete Reference* also by Stephen Coffin.

Why This Book Is for You

Using SCO UNIX is designed to make it as easy as possible for you to become productive with SCO UNIX. The book is task oriented and contains numerous examples that carefully guide you through the learning process.

If you are new to SCO UNIX, you will find that the early chapters are written in an easy-to-read style that quickly gets you up and running with SCO UNIX. Once you've mastered the basics, the later chapters in the book allow you to explore the program's more complex features.

For intermediate users, this book contains a variety of tips and techniques that you can use to hone your SCO UNIX skills. You'll find the chapters on filters, shell programming, system administration, and communications especially informative.

Whatever your skill level, *Using SCO UNIX* provides a much-needed preliminary step to exploring the SCO UNIX manuals that accompany your system. The manuals are often terse and difficult to understand for all but the most knowledgeable users; this book provides more extensive explanations and examples that pick up where the manuals leave you hanging.

CHAPTER

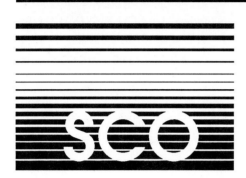

1

An Overview of SCO UNIX

SCO UNIX is a version of the UNIX operating system sold by the Santa Cruz Operation (SCO). In the last few years, SCO UNIX (and its predecessor SCO XENIX) has enjoyed a surge in popularity as affordable hardware capable of running the system has become available, and users have recognized its power and cost effectiveness.

This chapter presents a brief overview of the SCO UNIX system. It begins with the history of AT&T UNIX, and describes SCO XENIX and UNIX's relationship to AT&T UNIX. Then SCO UNIX's features and benefits are covered. The final part of the chapter describes the application programs available for SCO UNIX.

The Development of SCO UNIX

The development of SCO UNIX and its predecessor SCO XENIX is deeply intertwined with the development of UNIX as a whole. In addition, though, SCO UNIX and XENIX have their own unique history, which is also described here.

Early UNIX

The original UNIX was supposed to be a generally useful, portable, multi-user, multitasking operating system: nothing more, and—with the talented group developing it—certainly nothing less than a solid piece of software. But UNIX turned out to be far more than just software, and indeed more than a single system.

UNIX was conceived in 1969 at AT&T's Bell Labs by a group of researchers who designed the system for their own use. Prior to this project, the group was involved in a massive operating system project known as MULTICS, which was a joint development effort of AT&T, MIT, and General Electric. MULTICS was one of the first operating systems designed to handle several users simultaneously. Unfortunately, MULTICS grew to be so complicated and unwieldy that AT&T withdrew from the project.

Ken Thompson, Dennis Ritchie, and Rudd Canaday—all members of Bell Labs' original MULTICS design team—had devised a filesystem structure for their own use that they implemented as the original version of UNIX. They began using this version on a Digital Equipment PDP-7, a computer with only 18K of RAM (minuscule by today's standards), and then moved on to more powerful versions for the PDP-11 computer. Gradually UNIX spread throughout AT&T, and additional features were added to adapt the system to companywide use. In the process, UNIX grew in size and complexity.

Like most operating systems, UNIX was originally written in *assembly language*. The advantages of assembly language are its speed and its ability to deal directly with a computer's hardware; however, because hardware differs significantly from one type of computer to the next, programs written in assembly must be completely rewritten before they can be ported from one type of machine to another.

To make UNIX less machine-dependent, one of the developers of UNIX decided in the mid-1970s to rewrite the system in the C programming language. C was developed as a general-purpose programming language that combined much of assembly's power (such as its ability to deal directly with characters, numbers, and addresses) with the convenience of higher level programming languages (including the ability to perform logical tests, looping, and subprograms). Another principal advantage of C is its portability. Because C was and is available on a wide variety of computers, it's easy to port UNIX to other styles of machines.

Versions of UNIX

There are three kinds of UNIX today: AT&T UNIX, Berkeley UNIX, and XENIX. This section describes these different versions.

AT&T Versions   Over the years, AT&T has licensed numerous versions of the UNIX system. Initially, UNIX Version 6 was offered mostly to academic institutions, as a distribution of Bell Labs' research effort rather than as a product. Recently, however, UNIX has become more popular, and the release of each new version has grown more formal and is treated with great anticipation by the UNIX community.

The earliest versions of UNIX were named for editions that came out of Bell Labs' research department. For example, Version 6 was the first licensed version of UNIX, and Version 7 was the first commercially licensed version. In the late 1970s, AT&T changed its naming convention for new versions of UNIX to System III and System V. (System IV was developed but never licensed outside AT&T.) System V, the latest version of UNIX, was first introduced in January 1983. Since then, AT&T has added release numbers following the system number, as in System V Release 2 and System V Release 3.

Berkeley UNIX (BSD)   The University of California at Berkeley has been very active as a UNIX think tank since the late 1970s. Starting with

UNIX Version 6, it has produced many unique UNIX utilities and its own version of UNIX known as the Berkeley Software Distribution (BSD), or simply as Berkeley UNIX. The most recent version of Berkeley UNIX is BSD Release 4.3, and it is the dominant version in the university and engineering communities. It is also the version most frequently used by workstation vendors, such as Sun Microsystems.

XENIX   Because AT&T licensed the UNIX Version 7 software but reserved the UNIX trademark for itself, licensees could not use the UNIX name on their versions of UNIX. They were forced to come up with their own names, which met with varying degrees of success. Some names that emerged were XENIX, Vinex, Ultrix, Dynix, AU/X, and AIX.

In 1978, Microsoft coined the name XENIX for its version of UNIX developed from AT&T's Version 7 and optimized for Intel-based systems. Like its other operating system products, Microsoft did not sell XENIX directly to end users. Rather, it offered XENIX to original equipment manufacturers (OEMs), such as IBM and Radio Shack, who then customized XENIX for their hardware.

The story of SCO and its involvement with XENIX begins a bit earlier. As the story goes, Doug Michels had been a student at the University of California at Santa Cruz in the mid-1970s and hoped to find a job that would let him remain in that popular beach town across the mountains from the heart of Silicon Valley. Given the limited job opportunities in Santa Cruz, however, he was forced to take a job elsewhere. He became a systems consultant for TRW, where he was assigned the task of learning the UNIX operating system. At the time, TRW was just beginning to use UNIX as the foundation for its large telecommunications systems. The advantage of UNIX for TRW was that it insulated them from the perpetual problem of adapting their software each time a new operating system and new hardware were introduced.

The huge potential of UNIX was immediately apparent to Doug Michels, and he suggested it as a possible business opportunity to his father Larry Michels, an entrepreneur who had sold a credit-card verification company to TRW and was then a VP at TRW's Advanced Product Laboratory (APL). In particular, the opportunity to bring the powerful features of UNIX to microcomputers seemed promising to the two. In 1979, they transformed APL into what is now the Santa Cruz Operation.

In 1981, SCO joined forces with Microsoft to further develop and market XENIX. SCO's timing couldn't have been better; Microsoft was becoming increasingly consumed by its DOS development and welcomed a strategic partner who could take XENIX and run with it. Microsoft and SCO signed an exclusive joint agreement for the cooperative development and marketing of XENIX and XENIX-related technologies.

Here are some subsequent key events in the evolution of XENIX:

- In 1983, SCO and Microsoft introduced the first XENIX operating system and XENIX-based applications for the Intel 8088 and 8086 PC environments to be made available directly to end users.

- In 1985, SCO and Microsoft introduced SCO XENIX System V for the 80286 environment.

- In 1987, Microsoft and SCO delivered SCO XENIX System V as the first multiuser operating system for 80386-based PCs.

Today, XENIX System V Release 2.3 is available for industry standard 80286- and 80386-based systems and for Micro Channel machines (IBM PS/2s and compatibles). XENIX System V has three parts, each sold separately.

- The operating system, with a full set of utilities to perform system administration, edit files, run applications, and send and receive electronic mail

- A development system, with all the tools necessary to write C and assembly language programs (see "The Development System" later in this chapter for details)

- A text processing system, which includes the **nroff** text formatters (see "Text Processing" later in this chapter for more information)

In addition, SCO offers a variety of separately packaged business applications (see "SCO Business Applications" later in this chapter).

To optimize XENIX for Intel-based systems, XENIX offers several enhancements not found in standard AT&T UNIX. Here are some examples:

- Support for all leading floppy disk formats and tape drives

- Support for EGA and VGA monitors

- Mouse support

- Enhanced memory management optimized for Intel-based PCs

- Device drivers for many types of standard (and nonstandard) PC hardware, including SCSI and ESDI disk controllers

Enter SCO UNIX

In 1989, sensing the need for greater compatibility with AT&T System V, SCO and Microsoft released SCO UNIX System V/386 Release 3.2. This version of UNIX offers true binary compatibility with AT&T UNIX System V. In other words, *all* programs capable of running under AT&T UNIX System V can also run without modification under SCO UNIX System V/386.

SCO UNIX System V/386 is available for 80386- and 80486-based systems using all the most popular architectures, such as

- Industry Standard (ISA)

- Extended Industry Standard (EISA)

- Micro Channel (MCA)

Due to AT&T's recent loosening of the UNIX trademark, SCO decided in August 1989 to use the name SCO UNIX in favor of XENIX on all of its future products. In early 1989, Microsoft purchased a 20 percent stake in SCO, formalizing their long-standing relationship.

SCO UNIX System/386 brings a number of enhancements to the SCO System V family of products. Some of the more prominent ones are

- *POSIX conformance* The Institute of Electrical and Electronic Engineers (IEEE) has developed the portable operating system standard (POSIX), which establishes a standard set of system calls and library routines for UNIX. SCO UNIX System V conforms to the latest POSIX standard (P10003.1) with only minor exceptions.

- *X/Open conformance* The X/Open specification is published by X/Open, and covers systems and application software, including language and database systems. SCO's entire product line is compatible with the X/Open specification, ensuring compatibility with international markets.

- *Enhanced security* SCO UNIX runs as a "trusted" system in accordance with guidelines published by the Department of Defense. (The system has facilities to run at C2 security level and beyond.)

- *The Acer Fast File System (AFS)* This filesystem offers as much as a 600 percent increase in disk throughput compared to other filesystems. (SCO licensed AFS from Acer America Corporation, a maker of several popular high-end 80386-based systems.)

- *Additional device drivers* SCO has added support for a variety of standard PC peripherals.

Which SCO System Is Best?

Which SCO system is best for you depends on your equipment and your needs. Here are some guidelines for choosing the appropriate system:

- SCO XENIX 286 is for the installed base of 80286-based systems. If you have an 80286 system on which you want to run the operating system, this is your only choice, and it is a good one.

- SCO XENIX 386 is targeted to those who want to take full advantage of the 80386 processor's capabilities, yet retain XENIX's compact size and speed. SCO XENIX 386 offers the additional advantage of having been fine-tuned for several years.

- SCO UNIX System V/386 is for those who want the most advanced features, standards conformance, and security. On the other hand, SCO UNIX is not as fast as SCO XENIX and requires substantially greater system resources (additional RAM and hard disk space) than does SCO XENIX. See Chapter 2, "Installing the System," for more information on system requirements.

SCO UNIX Features and Benefits

SCO UNIX offers a dynamic blend of file and record locking, sophisticated user security, multitasking, advanced electronic mail and communications, networking, and remote file sharing. While other systems, such as OS/2, offer similar capabilities, SCO UNIX is especially good at making all these features work together efficiently and smoothly on Intel-based systems. The sections that follow describe many of these important features and benefits in detail.

Inexpensive and Diverse Hardware

The market for SCO XENIX and UNIX has grown in recent years, partly due to their availability on Intel 80286- and 80386-based systems. The low cost and easy availability of these systems and the variety of peripherals available for them can mean substantial savings.

In addition, many observers believe that the Intel 80386 chip has done more to advance the SCO XENIX and UNIX operating systems than any other single improvement in hardware. By exploiting the virtual 8086 mode of the 80386 chip, SCO XENIX 386 and SCO UNIX System V/386 take full advantage of the chip's 32-bit processing power—its raw speed and huge address space.

SCO UNIX on 80386-based PCs brings to the desktop power that rivals minicomputers at a fraction of the cost. Whereas a 15-terminal minicomputer system costs in the neighborhood of $200,000 in the 1970s, a similar

80386-based PC system may cost as little as $15,000 today. Single-user systems are available for less than $5,000, making UNIX by far the most economical multiuser system.

Multiuser and Multitasking

One of SCO UNIX's major advantages is that it was designed from the ground up as a *multiuser* operating system. In a traditional SCO UNIX system, a single computer with multiple users in a time-shared system does all the work for a number of "dumb" terminals, that is, terminals that provide little or none of their own processing power but rely for processing on the computer to which they are linked. (On the other extreme are computer workstations that do a great deal of their own local processing in a distributed processing environment.) As a multiuser system, UNIX supports built-in protection schemes such as passwords and file permissions. This allows a group of users to have individual accounts, each with their own home directory for easy access.

As a *multitasking* operating system, SCO UNIX can support many programs running at the same time on the same computer. It lets you *run* several programs simultaneously, not just keep them active. This means, for example, that in the midst of running an application program such as a spreadsheet, you can launch another application such as a word processor to draft a letter, all the while receiving electronic mail without any interruption of your work.

Hierarchical File Structure

In a multiuser environment, the number of files can multiply quickly. SCO UNIX's hierarchical file structure lets users group files in a coherent and accessible fashion. The file structure resembles an inverted tree whose trunk is the root directory. Other directories branch from the root directory, with each directory containing one or more files. Grouping files in this way makes it easy to locate them and perform operations on them. UNIX's file structure has become the foundation for many other operating systems, including MS-DOS and OS/2 for IBM PCs. Chapter 4, "Files and Directories," covers UNIX's hierarchical file structure in detail.

Utilities

In addition to the operating system itself, SCO UNIX provides a host of built-in commands, often called *utilities*, or *tools*. These tools are executable programs written with the idea that each tool should do one job well. In addition, the output from one utility is expected to be the input for another.

The advantage of the tools approach is its flexibility. It allows you to customize your environment by combining separate programs to do specific jobs. The UNIX utilities are discussed throughout this book. Chapter 3, "Using Your Account," and Chapter 5, "Command Line Fundamentals," provide introductions to these tools.

I/O Redirection and Pipes

By default, SCO UNIX displays the output of most commands on the screen. For example, if you use the **ls** command, which lists the contents of a directory, UNIX displays those contents on the screen. You can have UNIX direct output to a file, however, by using I/O (input/output) redirection. *I/O redirection* simply means reassigning the source of a command or program's input and the destination of its output.

Piping is a special form of I/O redirection that lets you make the output from one command or program become the input to another. Like UNIX's hierarchical file structure, I/O redirection and piping have also become part of other operating systems. See Chapter 5, "Command Line Fundamentals," for more on these topics.

Shells

A *shell* is a command interpreter that controls the interaction between the user and the kernel. (The *kernel* is the core UNIX program that serves as an interface between the hardware and the operating system.) The two shells that are bundled with SCO UNIX are the Bourne Shell and the C Shell. See Chapter 10, "The Bourne Shell," and Chapter 11, "The C Shell," for more information on shells.

In addition to interpreting commands that you type from the keyboard, shells can also interpret commands that are stored in a file. When you store commands in a file, that file is known as a *shell script*. The commands you can place in a shell script can be selected from among the many utility programs UNIX provides. They can also be any of the special flow of control commands the shell offers for controlling the order in which commands are executed in the shell script. For example, the Bourne shell offers the **for** command, which lets you execute a group of commands a specified number of times. By using flow of control commands in a shell script, you can create a variety of sophisticated application programs.

Text Processing

SCO XENIX and UNIX offer a comprehensive set of tools for creating, editing, and formatting documents. These are the same tools that are found in almost all UNIX systems. The following sections describe these text processing utilities.

 NOTE   You may find it easier to use a word processor instead of the UNIX text processing tools described here. There are two word processors available for SCO XENIX and UNIX systems: SCO Lyrix and Microsoft Word. See "SCO Business Applications" later in this chapter for information on these word processors.

The vi Editor   The original editor for UNIX was **ed**, a simple line-oriented editor that accepts the editing commands you enter and performs the requested operation on the contents of a particular line or group of lines within a text file. Although the **ed** utility is offered on all UNIX systems, it is rarely used today because a superior editor, **vi**, is widely available.

The **vi** (for visual) editor is an interactive, full-screen program that is the most popular editor among UNIX users today. (The **vi** editor is bundled with the SCO XENIX and UNIX operating systems.) As a full-screen editor, **vi** provides a window onto your text file, which shows approximately 20 lines of text at a time. To edit text in **vi**, you simply move the cursor around the window using single-character commands. After positioning the cursor at a chosen spot within the text file, you use **vi**'s editing commands to insert, delete, and change text according to your needs. You can also use other editing commands to affect groups of lines within the document or the document as a whole. See Chapter 7, "Editing and Text Processing," for a more thorough description of **vi**.

The nroff Text Formatting Tool   After creating a document with **vi**, the next step is to format it for printing using the **nroff** text formatter. With **nroff**, you can control many different aspects of your document's appearance, including text justification, line spacing, page length, line indention, and page headers and footers.

You format a document by using an editor to place formatting commands within the text. The **nroff** utility interprets any text that begins with a period in the first column of an input line as a command. For example, the command **.ls 2** within your input file instructs **nroff** to double-space your document.

The **nroff** utility provides sets of macros for controlling your output. A *macro* is a set of ready-made functions that let you perform with a few simple commands tasks that would otherwise take several **nroff** commands to accomplish. See Chapter 7 for more information on the **nroff** text formatting utility and its related macros.

 NOTE   The **nroff** utility is part of the SCO XENIX Text Processing System, which you must purchase separately. Your system may or may not include the Text Processing System. What's more, at the time of this writing, SCO does not offer **nroff** (or any other text formatter) for SCO UNIX. If you want this utility for your system, you must purchase it from a third-party vendor (see "Third-Party Products" later in this chapter).

Mail

SCO UNIX includes powerful electronic mail capabilities. Each user on a system has a *mailbox* to receive incoming mail. The **mail** utility enables you to send and receive electronic mail from different mailboxes.

To send mail to another user on the same SCO UNIX system, you just need to know the other user's account name. To send mail to a user on another UNIX system, you need to know that user's system or network address. Either way, once you have an appropriate address, you can easily send a message to another user, even if that user is across the country or around the world. Chapter 9, "Sending and Receiving Mail," covers electronic mail in detail.

The Development System

SCO UNIX offers a powerful software development environment that you can use to create your own C and assembly language programs. The required tools are part of the SCO XENIX or UNIX Development System, which you must purchase separately from the base operating system. Microsoft and SCO have collaborated to make the Development System particularly rich in features. It includes both the Microsoft and AT&T C compilers. Microsoft's CodeView debugger and MASM macro assembler are also part of the Development System, as are SCO CGI (a powerful graphics interface development system) and libraries for cross development of software for XENIX, DOS, and OS/2 programs. Because each tool in the Development System could easily be the subject of a separate book, these tools are not covered here.

Linking to Other Systems

One of SCO UNIX's great strengths is its system-to-system communications. In particular, the UUCP system is especially handy for connecting UNIX systems to exchange files and electronic mail over ordinary phone lines. You can also use the UUCP system to execute commands remotely on other UNIX systems and communicate interactively with other UNIX and non-UNIX systems. See Chapter 13, "Communicating Using the UUCP System," for more details.

Besides the UUCP system, which comes with the base operating system, SCO also provides powerful communications and networking software that you can purchase separately. For example, SCO offers a TCP/IP (Transmission Control Protocol/Internet Protocol) product for building high-performance Ethernet network connections between UNIX and non-UNIX systems. (TCP/IP is a Department of Defense standard protocol for networked systems.) Using TCP/IP, you can connect to remote networks and transfer files back and forth.

In addition, SCO's NFS (Network File System) product provides file sharing across a TCP/IP network. NFS was originally developed by Sun Microsystems and later adopted by SCO (and many other vendors). NFS runs on top of TCP/IP and allows systems to share disk drives, distribute files across a network, and run electronic mail across a variety of dissimilar machines. NFS networks can mix different computers—such as DEC Vaxes, Sun workstations, IBM-compatibles, and Apple Macintoshes—all running their own version of UNIX with NFS.

 NOTE   The SCO TCP/IP and SCO NFS products are sold separately from the base operating system. Both are part of Open Desktop (see "Open Desktop" later in this chapter).

The Structure of UNIX

UNIX is a complex operating system that includes literally hundreds of commands and options. Nevertheless, it has a consistent structure that applies regardless of the hardware on which it is running. Whether you approach UNIX as a beginner or an experienced computer user, it helps to know the system's structure. This section describes the various components of that structure.

A Typical Hardware System

Figure 1-1 shows a typical SCO UNIX system. It consists of the following components:

- *An 80286-, 80386-, or 80486-based PC* with a display, keyboard, at least one floppy drive, and a large disk drive provides the backbone of the system. This PC is often referred to as the *console.* System error messages are displayed on the console, and system administration is usually controlled from the console as well; however, the console can also function as an ordinary user terminal.

- *A tape drive* is often used to make backup copies of files or filesystems in case files are accidentally removed or destroyed.

- *User terminals* are either directly connected to the PC or connected remotely via modems and telephone lines. SCO UNIX supports many brands and models of terminals. You can also use a standard PC as a terminal, provided the PC is running a communications program that emulates a supported terminal. Two good communications programs for DOS systems are Procomm Plus and Crosstalk.

Figure 1-1.

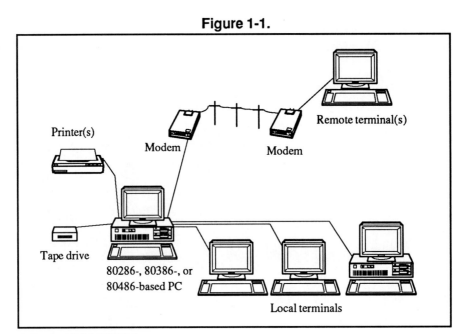

A Typical SCO UNIX System.

 NOTE   If you want to connect a PC directly to your SCO UNIX system using a standard serial line, make sure you have a null modem connector on the line.

- *Multiport boards* like the one shown in Figure 1-2 are often installed in the PC to allow several terminals to connect to the system at once.

- *Modems* are used to connect remote terminals to the SCO UNIX system or to connect one SCO UNIX system to another.

- *Printers* of many different kinds can be used with an SCO UNIX system, from simple impact printers (such as dot-matrix printers and letter-quality printers) to laser printers.

See Chapter 2 for more information about SCO UNIX hardware.

Figure 1-2.

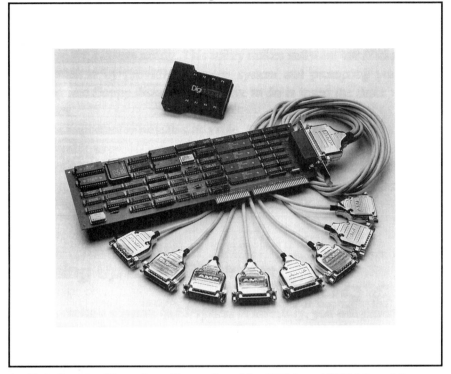

An Eight-Port Intelligent Input/Output Board for 80286- and 80386-Based Systems.
(Courtesy of DigiBoard, Incorporated)

Software Components

There are many tasks involved in running an operating system, each of which must be controlled by some aspect of the SCO UNIX software. For example, an SCO UNIX system is capable of supporting many users at the same time, each one running different programs. The software that manages this scheduling is not invoked by users, but runs automatically whenever SCO UNIX is active. Other software is employed by users to do specific tasks. This section describes several behind-the-scenes components of the system.

The Kernel The core of the SCO UNIX system is the *kernel.* The kernel communicates directly with the system hardware, and therefore must be adapted to the unique features of each hardware device. It is the kernel that insulates users from the differences in diverse hardware.

Besides communicating with the hardware, the kernel also coordinates the many internal functions of the operating system. One of these functions is allocating memory and other system resources to the processes going on at any given time. Because SCO UNIX is a multiuser, multitasking operating system, the kernel must oversee all the scheduling and memory management issues involved in such a complex environment. The kernel enables many programs or applications to run at the same time without interfering with one another.

The kernel also keeps track of who is logged in where and of the content and location of every file on the filesystems. Once the shell translates the commands that users type into instructions the computer can carry out, it is the kernel that actually implements these instructions. The kernel also maintains records of system activity and of individuals' system use for accounting purposes.

CPU Scheduling SCO UNIX is a time-sharing operating system. As such, it must provide each user with the illusion of having the entire computer to him- or herself. Because there is only a single processor in an SCO UNIX system, however, only one process can run at a time; thus, processes must be activated and deactivated at high speed, so that they appear to run continuously. Every few ticks of the system clock (milliseconds), the SCO UNIX system interrupts the current process and switches execution to another process, a mechanism known as *preemptive scheduling.* Because of the CPU's speed, the period required for the CPU to switch between processes is very brief. Everything about a process's context is saved, so when UNIX returns to a process, it can continue running it just as before.

For processes to appear to run in an uninterrupted fashion, the kernel must schedule processor time equitably. To do so, it uses a round-robin approach. That is, it skips from one process to the next using a priority system. In general, to ensure the smooth running of the system, system processes have a higher priority than user processes do. No single process completes as quickly using a round-robin approach, but the processing power of the system is evenly distributed among the system's users.

Processes   Every time you execute a utility or a program in SCO UNIX, you initiate a *process*. As a multiuser, multitasking operating system, UNIX is capable of running multiple processes simultaneously. The UNIX kernel controls the timing and priority of process execution. It allows processes to be created (by loading utilities for example) and terminated.

There are two types or levels of processes in SCO UNIX: user processes and system (or kernel) processes. Whenever you execute a UNIX utility (for example, to display the amount of available disk space), you initiate a user process. System processes, on the other hand, are initiated by the kernel to maintain the smooth operation of the system. For example, the kernel initiates a system process (or system call) whenever a program needs memory to execute. System processes are, for the most part, invisible to users.

Every time a user process needs to access a system resource, the kernel processes the request. For example, if you run a UNIX utility that needs to read a file on the disk drive, the utility makes a system call to the kernel to read from the disk. Thus, the kernel is the driver of the UNIX system. It interfaces with the hardware to provide a file system and coordinates the execution of processes. See Chapter 5, "Command Line Fundamentals," for additional information on processes.

SCO Business Applications

SCO offers several business applications for XENIX and UNIX. For example, the SCO Office Portfolio is a full suite of integrated application programs that run on XENIX and UNIX. In addition, SCO offers several standalone products that it has licensed from other companies, including SCO FoxBASE+, Microsoft Word, and Multiplan. Besides SCO, third-party vendors provide a host of products and services that are compatible with SCO XENIX and UNIX.

The SCO Office Portfolio

The SCO Office Portfolio is a family of business application programs and desktop accessories that all use the same menu interface. You can use each program in the Office Portfolio independently or use them together to form a comprehensive tool set. The programs available in the Office Portfolio are as follows:

- *SCO Manager* includes a clipboard that you can use to copy and paste data between applications in the Office Portfolio. You can also use the Manager to run several Office Portfolio programs simultaneously and jump between them. Built-in electronic mail is another popular feature offered by SCO Manager.

- *SCO Lyrix* is a full-featured, menu-driven word processor that includes a spelling checker and thesaurus. You can use Lyrix to perform simple writing tasks, like creating and editing shell scripts, or for working on complex documents that include special formatting (boldface, underlining, overstrike), footnotes and endnotes, columnar tables with math, and more.

- *SCO Professional* is a 1-2-3 Version 2.01 work-alike that reads and writes the Lotus .WK1 file format. Like 1-2-3, SCO Professional incorporates spreadsheet, database, and graphics capabilities in one product; however, unlike 1-2-3, SCO Professional lets you use SQL commands to create dynamic links between your spreadsheets and SQL databases, such as those created with SCO Integra.

- *SCO Integra* is a fully relational SQL-based database system that lets you create and manage tables of information. You can also create custom forms for data entry and custom reports for displaying information in SQL databases.

- *SCO ACCELL* is an integrated development system that serves as a complement to SCO Integra. Using SCO ACCELL, you can create your own custom applications that use specially designed screens and pop-up windows.

- *SCO Masterplan* is a project planning and resource management program that provides extensive graphics and reporting capabilities.

With SCO Masterplan, you can, for example, create Gantt charts, Network and PERT charts, perform critical path analysis, and more.

- *SCO ImageBuilder* is an integrated graphics program that lets you create graphs, charts, and diagrams using a variety of predefined formats. You can also enhance your graphs by adding objects (such as lines, arrows, and text notations), and by incorporating freehand graphics. SCO ImageBuilder supports both the keyboard and a mouse, and lets you send your output to a variety of printers and plotters.

- *SCO Statistician* is a comprehensive statistical package that incorporates powerful graphics and report generation capabilities. You can use SCO Statistician for a variety of statistical applications, including analysis of variance, regression analysis, and correlation analysis.

 NOTE   The SCO Office Portfolio Suite includes four programs—SCO Manager, SCO Lyrix, SCO Professional, and SCO Integra. In fact, if you order the SCO Office Portfolio from your dealer, you are bound to get the four programs in the SCO Office Portfolio Suite.

See Chapter 15, "An Overview of SCO Business Software," for more details on these products.

Other Licensed Products

SCO provides the following three programs for XENIX and UNIX that are licensed from other vendors but sold directly by SCO.

- *SCO FoxBASE+* is a dBASE III PLUS work-alike licensed from Fox Software. SCO FoxBASE+ provides complete source language and data file compatibility with Ashton-Tate's dBASE III PLUS.

- *Microsoft Word* is a version of the popular word processing program that is available for DOS and OS/2. Microsoft Word offers a variety of advanced features, including outlining, the ability to incorporate text and graphs in a single document, automatic revisions (redlining), annotation (allowing users to include comments along with a document), and "hot-linking" to spreadsheets such as SCO Professional and Microsoft Multiplan.

- *Microsoft Multiplan* is a version of the popular DOS spreadsheet that has long been known for its ability to link worksheets.

See Chapter 15, "An Overview of SCO Business Software," to learn more about SCO FoxBASE+ and Microsoft Word.

Third-Party Products

UNIX applications span a broad range of "horizontal" applications, such as spreadsheets, database management, communications, and word processing. These applications are horizontal in that they are intended to appeal to the entire UNIX marketplace. In addition, UNIX offers many "vertical" applications, such as financial modeling, robotics, computer-aided design (CAD), computer-aided software engineering (CASE), and medical billing. These vertical applications are targeted to a particular segment of the UNIX market, such as financial managers, engineers, or doctors. The next sections describe some of the major categories of horizontal applications. See the section "Who Buys SCO UNIX Systems?" later in this chapter for a discussion of vertical market applications.

Word Processors   Although UNIX provides powerful editing and text-formatting tools, they are not as interactive as most popular word processors for PCs. As XENIX and UNIX have become more common on PCs, many of the most frequently used word processors for DOS have made their way to these systems. As mentioned, Microsoft Word is one word processor that is available on UNIX. Others are WordPerfect and Samna Plus.

Database Management   SCO UNIX plays host to several powerful database management programs, for example, Oracle Corporation's ORACLE, Informix Software's INFORMIX-SQL, and Ingres Corporation's INGRES. These are all relational database management systems that made their reputation on minicomputer systems and are now available on PCs running UNIX.

The SCO System V Directory   To help you locate XENIX- and UNIX-related products and services, SCO publishes the *SCO System V Directory*. This directory also provides a comprehensive list of hardware, software, consultants, and training companies. It is especially helpful for locating vertical market software for anything from accounts receivable management to wholesale distribution.

The XENIX and UNIX System Documentation

Every XENIX and UNIX system provides a copy of the *User's Reference*. This is the official documentation, which describes the shells and utility commands for the system. (The term *man page* is often used to refer to an entry in the *User's Reference*, although the entry may actually occupy more than one page.)

The system also comes with the *User's Guide*, a more down-to-earth description of the most frequently used UNIX utilities. Some example topics in the guide are "vi: A Text Editor," "mail," "Communicating with Other Sites," "The Shell," and "The C Shell." You'll find this guide quite helpful when you are learning to use UNIX, and later on as you expand your knowledge to new areas.

The XENIX system includes an additional book called *Installation and Maintenance*. This book holds three references: the *Installation Guide*, the *System Administrator's Guide,* and *System Administration*. As you might expect, all these guides contain information that pertains to system administration.

For the UNIX System, there are two system administration books: the *System Administrator's Guide* and the *System Administrator's Reference*. In this case, the *System Administrator's Reference* also includes the *Installation Guide*.

Besides the books that come with your system, AT&T offers a standard set of documents that describes UNIX System V. These books, which are written by AT&T and published by Prentice Hall, are AT&T's official reference works on UNIX and are available at most major bookstores. Here are some of the more important books available in the UNIX System V library:

- *UNIX System V/386 Release 3.2 User's Guide* provides an overview of the UNIX system with tutorial sections on using text editors, mail, and simple shell programming.

- *UNIX System V/386 Release 3.2 Programmer's Guide Volumes I and II* provides an overview of UNIX's programming environment with tutorials on its programming tools.

- *UNIX System V/386 Release 3.2 Programmer's Reference Manual* provides information for UNIX programmers, including descriptions of UNIX system calls, file formats, libraries, and subroutines.

- *UNIX System V/386 Release 3.2 System Administrator's Guide* describes how to perform administrative tasks on a UNIX system.

- *UNIX System V/386 Release 3.2 System Administrator's Reference Manual* provides technical information for system administrators, including commands, file formats, and other miscellaneous information.

In UNIX, you can access an on-line help facility to find information about a UNIX command and its available options. The on-line help facility includes all the pages in the *User's Reference.* To access the on-line manual, type **man** *command,* where *command* is the name of the command you need information about. (In XENIX, the on-line help facility may or may not be installed on your system. An easy way to find out is to try the **man** command and see if you get a response.)

Other Standard Operating Systems

Besides UNIX, there are two other important standard operating systems: MS-DOS and OS/2. MS-DOS from Microsoft Corporation is the leading single-user, single-tasking operating system for 16-bit personal computers and is important to UNIX users because of the wealth of application programs available for it. In addition, you can use many MS-DOS commands from within UNIX. For example, the **dosmkdir** command lets you create a directory on a DOS disk, and the **dosdir** command lets you list DOS files in the standard DOS-style directory format. (You can use the DOS commands to access files in a nonactive DOS partition.) What's more, you can run existing DOS applications under XENIX or UNIX using the SCO VP/ix package. Chapter 14, "Using MS-DOS Under UNIX," provides a complete description of how to use the DOS commands and the VP/ix package.

OS/2, also from Microsoft, is a single-user, multitasking operating system for 16-bit computers, although it will soon be offered for 32-bit computers. Besides multitasking, OS/2 and UNIX share many other common features, including a hierarchical file structure, protection, and inter-process communication. Here are some of the major differences between OS/2 and UNIX:

- *Single User* Although OS/2 was designed as a multitasking operating system, it was also designed for a single user, with priority given to system performance for that user.

- *Portability* Unlike the designers of UNIX, Microsoft did not develop OS/2 with portability in mind. The OS/2 core contains a larger volume of assembly language than does UNIX's core, which is written almost entirely in the C language. In addition, Microsoft wrote the initial versions of OS/2 to exploit and overcome the features of the Intel 80286 processor. However, OS/2 Version 2.0 will take full advantage of the Intel 80386 processor's ability to run in protected mode.

- *Presentation Manager* This is a subsystem of OS/2 that manages the windows-based graphics user interface. Presentation Manager is a standard component of the OS/2 operating system. The standard SCO UNIX system does not include a graphics user interface, although you can purchase one separately, or through Open Desktop (see "The Future of the SCO UNIX System" later in this chapter).

Who Buys SCO UNIX Systems?

For years, UNIX was viewed as the ugly duckling of operating systems. People thought it was strictly the province of engineers or research and development labs with technically proficient users. It is true that as UNIX evolved many of its commands and options became too complex for the average layperson to master. Yet phone companies and the federal government standardized on UNIX, while hundreds of value-added resellers (VARs) and dealers prospered by selling low-cost UNIX multiuser systems. All the while, SCO was establishing itself as the world leader in microprocessor-based UNIX, and it now claims over 90 percent of the market worldwide.

SCO XENIX and UNIX have been particularly popular with VARs who fill the demand for customized applications that run on multiuser platforms where MS-DOS is not a major consideration. VARs typically specialize in vertical markets like health care, accounting, and legal offices. For a low cost per user, they can put together multiuser computer systems custom-fitted to the vertical market's needs.

The growing strength of the SCO XENIX and UNIX platforms is evidenced by the number of major MS-DOS applications that are making their way to them. For example, AutoCAD, the leading computer-aided design (CAD) package for DOS, is now available for SCO XENIX 386 and for SCO UNIX. According to recent benchmark tests, AutoCAD's performance on the SCO XENIX 386 operating system far outstrips its performance on MS-DOS systems.

The Future of the SCO UNIX System

The original UNIX system was not designed for graphics display devices. Instead, UNIX is geared towards supporting many users through inexpensive, character-based terminals. Nevertheless, the UNIX community pioneered the use of graphics in workstations. UNIX is the favored system for the high-end scientific and engineering workstation market.

UNIX's character-based approach has its advantages. For the experienced user, a character-based system is quick and convenient. It also lends itself to the software tools approach for which UNIX was designed. However, to become proficient at using a character-based system, the user must know quite a bit.

In an effort to expand UNIX's appeal, a number of companies are now providing graphics user interfaces (GUIs) for their UNIX systems. Most are based on the X Window System, developed by MIT. For example, AT&T and Sun are producing OPEN LOOK, which AT&T plans to incorporate into UNIX System V Release 4.

In response to AT&T's and Sun's efforts, a consortium of leading original equipment manufacturers (OEMs) have banded together to form the Open Systems Foundation (OSF). This group was established in May 1988 to produce another standardized, but more open, version of UNIX. Members of OSF include IBM, Digital Equipment Corporation (DEC), Apollo, Hewlett-Packard, and Toshiba, among others. As part of their alternative UNIX standard, OSF has proposed a graphics user interface standard known as Motif. Currently, the only Motif-compatible GUI shipping is SCO's Open Desktop.

Yet another forthcoming graphics user interface for UNIX is PM/X from Microsoft. This is a version of Presentation Manager that originated with the OS/2 operating system. The advantage of PM/X is that software vendors easily will be able to port their OS/2 applications to SCO UNIX, thereby making available the various application programs expected for OS/2 within the next few years.

Open Desktop

Open Desktop, SCO's graphical operating system, is designed to bring advanced workstation capabilities to industry standard 80386- and 80486-based microcomputers. Open Desktop gathers several industry standard products under one umbrella. These are

- *SCO TCP/IP* and *SCO NFS*, two programs that provide Ethernet network communications and distributed file system support (see "Linking to Other Systems," earlier in this chapter)

- *Merge 386*, an extension of the UNIX operating system that allows simultaneous operation of MS-DOS and UNIX applications (this product is licensed from Locus Computer Corporation and is similar to SCO VP/ix described previously; however, AT&T provides direct support for the Merge 386 interface in the source code for UNIX System V/386 Release 3.2)

- *INGRES/386*, a SQL-based database management system licensed from Ingres Corporation that is tailored to graphical windowing environments

Figure 1-3.

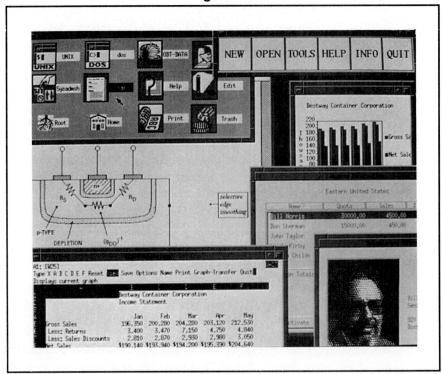

A View of Open Desktop's Graphical User Interface.

Figure 1-3 shows an example of the Open Desktop interface. With Open Desktop, SCO hopes to set a new standard for power and ease of use for microprocessor-based UNIX systems.

In its brief history, SCO UNIX has developed a level of maturity unmatched by other multiuser, multitasking operating systems for Intel-based systems. It provides a wealth of commands, text formatting tools, and communications facilities as well as a rich software development environment. It also offers a variety of applications programs that are available directly from SCO or from third-party vendors. In recent years SCO UNIX has proven to be an inexpensive, yet extremely powerful, operating system for general business use.

Installing the System

Installing your SCO UNIX system may at first seem a monumental task, but the installation program provided on the installation floppy disks, the *SCO UNIX Installation Guide,* and this chapter are all designed to make the installation process as simple and understandable as possible. The installation program is quite easy to use, only requiring you to respond to questions and insert the appropriate floppy disks. The *SCO UNIX Installation Guide* takes you carefully through the steps involved in the installation procedure, explaining the questions asked by the installation program and helping you make choices. This chapter explains some of the concepts discussed in the guide and gives additional insights into some of the steps involved in getting your system up and running. It is not intended to replace the guide that comes with your SCO UNIX or XENIX system, but is to be used in combination with it.

It is a good idea to plan your installation before you actually sit down at the computer and start inserting disks. The things you should take into consideration include what hardware components your system will consist of, how much space you have on your hard disk, how you will organize that space, and what parts of the operating system and other software you will install. Use the "Hardware Checklist" and "Software Considerations" sections in this chapter to help you plan your installation. The remaining sections, used in conjunction with the *SCO UNIX Installation Guide,* will show you how to install and configure your system.

Hardware Checklist

This section presents a checklist of hardware components you will need to install your SCO UNIX system. Some familiarity with hardware components and with the basic setup of a computer is assumed. You probably already have most or all of the components discussed here, but this is your opportunity to learn a little more about these components and the roles they play in a UNIX system, and to make sure that you have the appropriate hardware.

Memory

SCO UNIX requires at least 3MB (megabytes) of RAM (Random Access Memory), and it is recommended that you have at least 4MB for optimum performance. If you want to install the development system, you will need a minimum of 4MB. For optimum performance, SCO also recommends that you have .5MB of RAM per user in addition to the required minimum. For example, the recommended amount of RAM for a ten-user system with the Development System installed would be 9MB — 4MB for the operating system plus 5MB for the ten users (.5MB multiplied by ten).

XENIX   XENIX requires less memory than UNIX: a minimum of 1MB for the operating system and 2 or more MB if you plan to install the Development System. As with UNIX, SCO recommends that you have an additional .5MB of RAM per user on your XENIX system.

If you plan to install additional memory on your machine, you should fill the space allotted for RAM on the motherboard before you add additional memory cards. In general, RAM on the motherboard is faster than RAM connected to the bus.

Hard Disk

The hard disk is the data storage medium where the system software and user files are stored. When you install your UNIX system, information from the installation floppy disks is copied onto the hard disk. The hard disk is the slowest device in the computer and has the greatest impact on speed.

You will need at least a 40MB hard disk to install the SCO UNIX operating system. If you want to install additional software, such as the Development System or business software, you will need a larger hard disk. In fact, even an 80MB hard disk would quickly run out of space if you had the operating system, the Development System, some applications software, and a large number of user files on it. The actual requirements for your SCO UNIX system will depend on how much software you want to install. Appendix B, "Software Reference," lists the size of various SCO UNIX applications.

NOTE   Disk space in megabytes refers to usable, formatted space.

XENIX   Though the XENIX installation notes say that 20MB is the minimum size required for a XENIX operating system, the actual size needed to accommodate the entire set of operating system utilities, swap space, and a recover area, is somewhat larger. You would have to remove parts of the operating system to fit it on a 20MB hard disk. To allow space for software as well as the operating system, you should have a 40MB or larger hard disk.

Hard Disk Controller

There are four common types of hard disk controllers: MFM (Modified Frequency Modulation), RLL (Run Length Limited), SCSI (Small Computer System Interface), and ESDI (Enhanced Small Device Interface). Each type of controller uses a different hard disk interface. Both RLL and MFM controllers use the standard interface, ST-506. You must know which type of controller you have before you begin the installation procedure, because the different types of hard disks are formatted differently.

Serial Cards

To use terminals and modems on your SCO UNIX system, you need a serial I/O card, which is supplied with most computers. The typical serial card supports two COM ports, called COM 1 and COM 2. Be aware, however, that a card that *supports* two COM ports is not always *set up* for both ports when you buy it; in fact, most are initially set up for only one COM port. In order to use both COM 1 and COM 2 on your computer, your serial card must be fully populated with chips. You should be able to tell by looking at the card whether there are any empty slots for chips. If there are, you must get the missing chips and upgrade your serial card to use both COM ports. The additional chips are often sold in computer stores as serial card upgrade kits.

 CAUTION   If you install a parallel printer on the parallel port included on your serial I/O card, you must make sure that the port is wired to IRQ 5, not IRQ 7, as many cards are when delivered. If it is not wired to the correct IRQ line, it may result in very slow printing. To select a different IRQ line for your second parallel port, you need to change the switch settings on your I/O card. Consult your manual for the proper switch settings to use.

Multiport Boards

If you have a system with multiple users, a serial printer, and a modem, you will soon find the two COM ports provided by a serial I/O card inadequate for your needs. A multiport board that supports 8 or 16 terminals is indispensable to most UNIX systems. A multiport board is a card you insert in your computer's bus. The multiport board generally has some memory of its own to help handle input and output between the UNIX system and the terminals connected to the board.

Some multiport boards are "intelligent," while others are not. Whereas a standard multiport board usually provides 8 to 16 serial communication ports, an intelligent board also includes its own on-board processor and additional memory to improve the management of those ports. In addition, intelligent boards include software that allows them to take over some of the processing load from the host PC.

A multiport board usually comes set to use certain hardware IRQ lines and memory map addresses. These can be changed if they conflict with the interrupts used by your existing hardware.

There are different types of multiport boards for different types of buses—ISA (Industry Standard Architecture, or PC-standard bus), MCA (Micro Channel Architecture, IBM's bus for newer PS/2 models such as the 70 and 80), and EISA (Extended Industry Standard Architecture, supported only by some newer hardware). Make sure that your multiport board is the correct type for your computer's bus.

Terminals

If you need a bit-mapped device for a UNIX or DOS application on your system, you will need a display card in your computer. For most UNIX applications, you do not need a bit-mapped device. In this case, you can use ordinary video display terminals. The WYSE 60 terminal is probably the best supported terminal for SCO UNIX applications, but it is only one among many terminals SCO UNIX supports. For a full list of terminals supported by SCO UNIX, refer to the *SCO UNIX User's Reference.*

Terminals are where users log in to a multiuser UNIX system. If you do not have a bit-mapped console, you can also use a terminal as a serial console, where you will see the information displayed by the installation program and enter the input it requests. Terminals can be connected to serial ports on the computer, to multiports on a multiport card, or by a telephone line and modem.

Computer

SCO UNIX must be installed on an 80386 computer. There are versions of XENIX for both 80286 and 80386 computers. If you are installing XENIX, be sure you have the correct version for your computer before you open any of the software packets.

If possible, before you install SCO UNIX on a new computer you should first test the computer with DOS, because it is easier to troubleshoot hardware problems with DOS than with UNIX.

Floppy Disk Drive

You need at least one high density (1.2MB 5.25-inch, 720K 3.5-inch, or 1.44MB 3.5-inch) floppy disk drive to install your SCO UNIX system. When you first begin the installation procedure, the computer boots from the N1 floppy disk included in your set of installation disks. After that, the data on the remainder of the N,B, and X installation disks and other software disks is copied to your computer's hard disk.

Tape Drive

Many computers running SCO UNIX systems have tape drives in addition to floppy disk drives. Tape drives are especially valuable for doing system backups, because tapes hold much more data than floppy disks. Also, a tape backup does not require the system administrator to be on hand to insert disks; backups can be done automatically with the **cron** command.

While some tape drives, such as the Archive, Wangtek, Everex, and Mountain drives, have built-in device drivers on SCO UNIX and XENIX, others require special device drivers that you must install from software supplied with the drive. If you have a drive or controller that is not directly supported by SCO UNIX, be sure you have the appropriate software to install it.

 NOTE   Device driver software for XENIX systems will not work on UNIX systems, and vice versa. Make sure you have the correct installation disks for your system.

A Typical SCO UNIX System Setup

A typical SCO UNIX business system includes all or most of the following hardware components:

- An Intel 80386 microprocesser running at 25 or 33 megahertz

- 8MB of 32-bit RAM

- A 300MB formatted ESDI drive

- An 8- or 16-port multiport board, and a corresponding number of terminals

- A 150MB tape drive and controller card for backups

- A monochrome monitor and card on the console (this usually includes one parallel port)

- One serial AT I/O card that includes two serial (RS232) ports and a second parallel port

- A 2400-baud modem

Software Considerations

The software component of your UNIX system is just as important as the hardware component. Once your system is up and running, you can pretty much forget about the hardware (as long as there are no problems with it); however, you will interact directly with the software every time you use SCO UNIX. A mistake you make while installing the system software or supported applications can be difficult to correct later, so it is important that you understand and carefully follow the directions in the installation manual. This section provides some additional information you need to consider before installing your SCO UNIX system.

Separate UNIX and DOS Partitions on the Same Hard Disk

If you plan to install DOS and UNIX on separate partitions on the same hard disk, there are several things to consider. If the DOS partition already exists, you must be sure enough space remains on the disk to accommodate your UNIX system. If DOS has not been installed, you must install it before you install UNIX, because DOS must be the first partition on a disk; you cannot install DOS on a disk on which another operating system has already been installed. Finally, you must be sure you've allocated enough space to each operating system.

 REMEMBER   Once you have created a DOS partition, you cannot later remove it and replace it with a UNIX filesystem. To do so, you would have to run the **fdisk** program to repartition the disk, and this would destroy the current contents of *both* the DOS and the UNIX partitions, requiring you to reinstall your UNIX system.

The Operating System and Other Software

One of the most important considerations when you are installing your SCO UNIX system is the amount of space the software you want to install on the system is going to take up. Be sure to check the sizes of the packages you plan to install before you install them. The sizes of all SCO UNIX applications are listed in Appendix B.

Swap Space

A large section in the *SCO UNIX Installation Guide* deals with calculating the swap space for your system. *Swap space* is an area of the hard disk where running processes can be stored when the RAM is full. The availability of a swap area is one of the things that allows a UNIX system to work on many processes almost simultaneously. If you do not elect to specify the size of the swap space, the **divvy** program will determine the size for you during the installation procedure. In most cases, the default amount of swap space is enough, but problems can arise because the installation program has no way of knowing what software you will install on your system and how much use the system will get. Obviously, the greater the number of people who use the system at one time, and the more large processes those people run, the more swap space you need. Although the calculations for determining swap space may seem quite complex, you can make these calculations with a minimum of information.

- *The number of users on the machine.* All the users on your system may never be logged on at the same time, but for the purposes of determining the swap space you should assume that they will be. This will give you leeway for one user to run more than one large process at a time, or for adding additional users later.

- *The size of the largest process normally run on the machine.* The number to use here is the amount of RAM recommended by the manufacturer for the application in question. This amount is generally somewhat larger than the size of the running binary file, but using the recommended amount allows space for the user files that the process is running on. For example, suppose the largest process users run on your system is the SCO Development System. Near the beginning of the release notes SCO supplies with each product is a table showing the recommended amount of RAM needed for that product. Other manufacturers may list this number in a different place, but it should be supplied. If you plan to install a non-SCO application on your system that you know is large, but you cannot find a recommended amount of RAM, contact the manufacturer to get this number before calculating the swap space.

- *The amount of memory (RAM) installed on your system.* You should already know how much RAM your system has, because you will have had to verify that you have the amount of RAM required to install the system.

Note that the numbers you use to calculate the swap space are in megabytes. Since **divvy**—the program that prompts you for the swap space—uses kilobytes, you must convert the number you determine for swap space into kilobytes. To do this, multiply the number of megabytes by 1024. The size of a typical swap space is from 6 to 15MB.

Filesystems

A filesystem is an area of a hard disk. For the purposes of UNIX pathnames and commands, a filesystem is treated just like a directory. However, there are significant differences between a filesystem and a directory. First, a filesystem may be mounted and unmounted on the system. The files and directories on a given filesystem are accessible only when that filesystem is mounted. Files in an ordinary directory are intermingled with files in other directories in the same filesystem, so you cannot mount or unmount a directory. The second difference between filesystems and directories is that while a directory merely contains pointers to the files associated with it, a filesystem actually holds the files themselves.

One advantage of splitting your SCO UNIX system into more than one filesystem is that it makes file access time quicker. The computer can search a small filesystem more quickly than a large one. Having separate filesystems also reduces *fragmentation,* which occurs when files are stored in small pieces in many different locations on the disk. Fragmentation is not a problem in itself, but it does slow down disk access. Thus, the operating system can make the most efficient use of the space on the hard disk if you store files in separate filesystems.

By separating user files—which generally grow fairly often, and thus become more fragmented—from system files—which do not grow very often—you reduce the effects of disk fragmentation. Also, storing all (and only) user files in one filesystem, makes creating backups of your data much easier. Since user files are generally modified far more often than system files, you need to back up user files more frequently than system files. If the user files are interspersed with system files in the **/usr** directory, it takes a number of commands to back up just the user files; however, if all the user files are stored together, they can be backed up with a single command.

Keep in mind that once you've created a filesystem, you cannot change its size without losing the data in it. The same is true of the root filesystem, so you cannot enlarge one filesystem and reduce another without having to restore both of them.

A /u Filesystem?   Some administrators choose to have a separate filesystem for users' home directories. As explained in the previous section, there are several advantages to having a separate filesystem for user files: It makes backups easier, and also makes it easy to save and transfer all user files if you get a new disk or reinstall the system. This type of filesystem is conventionally called **/u**, but this name can be changed.

CAUTION   Technically, you can give the user filesystem any name except **root**, but if you're not careful, you could give it a name that is already the name of a directory in /, such as **/usr**. Such an oversight could have disastrous results. Thus, you should name your user filesystem something other than **/u** only if you have a good reason to do so, and only if you are an experienced UNIX user who knows which names are allowable and which are not.

On UNIX, you are only given the option of creating a /**u** filesystem if you have a large hard disk (140MB or more).

XENIX   On XENIX, you can create a /**u** filesystem on any disk that is large enough to accommodate the operating system. However, it is not a good idea to create a separate /**u** filesystem on a disk smaller than 80MB. If you create a /**u** filesystem on a smaller hard disk, you may end up with more space than you need for user files and not enough room for all the software you want to install.

If you do not have a large enough disk for a /**u** filesystem, or you simply decide not to create one, it is still a good idea to create a separate /**u** *directory* for users' home directories. Though this does not have the advantages of quicker access times and less disk fragmentation in the root filesystem, it still makes it easier to back up and restore user files.

The /tmp Directory

Though you do not determine the size of the /**tmp** directory during the installation procedure, you should take it into account. The /**tmp** directory is used by many UNIX programs to store the files that are being worked on; therefore, there must be sufficient space on the disk for this directory to hold a copy of the largest file users will operate on.

Free Space

Throughout the *SCO UNIX Installation Guide,* you are warned that you must leave at least 10 to 20 percent of your disk unused. This may seem like a large amount, but when you consider all the temporary files and backup files created by UNIX processes and by users themselves, it is not an unreasonable amount of space. As more and more space on the disk is used, processes searching for free space take longer to search the disk. A very full hard disk therefore slows the system considerably. Keep in mind that the free space on your disk does not include the user files. There must be 10 to 20 percent (20 percent is strongly recommended) of the disk free *after* all user files have been created. This means that when you are installing your system, you must leave more than 20 percent of the disk empty.

Installation Procedure

Before you begin installing your SCO UNIX operating system software, you should read the preceding sections to make sure that you have all the information you need about your software and hardware configurations. You should also read through the *SCO UNIX Installation Guide* so that you are familiar with the installation procedure before you start. The installation procedure, as discussed in the guide, consists of several steps: installing the basic operating system utilities, installing the extended operating system, and configuring the system using the **sysadmsh**. The **sysadmsh** is a visual shell that lets you perform certain system administration tasks by choosing menu items instead of typing commands. It also provides help on topics related to each menu item. During the installation procedure, you are automatically placed in this shell. In ordinary operation mode, you must enter this shell by typing the **sysadmsh** command. For more information about the **sysadmsh**, see Chapter 12, "System Administration."

The following is a brief summary of the steps involved in the installation procedure. For best results, you should follow the order shown here in installing your system.

1. Install the basic operating system utilities. These are on the installation floppy disks N1 through N5 and B1 through B8.

2. Install the extended operating system utilities on installation floppy disks X1 through X10. To make sure that everything gets properly

installed, you should install the entire set of extended utilities and remove any parts you don't want later.

3. Install any maintenance supplements or system updates supplied with your release. For example, SCO UNIX release 3.2.0 comes with two maintenance supplement disks, UF1 and UF2.

4. (Optional) Install CGI (Computer Graphics Interface) disks 1 through 4. The CGI driver allows you to use graphics with programs and monitors (CGA, EGA, or VGA) capable of supporting graphics. If you do not plan to run any graphics applications, you do not need to install the CGI.

5. Create any additional filesystems you have set up during the installation procedure. To do so, select the **sysadmsh** command **Filesystems** and select **Add** from the Filesystems menu. The **sysadmsh** invokes the command

   mkdev fs /dev/u /u

   to make the filesystems.

6. Mount any filesystems you have just created.

7. (Optional) Install the tape device driver. Select the **sysadmsh** command **Hardware** and select **Tape** from the Hardware menu. The **sysadmsh** invokes the command

   mkdev tape

   to create this device driver. Even if you do not plan to install the tape drive itself until later, you can install the device driver now. If you do not plan to install a tape drive, you can skip this step.

8. (Optional) If there are parts of the operating system you do not need and want to remove to save space, use **custom** to remove these parts now.

9. Make a backup of the operating system on tape (if you have installed a tape drive) or on floppy disks. Then if anything goes wrong while you are configuring the system, you can restore the basic operating system without having to repeat the whole installation procedure. Chapter 12, "System Administration," explains how to make backups of your system.

10. Set up any data directories you need in **/u.**

11. Install any device drivers required for additional hardware you plan to install, such as a multiport board or an Ethernet card. Verify that these device drivers work by testing the hardware, and then make another backup.

12. Install any add-in applications you want on your system. These might include SCO UNIX products such as the Office Portfolio, non-SCO applications such as special databases, or other programs for your business.

Automatic Installation

UNIX provides an automatic installation procedure that requires very little user participation. In fact, if you choose the automatic installation option the bulk of your work will be inserting floppy disks as prompted by the installation program. Look over the sections in this chapter and in the *SCO UNIX Installation Guide* concerning filesystems and swap space. If you are sure the applications you will be running will not require extra swap space, you can use the automatic installation option.

Primary Formatting of the Hard Disk

Before an operating system can write to and read from a hard disk, the disk must be formatted. Formatting a hard disk means defining its dimensions and parameters. More often than not, hard disks now come formatted by the manufacturer. Thus it is technically possible to install your SCO UNIX system without doing a primary format of the disk; however, it is common practice to do a primary format before you begin the installation procedure. You can use the formatter that is built into your hard disk controller to do a primary format. Or, you can use a DOS formatting utility such as Speed Store or Disk Manager.

By doing a primary format of the disk before you begin installing the operating system, you make sure the disk has the correct settings, and you get a chance to test the disk to be sure it works. Whatever formatter you use, you should format the drive only after it is warm. This ensures that the disk is formatted in the same state it will be in when it is in use.

 NOTE   Some UNIX technicians suggest not only formatting the hard disk under DOS, but also using DOS to read and write to the disk extensively. The rationale for this is that SCO UNIX is more likely to run with fewer errors on a burned-in hard disk.

If you do a primary format, you must have some information about your disk. This information includes such things as the number of heads, the number of cylinders, and the number of sectors per track. This information should be supplied with the documentation that comes with your hard drive.

Installing the Distribution Floppy Disks

The first step in installing an SCO UNIX system is to install the operating system itself. For the most part, this is a simple procedure that requires you to insert floppy disks when prompted and answer a number of questions. Once you install the operating system software as instructed in the *SCO UNIX Installation Guide,* you will have a working UNIX system, but you must take several more steps before your system is ready for full multiuser operation. The remainder of this chapter guides you through the major steps involved in getting your system up and running, and directs you to appropriate sections in the SCO manuals.

You must install all of the basic operating system utilities (those on distribution floppy disks N1 through N5 and B1 through B8). Begin with the floppy disk labeled Volume: N1. This volume is also known as the *Boot Floppy.* The *SCO UNIX Installation Guide* takes you through the steps involved in installing the floppy disks. After you have installed the basic operating system utilities and loaded the operating system from the hard disk, you are presented with the following menu:

```
1. Finish installation
2. Install additional software now
```

If you select **1**, you are choosing *not* to install the extended operating system utilities, but instead to configure your system using the **sysadmsh**. The *SCO UNIX Installation Guide* states that you may not need the extended operating system utilities on disks X1 through X10 if your SCO UNIX system is going to serve only as a base for an application; however, some applications may call for some of the extended utilities. It is a good idea to install the extended operating system utilities unless you are absolutely sure you won't need them.

 NOTE   It is possible to finish the installation now and add the extended operating system utilities later, but if you know you're going to install them anyway, it is recommended that you install them now.

If you are installing the extended utilities, you should install *all* of them, even if you don't think you will need them all, and then remove the unnecessary packages. There are two reasons for this: first, installing only selected packages takes longer than installing all packages because you have to select each one you want to install, and second, installing all packages leaves less room for error and ensures that the packages you do want are completely installed.

XENIX   The XENIX distribution consists of fewer volumes than the UNIX distribution; it has three N volumes, two B volumes, and four X volumes. However, you follow the same procedure to install the XENIX operating system that you do to install UNIX. That is, you install all of the basic and extended utilities, and then go back and remove the ones you don't want.

The packages included in your UNIX distribution are described near the beginning of the release notes provided with your software. Refer to these descriptions to determine which packages you don't think you will need, and then use the **custom** utility to remove these packages. Refer to the "Installation Procedure" section of this chapter for the appropriate stage at which to remove the operating system packages that you don't want. To remove the operating system packages, use **custom** and select option **2. Remove one or more packages.**

Installing Device Drivers

Many hardware devices have built-in device drivers in SCO UNIX. For example, serial I/O cards with two COM ports, floppy disk drives, and modems are directly supported, and do not require any additional device drivers to be installed. Other hardware components are not directly supported by SCO UNIX, so you must install the appropriate device drivers when you install the hardware. For example, different multiport boards have specific device drivers—usually supplied by the manufacturer on floppy disks—that you can install with the **custom** option

```
4. Add a supported product
```

When you install or remove a device driver, the SCO UNIX kernel must be relinked. Until you shut down and reboot the system, the new kernel will not operate. When you install or remove a device driver, **custom** exits to a root prompt (#), and you see the message

```
Reboot system to install new kernel.
```

This message does not mean that you should simply press the reset button or turn off the computer. To reboot the system, shut it down with the command

```
# /etc/shutdown
```

Then wait for the prompt

```
** Safe to Power Off **
         -or-
** Press Any Key to Reboot **
```

and press a key to reboot the system. If you shut down the system by turning off the power or resetting it, it will probably not be a disaster, but there is no guarantee that the new kernel will be saved to the hard disk.

Installing Additional Software

To install SCO UNIX software or other UNIX software on your system, you use the **custom** utility. This utility makes software installation simple and painless by providing a menu system and prompting you for the appropriate floppy disks. All you have to do is insert the disks and press RETURN.

It is important to note that as a rule, XENIX applications are not simply transferable to a UNIX system. Although it is sometimes possible to make XENIX applications run on an SCO UNIX system, you should not simply assume that they will be compatible. The same is true in reverse—most UNIX applications are not set up to run on XENIX.

Setting Up Data Directories

If you create a separate /**u** filesystem or directory, you will probably want special data directories in /**u**. For example, you may want to establish a /**u/bin** directory for user-created binary programs and shell scripts. This allows for easy separation of these homemade scripts and binaries from the SCO distribution binaries and scripts, which are stored in /**bin** and /**usr/bin**. You may also have special databases that you want to store in subdirectories of /**u**. To create these directories, use the command

   mkdir x

where x is the name of the directory you want to create. For example, to create the directory /**u/bin**, use the command

```
# mkdir /u/bin
```

Since you will want to let users read and execute the files in this directory, you will have to give users read and execute permission for the directory. If you also want to let users place their own files in this directory, you will need to give all users write permission. The following example shows how you would give read, execute, and write permission to **root** and give only read and execute permission to all other users.

```
# chmod 755 /u/bin
```

To allow other users to write to this directory as well as to read and execute it, you would use this command:

```
# chmod 777 /u/bin
```

For more information about file and directory permissions, see Chapter 4, "Files and Directories."

Adding User Accounts

Even if only one person is going to use your SCO UNIX system, that person should have a user account separate from the **root** account because a person logged in as **root** has the power to remove or change any file on the system. To prevent accidental loss or corruption of system files, this account should not be used for routine tasks. Although you may add new user accounts at any time, adding them as part of the installation process ensures that your system will be fully functional as soon as you start it up in multiuser mode. Use the information and suggestions in this section in conjunction with Chapter 10, "Administering User Accounts," in the *SCO UNIX System Administrator's Guide*. For more information on administering user accounts, see Chapter 12, "System Administration," in this book.

XENIX　In addition to the appropriate portions of the following sections, see Chapter 10, "Preparing XENIX for Users," in the *SCO XENIX System Administrator's Guide* for information about the XENIX **mkuser** command and various other aspects of user accounts.

Creating an Account

On UNIX, user accounts are created by selecting the **sysadmsh** command **Accounts,** selecting **User** from the Accounts menu, and selecting **Create** from the User menu.

This series of commands has replaced the XENIX **mkuser** command. To create a user account, the **sysadmsh** does the following things:

- Creates the user's home directory

- Assigns a login shell to the account

- Assigns an ID number to the user

- Assigns the user to a login group

- Places the appropriate initialization files (the **.profile** file if the login shell is the Bourne shell, or the **.login** and **.cshrc** files if the login shell is the C shell) in the user's home directory

- Assigns an initial password for the account

- Assigns a comment about the user

XENIX On XENIX, there are two ways to create user accounts. You can select the **sysadmsh** command **Users** and select **Add** from the User menu. You can also use the **mkuser** command. The **sysadmsh** command sequence and the **mkuser** command do exactly the same thing, so you can use whichever method you prefer. These commands accomplish all of the same things that the UNIX **sysadmsh** command sequence does.

Setting Up an Account

With the UNIX **sysadmsh** commands for creating accounts, you can choose either to use the default settings for all aspects of the account or to change these defaults. The settings include such choices as where the user's home directory will be located, what the login shell for the account will be, and what login group the account will be part of. The changeable parameters of user accounts are discussed in Chapter 10 of the *SCO UNIX System Administrator's Guide*, "Administering User Accounts."

Once you have elected to use the defaults or have changed the defaults for an account, the next step in creating a user account is to enter a comment field and a password for the user. The comment field can contain any information (up to 35 characters maximum), but the suggested format is

full name, location (office number, etc.), extension, home phone

Note the commas separating the fields. This format is recommended because this information is used by the **finger** command to display information about users. See Chapter 3, "Using Your Account," for more information about the **finger** command. The **finger** command displays the information in the comment field with the headings In Real Life:, Office:, and Home Phone:. If you do not use the recommended format, these fields will either be blank or contain incongruous information. The **/etc/passwd** file contains a line for each account on the system. The line consists of several pieces of information separated by colons. Below are some sample lines from an **/etc/passwd** file.

```
myrmur:*:205:60:Mrs. Murray, 805, x6415,565-3344:/u/myrmur:/bin/csh
moms:*:919:60:Mom's Soup,Fremont,No ext,498-0083:/u/moms:/bin/rsh
dbg:*:921:53:D.B. Gay,Consultant,x523,423-7575:/u/dbg:/bin/sh
sshadeed:*:923:53:S. Shadeed,23,x009,925-8791:/u/sshadeed:/bin/sh
```

The first field of the entry shows the user's login name. The second field contains an asterisk (*), which is an unreadable representation of the password for the account. This file is usually readable by all users, so the actual password must not be printed.

XENIX   On XENIX, the second field in the **/etc/passwd** file contains an *encrypted* version of the user's password, which is a coded, unreadable sequence of characters.

The third and fourth fields are the user's user and group ID numbers. The fifth field, which encompasses everything between the fourth and fifth colons, is the comment field. The sixth field shows the pathname of the home directory for the account, and the final field shows the login shell or the program executed on startup.

 CAUTION Do not edit the file **/etc/passwd** on an SCO UNIX system. If you want to change any of the information in this file after you create a user account, select the **sysadmsh** command **Accounts**, select **User**, and then select **Modify**. With this command sequence, you can change most of the information and parameters for a user.

XENIX On XENIX, editing the **/etc/passwd** file is the only way to change certain information for a user. For example, the XENIX **sysadmsh** does not have an option to change the comment field for a user. If you must edit the **/etc/passwd** file, do so with caution. A mistake in this file could result in lost files or prevent a user from logging in.

There are some restrictions on creating user accounts in UNIX that do not apply in XENIX. For example, on UNIX, once an account has been retired—or removed—you can never restore this account (or an account with the same name) to the system.

Home Directories

As mentioned earlier in the "Filesystems" section, it is a good idea to create a separate filesystem, or, if this is impractical, a separate directory, in which to place users' home directories. By default, users' home directories are created in the directory **/usr**. This directory also holds a number of other directories that contain important system files. It is far easier to manage and back up user files if they are all located in a single location that is uncluttered with system files. It is strongly recommended that you create all of your user accounts in either a **/u** filesystem or a **/u** directory.

If you elect to have a separate **/u** filesystem, the default location for user accounts on your system will automatically be set to **/u** during the installation procedure. If you do not create a **/u** filesystem, but do want to locate user accounts in a **/u** directory, you must make some adjustments to your system. You can use the **sysadmsh** to change the default home directory by selecting the **system** command, selecting **Configure** from the System menu, selecting **Defaults** from the Configure menu, and finally, selecting **Home** from the Defaults menu. This puts you in **vi** in the file **/etc/default/authsh**. Find the line that says

```
HOME=/usr
```

and change that line to read

```
HOME=/u
```

Since the **sysadmsh** uses the **vi** editor, you must know how to use **vi** to edit this file through the **sysadmsh**. If you want to use a different editor, edit the file with a shell command. Once you exit this file, the new directory you have specified will be the default directory. You can still choose another directory each time you create a new account.

 REMEMBER   If you have chosen a name besides **/u** for your user filesystem or directory, enter that name instead of **/u** in this file.

XENIX   On XENIX, you are not given a choice of home directories each time you create a user account. Instead, the default location is always used. To make the default home directory something besides **/usr**, edit the file **/etc/default/mkuser**. Edit the file as shown in the preceding paragraph. All new user accounts will now be automatically created in this directory. However, any accounts you created before making this change will remain in their old locations.

Login Shells

Each time you create an account, you assign a login shell to that account. The *login shell* for an account is the shell that the user interacts with when he or she first logs in. The default login shell on SCO UNIX is the Bourne shell. If you elect not to use the defaults for an account, you can choose a different login shell. Many users prefer the Bourne shell (**sh**) because it is the standard SCO UNIX shell, and because it provides a highly accurate shell programming language. Others like the C shell because of its history substitution features, which archive commands. While Bourne shell scripts can be created and run from the C shell, the reverse is not true. The restricted shell (**rsh**) can be used for accounts whose activities you want to restrict. SCO UNIX commands that allow users to change directories or to view or change important files are off limits to the restricted shell. See the *SCO UNIX User's Reference* for more information about each of the shells. If you are not sure which login shell your users prefer, you might want to assign the same shell to all new accounts, and then change them on an individual basis as users request you to do so.

Groups

By default, all nonadministrative users are assigned to the same login group. The *group* a user belongs to determines which files and directories that user has access to. File permissions are assigned for the owner of a file, for users in the same group, and for users not in the same group. For example, the members of one group may have write permission for a file, while users not in that group have only read permission. Each account must be associated with at least one group. You can assign an account to more than one group, in which case that user will be able to change her or his group association so that he or she has the permissions associated with the new group. See Chapter 4, "Files and Directories," for more information about groups and file permissions.

Installing an SCO UNIX system involves many different tasks. First, you must select the appropriate hardware for your system and for your own needs. Then, you must make a number of decisions about the software component of the system. For example, you must decide whether or not to have a separate user filesystem and whether you need extra swap space. You will also need to add hardware, additional applications, and user accounts. These and other tasks involved in getting your system up and running have been discussed in this chapter. For additional information about administering your SCO UNIX system, see Chapter 12, "System

Administration." Chapter 12 explains some of the routine tasks of system administration, such as backing up the system and monitoring user activity, and also supplies additional information about several topics discussed in this chapter.

3

Using Your Account

Every person who uses a SCO UNIX system must have an account on that system. A *user account* consists of several elements, which, in combination, allow you access to an SCO UNIX system. First, your account has a unique name, called your *account name, login name,* or *user ID,* which identifies you to the computer and to other users. A *password* is also assigned to each account to ensure that only the person authorized to use the account can log in to it. Finally, your account is assigned a *home directory,* in which you can create other directories and store your files. Once you log in, or gain access, to your account, you have access to a wealth of information and commands that allow you to use SCO UNIX for hundreds of different tasks. The commands discussed in this chapter will introduce the components of a user account and help you become comfortable with the SCO UNIX command-oriented operating system.

Logging In

The first step in using your account is to log in to the computer. *Logging in* means identifying yourself to the computer so that you can be placed in the proper home directory, and given access to the appropriate files and commands.

The Login Prompt

The login prompt is a message that appears on a terminal that is ready to use. Sometimes a system-specific message, such as the name of your particular system, is displayed before the login prompt, but the login prompt itself always ends with

```
login:
```

If this prompt does not appear on your terminal, press the RETURN key (several times if necessary), the DEL key, or CTRL-d. If the prompt still does not appear, you will have to try another terminal or talk to the system administrator. If you are the system administrator and can't get a terminal to respond, see the section "Terminals" in Chapter 12, "System Administration."

Once you see the prompt, type your user or login name exactly as it has been assigned to you. Because SCO UNIX is sensitive to case, you must match upper- and lowercase letters. For example, if your login name were hayes, you would type **hayes**, not Hayes or HAYES.

 NOTE   If your terminal is only capable of printing uppercase characters (as is the case with some very old terminals), simply type your login name in all uppercase letters. The system will display a message to warn you that it will consider your terminal an uppercase-only terminal unless you enter your login name in lowercase letters. Then it will again prompt you for your login. Typing your login name in uppercase again notifies SCO UNIX that your terminal does not support lowercase, and that it must expect and send you only uppercase characters.

If you type your login name in uppercase on a terminal that *does* support lowercase characters (say, if your CAPS LOCK key has been pressed), SCO UNIX will assume that you are on an uppercase-only terminal and will display its warning message. In this case, you must enter your login name again, this time in lowercase (perhaps by first disabling CAPS LOCK).

XENIX   On XENIX, once your terminal is set in uppercase-only mode, disabling CAPS LOCK will not work. Instead press CTRL-d to get out of uppercase-only mode.

The Password Prompt

After entering your login name and pressing RETURN, you will see the password prompt:

```
Password:
```

At this prompt, type your password, again matching upper- and lowercase letters exactly. To ensure that your password will not be read by other users, it will not appear on the screen as you type it.

   Some accounts—usually public accounts that will be used by a number of people—do not require a password; however, on UNIX, the password prompt is still displayed, and you must press RETURN to gain access to these accounts.

XENIX   On XENIX, a public account with no password does not display the password prompt, so you can ignore the instructions regarding passwords if you are using one of these accounts on XENIX.

   If you have typed both your login and your password correctly, you will be logged in to your account. If you've made a mistake typing *either* your login name *or* your password, you will see this error message:

```
login incorrect
login:
```

In response to this message, type both your login name and your password again, at their respective prompts.

System Messages

Once you have successfully logged in, you may see some system messages. These may include information about the release of XENIX or UNIX that your system is running; the amount of hard disk space that is available for data storage; a system-wide message of the day from the system administrator; a message telling you that you have electronic mail; and a list of system news items. You'll learn how to read system news items in the section "System Information" later in this chapter.

Setting Your Terminal Type

After any system messages have been displayed, you will see the terminal type prompt. The SCO UNIX system needs to know what kind of terminal you have so it can properly set up the screen for utilities like **vi**, the full-screen editor. Each brand and model of terminal supported by SCO UNIX has a unique code associated with it, and it is this code that you enter when UNIX prompts you for your terminal type.

If you don't know the code for your terminal, the simplest way to find out is to ask another user or the system administrator. Most user accounts have a default terminal type, which is set in a file containing commands that are executed every time you log in. In the C shell, this file is called **.login**, and in the Bourne shell it is called **.profile**. See Chapters 10, "The Bourne Shell," and 11, "The C Shell," for instructions on changing your default terminal type. The default for your account is displayed after the prompt. For example, if the default for your account is a WYSE 50, you will see:

```
TERM = (wy50)
```

If the terminal you are currently using is the same as the default type, all you have to do is press RETURN. If your terminal type is not the same as the default, type the code for your terminal type at this prompt and then press RETURN.

 NOTE   If you are unable to find out from another user what the code for your terminal is, there is a way you can log in anyway. At the prompt, type

tty

and your terminal type will be set to a basic type, tty33. Then, once you have logged in, send mail to your system administrator and ask her or him for the appropriate code.

If there is only one kind of terminal on your UNIX system or if you are working at the console, you may not be prompted for a terminal type.

Communicating with the Computer

As soon as you have completed the begin procedure you will see a shell prompt. A *shell* is an interface between you and the SCO UNIX kernel that translates each command you type into instructions to run a certain program or programs. A shell prompt is the signal that the shell is ready to carry out your next command. The two most common shells are the Bourne shell and the C shell. One of these will be your *login shell,* the shell that serves as your interface when you first log in. The prompt tells you which of the two shells you are in. A percent sign (%) is usually the C shell prompt, while the Bourne shell prompt is usually a dollar sign ($).

 NOTE   The % and $ signs are only the default prompts. The actual prompt for your account may be different. In Chapters 10, "The Bourne Shell," and 11, "The C Shell," you will learn how to change your shell prompt to a string of your choice if you don't like the default prompt for your account.

At any time, you can use a shell other than your login shell. Chapters 10 and 11 describe some of the features of each of the two shells, and tell you how to change your shell. For now, the commands discussed here will work in either shell.

Using SCO UNIX Commands

SCO UNIX is a command-oriented operating system; once the shell prompt appears on the screen, the computer waits until you tell it what to do by entering a command. You do this by typing the name of an SCO UNIX program, and then pressing RETURN. The computer will not execute your command until you press RETURN. All SCO UNIX command names are one word long, and most include only lowercase letters. Some commands, such as **date**, are actual English words; others, like **ls**, are not. Most commands that are not English words are somewhat mnemonic; for example, **ls** stands for *list* and **mkdir** stands for *make directory*.

SCO UNIX commands vary with respect to the type of input they require and the type of output they produce. You can execute some commands by typing the name of the command alone. Others require you to specify the name of a file or directory on which the command will operate. Any file names or other words that you type after the name of a command are *arguments* to the command. Most commands also have *options*, extra letters or numbers typed after a hyphen that allow you to achieve slightly different results with the same command. Whenever you type something (either an argument or an option) after a command name, it must be separated from the command name by a space.

Correcting Mistakes

If you make a mistake as you type an SCO UNIX command, there are several ways to correct either individual characters or whole lines. Some of these will work for you, and some will not, depending on how your terminal is set up. By pressing the BACKSPACE key, you can back up one space at a time until you reach the mistake. As you back up, the letter the cursor is on may or may not disappear from the screen; however, it will be erased from your input.

The key combination CTRL-h usually works exactly like the BACKSPACE key. Some users find it easier to use CTRL-h than BACKSPACE because on many keyboards the CTRL and h keys are easier to reach than the BACKSPACE key. Sometimes you can use CTRL-h even if your BACKSPACE key is not working correctly. Keys that erase one character at a time are called *erase keys*.

Sometimes you will type a whole line and then decide that you don't want to execute the command, or discover that you've made a mistake at the beginning of the line. In this case, you may want to erase the entire line in one fell swoop, rather than backing up one character at a time. Keys or combinations of keys that erase a whole line or cause the computer to ignore the line are called *line-kill keys*. One way to erase a whole line is by pressing CTRL-u. CTRL-u will not actually erase the line from the screen, but it will cause the command to be ignored so that it is not executed.

The *interrupt key,* which is usually set initially to the DEL key, does the same thing as a line-kill key. This key can also be used to exit a program, even after it has already started running. See the section "Displaying and Setting Terminal Parameters—stty" for instructions on how to change the erase, line-kill, and interrupt keys if you do not like their initial settings for your account.

System Information

Information about the operating system and other topics is available at all times. You can use UNIX commands to find out the time, obtain information about other users, get instructions for using other commands, and much more. The commands discussed in this section will introduce you to the resources SCO UNIX provides.

Displaying the Date and Time — date

The **date** command without any arguments prints the current date and time using a 24-hour clock, as in the following example.

```
$ date
Thu May 24 15:12:59 PDT 1990
```

You can make the **date** command display the date in many other formats. See the *SCO UNIX User's Reference* or the on-line manual pages for more information about the **date** command.

Displaying a Calendar — cal

The **cal** (short for *calendar*) command used without arguments displays a calendar for the present month and the two adjacent months. To display calendars for months or years other than the present month and year, you can type the months and years you want as arguments to the command. Months can be typed either as numbers (**1** through **12**) or as the first few letters (all lowercase) of the month name (**d** for *December,* **mar** for *March,* and so on).

 NOTE   If you type only one number as an argument to the **cal** command, it will be interpreted as a year, not as a month.

The following example shows one way to display a calendar for November of the current year.

```
$ cal nov
   November 1990
 S   M  Tu   W  Th   F   S
                 1   2   3
 4   5   6   7   8   9  10
11  12  13  14  15  16  17
18  19  20  21  22  23  24
25  26  27  28  29  30
```

The complete month name is also acceptable.

You must type years as four digits. That is, the number 90 would be interpreted as the year 90, not as 1990. The following example displays a calendar for June of the year 2000.

```
$ cal 6 2000
    June 2000
 S   M  Tu   W  Th   F   S
                 1   2   3
 4   5   6   7   8   9  10
11  12  13  14  15  16  17
18  19  20  21  22  23  24
25  26  27  28  29  30
```

Displaying Your User Name and Number—id

The **id** command displays your user (uid) and group (gid) ID numbers and your user and group names in the format shown here:

```
$ id
uid=201(shirleyb)  gid=50(group)
```

Listing Other Users on the System—who

The **who** command displays an alphabetized list of users currently logged in to the computer, the terminals they are using, and the time each one logged in, as in the following example.

```
$ who
root        tty02         Jan 24 09:25
myrmur      ttyilc        Jan 24 11:06
```

The command **who am i** prints this information for you only, as shown here:

```
$ who am i
myrmur      ttyilc        Jan 17 11:06
```

With the **-T** option, **who** displays some extra information. In addition to the name, terminal, and login time of each user, the *state* of the user's terminal is also displayed in a new second column, as in the following example.

```
$ who -T
root       - tty02      Jan 24 09:25
myrmur     + ttyi1c     Jan 24 11:06
```

A **+** in this column indicates that the user's terminal is *writable*, that is, you can send this user messages with the **write** or **hello** command. See the section "Communicating with Other Users" for more information about writable terminals.

With other options, the **who** command displays entirely different information. For example, the **-b** option causes **who** to display the time the system was last booted, while the **-t** option displays the time the system clock was last reset. With the **-l** option, **who** lists all data lines (lines connected to terminals) on which no one is currently logged in.

Displaying Information About a User—finger

On SCO UNIX, you can use the **finger** command to get information about users, even those who are not currently logged in to the system. Without arguments, **finger** displays information about all the users who are currently logged in. The information **finger** displays is much the same as that displayed by **who**; however, the **finger** command displays the user's real name and office location (if this data was entered by the system administrator when he or she created the user's account), as well as the terminal the user is working on, and the date she or he logged in. Like **who** with the **-T** option, **finger** also tells you whether or not a user's terminal is writable. Compare the following example to the example of the **who** command without arguments in the preceding section.

```
$ finger
Login       Name            TTY    Idle   When         Office
root        Superuser       *01    1:31   Wed 09:25    104
myrmur      Myrtle Murray   i1c           Wed 11:06    333
```

You can get additional information about any user, whether that user is logged in or not, by typing his or her login name as an argument to the **finger** command. When you use **finger** to display information for a specified user, it displays the user's home directory, the date of her or his last login, and the login shell assigned to her or his account, as well as the personal information normally displayed with **finger**. If the user's terminal is *not* writable, **finger** also prints "(no messages)." The following example shows the format the finger command uses to print information for specified users.

```
$ finger jeffa
Login name: jeffa              In real life: Jeff Anderson
Office: LBG, 333               Home phone: 555-3451
Directory: /u/jeffa           Shell: /bin/csh
Project: Hypochondria Study
Plan:
I am currently at work on a study of the effects of
hypochondria on the work habits of American males. In the
fall I will extend my study to cover European males.

I can be reached at x6200, usually between 8:00 and 5:30 or
so.
```

In addition to the standard information displayed for all users, a project and a plan may be displayed for the user. If you create a file in your home directory called **.project**, a line labeled **Project:** in the output of **finger** will display the first line of that file. If you create the file **.plan**, whatever is in that file will be printed below a line that reads **Plan:**. For the information in these files to be available to other users who use **finger**, you must make these files readable by all users. See Chapter 4, "Files and Directories," for information about making files readable by other users.

Reading System News Items—news

The **news** command displays system news items, which are found in files in the directory **/usr/news**. Without arguments, **news** displays the contents of all files in this directory that have been modified more recently than the file **.news_time** in your home directory. Then, the modification time of this file is changed, so that you only see files you have not seen before.

With the **-a** option, **news** displays all items, including those you have already seen. The **-n** option causes **news** to display only the names of current files that you have not seen. Finally, if you want to select certain items to read, you can type the names of those items as arguments to the **news** command. The following example shows how you would first list the names of items you had not seen, and then select two of them to read.

```
$ news -n
news: sched.update printer.fixed copier party
$ news party printer.fixed
```

The two files **party** and **printer.fixed** would be displayed.

On UNIX, the **news -n** command is executed when you log in, so you automatically see a list of the current news items. Also, initially, ordinary users have permission to place their own news items in the directory **/usr/news**; however, individual system administrators may revoke this privilege.

XENIX   On XENIX, ordinary users are initially denied permission to place files in the **/usr/news** directory, but the system administrator may grant that permission.

Displaying Your Terminal Line — tty

Hardware components such as terminals and printers connected to an SCO UNIX system are associated with special *device files*. The **tty** command displays the name of the device file associated with your terminal, as in the following example.

```
$ tty
/dev/ttyi1c
```

This device is a special file in the **/dev** directory. There are times when you will want to direct the output of a command to your terminal, and will need to know the name of the file that it is associated with. You may also need to know the name of your terminal device if you are communicating with other users via the **write** or **hello** command.

Viewing the On-Line Manual Pages—man

You can learn how to use any of the standard SCO UNIX utilities on your system with the **man** command. This command displays the on-line manual pages (**man** pages) for the command whose name you give as an argument. For example, to display the pages for the **date** command, you would type

```
$ man date
```

The first **man** page will be displayed, and if there is more than one page, a colon (:) prompt will appear at the bottom of the screen. When you are ready to look at the next page, simply press RETURN at this prompt. Repeat this procedure until all the pages have been displayed. If you want to quit the **man** program before you have seen all the pages for a command, type **q** at the colon prompt, and then press RETURN.

The **man** pages initially included with the SCO UNIX system cover only those utilities supplied with the operating system. Any special applications software that runs on your system will not be covered in the **man** pages unless your system administrator has installed pages pertaining to that software. You may have to consult the system administrator for information about special applications.

Modifying Your Environment

You have a great deal of control over your UNIX account and over the terminal you are using while you are logged in. For example, you can clear the terminal screen of old output or lock your terminal temporarily to reserve it. You can also control the way certain keys are interpreted by the computer. This section covers just a few of the ways you can modify your login environment and your terminal.

Clearing the Terminal Screen—clear

Notice that as you execute commands, previous commands and their output remain on the screen until they scroll off the top as the screen fills up. The **clear** command clears the screen of old commands and output and displays a new prompt at the top of the screen. This can be advantageous if there is something on your screen that you do not want other people to see, for example, a mail message you have just typed. Clearing the screen also makes it easier to focus on the next command's output.

Locking Your Terminal—lock

The **lock** command locks your terminal so you can leave it without worrying about anyone getting into your account or taking over your terminal. After you type **lock**, you are requested to enter and verify a password. You can choose any password you want; it need not be the password to your account. The echo to the terminal is turned off while you type the password, just as it is during the password portion of the login procedure. The terminal will only be unlocked when you type that password again, followed by a RETURN. Once you have typed and verified your password for **lock**, a message is printed telling others who locked the terminal and how long ago it was locked, as shown here:

```
$ lock
Password:
Re-enter password:
terminal locked by margyv 0 minutes ago
```

If you do not return and unlock your terminal within a certain amount of time, you are automatically logged out and the terminal is unlocked. This time period depends on the default time for your system. You may also specify a number of minutes as an option to the **lock** command, and lock the terminal for an amount of time different from the default. For example, to lock the terminal for 45 minutes, you would use the command

```
$ lock -45
```

Each system has a maximum allowable number of minutes before logout. If the number you type exceeds this maximum, the maximum time is used.

With the **-v** option, **lock** temporarily clears the screen of whatever you were doing and displays a large message stating that the terminal is locked.

Keeping Your Account Secure—passwd

From time to time, you should change your password to reduce the chance of unauthorized people logging in to your account. If other people could gain access to your account, they could not only read all of your files, but could also remove or change them. You use the **passwd** command to change your password. To do this, type **passwd**; you will see the following prompt:

```
Old password:
```

In response, type your old password. This step prevents someone else from changing your password if they are using your account (either with or without your authorization). Remember, your password does not print on the screen as you type it. If you type it incorrectly, the **passwd** program will fail and you will get an error message. On UNIX, you get the error message shown in the following example.

```
$ passwd
Old password:
Sorry.

Password request denied.
Reason: invalid old password.
```

XENIX   On XENIX, the **passwd** error message is less explicit than it is on UNIX. It looks like this:

```
$ passwd
Old password:
Sorry.
```

If you have typed your password incorrectly, the only remedy is to type the **passwd** command again, and start over.

Once you've typed the old password correctly, you are requested to enter a new password. On UNIX, there are two steps to entering your new password. First, you are asked to choose whether you want to pick your own password or have one generated for you. If you elect to choose your own, you will see the **New password**: prompt. If you elect to have a password generated for you, a list of passwords will be presented to you, one at a time. Keep pressing RETURN until you see one that you like, and then type that one.

XENIX   On XENIX, you are simply prompted for a new password, as follows:

```
New password:
```

On either UNIX or XENIX, if you choose your own password, choose one that will be hard for anyone else to guess. For example, do not use your name or nickname, or any word in the dictionary. (Someone who really wanted to find out your password could systematically check every word in the UNIX system dictionary to see whether it matched your password.) On the other hand, you should select a password that will be easy for you to remember. You should *never* write your password down. A word or name with numbers inserted between or in place of some of the letters is a good password.

When you have typed your new password once, you will be asked to confirm it by typing it again. This ensures that you have not made a mistake while typing your password. If the two entries match, **passwd** returns a shell prompt, and your password is changed. If they don't match, **passwd** asks you to type the new password again.

If you forget your password, do not panic. You can simply ask your system administrator to assign you a new password, which you can then use to log in.

Displaying and Setting Terminal Parameters—stty

You can use the **stty** command to display and change certain aspects of your terminal's behavior. These parameters include such things as rates of data transmission, the way lines are handled by the terminal, and which keys function as the erase, line-kill, and interrupt keys for your terminal. This section discusses how to use **stty** to change the key assignments. For a full description of the **stty** parameters, see the *SCO UNIX User's Reference* or the on-line man pages.

Without any arguments, the **stty** command displays a limited list of terminal parameters and their values, including the value of the interrupt key. To display the values of the erase and line-kill keys you must use the **-a** option, which causes **stty** to display all the parameters it normally displays, plus many additional parameters, as in the following example.

```
$ stty -a
speed 9600 baud; ispeed 9600 baud; ospeed 9600 baud;
line = 0; intr = DEL; quit = ^\; erase = ^H; kill = ^U;
eof = ^D; eol = ^@; swtch = ^@; susp = ^];
-parenb -parodd cs8 -cstopb hupcl cread -clocal -loblk
-ctsflow -rtsflow -ignbrk brkint ignpar -parmrk -inpck
istrip -inlcr -igncr icrnl -iuclc ixon ixany -ixoff
isig icanon -xcase echo echoe echok -echonl -noflsh -iexten
-tostop opost -olcuc onlcr -ocrnl -onocr -onlret -ofill
-ofdel
```

The last five lines of this output deal with parameters that, for the most part, define data transmissions between your terminal and the computer. These parameters take binary values, and the presence or absence of a minus, before the name of the parameter indicates the value. If the output of **stty** seems a bit intimidating, rest assured that you will rarely, if ever, need to use most of the information **stty** displays.

The second and third lines of the input list parameters that take character values, such as the erase and line-kill keys. In this example, the interrupt key (intr) is set to DEL, the erase key is CTRL-h (printed as ^H), and the line-kill key is CTRL-u (printed as ^U).

Suppose the interrupt key for your terminal is initially set to the DEL key, and you would rather use a different key. To change a parameter that takes a character value, type the name of the parameter and the character you want to set it to after the **stty** command. To indicate a control character, use a lowercase letter preceded by a caret (^) and enclosed in single quotes. For example, to set the interrupt key to CTRL-c, you would use the following command.

```
$ stty intr '^c'
```

You would use the same form for any other control character. For example, to set the erase key to CTRL-h, you would use this command:

```
$ stty erase '^h'
```

The next command sets your terminal parameters to reasonable values in the event that your terminal's settings become scrambled.

```
$ stty sane
```

Instead of pressing RETURN after entering this command, you press CTRL-j. If your terminal's settings are scrambled, the RETURN character may not function properly. CTRL-j is the *line-feed key,* which is different from RETURN. If you are ever faced with a frozen terminal or strange-looking output, try typing this command. Even if the command does not appear on the screen as you type, it may restore your terminal to its normal state.

Communicating with Other Users

One advantage SCO UNIX provides as a multiuser operating system is the ability to communicate with other users on your own and other UNIX systems. The **write** and **hello** commands let you instantly send messages to other logged-in users. The **mail** command lets you send messages through the electronic mail system to users who may or may not be logged in. When you send a message through the **mail** program, the recipient sees the message only if she or he decides to read it.

Writing to Another User's Terminal—write and hello

With the **write** command, you can instantly communicate with another user; however, that user's terminal must be writable, and your terminal must also be writable for you to receive a reply. (The next section, which covers the **mesg** command, explains how to make your terminal writable.)

You can use the **who** command with the **-T** option or the **finger** command to find out if the person you want to write to is logged, in and whether or not his or her terminal is writable. Once you have selected a user to write to, specify her or his user name as an argument to the **write** command. For example, to write to a user called **jitters**, you would use this command:

```
$ write jitters
```

As soon as you type this command and press RETURN, a message is sent to the other user saying that you are about to write to his or her terminal. The **write** command establishes only one-way communication. It lets you write to the other user's terminal, but does not let them respond. If the other user wants to respond to your message, he or she must also use the **write** command, but must specify *your* user name as an argument.

When the cursor is on a blank line, you can type your message. As soon as you press RETURN at the end of a line, that line is sent to the other user's terminal. Lines that the other user types appear on your screen in the same manner.

 TIP   Users often establish a convention to let one another know that they have finished writing. For example, you could use a slash or some other punctuation to indicate that you had finished typing your message, so the other user could respond. If both users type messages simultaneously, the lines will be interspersed on the screen, which can be confusing. When you have finished communicating with another user, press CTRL-d on a new line. The **write** program sends the message "(End of message)" to the other user's terminal, and you will be returned to the shell prompt.

The **hello** command is similar to the **write** command. Like **write**, it sends messages directly to another user's terminal.

XENIX   On XENIX, once you establish contact with another user with the **hello** command, whatever you type appears on the other user's screen immediately, without your pressing RETURN. Thus, one user doesn't have to wait while the other types a whole line.

On UNIX, **hello** functions like the XENIX **hello** command only for the superuser. For ordinary users, it behaves exactly like **write**.

Making a Terminal Writable—mesg

You can use the **mesg** command to make your terminal writable or not writable. When your terminal is writable, other users can send messages to your terminal with the **write** or **hello** commands. When your terminal is not writable, no user except the superuser may send you messages. If you attempt to write to a terminal that is not writable, you will get an error message, as in the following example:

```
$ write celie
Permission denied.
```

To make your terminal writable, issue this command:

```
$ mesg y
```

Terminals are generally writable by default, so you should not have to make your terminal writable unless you have made it not writable in the past.

To make a terminal not writable, issue the command

```
$ mesg n
```

 NOTE If your terminal is writable, your screen may be temporarily scrambled when another user writes to you, especially if you are using a utility that fills the whole screen, such as **vi**, the visual editor. For this reason, some users prefer to make their terminals not writable while they are using such programs. See Chapter 7, "Editing and Text Processing," for instructions on making your terminal not writable.

Sending and Reading Electronic Mail—mail

The **mail** program allows you to communicate with other users on your system or other connected UNIX systems. Mail is discussed in more detail in Chapter 9, "Sending and Receiving Mail." This chapter explains briefly how to read and respond to your mail messages and send mail of your own.

So that you have some mail to read as you try out the mail program, follow the steps below to send a mail message to yourself. You can send mail to any other user whose login name you know by following the same steps, but be sure to insert their login name in place of yours. First, type your login name as an argument to the **mail** command. For example, if your login name were **jackb**, you would type:

```
$ mail jackb
```

The command will prompt you for the subject of your message, as follows:

```
Subject:
```

The first line you type will be the subject of the message. When you press RETURN, whatever you type next will be the body of the message. Type as you ordinarily would, using the BACKSPACE and line-kill keys when necessary. Be sure to press RETURN at the end of each line, or your message will appear on one long line. When you have finished your message, type CTRL-d on a new line. You will see the message "EOT," and be returned to the shell prompt.

XENIX On XENIX, you will see "(end of message)" instead of "EOT."

Now that you've sent yourself some mail, you are ready to read that message and any others you might have. To read your mail, simply type the **mail** command without any arguments. You will see a list of messages. The list contains a number for each message, assigned according to the order in which it was received. It also includes the login name of the sender; the date and time the message was received; some information about the length of the message; and its subject, if any. Below the list you'll see the mail prompt, which is a question mark (?) on UNIX.

XENIX The mail prompt on XENIX is an underscore (_).

Once the list of messages is displayed, you can choose one to read by simply typing the number of the message followed by RETURN at the mail prompt. When you select a message to read, mail displays that message, together with some information about the sender, the date the message was sent and received, and the addressee. When the entire message has been displayed, you are returned to the mail prompt. Then, you can choose another message to read by following the same procedure outlined above, or you can respond to the message you just read. To respond to a message, type a lowercase **r** at the mail prompt after reading the message. This starts a new message, which will be mailed to the person who sent the message that you just read. An uppercase **R** sends the message that follows it to everyone who received the original message.

To leave the **mail** program, you can use the **quit (q)** or **exit (x)** command. On UNIX, if you type **q**, any messages that you have read are saved in a file called **mbox**, in your home directory, while those you have not read are saved for the next time you execute the **mail** program.

XENIX Messages are not automatically saved in your **mbox** file on XENIX. Instead, all messages that you do not delete or save as files are saved in the *mail spool,* the place where your new messages are stored.

On either XENIX or UNIX, if you type **x** to leave the **mail** program, all messages are saved for the next time you execute **mail**.

Logging Out

When you are ready to end an SCO UNIX login session, you must *log out* of, or exit, your account. This prevents others from using your account and frees the terminal for someone else to use. There are three ways to log out of your account. In either the Bourne shell or the C shell, you can use the **exit** command. To make sure you are logged out, wait until you see a new login prompt on the screen indicating that the terminal is ready for another user to log in. In the C shell, the **logout** command works just like the **exit** command.

If your login shell is the Bourne shell (your prompt will be $), you can also log out by pressing CTRL-d. CTRL-d sometimes logs you out in the C shell as well, but your account may be set up not to allow this. In this case, if you type CTRL-d, you will get the following error message.

```
Use "logout" to logout.
```

When you log out, whatever is on your screen stays there for the next user to read. If you don't want this to happen, clear the screen with **clear** before logging out.

You now know how to log in to your SCO UNIX account and execute a number of useful commands. To make full use of your SCO UNIX account, you will need to create files and directories. Chapter 4 explains the concepts of files and directories and covers the commands you will use to create your own directory structure and the files in which you will store your data.

In this chapter, you also learned to make certain changes to your environment for a particular login session. You will probably want to make some of these changes take effect every time you log in to your account. Chapters 10, "The Bourne Shell," and 11, "The C Shell," explain how you can do this.

Files and Directories

A UNIX filesystem contains a hierarchical structure of files and directories. Some people find it helpful to think of a filesystem as an inverted tree. At the top of the structure is a single directory, called the *root,* or **/** (slash) directory, which branches off into a number of other directories, just as a tree trunk branches into limbs. Each of these directories may in turn branch into other directories and files. Between the root directory and the files are other directories. The directories of a UNIX filesystem can be thought of as the branches of the tree: they lead from the trunk to other directories and finally to individual files. The system of directories provides a way of addressing a file, so that SCO UNIX can access it quickly and efficiently.

Figure 4-1 shows a partial structure of a typical UNIX filesystem. A diagram of all the files and directories on a UNIX system would be too large to show here, so only a few directories are included. Examine this figure to familiarize yourself with some of the terminology you will see throughout this chapter.

Any directory that is inside another is called a *subdirectory*. In Figure 4-1, **usr** is a subdirectory of **/**; **lib**, **pub**, and **tmp** are subdirectories of **usr**, and so on. Any directory that contains a file or subdirectory is called the *parent directory* of that file or subdirectory. In Figure 4-1, **/** is the parent of several directories, including **bin**, **dev**, **u** and **usr**; **kirkwood** is the parent directory of **articles** and **reports**, and so on. Finally, **acid.rain** is a file in the directory **articles**.

At any level in the filesystem you may find files, directories that branch into files, or directories that branch into other directories. Once you are familiar with the commands used for creating and manipulating directories, you will be able to create a system of directories and subdirectories in your UNIX account in which to store your personal files.

Figure 4-1.

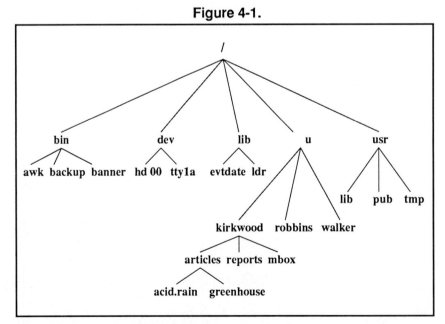

Partial Structure of a UNIX Filesystem.

Getting Acquainted with Files and Directories

Before you begin creating files and directories of your own, there are several concepts you should be familiar with. You should understand what files and directories are, the way they are addressed, and how the operating system keeps track of the huge number of files on an SCO UNIX system. The following sections explain many of the concepts that are integral to working with files and directories.

What Is a File?

A file is a collection of data, usually either text or machine code. Most of the files you create will be text files, while most programs that run on SCO UNIX are machine code files. Whenever you execute an SCO UNIX command, you are telling the computer to execute the commands in a certain file or set of files. As a user of UNIX, you will be able to create, edit, read, change, search, and remove your own files. In this chapter you will learn how to create your own files, and how to move, copy, rename, remove, and change the permissions on files—in short, most of what you need to know to work with UNIX files.

What Is a Directory?

Every file in a UNIX system is part of some directory. This arrangement keeps files organized and reduces the time it takes the operating system to find a particular file. If all the files in the system were stored together in one place, it would take UNIX a long time to search through all of them and find a particular file. Directories provide a way of addressing files so they can be accessed quickly and easily.

 NOTE   Actually, a file is not physically *in* a directory. Rather, the file is associated with a directory, and the inode that contains information about the file is part of the directory. The inode of a file contains pointers to the data blocks that make up a file, which may be located in several different places on the hard disk. For our present purposes, however, it is safe to say that a file associated with a directory is *in* that directory.

File and Directory Access Permissions

All files on an SCO UNIX system are part of one large filesystem and could, in principle, be accessed by any user of the system. To prevent users from gaining unauthorized access to files, each file and directory on an SCO UNIX system is associated with an owner—usually the person who created it or a system administrator—and with a group—usually (but not necessarily) the login group that the owner belongs to. In addition, access to each file and directory is controlled by a set of *permissions* that determine which users can read, or view, the file; write, or make changes to the file; and, if the file is executable as a program, run that program. As they pertain to directories, read and execute permissions allow the user to list the contents of a directory, while write permission allows the user to create files in the directory.

You can change the permissions of any file or directory that you own with the **chmod** (for change mode) command. See the section "Changing Access Permissions of a File or Directory" later in this chapter for information about changing the permissions of your files.

You can view the permissions, owner, and group for a file or directory with the **ls -l** command. The **l** command works exactly the same as the **ls -l** command, and you may find it easier to remember. See the section "Listing the Contents of a Directory" later in this chapter for more information about viewing the permissions for a file or directory.

Pathnames

Every file and directory on a UNIX system has a unique address, called a *pathname*. A pathname is so called because it consists of a list of directories that lie along the path from the root directory to the file in question. Every absolute pathname begins with a **/** (slash), which is the name of the root directory. A **/** also separates the names of the directories in the pathname. Figure 4-2 shows a UNIX filesystem that has as one subdirectory a user account called **harrymu**. The directories that lie along the path of the home directory of this account are shaded in the figure. The pathname of this directory would be **/u/accounting/harrymu**. As you can see in Figure 4-2, **harrymu** is a subdirectory of a directory called **accounting**, which is in turn a subdirectory of a directory called **u**. Finally, **u** is a subdirectory of **/**, the root directory. If **harrymu** contained a subdirectory called **music**, the pathname of that subdirectory would be **/u/accounting/harrymu/music**.

When you use an SCO UNIX command that operates on a file or directory, you must specify the name of the file or directory you want to operate on. If the file to be operated on is in the current directory, you can simply type its base name. The *base name* of a file or directory is the part of the pathname that follows the final slash—or the name that appears when you list the contents of a directory with the **ls** command. The reason you do not have to type the pathname of a file or directory in the current directory is that the system always keeps track of your current directory and can fill in that part of the pathname itself.

An *absolute pathname* consists of the complete path from the root directory to a file, and a *relative pathname* specifies the pathname from the

Figure 4-2.

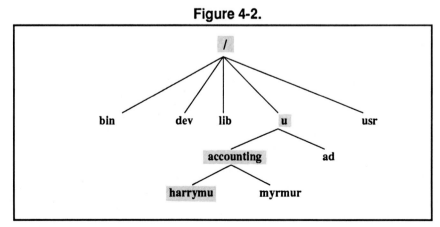

The Path of User Account **harrymu.**

file in question to a predefined directory such as your home directory or the current directory. The shell supplies the part of a relative pathname that precedes the predefined directory. For example, to specify a pathname relative to your home directory, you can begin the pathname with **$HOME**. The shell then replaces **$HOME** with the value of the **HOME** variable. For example, if your home directory were **shirleyb**, your **HOME** variable might stand for **/u/shirleyb**. The **HOME** variable works in all shells. In the C shell, you can also use the single character **~** (tilde) to represent your home directory. That is, the C shell replaces the tilde with the pathname of your home directory. If you are using the C shell, you can substitute a **~** for **$HOME** whenever it appears in examples. If you follow the tilde with the name of another user, the C shell provides the pathname of that user's home directory. For example, **~nancig** represents the home directory of the user **nancig**.

Suppose you have subdirectories in your home directory called **sales** and **addresses**. If your current directory is **sales** and you want to refer to **addresses**, you can't just use the base name of the directory **addresses** because addresses is not in the current directory. Instead you could use its pathname relative to the home directory, which would be either **$HOME/addresses** (in any shell) or **~/addresses** (in the C shell). In this case, the home directory is also the parent directory of the current directory, so there is yet another way you can refer to the subdirectory **addresses**. You can use **..** in the pathname to represent the home directory, as follows: **../addresses**. The special file **..** (dot dot) always stands for the parent directory of the current directory. Figure 4-3 illustrates this situation.

Figure 4-3.

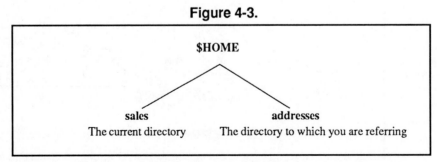

Referring to a Directory Outside the Current Directory.

To specify a pathname relative to the current directory, you can begin the pathname with either **.** or the name of the first subdirectory in the path. (The special file **.** (dot) stands for the current directory.) Suppose that your current directory contains a subdirectory called **schedule**, which in turn contains a file called **lectures**. If you want to refer to the file **lectures** without changing your current directory, you can refer to it as either **./schedule/lectures** or **schedule/lectures**. The reason the **.** is optional in this case is that if the pathname doesn't start with a **/**, UNIX assumes you want it to start with the current directory. See the section "The Current Directory" later in this chapter for more information about the **.** file.

When you type a UNIX command that operates on a file or directory, you can type the base name of the file or directory providing it is in your current directory; if it is not in your current directory you must type a full or relative pathname. Here are examples of the full pathname, base name, and relative pathnames of one file:

Full pathname (You can use this name no matter what the current directory is)	**/u/owens/supplies/paint**
Base name (the current directory must be **/u/owens/supplies**)	**paint**
Pathname relative to home directory (home directory is **/u/owens**)	**$HOME/supplies/paint**
Pathname relative to current directory (current directory must be **/u/owens**)	**./supplies/paint** or **supplies/paint**

Wildcard Characters

There are times when you may want to perform the same operation on every file in a directory or on all the files that have similar names. For example, you might want to move all the files from one directory into another directory. If there were a large number of files in the directory, it would be tedious to move each one individually. Fortunately UNIX has special symbols called *metacharacters* or *wildcard characters,* that allow you to refer to several files with one general name. There are three wildcard characters: the * (asterisk), the ? (question mark), and the [ ] (square brackets). These characters can be typed in place of, or combined with, file names to make a command operate on more than one file or directory at a time.

The * alone matches any file name consisting of any number of characters. The only file names the * does not encompass are those that start with a period (.), sometimes called *dot files*. The * *does* match a period in the middle or at the end of a file name. You can type an * alone in place of a file name when you want to perform some operation on all the files in the current directory. For example, to find out the type of all the files in the current directory, you would type

```
$ file *
```

See the section "Determining File Types" later in this chapter for more information about the **file** command.

 REMEMBER   The output of this command will *not* include files whose names begin with a . (dot).

Wildcard characters always refer to directory names as well as file names. Whenever you type a file name with an *, UNIX will perform, or attempt to perform, the named operation not only on files, but also on any directories that fit the pattern.

The * alone is useful for performing operations on all the files and subdirectories in a particular directory, but perhaps an even more useful function of the wildcard characters is to perform operations on a certain set of files or directories. If you combine the * with a partial file name, it still matches any number of characters, but the file names it matches must contain the partial name as well. Here are some sample names with an * in them, along with examples of file names they will match:

- **∗t** will match any number of characters followed by a *t,* that is, any word that ends in *t.* For example: **t** (the number of characters before the **t** in this case is zero), **last, fact,** and **account,** (**accounts** would not be matched, because *t* is not the last character).

- **∗temp∗** will match any name with *temp* in it. For example: **temp, 1temp, temp.list,** and **1.temp.acct**.

- **pr∗t** will match any name that begins with *pr,* ends with *t,* and has any number of characters in between. For example: **prt, product,** and **profit.chart**.

 TIP   A common UNIX trick is to name files that have a similar purpose in a way that allows them all to be matched by a single pattern using a wildcard character. For example, if you have several files that contain information about companies who have accounts with you, you might want to append **.a** to the name of each file, just to remind you what these files are all about. Then, whenever you want to do some operation on all the account files, you can refer to them as **∗.a**.

The wildcard character **?** matches any single character, except a **.** that is the first character in a name (that is, it does not match the period in dot files). It can be used alone, or together with a partial name. Used alone, the **?** will only match file names that are one character long; **??** will match names that are two characters long, and so on. Like the **∗**, the **?** is generally more useful when it is combined with a partial name or used in conjunction with the **∗**. Here are some sample patterns that contain a **?**, sometimes in conjunction with an **∗**. Examples of names each pattern will match are also included.

- **?s** will match any one character followed by *s* and any two-letter word that ends in *s.* For example: **ls, cs,** and **ts**.

- **x??** will match any three-character name whose first character is *x.* For example: **xaa, xbt, x.1, x13**.

- **account?** will match any name that begins with **account** and ends with one more character. For example: **accounts, account1,** and **account2**.

Any number of characters enclosed in [ ] (square brackets) matches any one of the characters enclosed therein. For example, [abc] will match **a** or **b** or **c**. A range of characters separated by a hyphen matches any character in the range. For example, [1-5] will match any number from 1 to 5. Here are some sample patterns that include square brackets and some file names that they match:

- **account[123]** will match **account1**, **account2**, or **account3**.

- **file.[a-z]** will match any file name whose name begins with *file.* and ends with one lowercase letter. For example: **file.a**, **file.b**, and **file.z**.

- **te[ms][pt]** will match **temp**, **test**, **temt**, and **tesp**.

- **.[a-z]*** will match any name that begins with a dot and a lowercase letter. For example, **.cshrc**, **.exrc**, **.login**.

You can also use patterns whose names are a combination of several wildcard characters. Here are some examples of patterns that include the *, the **?**, and the [ ] along with some file names that they match:

- ***.?** will match any name that begins with some sequence of characters, followed by a **.**, and one character after the **.** (dot). For example: **account.1**, **appts.c**, and **funds.8**.

- **b[eu]rt*** will match any file whose name begins with *bert* or *burt*. For example: **bert**, **burt**, **bertrand**, and **burton**.

Whenever you use a wildcard character in place of individual file names, you risk doing an operation on a file that you've forgotten about, which coincidentally matches the pattern with the wildcard character. With commands like **rm**, which removes files, this can be disastrous. You may want to list the files that match the name you are using before you do any potentially dangerous operation. To do this, type

ls *name*

where *name* is the pattern containing wildcard characters that you plan to use. For example, to list all files that begin with *temp,* you would use the following command:

```
$ ls temp*
```

See the section "Listing the Contents of a Directory" later in this chapter for more information about the **ls** command.

Working with Files

There may be a few files already in your account when you first log in. For example, a file called **.profile** or **.login** will be in your home directory. For the most part, however, the files you work with will be files that you create. The following sections acquaint you with some of the commands you need to create and manipulate your own files.

Creating and Viewing Files

SCO UNIX has a number of utilities you can use to create files. Many of these are quite complex, and are covered in later chapters of this book; however, one simple way to create a file is with the **cat** command. Before you create a file, you must choose a name for it. A directory or file name may consist of up to 14 characters, including upper- and lowercase letters, numbers, and all characters but the special characters discussed in Chapter 5, the wildcard characters discussed earlier in this chapter, and the **/**. Since you may type certain file names quite often, it is a good idea to keep file names under the 14-character limit. You must also make sure you are in a directory in which you have write permission, or you will not be allowed to create a file. You can use the **pwd** command to determine the name of the current directory. See the section "The Current Directory" later in this chapter for more information about the **pwd** command.

To create a file, type

    cat > *filename*

where *filename* is the name of the file you want to create, and then press RETURN. Now type any text you want, making sure to press RETURN at the end of each line. If you do not press RETURN when the text reaches the right edge of the screen, it will appear to wrap around to the next line, but it will really be one long line. Everything you type on the lines that follow the **cat** command will go into the new file. When you are done typing, press RETURN to move to a new line and then press CTRL-d. The following example shows the creation of a file called **test**. To make sure you are in a directory where you are allowed to create files, first change to your home directory with the **cd** command. The **^D** below the last line of text shows that the user in the example pressed CTRL-d to return to a shell prompt.

```
$ cd
$ cat > test
This is a test. It is only a test. If this had been a real
file, it would have contained some information worth
reading. It sure is fun to create files on UNIX!
^D
$
```

Create a few files of your own so that you will have some files with which to practice the commands discussed in the next few sections. Remember that each file must have a different name. If you specify the name of a file that already exists, one of two things will happen. In the Bourne shell, the already existing file will be replaced by the new text you type. If you are using the Bourne shell, be careful when creating new files lest you overwrite an important existing file. In the C shell, there is a variable called **noclobber**. When this variable is set, the shell will not let you overwrite an existing file in this way. If it is not set, you can overwrite a file just as you can in the Bourne shell. The **noclobber** variable may be automatically set from your **.cshrc** file. See Chapter 11, "The C Shell," for more information about setting variables.

You can use the **cat** command to view, as well as create, a file. To view the file you just created, type

    cat *filename*

where *filename* is the name of the file. Note that you do not use the > symbol to view a file with **cat**. The **cat** utility will now display the contents of the file on the screen, as shown here:

```
$ cat test
```
This is a test. It is only a test. If this had been a real
file, it would have contained some information worth
reading. It sure is fun to create files on UNIX!

If a file is very long, it will scroll continuously, moving off of the screen before you can read it. You can stop the scrolling by pressing CTRL-s at any point; then press any key to resume scrolling.

The examples of the **cat** utility presented in this section show only a few of its many uses. For more information about the **cat** utility, see Chapter 6, "Filters." Chapter 6 also covers other ways to create and view files.

Removing Files

When you no longer need a file, you can remove it from your account with the **rm** command. Specify the name or names of the file or files you want to remove as arguments to the command. For example, to remove a file called **temp**, you would use the command

```
$ rm temp
```

To remove all the files in the current directory whose names begin with *temp,* you would use the command

```
$ rm temp*
```

To remove the files **temp, junk,** and **test,** you would use the command

```
$ rm temp junk test
```

Once you have removed a file, you can only retrieve it if it was backed up when the system administrator did the last system backups, and even then it is not a simple matter. Therefore, use **rm** with great caution, especially if you use a wildcard character such as * to remove more than one file at a time.

If you want to give yourself one last chance to decide before you remove a file, you can use **rm** with the **-i** (for interactive) option. When you use the

rm -i command, **rm** prompts you to confirm that you really want to delete the file (or files if you've named more than one), as in this example:

```
$ rm -i temp
temp: ?
```

Type **y** (for yes) if you really want to remove the file. If you do not want to remove the file, type **n** (for no) or simply press RETURN. If you use the C shell, you can modify your **.cshrc** file, which controls your shell environment, so that **rm** always uses the interactive option for you. See Chapter 11, "The C Shell," to learn about modifying your **.cshrc** file.

Copying Files

The **cp** (for copy) utility makes a copy of a file. If the copy is in the same directory as the original, it must have a different name. If it is in a different directory, it can have a different name or the same name as the original. You can use the **cp** command to make backup copies of important files or to copy files that you want to change. You can also copy files that you have only read permission on, and since you own the copy, you can make changes to it. If you want to keep copies of a file in different directories, you can also use the **cp** command to copy a file into a different directory. To make a copy of a file in the current directory, type

   cp *filename1 filename2*

where *filename1* is the name of the original file and *filename2* is the name you want to give the copy. To make a copy of a file in a directory, you must have write permission in that directory. Try copying a file in the same directory, but first make sure that you are in your home directory or one of its subdirectories. For example, to make a copy of a file called **test**, and name the copy **test.2** you would use the command

```
$ cp test test2
```

Try copying some of the files you have created. Remember that no two files in the same directory can have the same name.

 CAUTION   If the second filename you specify is the name of a file that already exists in the current directory, **cp** will replace the old file with the copy it creates. To avoid overwriting a file that you want to save, always check to make sure the name you want the copy to have doesn't belong to an existing file before you use the **cp** command.

To copy a file into a different directory, type

cp *filename dirname*

where *filename* is the name of the file you want to move and *dirname* is the name or pathname of the directory you want to move it into. For example, you can copy the file **/etc/passwd** into your home directory with the command

```
$ cp /etc/passwd $HOME
```

Now a file called **passwd** will be in your home directory. Assuming you have a subdirectory called **system**, you can copy **passwd** into that subdirectory with the command

```
$ cp /etc/passwd $HOME/system
```

Now the **system** directory will also contain a file called **passwd**. Again, when you are copying a file into a different directory, make sure that no file with that name already exists in the target directory. By default, **cp** gives the copied file in the new directory the same name as the original. This is possible because the two files do not have the same pathname. If you want the copy in the new directory to have a *different* name from the original file, append the new name to the directory name after a /. For example, to copy the file **/etc/passwd** to your home directory and name the copy **etc.pass** instead of **passwd**, you would use the command

```
$ cp /etc/passwd $HOME/etc.pass
```

As long as **etc.pass** is not the name of a directory in your home directory, **cp** will know that this should be the name of the copy, rather than a directory to copy the file to.

Moving and Renaming Files

You can use the **mv** utility to move a file into a different directory or to change the name of a file. To rename a file, type

    mv *name1 name2*

where *name1* is the old name or pathname of the file and *name2* is the new name you want to give it. For example, to give a file called **murray** in the current directory the new name **shannon.m,** you would use the command

```
$ mv murray shannon.m
```

 CAUTION   Make sure that the new name of the file is not the name of an existing file. If it is, the old file will be replaced by the one you are moving.

To change the name of a file, you must have write permission on both the file and on the directory it is in. Before you try using the **mv** command, make sure you are in your home directory or one of its subdirectories.

    To move a file into a different directory, type

    mv *filename dirname*

where *filename* is the name of the file you want to move and *dirname* is the name or pathname of the directory you want to move it to. For example, you could move a file called **lunches** from your home directory into a subdirectory called **expenses** by typing

```
$ mv lunches expenses
```

In this example, both the file **lunches** and the directory **expenses** are members of the current directory. If your current directory did not contain the file **lunches** and the directory **expenses,** you would have to specify their pathnames, as in this example:

```
$ mv $HOME/lunches $HOME/expenses
```

To move the file **$HOME/lunches** into the current directory, you would use the following command. Note that this command will only work if the current directory is *not* your home directory.

```
$ mv $HOME/lunches .
```

Remember, **.** is the name that represents the current directory.

When you use **mv** to move a file into a different directory, the file you move will have the same name in the new directory as it did in the old one unless you specify a new name by appending it to the directory name after a slash. For example, suppose you wanted to move the file **lunches** from your home directory to the subdirectory **expenses,** but you wanted the file in **expenses** to be named **bus.lunches.** To do this, you would type

```
$ mv $HOME/lunches $HOME/expenses/bus.lunches
```

Now the directory **expenses** contains a new file called **bus.lunches.** Use the same caution when moving files into different directories that you would when renaming a file in the current directory. If there is already a file in the target directory that has the same name as the file you are moving (or the new name you are giving it) that file will be deleted before the new one is moved.

Determining File Types

There are several types of UNIX files. The kind you will probably use most is the *text file*. A text file contains only ASCII characters (letters, numbers, and punctuation) and can be read by a person. In Chapters 10, "The Bourne Shell," and 11, "The C Shell," you will learn how to create text files that are also executable programs. The text in shell scripts consists of SCO UNIX command lines that are interpreted by the shell when you execute the script. A *compiled program* consists of machine code that can't be read by most people or printed on terminal screens. *Device files* are special files that serve as interfaces between the operating system software and hardware components. Each hardware component is associated with at least one device file, and this file gives the computer a way to address the hardware component and send data to it.

Although only text files are readable, in most respects compiled programs, device files, and other special files behave just like text files. You can locate, remove, move, and copy any file that you have access to, regardless of its type. The examples in this chapter deal primarily with text files; however, except for commands that deal with creating and viewing files, the commands discussed here will work on any type of file.

You use the **file** command to determine the type of a file. You can specify either the full pathname of a file or the base name of a file in the current directory as an argument to **file**. A file must be readable by you for you to use **file** on it. You cannot use **file** to determine the type of another user's file or a command file in **/bin**, for example. The **file** utility is capable of distinguishing many different types of files. Here is a list of the most common file types:

English text	An ordinary text file that contains English words and punctuation.
ASCII text	Text that consists of ASCII characters (letters, numbers, and punctuation), but that is not identifiable as English sentences. Lists of names, tables, and text that includes a large number of special punctuation marks qualify as ASCII text.
directory	Self-explanatory.
commands text	An executable shell script. A shell script will qualify as ASCII text or English text if it is not executable.
block special	A device file that handles blocks of data.
character special	Any device file that reads and writes character by character.

fifo   A fifo, or named pipe. A fifo file serves as a communication path between two programs.

executable   A compiled program file. There are different types of executable files, identified by a preceding word or code, as you'll see in a moment.

a.out   A compiled C program. There are many types of C programs, and **file** is able to differentiate between some of them. The exact description **file** presents for a C program may vary, so look for the **a.out** portion of the description. You'll find one of these files in the next set of examples.

XENIX   The XENIX **file** command may produce different file descriptions than those shown here for certain types of executable files.

The following examples illustrate several **file** commands. All of these examples are executable by ordinary users (on a system with default permissions). With the exception of the two examples involving **tarskip** and **tarskip.c**, all the files mentioned in these examples should be on your system. Remember that you can also use **file** to determine the type of your own files.

```
$ file /etc/motd
/etc/motd:       English text
$ file /etc/passwd
/etc/passwd:     ascii text
$ file /bin/clear
/bin/clear:      commands text
$ file /usr/spool/mail/$LOGNAME
/usr/spool/mail/laurag:      unix-rt ldp
$ file /dev/tty1A
/dev/tty1A:      character special (5/128)
$ file /usr/lib/cron/FIFO
/usr/lib/cron/FIFO:      fifo
$ file /dev/fd048ds9
/dev/fd048ds9:   block special (2/4)
$ file /u/bin/tarskip.c
/u/bin/tarskip.c:          ascii text
```

```
$ file /u/bin/tarskip.
/u/bin/tarskip: Microsoft a.out separate pure segmented
word-swapped not-stripped 386 executable
$ file /bin/rm
/bin/rm:        iAPX 386 executable
```

 NOTE   The **file** utility is not 100 percent accurate. It sometimes wrongly assesses a shell script as C program text, while an uncompiled, unexecutable C program may be assessed as ASCII text.

Changing Access Permissions of a File or Directory

By default, your own files are usually readable and writable, but not executable, by you, while your directories are readable, writable, and executable. The default permissions on files that you create are determined by the **umask** command. This command is usually executed from your **.profile** file (in the Bourne shell) or your **.login** file (in the C shell), which means it is executed automatically every time you log in. To give a file access permissions different from the default, use the **chmod** (for change mode) command.

There are two ways to change the permissions of a file with **chmod**. Probably the simplest is to use *symbolic mode,* in which the arguments to **chmod** are symbols that represent certain groups of users and certain permissions. The syntax for changing permissions with symbolic mode is

   chmod *users operator permissions file*

where *file* is the name of the file whose permissions you want to change, and *users, operator,* and *permissions,* can be replaced by the symbols listed here:

   users (the users or groups of users for whom permissions are granted or denied)

   u (user)   The owner of the file.

g (group)	The login group to which the file belongs. (A file may belong to a group other than its owner's group.)
o (others)	All other users besides the owner and the owner's group.
a (all)	All users, including the owner, the group, and all others.

operators (these grant and deny permissions)

+	Grants the permissions following the symbol to the specified classes of users.
–	Removes the permissions following the symbol from the specified classes of users.
=	Assigns the permissions following the symbol to the specified classes of users and takes away all other permissions for those users. If no permission is assigned, all existing permissions are removed.

permissions

r	Permission to read a file or search a directory.
w	Permission to make changes to a file or add files to a directory.
x	Permission to execute a file as a program or change to a directory.
s	Sets the user or group ID to that of the owner upon execution of the file. If the specified user is **u**, the user ID is set. If the specified user is **g**, the group ID is set.
t	Sets the *sticky bit,* which causes a program to be saved in memory when it is executed. Only the superuser can set this permission.

No matter what permissions you have set on your files, the superuser has read and write permissions on all files on the system and execute permission on all files that have execute permission for anyone. Remember, you can only change the permissions for files that you own.

Let's look at some examples that show you how to grant and deny various permissions to different users. To give other users in your login group permission to list the files in your home directory, you would use the command

```
$ chmod g+r $HOME
```

This specifies that read permission for the users in your group (**g**) will be added to your home directory.

To make a file called **/u/burnett/mkchart** executable by all users, use the next command. The **l** command shows the permissions on the file before and after the **chmod** command is executed.

```
$ l /u/burnett/mkchart
-rw-------    1 burnett group      2481 May 15 11:37 /u/burnett/mkchart
$ chmod a+x /u/burnett/mkchart
$ l /u/burnett/mkchart
-rwx--x--x    1 burnett group      2481 May 15 11:37 /u/burnett/mkchart
```

Remember, for a command like this to succeed, you must own the file. This gives all users (**a**) permission to execute the file as a program. Of course, the file must contain executable commands or it will not be executable, even if you do have execute permission. See Chapters 10 "The Bourne Shell," 11 "The C Shell," and 12 "An Introduction to Program Development," for further information about creating executable files.

To remove execute permission for your home directory from users who are not in your group, use the command

```
$ chmod o-x $HOME
```

This protects your home directory so users who are not in your group cannot change to your home directory using **cd**; however, users who retain read permission can still list the contents of your home directory with **ls**. To remove this permission as well, use the command

```
$ chmod o-r $HOME
```

To take away all permissions for all other users on a directory called **private**, you would use the command

```
$ chmod go= private
```

The second way to change the access permissions for a file or directory is with *absolute mode,* in which the argument to **chmod** is a single number that sets all permissions for all users. Although the numbers you use with absolute mode are a bit more complex than the symbolic codes, they are more convenient because you can set *all* the permissions for a file with one command. Each permission is represented by an octal number. To set all the permissions, simply combine the numbers representing the individual permissions you want the file to have. The numbers assigned to the permissions are listed next, followed by some examples of absolute modes.

The first digit determines the special permissions the file is to have. These permissions are normally used only with system files that are executed by nonowners. You will probably never need to create files that have these three permissions:

4000	Sets the user ID (SUID) when the program is executed
2000	Sets the group ID (SGID) when the program is executed
1000	Sets the sticky bit

The second digit determines permissions for the owner of the file.

0400	Read permission for the owner
0200	Write permission for the owner
0100	Execute permission for the owner

The third digit determines permissions for users in the login group the file is associated with.

0040	Read permission for the group
0020	Write permission for the group
0010	Execute permission for the group

The last digit determines the permissions for users who are not in the login group with which the file is associated.

0004	Read permission for others
0002	Write permission for others
0001	Execute permission for others

Note the symmetry in the previous lists: a 1 always represents execute permission; a 2 always represents write permission; and a 4 always represents read permission. When the first digit in a mode number is 0 (there are no SUID, SGID, or sticky bit permissions set for the file), you do not have to include it in the mode number. For example, **0600** and **600** have the same meaning.

The following examples show you how to assign various sets of permissions using absolute mode. To set read permission only for the owner of the file on a file called **california,** you would use the command

```
$ chmod 0400 california
```

Once this command had been executed, no other users would have any permissions for this file. Since the first digit in this number is 0, it can be eliminated. The following example sets the same permission:

```
$ chmod 400 california
```

For the remaining examples, the first digit will be left off if it is 0.

To make the same file executable only for the owner, you would use the command

```
$ chmod 100 california
```

The number that represents both read and write permissions for the owner only is 0600, the sum of the numbers for the individual permissions. To set both of these permissions, you would use the command

```
$ chmod 600 california
```

Note that the sum of any two octal numbers is distinguishable from any other octal number. For example, the only way you can get the mode 0600 is by adding 0200 and 0400.

To set read, write, and execute permissions for just the owner, you would use the command

```
$ chmod 700 california
```

To set all permissions for the owner and read only permission for the group and other users, you would use the command

```
$ chmod 744 california
```

To set read and execute permissions for all users, you would use the command

```
$ chmod 666 california
```

All of the files and directories on a UNIX system are controlled by an associated set of access permissions; therefore, unless you are the superuser, there are probably many files and directories that you cannot read or change. These include files that contain the machine code for running UNIX programs, files used in system administration, and other users' personal files. For some system files, you may be allowed read but not write permission, or execute but not read or write permission. If you attempt to access a file for which you have no permissions, you will see an error message telling you that permission is denied. If you attempt to modify a file for which you have only read permission, you will be told the file is read-only.

You can change the ownership of a file that you own with the **chown** command; however, once you've done so, you cannot change it back, because the file is no longer yours to change. You now have the same access permissions as the other users in your group. If the file is readable and writable by your group, you can change it. If it is not, you will see the message "Permission denied" when you try to access the file. If you do not change the group association as well, the file will remain associated with your login group. The **chown** command takes two arguments: the login name or ID number of the user who is to be the new owner, and the name or names of the file or files whose ownership you want to change. The following example shows how you would change the ownership of a file called **smith.acct** to the user **mcdowell**. The l command displays the permissions and ownership of the account before and after the **chown** command.

```
$ l smith.acct
-rw------- 1 murray group       3754 May 14 11:04 smith.acct
$ chown mcdowell smith.acct
$ l smith.acct
-rw------- 1 mcdowell group     3754 May 14 11:04 smith.acct
```

You can change the group ownership of any file that you own with the **chgrp** (for change group) command. This means that the file is still owned by you, but it is now associated with a login group other than the one you belong to. This is useful if you have a file that you want to make readable or writable for a group other than your own, but not for everyone on the system. The **chgrp** command takes two arguments: first, the name of the group, and then the name or names of the file or files whose association is to be changed. For example, to change the group ownership of a file called **wanda.w** to the group **accounting**, you would use the following command. The **l** command displays the permissions and ownership of the file **wanda.w** before and after the **chgrp** command.

```
$ l wanda.w
-rw-------    1 cmorgan group        1021 May 9 19:24 wanda.w
$ chgrp accounting wanda.w
$ l wanda.w
-rw-------    1 cmorgan accounting   1021 May 9 19:24 wanda.w
```

As the owner of the file, you still have the original permissions for the file, but the members of your login group are now classified as *other* users for the purposes of accessing this file, while users in the group **accounting** now have group permissions.

Working with Directories

When you first log in to your account, you are in a subdirectory of the UNIX system, called your *home directory*. You will probably need to create some subdirectories in your home directory in which to store your files. You'll discover that it is easier to locate and keep track of your files if you group them in directories by subject or type. The operating system can also search small directories more efficiently than large ones, so try to keep your directories as small as possible. If you find that a directory contains more than about 30 files or subdirectories, you should create new subdirectories for some of them. The following sections will acquaint you with the commands you need to create directories, as well as move and copy files between directories, list the contents of directories, and change the directory you are in.

Your Home Directory

You are placed in your home directory when you log in to your UNIX account. In most cases, the name of your home directory is the same as your login name.

Users' home directories look just like other kinds of directories in a diagram of a file system. (For example, in Figure 4-1, **kirkwood** is a user's home directory.) However, as the top directory in your account, your home directory has a special status. Every time you log in, UNIX sets up a variable called **HOME** that identifies your home directory. UNIX uses the value of the **HOME** variable as a point of reference by which it determines what files and directories in the filesystem you have access to, and how to move you when you change directories.

Certain files that determine your working environment are kept in your home directory. For example, if your login shell is the Bourne shell, your home directory will contain a file called **.profile**, and if your login shell is the C shell, your home directory will contain the files **.login** and **.cshrc**. These files contain commands that are executed each time you log in to your account. The commands in these files determine such things as your prompt, your login shell, and other aspects of your environment. See Chapters 10, "The Bourne Shell," and 11, "The C Shell," for more information about these files. Other files in your home directory set up specialized aspects of your environment, such as how the **mail** program works for you. These files are discussed in later chapters.

The Current Directory

The *working*, or *current*, *directory* is the directory you are in at any given time. For example, when you first log in, the current directory is always your home directory. If you then move to another directory, that directory becomes the current directory. UNIX always keeps track of your current directory during a login session, and unless you specify another directory for your commands to operate on, they are executed relative to the current directory. For instance, any file that you create becomes part of the current directory by default, as does any subdirectory you create.

Every UNIX directory contains a file called . (dot). This is a special file name that stands for the current directory. Whenever you need to refer to the current directory, you can use . to do so. Another file called .. (dot-dot) stands for the parent directory of the current directory. When you need to refer to this directory, you can use .. instead of the pathname of the directory.

To find out the name of the current directory, use the **pwd** (for print working directory) command. This command prints the full pathname of the current directory, as in this example:

```
$ pwd
/u/owens/art/paintings
```

The name following the last / is the base name of the current directory.

Listing the Contents of a Directory

You can use several commands to list the contents of a directory. The basic command is the ls command, which has a number of options. Several other commands work just like ls with one of its options. These commands are explained along with the options they mimic.

With no arguments, the ls command lists the files and subdirectories in the current directory in alphabetical order. If you specify a directory as an argument to the ls command, the contents of that directory are listed. For example, to list the contents of the / directory, use the command

```
$ ls /
```

If you specify a file name or file names as an argument to **ls**, it will display only those files. This is most useful if you include a wildcard character in the file name. For example, to list all the files in the current directory that end with **.a**, you would use the command

```
$ ls *.a
```

If you have a large number of files in a directory, the output of **ls** may fill more than one screen, so you won't have a chance to read the whole list before some of it scrolls off the top. To keep this from happening, instead of using **ls**, use the **lc** command, which displays the same output as **ls**, but arranged in several columns, instead of just one. The following example shows the contents of the **/** directory listed first with **ls,** and then with **lc**.

```
$ ls /
bin
boot
dev
dos
etc
install
lib
mbox
mnt
sfmt
shlib
tcb
tmp
u
unix
unix.old
usr
$ lc /
bin     dos       lib     sfmt     tmp     unix.old
boot    etc       mbox    shlib    u       usr
dev     install   mnt     tcb      unix
```

The **lc** command takes most of the same options as **ls**. It is the equivalent of the **ls -C** command (**ls** with the -C option).

The **lf** command lists the directory contents in alphabetical order and columnar format. It also marks each directory with a **/** after the name, and each executable file (that is, each file that can be executed as a command)

with an *. Ordinarily, directory names and file names look alike. The **lf** command is an easy way to distinguish the two. This example shows the **/** directory listed with **lf**:

```
$ lf /
bin/    dos       lib/    sfmt*    tmp/     unix.old
boot    etc/      mbox    shlib/   u/       usr/
dev/    install/  mnt/    tcb/     unix
```

The **ls -F** command is the equivalent of **lf**, except **ls -F** does not produce a columnar format.

The **lr** command recursively lists the contents of all subdirectories it encounters, as does **ls -R**; however, **lr** also displays the output in a columnar format. For example, the command

```
$ lr /
```

would first list the contents of **/**, followed by the contents of **/bin** and any of its subdirectories, followed by the contents of **/dev**, and so on, until all the directories in the entire system had been listed. The command

```
$ lr $HOME
```

would list all the files and directories in your home directory.

The **l** command lists the directory contents in long format. In this format not only the name of each file and directory is listed, but also some information about each file and directory. The **l** command is the equivalent of **ls** with the **-l** option.

 NOTE Because a long format listing takes up the whole width of the terminal screen, it cannot be printed in multiple columns. Therefore, the **-l** option overrides the columnar format of **lc**, **lf**, and **lr**.

The next example shows the **/** directory listed with **l**. The meaning of the different columns in this list is explained briefly following the output.

```
$ l /
total 2012
```

```
drwxr-xr-x    2 bin    bin        1984 Jun 25  1989   bin
-r--------    1 bin    bin       29246 Jun 23  1989   boot
drwxr-xr-x    4 root   backup     3296 Apr 30 18:11 dev
-r--------    1 bin    bin         577 Jun 23 1989 dos
drwxrwxr-x   17 bin    auth       2336 May 11 15:32 etc
drwxr-xr-x    2 root   other        32 Jun 25 1989 install
drwxrwxr-x    4 bin    bin         112 Jun 25 1989 lib
-rw-------    1 root   other     11455 May 13 17:25 mbox
drwxrwxrwx    2 root   root         32 Jun 25 1989 mnt
-rwx------    1 bin    bin        2850 Jun 23 1989 sfmt
drwxr-xr-x    2 bin    bin          64 Jun 25 1989 shlib
d--x--x--x    6 bin    bin          96 Jun 25 1989 tcb
drwxrwxrwt    3 sys    sys         336 May 13 19:51 tmp
drwxr-xr-x   14 root   other       240 Apr 29 18:22 u
----r-----    1 bin    mem      477063 Jan 5 16:38 unix
----r-----    1 bin    mem      477063 Jan 4 14:23 unix.old
drwxrwxr-x   18 root   auth        288 Jun 25 1989 usr
```

The first column of output consists of ten slots that may contain either a hyphen (-) or a letter indicating the access permissions or file type of the item, as illustrated in Figure 4-4. If the item is a directory, a **d** appears in the first slot. If it is a special file, a letter indicates what type of file it is. For example, a **p** in the first column indicates that the file is a named pipe. If the item is an ordinary file, a hyphen appears in this slot. Slots two through

Figure 4-4.

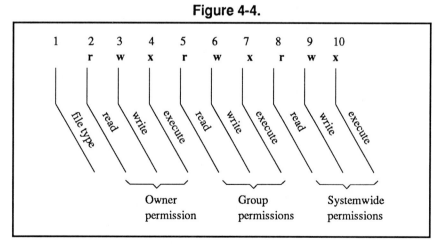

File Access Permissions as Displayed by **ls-1.**

four show the permissions the owner of the file has. Slots five through seven show the permissions for the group the file is associated with. Slots eight through ten show the permissions for users who are not in the group. If a permission is not granted, a hyphen appears in the slot instead of a letter. For more information about access permissions, review the section "File and Directory Access Permissions" earlier in this chapter. Other information displayed with l includes the number of links the item has, the owner of the file or directory (usually the person who created the file), the name of the group the file is associated with, the size of the item in blocks (one block being 512 bytes), the date the item was created, and in the last column, the name of the file or directory.

To better understand the information displayed with l, examine the entry for the file **sfmt** from the previous example. The line is as follows:

```
-rwx------    1 bin    bin    2850 Jun 23  14:22 sfmt
```

The hyphen in the first slot of the first column indicates that the item is an ordinary file. The next three slots show that the owner has read, write, and execute permissions, while the hyphens in the remaining slots show that other users have no permissions for the file. The number **1** is the number of links the file has. The file belongs to the user **root** and the group **other**. There are 2850 bytes in the file, which was last modified at 2:22 P.M. on June 23.

The l option is also useful for getting information about a particular file or set of files. For example, to see a long listing for just the file **webster**, you would use this command:

```
$ l webster
-rw-------    1 lewisc  group    2143 May 13  22:45 webster
```

To see a long listing for just the files that begin with *p*, you would use the command

```
$ l p*
-rw-------    1 rachel group   1021 May  9 19:24 plan
drwx------    1 rachel group   1626 May 14 21:12 portfolios
-rw-------    1 rachel group   1548 May 14 15:03 pratt
-rwx------    1 rachel group    704 Jun 12 11:53 print
```

Each directory contains at least two "hidden files" that are not displayed with **ls** alone. These are called *dot files* because their names begin with a period (.), or dot. The two dot files that every directory contains are ., which represents the current directory, and .., which represents the parent directory of the current directory. Your home directory contains special dot files that become part of your account when it is set up. To make the dot files show up when you list the contents of a directory, use the **ls -a** command. This option causes all files and directories, including dot files, to be listed. Dot files are only special in that they are hidden. You can create a dot file just as you would an ordinary file. Some users like to back up important files as dot files. Be sure to check for the presence of dot files in a directory before you attempt to remove it.

The **ls -t** command lists the files and directories in the order in which they were last modified, beginning with the most recently modified file or directory. This option is useful if, for instance, you have two versions of the same file with different names, and you want to know which one contains the most recent changes.

You can use any of the options for **ls** with its companion commands, **lc**, **lf**, **l**, and **lr**. For example, you can get a multicolumn list that includes the dot files by using **-a** with the **lc** command. The options discussed in this section are just a few of those possible for **ls**. For more information about **ls** see the on-line **man** pages or the *SCO UNIX User's Reference.*

Creating Directories

You can create a directory within your home directory (or any of its subdirectories) with the **mkdir** command. You can name a directory anything you like, as long as the name does not exceed 14 characters and does not include the wildcard characters discussed earlier in this chapter, characters that are special to the shell, the / character, or any spaces. Since the / is used to separate the names of directories in a pathname, file or directory names that contained a / would be interpreted as pathnames. The example files and directories used in this book have names that are all lowercase. No two files or directories in the same subdirectory can have the exact same name. If they did, the two items would also have the same pathname, and

UNIX could not determine which file or directory the pathname stood for. The following example shows how you would create a directory called **letters**.

```
$ mkdir letters
```

As with all commands that operate on directories, you can supply **mkdir** with a pathname instead of a short name if you want to create a directory that will not reside in the current directory. For example, to create a subdirectory **business** in the directory **letters**, which was created in the last example, you would use the command

```
$ mkdir letters/business
```

If your home directory is not the current directory, you will have to specify the pathname of the directory you want to create, as in this example:

```
$ mkdir $HOME/letters
```

Typing this command would create a directory in your home directory, not in the current directory.

The **mkdir** command does not print anything on the screen if it is successful; it just returns a prompt. If you attempt to create a directory where you are not permitted to, or if you already have a directory with the same name as the one you are trying to create, **mkdir** will display an error message. If you want to verify that a directory you've created is really there, use the **ls** command.

Removing Directories

To remove a directory that you no longer need, use the **rmdir** command. For example, to remove a directory called **fin89**, you would type

```
$ rmdir fin89
```

For a directory to be removable with **rmdir**, it must be empty. That is, it must not contain any files or subdirectories. Only the files . and .., which cannot be removed, may remain in a directory that is to be deleted. In the previous example, if the directory **fin89** had contained any files or directories, the directory would not have been removed and an error message would have been displayed, as in this example:

```
$ rmdir fin89
rmdir: fin89: Directory not empty
```

Remember that a directory may contain hidden dot files, so you might get an error message when you try to remove a directory that appears to be empty. Use the **ls -a** command to check for hidden files in a directory.

To remove a directory that does contain files or subdirectories, you must use the **rm -r** command. The **rm** command without any options removes files only. With the **-r** option, **rm** recursively removes all files and directories within the directory you specify. For example, to remove the directory **fin89**, all of its files, all of its subdirectories, and all the files in those subdirectories, you would use the command

```
$ rm -r fin89
```

 CAUTION Before you use the **rm -r** command, be absolutely certain that the directory you specify does not contain any files or subdirectories that you want to keep. You may want to use the **-i** option along with the **-r** option, so that **rm** asks you to confirm the removal of each file and each subdirectory. If you elect not to remove any item, the top directory will not be removed. For example, to remove all of the files and subdirectories in the directory **fin89** with confirmation, you would type

```
$ rm -ir fin89
```

You cannot remove either the current directory or the parent directory of the current directory because that would leave you in no directory at all; thus, you cannot specify **.** or **..** as an argument to **rmdir**. However, if you want to remove all of the files and directories in the current directory, but not the current directory itself, you can use the command

```
$ rm -r .
```

Again, use this command with caution. It is a good idea to use the **-i** option whenever you use **rm -r**.

Moving to a Different Directory

You can move to different directories in the directory structure with the **cd** (for change directory) command. Follow the **cd** command with the name or pathname of the directory to which you want to move. Each time you move to a new directory, that directory becomes the current directory. You can then access the files and subdirectories in that directory without typing their pathnames. For example, to move to the root directory (/), you would type

```
$ cd /
```

To move to the directory **/usr/bin**, you would type

```
$ cd /usr/bin
```

You can also use the special file name **..** to move to the parent directory of the current directory, as in this example:

```
$ cd ..
```

With no arguments, the **cd** command places you in your home directory. You can use the **pwd** command at any time to find out the pathname of your current directory.

Renaming Directories

You can use the **mv** utility to rename a directory, just as you would to rename a file. However, **mv** cannot move one directory into another. The **mvdir** command, which is available only to system administrators, accomplishes this task.

You can use **mv** to rename a directory by typing

mv *name1 name2*

where *name1* is the original name of the directory and *name2* is the new name you want to give it. The **mv** utility can tell that the first item you named is a directory, not an ordinary file, so it will make the new name a directory too; in fact, it will be the same directory with a different name. For example, to change the name of a directory called **expenses** to **bus.expenses**, you would use this command:

```
$ mv expenses bus.expenses
```

Since **mv** cannot move a directory to a new location, the old name and the new name must be in the same directory. That is, if you specify the pathname of the original directory, you must fill in the pathname of the second directory as well. For example, suppose you have a directory whose pathname relative to your home directory is **$HOME/expenses/personal**, and you want to change the name of **personal** to **my.own**. To do this, you would have to use the command

```
$ mv $HOME/expenses/personal $HOME/expenses/my.own
```

This command would *not* work:

```
$ mv $HOME/expenses/personal my.own
```

Actually, it would be simpler to move to the directory **expenses**; then you would not have to specify the pathname of the directory along with its new name.

Locating a File or Directory

You can use the **find** utility to locate any file or directory anywhere in the entire system. Although the syntax of this command can be quite complex, it is well worth learning, and you can do quite a bit with **find** without knowing everything about its syntax. The basic syntax of **find** is

find *pathname-list expression-list*

The *pathname-list* is the list of directories that you want to search in, and the *expression-list* determines the criteria that **find** will use to locate a file.

The **find** utility is useful both for locating a particular file and for finding groups of files that have similar characteristics. Suppose you want to find all the subdirectories in your home directory. The following command would locate each directory and print out its full pathname:

```
$ find $HOME -type d -print
```

The first argument, **$HOME**, tells **find** to look through your home directory and all of its subdirectories. You could also specify the pathname of your home directory here. The second argument, **-type**, is an expression that tells **find** to look for files of type **d**, which stands for directory. The final argument, **-print**, is an expression that tells **find** to print the names of any files or directories it locates that match the first criterion—in this case, that would be any items that are directories.

You now know two **find** expressions that can be used in the *expression-list*. Here is a list of some of the other expressions you can use with **find** (for additional **find** expressions, see the on-line manual pages or the *SCO UNIX User's Reference*):

-name *file*   Finds all files and directories whose names match *file*. If you want to include wildcard characters in *file* so that it will match more than one file name, you must enclose the entire *file* in single or double quotes. For example, the expression **-name '*temp*'** would find all the files and directories whose names contain the word *temp*.

-type *x*   Finds only files of type *x*, where *x* is **b** for block special file, **c** for character special file, **d** for directory, or **f** for ordinary file. For example, the expression **-type d** would locate only directories.

-user *uname*   Finds files belonging to the user whose login name is *uname*. For example, the expression **-user joyo** would find all the files that belong to the user **joyo**.

-group *gname*   Finds files associated with the login group specified by *gname*. For example, the expression **-group other** would find all the files and directories associated with the group **other**.

-mtime *n*   Finds all files last modified *n* days ago. For example, the expression **-mtime 3** would find files last modified three days ago. If you precede the number *n* with a hyphen, the expression finds files modified any time within *n* days. For example, the expression **-mtime -2** would find all the files that have been modified in the last two days.

-exec *cmd*   Executes the command *cmd* on files and finds those files for which *cmd* returns a zero exit status—that is, those files on which the command executes successfully. To execute a command on a file that is currently being searched, use the argument { } after the desired command. The entire command must also be followed by a semicolon preceded by a backslash (\;). For example, the expression **-exec grep "Taxes"** { } \ ; would find all files that contain the word *Taxes*. (The **grep** command looks for patterns in a file. See Chapter 6, "Filters," for more information about **grep**.)

-print   Prints the pathnames of any files that meet the criteria set by the previous expression or expressions. If there is no previous expression, **-print** prints the pathnames of all files and directories in the *pathname-list*. For example, the expression **-user alice -print** would find and print all files and directories whose owner is the user **alice**. Without the **-print** expression, other expressions locate files but do not print their pathnames. If you want to see the list of files that **find** locates, you must use the **-print** expression. If the **-print** expression precedes another expression, all the files in the *pathname-list* will be printed, just as though the other expression were not present.

When you combine one or more expressions, a file must meet the criteria set by both expressions to be found. For example, the expression **-type f -name rotary** would find only ordinary files with the name **rotary**. If you want to find files that meet either one criterion or another, you can separate the two expressions with the **-o** operator. For example, the expression **-name rotary -o -name moose** would find files or directories named either **rotary** or **moose**.

Ordinarily, expressions in an *expression-list* are evaluated linearly. For example, the expression **-name bin -o -name lib -print** would first check to see if a file's name was **bin**. If the file met this criterion, the expression would not be evaluated further. If it did not, **find** would check to see if the file's name was **lib**. If it was, **find** would go on to evaluate the rest of the expression, **-print**. The list of files named **lib** would be printed, but those named **bin** would not. To prevent the linear evaluation of expressions, you can enclose them in parentheses for grouping. Because parentheses have a special meaning to the shell, you must precede each parenthesis with a ****. For example, here is the command you would use to print the list of files in your home directory that are named either **bin** or **lib**:

```
$ find $HOME \( -name bin -o -name lib \) -print
```

You can search all directories on the entire system by specifying **/** as the pathname list. For example, to search the entire filesystem for a file named **uutry**, you would use this command:

```
$ find / -name uutry -print
```

Unless you are the superuser, you do not have permission to search every directory on the system; therefore the **find** command may return some error messages when you use it to search the **/** directory. Nonetheless, **find** will continue to search all the directories that you do have permission to search.

You can specify more than one directory for **find** to search. For example, to search both the directories **/u/bin** and **/u/lib** for files or directories that were last modified within the last three days, you would use the following command:

```
$ find /u/bin /u/lib -mtime -3 -print
```

Most of the work you do on SCO UNIX will either directly or indirectly involve files and directories. Knowing how to create your own system of files and directories is one of the most crucial steps in learning to use your

UNIX system. Before you can take advantage of the more powerful SCO UNIX utilities, you must know how to create and manipulate files. You now know how to create a system of directories and subdirectories that will serve as your base of operations.

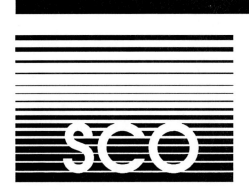

5

Command Line Fundamentals

Since you have already learned to use many SCO UNIX commands, you should be familiar with the basic *command line*. The command line is the line that contains the command, the options (if any), and any arguments to the command. As you'll recall, arguments to a command are the names of any files or directories the command is to operate on.

Each UNIX command has its own *syntax*, that is, a certain format in which you type the options and arguments. For example, some commands take file names as arguments, while others do not. The options for some commands may be combined after a single hyphen, but this is not true of every command. You'll find the complete syntax for every SCO UNIX command, including all options, in the *SCO UNIX User's Reference* and the on-line man pages.

In addition to the options and arguments to individual commands, certain symbols can be added to any SCO UNIX command line to execute commands consecutively, run programs in the background, or determine the source of the command's input and destination of its output. These symbols can greatly increase the power and efficiency of ordinary SCO UNIX commands.

Executing Commands Consecutively

If you want to execute two commands consecutively, you can type them either on consecutive command lines or on the same command line, separated by a semicolon (;). For example, to first change to a directory called **misc** (if **misc** is a subdirectory of the current directory) with the **cd** command, and then list the contents of that directory with the **ls** command, you could type

```
$ cd misc ; ls
cars
letter.dad
rent
things2do
```

As shown here, a list of the **misc** directory's contents would appear immediately, and then you would be returned to a shell prompt. You can even execute more than two commands consecutively, as long as you place a semicolon after each one (except the last one).

Executing Commands Conditionally

With the semicolon, each command is executed immediately upon completion of the previous command, no matter what the results of that command are. For instance, in the previous example, if there were no **misc** directory in the current directory, the **cd** command would return an error message; however, the **ls** command would still be executed, but it would be executed on the current directory.

SCO UNIX also provides symbols you can use to make the execution of one command dependent upon the success or failure of the previous command. These symbols are a pair of ampersands (**&&**) and a pair of pipes (**| |**). You may never need to use these symbols on an ordinary command line, but they can be useful when you begin creating your own *shell scripts,* simple UNIX "programs" that use shell commands and language instead of a programming language. See Chapters 10, "The Bourne Shell," and 11, "The C Shell," for more information about creating shell scripts.

In the Bourne shell, if you separate two commands with the **&&** symbol, the second command will be executed only if the first command is successful. For example, suppose you wanted to list the contents of the directory **/bin**, and change to that directory only if it contained a file called **nroff**. The following example shows how you would do this in the Bourne shell.

```
$ ls /bin/nroff && cd /bin
```

If you separate two commands with the **| |** symbol, the second command will be executed only if the first command is *unsuccessful*. For example, suppose you wanted to copy a file called **temp** into a directory called **execs** only if **execs** did not already contain a file called **temp**. In this case, you would type

```
$ ls execs/temp || cp temp execs
```

First, **ls** would check the directory **execs** to see whether it contained a file called **temp**. If it did not, the **ls** command would return an error message, and the **cp** command would be executed.

 NOTE   Remember, the preceding two commands work as described *only* in the Bourne shell.

In the C shell, these symbols work the opposite way. That is, if you separate two commands with the **&&** symbol, the second command will be executed only if the first command is unsuccessful. In the C shell, the following command line works the same as the previous one in the Bourne shell.

```
% ls execs/temp && cp temp execs
```

 NOTE   This command works as described *only* in the C shell.

If you use the **| |** symbol in the C shell, the second command will be executed only if the first command is successful.

Keep in mind that the definitions of *successful* and *unsuccessful* vary from command to command. The success of a command depends not upon whether the command does what you want it to, but upon its *exit status,* a numerical code returned upon its completion. Most commands are unsuccessful if they return an error message, but this is not always true. For example, the **cd** command does not return an unsuccessful exit status even if it does return an error message. If you plan to use the **&&** or **| |** symbol, you will have to experiment with the commands you want to use to find out what makes a particular command successful or unsuccessful.

Input and Output

All UNIX commands take some input and produce some output. The input to a command is the data upon which the command operates. This data may come from a file that you specify, from a UNIX system file, from the terminal, or from the output of another command. The output of a command is the result of the operation on the input. The output of a command may be printed on the terminal screen, sent to a file, or fed to another command.

Standard Input

Some UNIX commands have only one possible source of input. For example, the **date** command always uses the built-in system clock to determine the date and time. Other commands take their input from a source that you specify. With the latter type of command, unless you specify a file or other source of input, UNIX assumes that the input for the command is to come from the keyboard, that is, from what you type. Input derived from what you type on the keyboard is called the *standard input file,* or simply *standard input.*

Information from the keyboard goes directly to the computer, and as a convenience, UNIX also *echoes,* or sends a copy of, what you type to the screen. This lets you know that you've typed commands correctly and makes SCO UNIX more friendly to the user; however, it is not necessary for input to be echoed to your terminal. In fact, when you type your password during execution of the login procedure or the **passwd** command, it is important that what you type *not* appear on the screen, so the echo is turned off at those times.

Standard Output

Almost all SCO UNIX commands send their output to the user's terminal screen by default. Any output that is sent to a user's terminal is called the *standard output file,* or just *standard output.* Like standard input, standard output can be redirected to a destination other than the terminal, such as a file or another command.

Commands that change internal parameters—such as **rm, mv,** and **mkdir**—do not have output, so, when the command is successful, nothing prints on the screen.

Standard Error

Even commands that produce no output generate error messages when they are unsuccessful. This is because the terminal screen is also the *standard error file,* the place where error messages are sent by default. Do not confuse the standard error of a command with its standard output.

Redirection Symbols

There are three basic ways in which the standard input or output of a command can be redirected—that is, taken from or sent to files instead of to the terminal. With many SCO UNIX utilities you can simply supply the name of the file to be taken as input or output as an argument to the command. Remember, you can only specify a file name as an argument to a command that can take its input from a source you choose. For example, the **pwd** (print working directory) command cannot take a file name as an argument, because it always gets its input from the same source. Even with commands that take file names as arguments, it is usually only the input source, and not the output destination, that can be specified in this way.

Another way to redirect standard input, output, or error to or from a file is to use *redirection symbols.* Using a redirection symbol and a file name, you can direct a command to take its input from, or send its output to, that file. Though the Bourne shell and the C shell share some common redirection symbols, each shell also has a set of unique symbols. Both the shared and the unique redirection symbols are summarized in Table 5-1. With redirection symbols, you can save the output of a command in a file, and then perform other operations on that file. This allows you to manipulate one set of data in an unlimited number of ways.

A third way in which input and output can be redirected is with the pipe symbol (I), which sends the output of one command to the input of another. Pipes are discussed later in this chapter.

Table 5-1.

Symbol	C Shell	Bourne Shell
>	Directs standard output to new file	Directs standard output to file
>!	Directs standard output to old file	N/A
>>	Appends standard output to old file	Appends standard output to old file, or directs standard output to new file
<	Redirects standard input from file	Redirects standard input from file
>&	Directs standard output and error to new file	N/A
>&!	Directs standard output and error to old file	N/A
>>&	Appends standard output and error to old file	N/A
1>	N/A	Directs standard output to file
2>	N/A	Directs standard error to file
>&2	N/A	Combines standard output and standard error and directs the result to standard output

Input and Output Redirection Symbols in the Bourne and C Shells

Redirecting Standard Input

In both the Bourne shell and the C shell, the less than (<) symbol is used to read a command's input from a file instead of using the standard input. To use this symbol, type *command < filename*

where *command* is the name of the command and *filename* is the name of the file you want the command to take its input from. One handy use of < is to mail files to other users. Whereas **mail** normally takes its input from what you type, you can send a whole file to someone by typing

mail *user< filename*

where *user* is the login name of the user or users you want to send the file to, and *filename* is the name of the file you want to send. When you press RETURN, you will not see the **Subject:** prompt; instead, the file will be sent and you will be returned to a shell prompt. See Chapter 9, "Sending and Receiving Mail," for more information on mailing files.

In many cases, using < with a command is the same as simply specifying the file name as an argument. For example the command,

```
$ cat temp
```

would have exactly the same effect as the command

```
$ cat < temp
```

Both commands would tell **cat** to take the file **temp** as input.

Redirecting Standard Output

The symbols > and >> redirect the standard output of a command to a file instead of to the terminal, but each has a specialized function. The output redirection symbols work with any SCO UNIX utilities that produce output. In both the C shell and the Bourne shell, the > symbol sends the output of a command to the named file, regardless of whether that file already exists. If it already exists, any data in the file is overwritten. The following example shows how you would send the output of the **date** command to a file called **current**.

```
$ date > current
```

Since > will overwrite an existing file, you could lose an important file by accidentally redirecting output to it. If your login shell is the C shell, you can set an option called **noclobber** to prevent a file that you want to keep from being lost in this way. To set this option (in the C shell only), type

```
% set noclobber
```

See Chapter 11, "The C Shell," for instructions on setting this option automatically every time you log in.

Once you have **noclobber** set, the C shell will not allow you to overwrite an existing file with the > symbol. If you decide that you do want to overwrite the file, you can use **>!** to do so. For example, to send the output of **date** to a file called **log**, and overwrite the current contents of that file, you would type

```
% date >! log
```

The Bourne shell does not have the **noclobber** option, so use the > symbol with caution; be sure to check and see whether a file you are directing output to already exists. In addition to > and >>, in the Bourne shell you can also use the symbol **1>** to direct output to a new file. This symbol indicates standard output, and works exactly like >.

The append (>>) symbol behaves slightly differently in the two shells. In the C shell, this symbol can only be used with a file that already exists. The output you direct to the file is then appended to whatever was already in the file. An error message results if you attempt to use >> to append output to a nonexistent file. In the Bourne shell, if the file already exists, >> works the same as it does in the C shell. If the file does not exist, however, >> works just like >; it sends the output to a new file instead of generating an error message.

In Chapter 4, "Files and Directories," you learned how to create a file using **cat**. When you give the command

cat > *filename*

cat reads the standard input (what you type at the keyboard) and directs the output, not to the terminal screen, but to the file represented by *filename*. When you press the end-of-file character (CTRL-d), the input is terminated and the file is created. You will learn more about directing output to a file rather than to the screen in Chapter 6, "Filters."

Redirecting Standard Error

If you redirect the standard output with >, >>, or, in the Bourne shell, **1>**, commands still send their error messages to your terminal. For example, if you use this command to redirect the standard output of **cat**,

```
$ cat a b > file1
```

and the file **b** doesn't exist, an error message will print on the screen, although the output of **cat** (that is, the content of file **a**) has been redirected to **file1**. Both the Bourne shell and the C shell provide symbols you can use to redirect the standard error.

The Bourne Shell   In the Bourne shell, if you want to redirect the standard error to a file instead of to the terminal screen, you can use the symbol **2>**. For example, to send an error message from the **cat** command to a file named **file2**, you would use the command

```
$ cat a b 2> file2
```

You can even send the standard output to one file and the standard error to another file. For example, this command would send the standard output of **cat** to **file1** and the standard error to **file2**.

```
$ cat a b 1> file1 2> file2
```

The file **file1** would now contain the contents of the input files **a** and **b**. If either **a** or **b** did not exist, **file2** would contain the error message or messages generated by **cat**.

The C Shell   Although the Bourne Shell allows you to redirect the standard output and standard error separately, the C Shell does not. In the C Shell, you must combine the standard error with the standard output to redirect the standard error. You combine and redirect standard output and standard error with the **>&** symbol. The following example demonstrates redirection of the standard output and standard error of the **cat** command.

```
% cat a b >& newfile
```

The file **newfile** would now contain the contents of the input files (if they existed) and any error messages generated by **cat** (if one or both of the input files did not exist).

It is useful to combine and redirect standard error and output when you want to run a slow command in the background, and don't want its output cluttering up your terminal.

 TIP   If you have the **noclobber** option set, you can use the symbol **>&!** to direct the standard error and standard output to an existing file.

Pipes

Redirection symbols offer one way to perform more than one operation on the same input. By simply redirecting the output of a command to a file and then using that file as input to another command, you can accomplish anything you want to with SCO UNIX commands. Suppose, however, that you want to do five different operations on the same input. Each one would require a new file, but that file's only purpose would be to serve as input to another command. All you really want from the string of commands is the end result, not the intermediate files. In this case, using redirection symbols would clutter your account with files that you will never use again and will have to remove later.

To avoid creating a new file each time you perform an additional operation on your data, you can use a pipe (|) instead of a redirection symbol. On the keyboard and the terminal screen, the pipe key is usually represented as a broken vertical line. The | symbol is used to direct the output of one command to the input of another, instead of to the screen or a file. You can use as many pipes as you want on a single command line, each one directing the output of the previous command to the input of the next command. You use a pipe by typing a command and its arguments, if any, as you normally would, followed by a pipe and the command that you want the output of the first command sent to, like this:

command1 | *command2 . . .*

A line of commands separated by pipes is called a *pipeline*.

Suppose you wanted to use **find** to list all the files in your home directory and its subdirectories, and then view this list with **pg**. Using redirection symbols, this would take two steps: first, saving the output of **find** in a file, and then viewing the file with **pg**, as in the following example:

```
$ find $HOME -print > temp
$ pg temp
```

Using the pipe, you accomplish the same thing with one step, as follows:

```
$ find $HOME -print | pg
```

This command tells the shell that you don't want the output of **find** to go either to the standard output or to a file, but to the **pg** command, which will display it one screenful at a time. Once you finish looking at the output of **find** with **pg**, that output is gone forever, but if you use the redirection symbol >, you are left with an extra file, **temp**.

Not all UNIX commands will work successfully at every position in a pipeline. What commands you can use in a pipeline depends on the spot in the pipeline. The requirements for the different positions are as follows:

- The first element in a pipeline can be any SCO UNIX command that generates output. Some of the commands you have seen that generate output are **date, who, ls,** and **pwd**. Any of the filters you'll learn about in Chapter 6, "Filters," can also be the first command in a pipeline. Commands that adjust internal parameters, such as **mkdir, rm,** and **cd** have no output, so they are not candidates for the first element in a pipeline; nor do interactive commands qualify.

- If the pipeline consists of more than two elements, the intermediate elements must be commands that take input and produce output—namely filters. If the intermediate commands did not produce output, there would be nothing to send to the next command in the pipeline.

- The last element in a pipeline must be a command whose input you can specify. Commands that always take input from specific sources, such as **date** or **cal**, cannot follow a pipe, because no input can be sent to them.

In a moment you'll see some example command lines that use pipes. Because SCO UNIX filters are so often components of pipelines, some filters you have not yet encountered are included in these examples. The functions these filters perform are described briefly in the examples. For full descriptions of these filters, see Chapter 6, "Filters."

```
$ grep "overdue" march april | sort
```

This pipeline first finds all the lines in the files **march** and **april** that contain the word *overdue,* and then alphabetizes these lines using the **sort** utility.

```
$ last | grep "root" | head
```

This pipeline first lists the last login times of all users on the system with **last**. Then it extracts only those lines where the user **root** has logged in. Finally, it prints the first ten of those lines with the **head** command. The result is a list of the ten most recent login times for the user **root**.

```
$ sort accts | split -10
```

This pipeline first alphabetizes a file called **accts**, and then uses the **split** utility to split the alphabetized output into files ten lines long. The output files are named **xaa, xab, xac**, and so on.

Although the previous examples present relatively simple pipelines, they demonstrate the kinds of things you can do using pipes. Once you have learned to use the UNIX filters and become familiar with their functions, you will certainly find many occasions to create pipelines of your own.

The tee Command

The **tee** utility takes the standard input (usually the output of another command) and sends output both to the standard output and to one or more files specified as arguments. Thus, this utility acts as a combination output redirection symbol and pipe. The **tee** utility is so named because it is usually used to create a T in a pipeline, taking one set of input and producing two sets of output. This utility is useful if you want to see the output of a command on your terminal screen at the same time it is sent to a file, or if you want to save the output of one of the commands in a pipeline and also send the output to another command.

The following example shows a possible use of **tee** in a pipeline. The output from **nroff**, a text formatting utility, is piped to **tee**, and the output of **tee** is both saved in the file **report.n** and piped to **lp**, which sends the formatted version of the file to the default printer.

```
$ nroff report | tee report.n | lp
```

The Backquote

When you enclose a command and its arguments (if any) in backquotes, you create an expression that the shell replaces with the output of the command. This is known as *command substitution*. For example, the expression **'ls /'** would be replaced with the names of all the files and directories in the / directory. The expression **'date'** would be replaced with the current date, and so on. If you use such an expression as an argument to another command, that command will take as arguments whatever output is generated by the command enclosed in backquotes. A simple case is the following example, where **pg** takes as arguments all the files listed with the **ls** command.

```
$ pg `ls`
```

The **pg** command would display all the files listed with **ls**, one screenful at a time.

The preceding example is a rather trivial use of a command substitution. In this case, you could get the same results just as easily by using the wildcard character **∗**, as in the following example:

```
$ pg *
```

However, there are cases when this would not be possible. For example, suppose you wanted to find all the files in your home directory and its subdirectories whose names ended with **.acct** and join these files together in a new file using **cat**. Since the files may be in different directories, you cannot simply use a wildcard character to find them all. Instead, you would use the **find** command. By enclosing the **find** command and its arguments in backquotes, you could make **cat** take all of the files **find** reported as arguments, as in the following example:

```
$ cat `find $HOME -name "*.acct" -print` > $HOME/accounts
```

The backquote is also useful in shell scripts, where you can set a variable to equal the value of a command's output. Chapters 10, "The Bourne Shell," and 11, "The C Shell," explain how to do this.

Executing Commands in the Background

Many SCO UNIX commands execute almost instantaneously. However, some utilities such as **find** (see Chapter 4), which searches large directories, and the formatting utilities (see Chapter 7), take some time to run. If UNIX could run only one command at a time, you would not be able to type any more commands while these commands were executing. If you were searching a very large directory or formatting a large file, especially if there were many users on the system, you might have to wait several minutes before you could execute another command. Fortunately, SCO UNIX has the ability to put jobs in the background. This means that the job continues running, but you are returned to a shell prompt, so you can continue working.

To make a job run in the background, type an **&** (ampersand) after the command on the command line.

A command that is running in the background still prints its output on your terminal screen, interrupting whatever you are doing; therefore, you will probably want to redirect the output of background commands to a file so you can read it later. Suppose, for example, that you wanted to use **find** in the background to search the entire **root** file system for files whose names contain the word *mail* and save the output in a file called **mailfiles** in your home directory. To do this you would type

```
$ find / -name "*mail*" -print > $HOME/mailfiles &
1983
```

The number printed below the command line is the process ID number that SCO UNIX has assigned to this command.

Earlier in this chapter, you learned to execute commands consecutively by typing them all on the same command line and separating them with semicolons. An **&** at the end of such a command line places *all* of the commands on that command line in the background. This will not work for command lines that use the symbols **&&** or **I I**. The following example shows a command line that first joins all the files ending with **.acct** in a new file called accounts, and then removes the original files—all in the background.

```
$ cat *.acct > accounts ; rm *.acct &
2001
```

Since the command following a semicolon will not be executed until the previous command is finished, SCO UNIX initiates a new shell to control these background jobs and make sure they are executed in the proper order. The number that is printed for the previous command line is the process ID for this shell. If you execute a pipeline in the background, process numbers for each command in the pipe will be printed.

Interrupting Command Execution

Once you've given a command, you can stop its execution by pressing the interrupt key, usually DEL or CTRL-c. To find out what the interrupt key for your account is, use the **stty -a** command, discussed in Chapter 2, "Using Your Account." The interrupt key can be very useful if you are running a program that seems to be taking too long to execute, or if you mistype a command and get odd or unwanted results. For example, if you wanted to direct the output of a command to a file, but forgot to use a redirection symbol, the output of the command would go to your screen instead of the file. Pressing the interrupt key at any time while the command was still executing would prevent the command from producing further output or results.

To stop a process that is running in the background, you must use the **kill** command. To do so, type

kill *PID*

where *PID* is the process number of the process you want to kill. Remember, when you execute a command in the background, the process number of that command prints on the screen after you press RETURN. If you don't remember the process number of the command you want to stop, you can find it with the **ps** command. This command lists the process number of each command you are currently running, the **tty** you are using, the time each command has spent in process, and the name of each command. The following example shows how you could use the **ps** command to find the process number of a **find** command you were running in the background, and then stop that command with a **kill** command.

```
$ ps
 PID TTY TIME COMMAND
2453 ilc 0:06 csh
3420 ilc 0:14 find
3426 ilc 0:00 ps
$ kill 3420
```

Quoting Special Characters

In this and other chapters you have learned about a number of characters that have special meaning to the shell. These include wildcard characters such as *, redirection symbols such as >, the pipe (|), and slash (/). The space character is also special to the shell because it usually marks the end of a command line argument. If you need to use a special character *without* its special meaning, you must either enclose it in double or single quotes or precede it with a backslash (\). For example, the strings * and "*" both tell the shell to interpret the asterisk without its special wildcard character meaning. This is called *quoting*, or *escaping* a character.

If the special character is in the middle of a word, you can enclose the entire word in quotes. However, if you escape a character with a backslash, the backslash must immediately precede the character. Because the backslash and single and double quotes have the ability to remove the special meaning of other characters, they are themselves special characters. You must quote them just as you would any other special character if you want to use them without their special meaning. Throughout this book, special characters that must be quoted are pointed out, and examples of how they must be quoted are given.

 NOTE   It is not a good idea to give files names that include special characters, even if you quote them. If you do, you will have to quote the file name whenever you type it.

In this chapter you have learned about many useful UNIX tools. The semicolon (;) allows you to execute several commands consecutively. The ampersand (&) lets you run programs in the background. Redirection symbols and the pipe (|) allow you to manipulate the input and output of commands. In the next chapter, you will learn about a group of powerful SCO UNIX utilities called filters. When you combine filters with redirection symbols and pipes, you can find a way to do almost anything you want to a file or other input. In Chapter 10, "The Bourne Shell," and Chapter 11, "The C Shell," you will learn how to insert command lines that contain filters, redirection symbols, and pipes into shell scripts, so you can execute very complex tasks by typing a single command.

CHAPTER

6

Filters

A *filter* is a UNIX utility that takes the standard input or some other input that you specify, performs some operation on that input, and provides the result of the operation as standard output. As well as the standard input, most of the filters in this chapter can take as input a file specified as an argument on the command line. Many can even take multiple file names as arguments. It is important to understand that a filter does not make changes to the input. You can think of a filter as a change machine. You feed in a dollar bill, and a dollar's worth of change comes out. The dollar bill itself remains intact inside the machine; it has not been physically converted into coins, yet the change is your dollar in a different form. UNIX filters work similarly, giving you output that is a different form of the input without actually altering the input. With pipes and redirection symbols, you can redirect the input and output of filters to files or other utilities, and use filters as building blocks to make powerful UNIX command lines.

Viewing and Formatting Input

The filters in this section are generally used to put the input in a more readable form, or to view selected parts of the input. With the exception of **pr**, which paginates files and adds identifying headers, these filters do not change specific parts of the input, but instead arrange the input in a different way.

Sending Standard Input to Standard Output—cat

You have already had some exposure to the **cat** utility. In Chapter 4 you learned how to use **cat** to create and view a file. This section discusses some of **cat**'s more basic functions. The **cat** (for "catenate") utility takes as input one line of text (ending with RETURN) at a time. Its output is that same line of text. Although this may seem trivial, **cat** has a multitude of uses, including creating and viewing files, joining several files together, and getting input from the user of an interactive program. You do all of these things by specifying sources of input and output other than the standard input and output; however, before exploring these functions of **cat**, it will be helpful to see how it operates on the standard input and standard output.

If you type **cat** alone as a command and press RETURN, the cursor will move to the beginning of a blank line. You can then type whatever you want, pressing RETURN at the end of each line. After you press RETURN, the line you just typed will be printed on your screen.

 REMEMBER   The first time the line appears on the screen, it does so only because UNIX echoes your input to the screen as you type.

When you have finished typing, press RETURN and then CTRL-d as the first character on the next line; you will be returned to a shell prompt. You may never actually need to use **cat** in this way, but it will help you see exactly what **cat** does. Here is an example of what happens when you type **cat** alone as a command (The lines that appear bold are the lines you type.):

```
$ cat
You're barking up the wrong tree.
You're barking up the wrong tree.
Money doesn't grow on trees.
Money doesn't grow on trees.
The acorn never falls far from the tree.
The acorn never falls far from the tree.
^D
```

To make **cat** operate on a file instead of on the standard input, all you have to do is type the name of the file you want **cat** to operate on as an argument on the command line. As you'll recall from Chapter 4, to look at a file called **deeds**, you would type

```
$ cat deeds
```

The content of **deeds** would then be displayed on the screen. What **cat** does is copy one line at a time from the file and send it to the standard output.

To join several files together, you can type all of the file names as arguments to the **cat** command. The command

```
$ cat file1 file2 file3
```

would send the files **file1**, **file2**, and **file3** to the standard output, in that order. If you redirect the output of this command to a file, the contents of all three files would be sent to the new file, as in the following example.

```
$ cat file1 file2 file3 > file4
```

If you use a hyphen (-) as one of the arguments to **cat**, the standard input will be read in place of that argument. This is useful if you want to combine a file with the standard input. For example, suppose you want to put the current date and then a file called **memo** into another file called **ready**. You could do this with the command

```
$ date | cat - memo > ready
```

Displaying Input by Screenfuls—more and pg

Two similar filters, **more** and **pg**, take lines of input, arrange them in groups
that will fit on a single screen, and display them interactively, one screenful
at a time. Both **more** and **pg** work on either the standard input or on a file
specified as an argument to the command. The difference between **more**
and **pg** is the way you interact with the program. You can try both utilities
and see which one you prefer. However, you should be familiar with both
because certain other SCO UNIX utilities may use either **more** or **pg** to
format information. For example, the **man** utility, which displays on-line
man pages for SCO UNIX commands, uses **pg** by default to paginate its
files. Alhough the system administrator can change this, you should know
how to use **pg** to read the **man** pages.

To display a file with **more**, type

   more *filename*

where *filename* is the name of the file you want to look at. After one
screenful of the file is displayed, the message "More," followed by the
percentage of the file that has been displayed, appears in the bottom-left
corner of the screen. After you see this prompt, and when you have finished
looking at the first screenful, simply press the SPACEBAR to see the next
screen. You can continue to display the file in this way by pressing the
SPACEBAR after each screen until you reach the end of the file.

 NOTE   If you use **more** to display the standard input instead of a file, the
percentage of the file that has been displayed is not displayed as part of the
prompt. Instead, the prompt simply says "More."

Each time **more** displays its prompt at the bottom of the screen, you can
type one of several commands internal to **more** that do things besides
display the next screen. Some of the most useful of these commands are
described here:

- The **q** or **Q** (for "quit") command aborts the **more** program and returns you to a shell prompt.

- The **f** command instructs **more** to skip forward one screen.

- The **:f** command displays the name of the current file and the line number of the current line, which is the last line displayed on the screen.

- Typing a slash (**/**) followed by a regular expression causes **more** to search forward for the next occurrence of that regular expression and display the screen in which it is found. A regular expression may be a character, a word, or a phrase, or it may be a pattern that includes special characters that match several different characters. See the section "Regular Expressions," later in this chapter for more information about and examples of the special characters you can use in regular expressions.

- The **v** command starts up the **vi** editor at the current line. See Chapter 7, "Editing and Text Processing," for more information on **vi**.

- The **h** (for "help") command or **?** displays a list of all the **more** commands. Typing **h** while you are using **more** is a good way to learn and practice using the other commands.

Most of the **more** internal commands are not displayed on the screen, and you do not press RETURN after typing them. The one exception is the */regular expression* command. When you type the **/**, it appears at the lower-left corner of the screen, and the regular expression is also displayed there as you type it. When you are finished typing the regular expression to search for, press RETURN.

The **more** command also has several command line options that change the format in which the output is displayed. Here are some of the most useful of these options:

- The **-c** option causes **more** to draw each screen starting at the top instead of scrolling so you can begin to read the output before a whole screen is printed. This is useful for slow, unintelligent terminals that scroll by redrawing the screen for each line.

- The **-d** option causes **more** to prompt after each screenful with the message "Hit space to continue, 'q' to quit."

- The -s option compresses multiple blank lines in the input to a single blank line in the output. When you are viewing files that have many blank lines, such as **nroff** output, this option maximizes the actual text displayed on the screen.

If you follow the **more** command with a plus sign (**+**) and a line number, **more** will start displaying the file or standard input with the line you've specified. For example, to start displaying the file **miles** at line number 500, you would use the following command.

```
$ more +500 miles
```

By following the **+** with a **/** and a regular expression, you can instruct **more** to start at the first occurrence of that regular expression in the input. If the regular expression contains spaces, you must enclose the entire regular expression in quotation marks. For example, to start displaying the file **novel** at the first occurrence of the phrase *Chapter 2,* you would use the command

```
$ more +/"Chapter 2" novel
```

To display a file with **pg**, type

pg *filename*

where *filename* is the name of the file you want to display. Like **more, pg** pauses after a screenful of text has been displayed. Instead of showing the percentage of the file that has been displayed, **pg** uses a colon (**:**) as a prompt. To display the next screen, press RETURN. Again, like **more, pg** has a number of internal commands. Many of these commands are identical to **more**'s internal commands; however, **pg** internal commands *do* appear on the screen as you type them. In addition, you must press RETURN after typing **pg** internal commands. Here are some of the most useful of them:

- The **q** or **Q** command quits the **pg** program and returns you to a shell prompt.

- A slash (/) followed by a regular expression causes **pg** to search forward for the next occurrence of that regular expression and display the screen in which it is found.

- A question mark (**?**) followed by a regular expression causes **pg** to search backward for the preceding occurrence of that regular expression and display the screen on which it occurs.

- The **v** command starts up the **vi** editor at the current line. See Chapter 7, "Editing and Text Processing," for more information on **vi**.

- The **h** (for "help") command displays a list of all the **pg** commands. Typing **h** while you are using **pg** is a good way to learn and practice using the other commands. Notice that because the question mark is used to search backward for a regular expression in **pg**, you cannot type a **?** for help.

The command line options you can use with **pg** include the following:

- The **-p** *string* option tells **pg** to use *string* as a prompt instead of using the default prompt, **:**. If the prompt string you want to use contains spaces, you must enclose the entire string in quotes. For example, the following command would make **pg** display the file **memo** with the prompt "Next page . . .."

  ```
  $ pg -p "Next page..." memo
  ```

- The **-c** option clears the screen before displaying each new screen, and starts printing from the top of the screen instead of scrolling, so that you can read each line as it prints.

- The **-n** option causes commands to be executed as soon as they are typed. Ordinarily, you must press RETURN after typing any of the **pg** internal commands.

As with **more**, you can make **pg** begin displaying the file or other input at a particular line by following the command with a **+** and a line number. You can also follow the **+** with a slash and a regular expression to start displaying the file at the first occurrence of that regular expression. If the regular expression contains spaces, you must enclose the entire regular expression in quotes to prevent the shell from interpreting the second word as a file name. The following example would make **pg** start at the first occurrence of the words *For example* in the file **lecture**.

```
$ pg +/"For example" lecture
```

Besides displaying files with **more** and **pg** you can also pipe the output of other commands to these utilities. This can be useful if a command produces lengthy output that would otherwise scroll off the screen before you could read it. See the on-line **man** pages or the *SCO UNIX User's Reference* for more information about the **more** and **pg** utilities.

Paginating Input—pr

The **pr** utility arranges input lines into pages and provides formatted pages with headers and page numbers as output. Lines of text are not wrapped (broken and continued on the next line) if they are too long, or filled (stretched) if they don't reach the right margin, so **pr** cannot be used as a text formatter. However, it can be useful for dividing previously formatted text into pages or for printing files in a readable format. You can use a number of command line options with the **pr** command to produce output with a different format. For example, the **-n** option produces output with numbered lines, while the **-t** option suppresses the header and trailing blank lines normally printed with each page. Many of the **pr** options are discussed in Chapter 8, "Printing." See also the on-line **man** pages or the *SCO UNIX User's Reference*.

Regular Expressions

By inserting special symbols into a string of letters or numbers, you can make that string a *regular expression,* which is a general pattern that includes some variables so that it matches several different particular patterns. You can think of a regular expression as a description of a pattern, rather than an actual pattern; a regular expression matches any pattern that fits its description. Regular expressions are invaluable if you want to search for or make changes to a number of different words or strings that have something in common. For example, suppose you wanted to find all occurrences of either the word *father* or the word *mother.* You could do two separate searches for these two words, but notice that the last four letters of each word are the same. Likewise, suppose you wanted to find all occurrences of numbers following a pound sign (#). To search for every possible number individually would be tedious indeed. Thus, UNIX provides a convention by which searches such as these—and even more complex searches—can be combined in a single search.

The special symbols used in regular expressions are explained here:

- Enclosing characters in square brackets ([ ]) means "match any one of the characters inside the brackets." Thus, **[abc]** would match a or b or c. A whole range of ASCII characters (letters or numbers) can also be specified inside square brackets by separating the upper and lower limits of the range with a hyphen (-). To find any number from 0 to 9, you could use **[0-9]**. To find any lowercase letter, you could use **[a-z]**. The limits of a range of characters can only be specified with one character. For example, you could *not* find any number from 1 to 40 by using **[1-40]** in a regular expression; instead, this would match any number from 1 to 4, or 0. If the first character in the range is actually ordered after the second in the computer, the pattern will match either the first character or the second one, as if the hyphen were not there; thus **[3-1]** would match only 3 or 1.

- An asterisk (∗) means "match zero or more occurrences of the preceding character." Thus, **a**∗ would match any number of *a*'s, including none, and **[0-9]**∗ would match any number of digits.

 NOTE   The ∗ has a different meaning in regular expressions than it has as a wildcard character. As you may recall, as a wildcard character the ∗ stands for any number of characters, however, in regular expressions, it means any number of recurrences of the character that precedes it. Thus, while the ∗ can be used alone as a wildcard character, it does not have its special meaning in a regular expression unless it is preceded by another character.

- A period (.) matches any single character except newline, which is the character that represents the end of one line and the beginning of the next.

- A caret (^) as the first character in a regular expression signifies the beginning of a line. If a regular expression begins with a ^, only occurrences of the regular expression that are at the beginning of a line are matched.

- A ^ as the first character in square brackets changes the expression to mean "match any characters *except* those in the brackets." Thus, [^] would match any character that is not a space, and [^0-9] would match any character that is not a numeral.

- Any expression enclosed between \(and \) matches the same patterns that it would without the parentheses. This is useful because it enables you to refer to the expression later. Each time you set off an expression in this way, it is assigned a number, which can then be referred to by preceding that number with a \.

- A dollar sign ($) represents the end of a line. Any regular expression that ends with a $ will only match a pattern if it is the last thing on the line. For example, **broccoli$** would only find the word *broccoli* if it occurred at the very end of a line. If there were even a period after it, the word would not be matched.

- A backslash (\) "turns off" the special meaning of a following special character. This is useful if you want to find an actual occurrence of one of the special characters in the input. For instance, if you wanted to find a period, you could use \. in a regular expression. Because of the backslash's power to turn off special characters, it is itself a special character. Thus, if you want to find an actual backslash in a file, you need to precede it with another one in the regular expression (\\).

You can use regular expressions with a limited set of SCO UNIX utilities, including the filters **sed**, **more**, **pg**, **vi**, **ed**, and **grep**. The sections in this book that discuss each of these commands show how you can use regular expressions with them. The **egrep** (for "extended grep") utility recognizes most of the same regular expressions that the other utilities do, and it uses some additional special characters **grep** does not use. These are as follows:

- The **?** means "match zero or one occurrence of the preceding character." For example, **grants?** would match either *grant* or *grants*. A question mark can also match one or more occurrences of a string enclosed in parentheses. (See the example that follows the description of parentheses.)

- A pipe (**|**) between two regular expressions means "match either of these two regular expressions." For example **father|mother** would match either *father* or *mother*.

- Parentheses can be used to enclose some patterns or expressions that you want to group together. The expression **embezzle(ment)?** would match either *embezzle* or *embezzlement*. The question mark here matches one or more occurrences of the string grouped with parentheses. Parentheses do not have this special meaning when they are inside square brackets.

Several special characters can be used in a single regular expression, making it match even more patterns. Here are some sample regular expressions that contain more than one special character along with examples of the patterns they match:

- The expression **b[aieou]*d** would match a word or part of a word that begins with *b*, ends with *d,* and has any number (including zero) of vowels between. Examples include: **bead, bad,** and **bd,** but NOT **bond** or **ballad,** because these sequences have characters that are not vowels between the *b* and the *d*.

- The expression **^[0-9][0-9]\.** would match any two-digit number followed by a period at the beginning of a line. Examples might be: **29., 33.,** or **08.**

- The expression **[aA]ccrual** would match either *Accrual* or *accrual*. This is useful if you want to find a word either at the beginning or in the middle of a sentence.

- The expression **^[^A-Z]** would match the beginning of any line that does *not* start with an uppercase letter.

Selecting Part of the Input

The filters discussed in this section display only part of the input as output. Some, such as **head** and **tail** simply select a section of the input to display, while others, such as **grep** search for particular parts of the input and display only those parts.

Displaying the Beginning or End of the Input—head and tail

The **head** and **tail** utilities display the first and last parts of the input, respectively. By default, the **head** utility prints the first ten lines of the input. Likewise, **tail** prints the last ten lines. Both **head** and **tail** work on either the standard input or on a file specified as an argument to the command. You can use **head** or **tail** to view only part of a file, which is a good way to check the contents of a file when you don't want to look at the whole thing. For example, to view the first ten lines of a file called **returns**, you would use the command

```
$ head returns
```

To view the last ten lines of this file, you would use the command

```
$ tail returns
```

You can make **head** print a number of lines different from the default of 10 by typing the desired number after a hyphen as an option to the command. For example, the following command tells **head** to print the first 20 lines of the file **returns**.

```
$ head -20 returns
```

You can specify any number you want; if the number is larger than the number of lines in the file (or standard input), the whole file will be printed.

You can also make the **tail** command display a different number of lines from the default. By preceding the number with a - (hyphcn), you instruct **tail** to display that many lines from the end of the file. For example, to make **tail** display the last 30 lines of the file **returns** instead of the last 10, you would use the command

```
$ tail -30 returns
```

 NOTE   If you use **head** or **tail** to view a very long segment of a file (longer than the number of lines on the screen), the text will scroll off the screen before you can read it. To prevent this, you can pipe the output of **head** or **tail** to another filter, such as **more**, that displays the output by screenfuls. The following example shows how you would pipe the output of **tail** to **more**.

```
$ tail -50 /etc/termcap | more
```

You can also instruct **tail** to display a file starting a certain number of lines from the beginning of the input by preceding the desired number with a **+**. For example, the following command tells **tail** to display the file **returns** from line 45 to the end.

```
$ tail +45 returns
```

If the input to **tail** is a file and not the standard input, the **-f** option will cause **tail** to loop endlessly, pausing for one second and then displaying any new lines at the end of the file. This is useful for monitoring the progress of a file created by another command. For example, if the output of **nroff** or **find** is directed to a file, that file will grow as the process executes. Of course, the process that creates the file must be run in the background or from another terminal, or you will not be able to type the **tail** command. The following example shows how you would direct the output of **find** to a file called **temp** and then view the file **temp** continuously as it grows (the output of the **tail** command is not shown in the example).

```
$ find $HOME -print > temp &
4567
$ tail -f temp
```

To stop **tail**, you would have to press the interrupt key.

Searching for a Pattern—grep

The **grep** utility is a filter that looks for a specified regular expression in a line of input. If the pattern is *matched* (found) in the line, the line is printed as output. Otherwise, the line is not printed. This utility is very handy for checking whether a file or other input contains a certain word or phrase. The name *grep* comes from "get regular expression print." The **grep** command has two companion commands: **egrep** (from "extended grep") and **fgrep** (from "fixed string grep"). The difference between these three commands is in the types of patterns they match.

By default, **grep** takes the standard input, but it can also take a file specified as an argument. To search for a regular expression in a file, type

   grep *regular expression filename*

where *regular expression* is the word or other sequence of characters you want to search for and *filename* is the name of the file in which you want to search. The syntax for **egrep** and **fgrep** is the same as that for **grep**.

Create some sample files of your own on which to practice using **grep**. The following example shows how **grep** works on the file **funds**, which is first displayed with **cat**:

```
$ cat funds
We'd like to purchase all of the equipment you requested,
but there's a cash flow problem. As soon as the check from
the IRS is cashed, we may have the funds.
Cash the check immediately when we receive it!
$ grep cash funds
but there's a cash flow problem. As soon as the check from
the IRS is cashed, we may have the funds.
```

Since you are actually telling **grep** to look for a sequence of characters and not for a word, it will find that sequence even if it is a part of a longer word. For example, it would find the word *cashed* in the preceding example. It would also find the words *cashew, cashier,* and so on. If you wanted to find only those occurrences of *cash* where it was a whole word, you would have to put a space at either end. To do this, you would have to enclose the whole pattern in single quotation marks, as follows:

```
$ grep ' cash '
```

The quotes ensure that the shell will not interpret the spaces around the word as superfluous spaces in the command line.

In the preceding example, the line "Cash this check immediately." does not contain a matching pattern because the word *cash* begins with an uppercase *C.* If you wanted the word *cash* to be matched either at the beginning or in the middle of a sentence, you could do two searches—for **cash** and for **Cash**—or you could use the **-y** option with **grep**, which causes the case of letters to be ignored so that *cash* would match not only *cash,* but also *Cash, CASH, cAsh,* and all other possible combinations of upper- and lowercase letters. You can also use **grep** to search for more than one word. However, if you simply type both words as arguments to **grep**, **grep** will interpret the second word as a file name, and you will get an error message, as in the following example.

```
$ grep quality control production
grep: can't open control
```

In this example, **grep** would still go on to search for the word *quality* in the file **production**. To search for two (or more) words, you must enclose them in single quotes. For example, to search for the phrase "quality control" in the file **production**, you would type

```
$ grep 'quality control' production
```

 TIP It is a good idea to get in the habit of enclosing the pattern you want to search for with **grep** in single quotes. That way, they will always be there when you need them.

There are a few other **grep** options that you may find useful. For example, you can use the **-c** option to see how many lines in the input contain a regular expression, rather than looking at the lines themselves. The following example shows the results of **grep -c** on the file **funds**.

```
$ grep -c 'cash' funds
2
```

 NOTE   Since **grep** finds whole lines that contain matching patterns in the input and not individual occurrences of a pattern, a line containing two or three occurrences of the pattern will be counted only once.

The **-n** option causes the number of each input line that contains a matching pattern to be displayed at the beginning of that line. The example below shows how **grep -n** works on the file **funds**.

```
$ grep -n 'cash' funds
2:but there's a cash flow problem. As soon as the check from
3:the IRS is cashed, we may have the funds.
```

You can use any of the **grep** options in combination.

The difference between **grep**, **egrep**, and **fgrep** is in the kinds of patterns or regular expressions that they search for. While **grep** can match ordinary regular expressions, **egrep** uses an extended set of characters that give its regular expressions greater power and flexibility. The **fgrep** utility, on the other hand, does not recognize any of the special characters used in regular expressions and can only match fixed patterns. The **fgrep** utility runs faster than either **grep** or **egrep** because its parsing algorithms are not as complex. Though it would be ideal to have just one utility that combined the features of **grep**, **egrep**, and **fgrep**, only by separating the three can the trade-off between complexity and speed be achieved.

Finding Duplicate Input Lines—uniq

The **uniq** utility eliminates or reports duplicate lines in the input. By default, **uniq** prints each line that occurs in the input as output. Input lines that are not duplicated are not affected and are printed on the output. If a line is duplicated, **uniq** prints the line only once on the output. Two lines must be adjacent in the input to be considered duplicates. The following example shows the effect of **uniq** on the file **logdates**, which is first displayed with **cat**.

```
$ cat logdates
carolb    Oct    09
carolb    Oct    09
myrmur    Oct    10
daleb     Oct    12
daleb     Oct    12
daleb     Nov    01
carolb    Nov    05
daleb     Nov    06
myrmur    Nov    06
daleb     Nov    06
$ uniq logdates
carolb    Oct    09
myrmur    Oct    10
daleb     Oct    12
daleb     Nov    01
carolb    Nov    05
daleb     Nov    06
myrmur    Nov    06
daleb     Nov    06
```

The first and second lines in the input file are identical, as are the third and fourth; thus only one occurrence of each of these pairs is printed as output. Note that the last and the third from the last lines in the input file are both printed as output, even though they are identical. This is because they are not adjacent in the input. If you really want to find only unique lines, you should first use **sort** on the input to ensure that all duplicate lines are adjacent. The **sort** utility, discussed later in this chapter, alphabetizes the lines in the input.

By default, **uniq** takes the standard input and produces the standard output, but this command is unusual in that both its input and its output can be specified as arguments on the command line without the use of redirection symbols. If you specify one file name, that file is taken as the input (as in the preceding example), and the output is sent to the standard output, which may be redirected to a file or piped to another command. If you specify two file names, the first is interpreted as the input and the second as the output. The following example shows how you would make **uniq** operate on the file **logdates** and send the output to a new file called **updates**.

```
$ uniq logdates updates
```

You can also pipe the output of another command to **uniq,** but in this case you must send the output of **uniq** to the standard output as well. That is, you cannot specify an output file as an argument to the command if the input to **uniq** is the standard input. The shell interprets the first file name after **uniq** as the input file even if you tell **uniq** to read the standard input. The following example shows how you would pipe the output of the **sort** command to **uniq.** To save the output to a file, you would have to use the redirection symbol **>.** In the example, the output of **uniq** is redirected to the file **price.range.**

```
$ sort prices | uniq > price.range
```

Three command line options can be used to change the format of **uniq**'s output:

- The **-c** option causes **uniq** to precede each line of the output with the number of times that line occurred in the input.

- The **-d** option causes **uniq** to display one occurrence of *only* those lines that are repeated in the input.

- The **-u** option causes **uniq** to display only lines that are *not* duplicated in the input. Remember, if duplicate lines are not adjacent, they are counted as unique.

You can make **uniq** ignore certain parts of each input line and compare the remainder of the line. If you specify a number following a **-, uniq** will ignore that many fields—plus any whitespace characters that precede them—in each input line. A field is a sequence of nonwhitespace characters bounded by whitespace characters. For example, in the line "abc def ghi," there are three fields. If you specify a number following a **+, uniq** will ignore that many *characters.* The following example shows how you would make **uniq** ignore the first field in each line of the file **logdates.**

```
$ uniq -1 logdates
carolb    Oct    09
myrmur    Oct    10
daleb     Oct    12
daleb     Nov    01
carolb    Nov    05
daleb     Nov    06
```

Now even lines in which the first field (the name) are different will be counted as duplicates as long as the second two fields (the month and date) are the same.

 NOTE This technique only works correctly if the field separators in the file **logdates** are tabs, not spaces. Because **uniq** considers whitespace characters to be part of the second field, a different number of spaces before two occurrences of a month name would prevent those fields from being recognized as identical.

If you include both a number of fields and a number of characters to be ignored, **uniq** will ignore the number of fields you specify and the number of characters you specify after that. You might want to restrict **uniq** to comparing certain fields or characters in the input lines if, for example, each line in the input were numbered, but the text after the numbers might be the same. You could have **uniq** ignore the field or fields that contained the line numbers and still find duplicate lines.

Splitting Input into Output Files of Equal Length—split

The **split** utility splits the input into output files of equal length. The **split** utility is unusual in that its output is automatically redirected to files instead of to the standard output. By default, each output file is one thousand lines long, with the exception of the last file, which consists of the remainder. The following command would split the file **islands** into as many one thousand-line files as necessary.

```
$ split islands
```

Unless you specify otherwise, the output files are named **xaa, xab**, and so on, up to **xzz** if necessary. You can replace the *x* in the output file names with any prefix of your choice by following the input file name with the name you want the output files to have. The following example splits the file **islands** into one thousand-line files, just as in the previous example, but in this case the output files will be named **isletaa, isletab**, and so on.

```
$ split islands islet
```

NOTE   Because the second argument to the **split** command is automatically interpreted as a name prefix for the resulting files, only one file name may be specified as an argument to **split**.

To see the output files that are created by a **split** command, use the **ls** command, which lists the contents of the directory.

You can create output files of a different size from the default by putting the desired number after a hyphen and using it as an option to the **split** command. For example, the following command would split the file **trombones** into output files 76 lines long.

```
$ split -76 trombones
```

If the input to the **split** command is the standard input (the output from another command), and you want to specify a file name prefix for the output files, you must place a hyphen between the **split** command and the name of the output files. For example, the following command line sorts the file **balances** and sends the sorted output to **split**. The output files are named **balaa, balab**, and so on.

```
$ sort balances | split - bal
```

The hyphen tells the shell that the input to **split** is the standard input, and that the name after **split** is the name of the output file rather than the input. Without the hyphen, the shell would interpret **bal** as the name of the input file for **split**.

Editing or Altering Input

A number of filters allow you not only to print the input in a different output format but also to change parts of the input. For example, you can change one word to another with the **sed** editor, translate one character into another with **tr**, or perform complex calculations on the input with **awk**. These powerful utilities are somewhat complex, but once you've learned to use them, they can save you a great deal of time and effort.

Editing the Input—sed

The **sed** (for "stream editor") utility is a filter that takes lines of text as input, copies them, and performs some operation on specified lines. The operation **sed** performs depends on which editing command you specify. Finally, **sed** prints all lines— changed or not—as output. The **sed** utility is most useful for making global changes to one or more files.

By default **sed** takes the standard input and produces the standard output. It can also take as input a file specified on the command line. The syntax of **sed** is somewhat more complex than that of the other commands you've learned. Unlike some commands, **sed** must have at least one option or argument to do anything; typing **sed** by itself on a command line returns you to a shell prompt. In addition, two of **sed**'s three options take arguments of their own. The options are as follows:

- The **-e** option takes an editing command as an argument and causes the command to be executed on the input. An editing command following the **-e** option should always be enclosed in quotation marks. Editing commands are discussed later in this section.

- The **-f** option takes a file name as an argument. The file that you specify, called a *sed script,* must contain one or more **sed** editing commands. The commands in this **sed** script are executed on the input.

- The **-n** option suppresses the default output of **sed**. This allows you to select which lines you want printed as output, as explained later in this section.

Unlike the options for other commands, **sed**'s options cannot generally be combined after a single hyphen. For example, **-nf** is not interpreted as **-n -f**. However, you can use the options together, as long as you precede each one with a separate hyphen. For options that take their own arguments, the argument must immediately follow the option it goes with. That is, you would type

   -e *editing command* **-f** *script*

and not

   -e -f *editing command script*

Before you can use **sed**, you must be able to use some editing commands. An editing command has the following format:

   [*address*[,*address*]] *instruction* [*arguments*]

 NOTE   A **sed** editing command cannot be followed by any spaces. If it is, you will get an error message.

sed Addresses   The *addresses* in a **sed** editing command, which are optional, specify certain lines to look for. Any command that follows the address is performed on the addressed lines. The addresses can either be *relative* (line numbers) or *contextual* (marked by a pattern), and you can specify either one line or a range of lines, where the first line specified marks the beginning of the range, and the second line marks the end of the range. For example, to perform an operation on lines 1 and 2 of a file, you would specify the relative addresses **1,2**. Note that there can be no spaces between the addresses and the comma. To do the operation on lines 1 through 10, you would use the addresses **1,10**. If you want to change all the lines from a particular line to the last line in the input, you can use **$** to represent the last line, so you don't have to know the line number of the last line. For example, to change all lines from line 105 to the last line, the addresses would be **105,$**.

You can also use either one or two regular expressions as addresses. If you specify one regular expression, changes are made only to lines containing that pattern. You must enclose the regular expression in slashes (**/**). For example, if you wanted to make changes to all lines that contain the word *paid,* you would specify the address **/paid/**. If you wanted to change only those lines containing *paid* as a whole word, and not those containing *unpaid* or other words that include the sequence *paid,* you would surround the word *paid* with spaces (**/ paid /**). You do not need to enclose the pattern in quotes because it is already enclosed in slashes. You can also use special characters to make a regular expression that matches any number of lines. For example, the address **/^[0-9][0-9]∗\./** would match all lines that begin with a number followed by a period. Review the section "Regular Expressions," earlier in this chapter, if you need more information about regular expressions. If you specify two regular expressions separated by a comma, changes are made to all lines starting with the first line that matches the first regular expression and ending with the next line that matches the second regular expression.

You can also mix relative and contextual addresses. For example, you could change all lines from line 1 to the first line that contained the word *market* by giving the addresses, **1,/market/**. Likewise, you could change all lines from the first line that contained the word *market* to line 10 by giving the addresses, **/market/,10**.

sed Instructions   Once you have specified the addresses of the lines you want to change, you must specify the changes that you want to make. You do this with **sed** instructions, which specify what changes are to be made to the selected lines. If you do not specify an address, an instruction is applied to all lines of the input. Instructions are the only part of **sed** commands that are not optional, because without an instruction no changes would be made to the file. You can use **sed** instructions to make almost any change you want to a file. As **sed** examines each input line, that line is copied to a *pattern space*. There, any required changes are made, and the line is then copied to the standard output. Some **sed** instructions copy lines to or from a *hold space,* where lines are stored for later retrieval. The following sections discuss the **sed** instructions in greater detail.

The a\ (Append) Instruction   The **a** instruction appends subsequent text to the addressed lines. The text that follows it begins on the next line and must have a backslash at the end of each line except the last one, as in this example:

```
a\
Sincerely,\
Shirley L. Baldwin\
Director of Consumer Affairs
```

This instruction would append the three lines of text below the **a** to any lines that you specify.

NOTE   You can specify only one address, not a range of addresses, with the **a** instruction.

The i\ Instruction   This instruction inserts lines of text *before* selected lines. Otherwise, it functions exactly like the **a** instruction. Specify the text to be inserted as shown with the **a** instruction.

The c\ Instruction   This instruction changes lines of text by deleting them from the output and adding new lines specified in the same way as for the **a** instruction. If you specify two addresses with this command, all lines in the range specified by the addresses will be replaced with the new text.

NOTE   Use **sed** instructions that take following text arguments (**a\, i\,** and **c**) in a **sed** script with the **-f** option instead of on the command line with the **-e** option. Because these instructions extend over more than one line, they are tedious to type on the command line, and you cannot go back and correct a mistake that you've made on a previous line.

The p (Print) Instruction   The **p** instruction causes the addressed line or lines to be printed as output. This instruction overrides the **-n** option, which suppresses the output of **sed**. The **p** instruction is often used in conjunction with the **-n** option to print out *only* the selected lines as output. If you use the print instruction without the **-n** option, selected lines are printed as output twice, while nonselected lines are printed only once.

The w (Write) Instruction   The **w** instruction causes the selected lines to be written to a specified file. The name of the file the lines are written to must be separated from the write instruction by exactly one space. The following example shows a **sed** editing command that writes the first ten lines of the input to the file **newfile**.

```
1,10 w newfile
```

Use this instruction with caution. If the file named after the write instruction already exists, it will be written over by the new lines and the data in the original file will be lost.

The r (Read) Instruction   This instruction causes a specified file to be read, or integrated, into the output after the selected lines. As with the append (**a**) instruction, you can only specify one address with the read instruction.

The d (Delete) Instruction   The **d** instruction deletes selected lines from the output.

The s (Substitute) Instruction   This instruction causes one pattern to be substituted for another. The format for the substitute instruction is s/*oldpattern*/*newpattern*/*flags,* where *oldpattern* is the regular expression you want to be replaced by *newpattern.* For example, the following **sed** command replaces the word "Dr." with "Doctor."

```
s/Dr\./Doctor/
```

Note that the regular expressions, like the patterns in contextual addresses, must be enclosed in slashes. The backslash before the period is necessary because the period is a special character in regular expressions. Without the backslash, the regular expression **Dr.** would match Dro, Dri, and so on. The backslash ensures that the period matches only a period. Like all **sed** instructions, the substitute instruction applies only to occurrences of *oldpattern* on lines selected by the addresses, unless no addresses are specified.

If you want *newpattern* to include *oldpattern, newpattern* can contain an ampersand, (**&**) which will represent *oldpattern.* For example, suppose you wanted to change all occurrences of the word *interest* to *compound interest.*

Instead of typing **s/interest/compound interest/**, you could just type **s/interest/compound &/**.

NOTE   If a **sed** instruction includes spaces (such as the one in "compound interest" or special characters, you must enclose the instruction in quotes. In fact, you should get in the habit of enclosing **sed** instructions in quotes whenever you type them on the command line. This is not necessary if the instructions are executed from a **sed** script.

The **&** is even more useful when the pattern you want to replace is a complex regular expression. For example, suppose you wanted to add a period to all numbers that occur at the beginning of a line. Even though you don't know what each number will be, you can replace them all with the **&**, as in the following example.

```
s/^[0-9][0-9]*/&./
```

This instruction would replace 1 with 1., 23 with 23., and so on.

REMEMBER   The ampersand (**&**) is a special character to the shell, so this instruction must be enclosed in quotes if you use it on the command line after the **-e** option.

Review the section "Regular Expressions" earlier in the chapter if you need more information about regular expressions.

Three *flags*—**g**, **p**, and **w**—can be specified at the end of a substitute command. The **g** (global) flag makes the substitution apply to all occurrences of *oldpattern* on selected lines. Without the **g** flag, the substitution would apply only to the *first* occurrence of the pattern on any given line. The **p** (print) flag functions just like the print instruction, that is, it causes all lines on which substitutions have been made to be printed as output. If a line is addressed, but does not contain the pattern to be replaced, it is not printed as output. The **w** (write) flag functions like the write instruction. It causes the lines that are changed by the substitute instruction to be written to a file specified as an argument to the flag. See the **w** instruction for the format to use with the **w** flag.

The q (Quit) Instruction   This instruction causes **sed** to stop processing, or quit, when it reaches the selected line. The remainder of the input is not changed or printed as output.

The ! Instruction   The exclamation mark stands for "not." When you use this instruction in front of any other instruction, it tells **sed** to carry out that insruction only on lines *not* selected by the specified addresses. For example, if you wanted to delete all lines that do not contain the word *acquisition,* you would use the following command.

```
/acquisition/!d
```

The address here is specified with the pattern enclosed in slashes, and the instruction **d** is preceded by an **!**, so it will be carried out on all lines not selected by the address.

 NOTE   If you are using the C shell, you must precede the exclamation point with a backslash, even if the entire instruction is enclosed in quotation marks. This is not necessary if the instruction is executed from a **sed** script.

The h Instruction   This instruction replaces the contents of the hold space with the addressed line. Only one address can be used with this command. If more than one address is given, only the last addressed line is put in the hold space.

The H Instruction   The H instruction appends the addressed lines to the hold space. More than one line can be appended.

The g Instruction   The g instruction replaces the addressed lines with the contents of the hold space.

The G Instruction   The G instruction appends the contents of the hold space to the last addressed line.

The n Instruction   The n instruction copies the addressed line to the standard output and goes to the next line of input. This command can be used to make changes to the lines *following* lines that match a certain pattern, even if you don't know what the next lines will say. For example, by enclosing the **n** and **d** commands in braces, you could delete all lines that follow lines containing a particular word (see "Example sed Commands," later in this chapter).

The N Instruction   The **N** instruction copies the addressed line to the standard output and appends the next line of input with an embedded newline. Any commands enclosed in braces with the **N** command will affect both the addressed line and the next line (see "Example sed Commands," later in this chapter). This instruction writes the addressed lines to *file*.

The x Instruction   The **x** instruction exchanges the addressed lines for the contents of the hold space, and puts the addressed lines in the hold space.

The {} Instruction   Braces enclose a group of commands to be executed on the same selected lines. Each command within the group should be on a separate line, and a **}**, also on its own line, ends the grouping. For example, the following **sed** script executes three substitute commands on lines 1 through 10 of the input.

```
1,10 {
s/Miss/Ms\./g
s/girl/woman/g
s/his/& or her/g
}
```

 REMEMBER   A set of commands like that in the preceding example should be executed from a **sed** script, not from the command line. If you tried to type this example on the command line, you would have to follow each line with three backslashes, and the fourth line, which contains spaces, would have to be enclosed in quotes.

sed Arguments   The argument portion of a **sed** editing command varies depending on which instruction the command line contains. For example, when you use the append instruction, the argument is the following text, but with the write or read instruction, the argument is the file that you specify.

Example sed Commands   You have now learned everthing necessary
to try some sample **sed** commands. To start relatively simply, try using **sed**
with the **-e** option so that you can specify the command right on the command
line. After you type a command line with **sed**, the cursor moves to a blank
line, and waits for your input.

Suppose you wanted to replace all occurrences of the word *data* with the
word *information*. The first example shows how **sed** operates on the input
file **memo**, which is displayed first with **cat**.

```
$ cat memo
Here is the data you requested.
I am attempting to solve the problem, but
I need more data.
There is a lot of data to process,
so I expect this will take some time.
$ sed -e "s/data/information/g" memo
Here is the information you requested.
I am attempting to solve the problem, but
I need more information.
There is a lot of information to process,
so I expect this will take some time.
```

In this example, no address is specified, so the substitute instruction applies
to all input lines that contain the word *data*.

Now you can try creating a **sed** script, and using **sed** with the **-f** option.
The first step is to create a **sed** script using **cat** or **vi**. See Chapter 4, "Files
and Directories," for information on creating files with **cat**. Chapter 7,
"Editing and Text Processing," discusses creating a file with **vi**. You can
give your script any legitimate file name. The sample script in the following
example is called **script1**.

```
$ cat script1
1 s/Client/Potential &/
s/lawyer/legal professional/
$ a\
Sincerely,\
Arnold K. Smith\
Smith, Smith, Smith, Smith, and Smith, Attorneys at Law
```

The first command in this example selects line 1. On this line, the first
occurrence of the word *Client* is replaced with *Potential Client*. The

second line of the script instructs **sed** to replace every instance of the word *lawyer* with the words *legal professional*. Note that since there are no spaces around *lawyer* in the regular expression, this string will be replaced even if it is part of a longer word. This line does not specify any addresses, so this command will be applied to all lines of the input. The third command in the script appends three lines of text to the last line in the input.

In the following example, **sed** uses the script **script1** to make changes to the file **intro**, which is first displayed with **cat**.

```
$ cat intro
Dear Client,
    Please allow me to introduce the legal team of Smith,
Smith, Smith, Smith, and Smith. We are a qualified group of
lawyers who have been practicing law for a
cumulative time of 100 years. One of our best
recommendations is that our clients often include other
lawyers. We hope you will consider consulting
with our firm about your current legal situation.
$ sed -f script1 intro
Dear Potential Client,
    Please allow me to introduce the legal team of Smith,
Smith, Smith, Smith, and Smith. We are a qualified group of
legal professionals who have been practicing law for a
cumulative time of 100 years. One of our best
recommendations is that our clients often include other
legal professionals. We hope you will consider consulting
with our firm about your current legal situation.
Sincerely,
Arnold K. Smith
Smith, Smith, Smith, Smith, and Smith, Attorneys at Law
```

Translating Input Characters—tr

The **tr** utility translates the input characters you specify into different characters and then copies the input to the standard output. Unlike most of the filters discussed in this chapter, **tr** cannot take its input from a file specified as an argument to the command. The input to **tr** must be the standard input either piped from another command or redirected from a file. The **tr** command takes two command line arguments. The first argument specifies the input character or characters to be replaced, and the second specifies the output character or characters. The characters can be either an actual ASCII character or a one-, two-, or three-digit octal number that represents the character. For example, the octal code \012 represents a newline character. In the following simple example, **tr** translates all occurrences of the letter *p* in the file **words** into the letter *s*. The file **words** is first displayed with **cat**.

```
$ cat words
pit
pat
peat
pet
$ tr p s < words
sit
sat
seat
set
```

Here, the input to **tr** is redirected from the file **words** with the redirection symbol <. You could achieve the same result by piping the output of **cat** to **tr**, as in the following example.

```
$ cat words | tr p s
sit
sat
seat
set
```

If more than one character is specified as the input and output strings, input and output characters are matched one for one. That is, each input character specified is replaced with the corresponding output character. For example, the following command replaces each *p* with *P* and each *t* with *l* in the file **words**.

```
$ tr pt Pl < words
Pil
Pal
Peal
Pel
```

One function of **tr** that you may find useful is changing the case of the letters in an entire file. For example, if you have a file of uppercase text that you want to make lowercase, **tr** can do this quickly and easily, whereas doing it by hand would be time-consuming and tedious. The following command would change all uppercase letters to lowercase letters in the file **note**, which is first displayed with **cat**.

```
$ cat note
NOTE: UNDER NO CIRCUMSTANCES SHOULD YOU REMOVE THE REAR PANEL.
THIS PANEL SHOULD BE REMOVED ONLY BY A TRAINED MECHANIC.
$ tr "[A-Z]" "[a-z]" < note
note: under no circumstances should you remove the rear panel.
this panel should be removed only by a trained mechanic.
```

The square brackets indicate that the characters enclosed therein are a range of characters. Strings enclosed in square brackets must be enclosed in quotation marks because the square brackets are wildcard characters and would otherwise be interpreted by the shell. The input characters and the output characters must each be enclosed in a separate set of quotes, or the entire set will be interpreted as input characters.

Another useful operation **tr** can perform is to divide text into one-word lines. That is, it can replace spaces with newline characters so that each word of the input is on a separate output line. This is useful if you want to compare the words used in a file or if you are sending a file to a program that takes one word at a time as input. The following example shows how you would transform the file **note** from the preceding example into a list of this sort.

```
$ tr " " "\012" < words
NOTE:
UNDER
NO
CIRCUMSTANCES
SHOULD
YOU
REMOVE
THE
REAR
PANEL.
THIS
PANEL
SHOULD
```

```
BE
REMOVED
ONLY
BY
A
TRAINED
MECHANIC.
```

The first argument to **tr** in this example is a space enclosed in quotes so that it will not be interpreted by the shell. The second argument is the octal code that represents a newline character.

The **tr** utility is capable of even more complex operations than those illustrated in this section. For more information about **tr**, see the *SCO UNIX User's Reference* or the on-line **man** pages.

The Wonder Utility—awk

The **awk** program is one of the most powerful SCO UNIX utilities. In fact, it is similar to a programming language in both complexity and power. Among other things, it can perform mathematical calculations on numerical input, make changes to textual input, and rearrange lines or parts of lines to print the output in a completely different format from the input.

The **awk** utility operates by scanning input for particular patterns or fields and performing actions on lines or fields of the input. The patterns to search for and the actions to be performed on them are specified in the form of a *program*. An **awk** command may be typed in two formats. In the first format, you type the program that you want **awk** to execute as a command line argument, like this:

awk *'program'* [*file*]

In the second format, the program is contained in a program file specified as an argument to the **-f** option, like this:

awk -f *program-file* [*file*]

Like most filters, **awk** can take as input either a file specified as an
argument to the command or the standard input.

awk Programs   An **awk** program consists of a pattern and an action to
be taken on lines or portions of lines that match that pattern. The format of
an **awk** program is

pattern { *action* }

If the pattern portion of an **awk** program is missing, the action is carried out
on every line of the input. If you do not specify an action to be performed,
lines matching the pattern are simply printed on the output.

Patterns   A pattern in **awk** can be a regular expression enclosed in
slashes or a numerical value that matches a line or a particular field on a
line. A pattern can match either an entire line or a particular part of a line.
For example, the pattern **/Nov/** matches all lines that contain the sequence
"Nov," anywhere on the line. The pattern **123** matches a line whose
numerical value is 123. If you precede the pattern with an exclamation mark
(**!**), the action will be carried out on all lines that do *not* match the pattern.
For example, the pattern **!/Nov/** matches any line that does not contain the
sequence "Nov."
    To test whether a pattern matches a specific part of the line or a variable,
you can use the tilde operator (**~**) as follows:

variable~/regular expression/

The *variable* can be a line field, or another variable you want the pattern
to match. The next section, "Variables," explains how to refer to fields and
other variables. The operator **!~** tests for a field that does *not* match a pattern.
    A numeral not enclosed in slashes is treated as a number and can be used
to compare numerical values. The format for comparing numerical values
of variables is

variable operator number

where *variable* is the name of a field or other variable (as explained in the following section, "Variables") and *operator* is one of the following operators:

<	Less than
<=	Less than or equal to
==	Equal to
!=	Not equal to
>	Greater than
>=	Greater than or equal to

See the section "Examples of awk in Use," later in this chapter, for examples of how to use these operators.

 REMEMBER   These operators are part of the *pattern* portion of an **awk** program. They are used to evaluate whether a portion of the line has a certain value. Do not confuse these operators with those used in the *action* portion of the **awk** program.

Two patterns separated by a comma indicate a range of lines beginning with a line that matches the first pattern and ending with the next line that matches the second pattern. An action that follows two patterns separated by a comma will apply to all lines in the range.

Two patterns may also be separated by one of the two Boolean operators: II, which stands for "or" or **&&**, which stands for "and." That is, the pattern */Nov/* II */Dec/* would match all lines that contain either *Nov* or *Dec*. Likewise, the pattern */Nov/* **&&** */Dec/* would match only lines that contain both *Nov* and *Dec*.

The special pattern **BEGIN** allows you to specify actions to be performed before **awk** begins processing the input lines. The pattern **END** allows you to specify actions to be performed after **awk** has finished processing the input lines.

Variables   You can create your own variables to stand for anything you want. In addition, **awk** maintains a set of built-in variables that you can use in both the pattern and the action portions of an **awk** program. The built-in variables include the following:

NR	The current record number. By default, a record is one line, but you can change this by assigning a different value to the **RS** variable.
$0	The current record (all fields on the line).
NF	The number of fields on the current record.
$1-$n	The fields in the current record, where *n* is the last field in the record.
FS	The input field separator. By changing this variable, you can use different field separators in different lines of the input. By default, spaces and tabs are the input field separators.
OFS	The output field separator. By default, spaces are the output field separators.
RS	The input record separator. By default, this is a newline character, which means that a record is one line.
ORS	The output record separator. By default, this is a newline character.
FILENAME	The name of the current input file.

When you use the name of a variable in either the pattern or the action portion of an **awk** program, the name refers to the current value of that variable. You can change the values of these variables with any of the operators discussed in the section "Operators," later in this chapter.

Actions   The action portion of an **awk** program tells **awk** what action to take on the lines matched by patterns. If you do not specify an action following a pattern, lines that match the pattern will be printed as output.

You can use the **print** command to print one or more fields of a line, text, or the value of a variable. The format of the **print** command is

{print *x*}

where *x* is either the name of any field or other variable, or some ordinary text enclosed in double quotes. For example, to print the phrase "Number 1 is" and then the first field of a line, you would use the action

```
{print "Number 1 is " $1}
```

The previous section, "Variables," explains how to refer to fields and other variables. See the upcoming section "Examples of awk in Use" for more examples of the **print** command.

Operators You can use the following operators to perform mathematical operations on the values of variables.

e1 **+** *e2*	Adds the expressions *e1* and *e2*.
e1 **-** *e2*	Subtracts the expression *e2* from the expression *e1*.
e1 ***** *e2*	Multiplies the expression *e1* by the expression *e2*.
e1 **/** *e2*	Divides the expression *e1* by the expression *e2*.
e1 **%** *e2*	Takes the remainder of dividing the expression *e1* by the expression *e2*.
v **=** *e*	Assigns the value of the expression *e* to the variable *v*, where *v* is any built-in variable *or* any of the variables you have initialized. This works for assigning string as well as numerical values to variables.
v **++**	Increments the variable *v*.
v **--**	Decrements the variable *v*.
v **+=** *e*	Increases the value of the variable *v* by the value of the expression *e*.
v **-=** *e*	Decreases the value of the variable *v* by the value of the expression *e*.

v *= *e*	Multiplies the value of the variable *v* by the value of the expression *e* and assigns the result to the variable *v*.
v /= *e*	Divides the value of the variable *v* by the value of the expression *e* and assigns the result to the variable *v*.
v %= *e*	Divides the value of the variable *v* by the value of the expression *e* and assigns the result to the variable *v*.

Functions   Some of the functions you can use to manipulate numbers and strings are as follows:

length(*s*)	Returns the number of characters in the string *s*.
int(*n*)	Returns the integer portion of the number *n*.
sub(*old,new,in*)	Replaces the first occurrence of the regular expression *old* with the regular expression *new* in the string *in*. The regular expressions *old* and *new* must be enclosed in double quotes.
gsub(*old,new,in*)	Replaces *all* occurrences of the regular expression *old* with the regular expression *new* in the string *in*. The regular expressions *old* and *new* must be enclosed in double quotes.
index(*s1,s2*)	Reports the position in string *s1* where string *s2* first occurs. If the strings are regular expressions, they must be enclosed in double quotes.

 NOTE   Only the rudiments of the **awk** utility are explained here. For more information on **awk**, refer to the Bell Labs publication, *Awk—A Pattern Scanning and Processing Language*. This text is written by the creators of **awk**, Alfred V. Aho, Peter J. Weinberger, and Brian W. Kernighan.

Examples of awk in Use   The **awk** examples in this section all take as input the file **radio**, which is displayed here with **cat**.

```
% cat radio
Sun     10am    Breakfast-in-Bed        KZSC    88.1    $35
Mon     7pm     Closet-Free_Radio       KZSC    89.1    $35
Tues    12n     Latin-American_Music     KRMR    93.1    $10
```

```
Tues      9pm        The_Living_Spirit        KKUP    91.5    $60
Tues      9pm        Ragtime/Dixie_Show       KAZU    90.3    $40
Wed       9am        Spirit_of_Africa         KRMR    93.1    $10
Wed       9am        Brazilian/Cuban_Music    KZSC    88.1    $35
Thu       7pm        Just_Jean-Bluegrass      KKUP    91.5    $60
Fri       3pm        Roses_of_Portugal        KZSC    89.1    $35
Sat       5pm        African_Music,Etc.       KAZU    90.3    $40
Sat       7pm        Latin-American_Music     KAZU    90.3    $40
```

Each line in this file contains six fields separated by tabs. The fields show the day of the week, the time, the name of a radio show, a radio station, its position on the dial, and a subscription amount.

The following example shows how a simple **awk** program specified right on the command line operates on the file **radio**. The program selects all lines in which the first field contains the pattern **Tues** and prints the first four fields of those lines. The commas between the names of the field variables cause the output fields to be separated by spaces.

```
% awk '$1~/Tues/ {print $1,$2,$3,$4}' radio
Tues 12n Latin-American_Music KRMR
Tues 9pm The_Living_Spirit KKUP
Tues 9pm Ragtime/Dixie_Show KAZU
```

The next example uses a program in a file called **sort.by.day** to print some of the information in **radio** in a different format. The file **sort.by.day** is first displayed with **cat**.

```
% cat sort.by.day
NR == 1 {ST = $1
print ""
print "The shows on " $1 " are: "
print $3 " at " $2 " on " $4"."
}
$1 == ST {print $3 " at " $2 " on " $4"."}
$1 != ST {ST = $1
print ""
print "The shows on " $1 " are: "
print $3 " at " $2 " on " $4"."
}
```

This program first initializes a variable **ST** to be equal to the first field of the first input line, and then prints some text and some of the fields from that line. For each subsequent line, **awk** checks to see whether the first field matches the value of the variable **ST**. If it does, fields 3, 2, and 4 of the line are printed, along with some text. If it does not, the value of **ST** is reset to this new value and the process starts again. The following example shows the output of **awk** used with this program on the file **radio**.

```
% awk -f sort.by.day radio

The shows on Sun are:
Breakfast-in-Bed at 10am on KZSC.
Breakfast-in-Bed at 10am on KZSC.

The shows on Mon are:
Closet-Free_Radio at 7pm on KZSC.

The shows on Tues are:
Latin-American_Music at 12n on KRMR.
The_Living_Spirit at 9pm on KKUP.
Ragtime/Dixie_Show at 10pm on KAZU.

The shows on Wed are:
Spirit_of_Africa at 9am on KRMR.
Brazilian/Cuban_Music at 9am on KZSC.

The shows on Thu are:
Just_Jean-Bluegrass at 7pm on KKUP.

The shows on Fri are:
Roses_of_Portugal at 3pm on KZSC.

The shows on Sat are:
African_Music,Etc. at 5pm on KAZU.
Latin-American_Music at 7pm on KAZU.
```

The next example uses the program file **late** to print information about shows that begin at or later than 7 P.M. The file **late** is first displayed with **cat**.

```
% cat late
BEGIN {print "The late evening shows are:"
$2~/pm/ && int($2) > = 7 {print $3,"at",$2,"on",$4}
```

Before **awk** begins processing the input file, the **BEGIN** pattern causes text to be printed. Then two patterns select the lines from which fields are to be printed. The first pattern selects only lines where the second field contains the regular expression **pm**. The second pattern selects only lines where the integer portion of the second field is greater than or equal to 7. Because these two patterns are separated by the Boolean operator **&&**, both of them must be matched for a line to be selected. The following example shows the output of **awk** used with this program on the file **radio**.

```
% awk -f late radio
The late evening shows are:
Closet-Free_Radio at 7pm on KZSC
The_Living_Spirit at 9pm on KKUP
Ragtime/Dixie_Show at 10pm on KAZU
Just_Jean-Bluegrass at 7pm on KKUP
Latin-American_Music at 7pm on KAZU
```

The filters you have learned about in this chapter have a multitude of uses. By themselves, filters are useful for formatting, displaying, or changing files. In Chapter 5, "Command Line Fundamentals," you learned how to use pipes and redirection symbols to redirect the input and output of commands. Now you can combine these symbols with filters and other SCO UNIX utilities to create complex and powerful command lines and shell scripts. In Chapters 10, "The Bourne Shell," and 11, "The C Shell," you will learn how to put filters and other commands to work in shell scripts.

CHAPTER

7

Editing and Text Processing

SCO UNIX offers some full-fledged word processors such as Lyrix, Word-Perfect, and Microsoft Word. Lyrix is a part of the SCO Office Portfolio Suite, and Microsoft Word and WordPerfect are separate programs that you can purchase from SCO. The more traditional UNIX document preparation tools are **vi**, the visual text editor, and **nroff**, a text formatter. These two programs work together to create professional-quality documents. In fact, this book was written and originally formatted with **vi** and **nroff**.

With the **vi** text editor you can enter, erase, and rearrange text, both within a file and between files. The **vi** utility is *not* a text formatter. It does not perform such functions as line justification, line spacing, and indentation. For this reason, **vi** is especially well suited to creating files such as shell scripts and programs. Word processors usually insert special formatting characters into text, or automatically wrap and fill lines, so they are not practical for creating programs, which must be in a specific, text-only format.

Midway through this chapter, at the end of the **vi** section, you'll find a quick reference to **vi**. Once you've become acquainted with the basic **vi** commands and are familiar with how the program works, you can quickly and easily look up particular commands in this handy table.

To format your text, you can use one of the text formatting utilities. The most common UNIX text formatter is the **nroff** program. The **nroff** text formatter for SCO UNIX is not currently available from SCO, although similar text formatters such as **eroff** are available from other vendors. A version of **nroff** is available for SCO XENIX, but it is not included with the basic operating system and must be purchased separately. The **nroff** command may or may not be available on your system. This chapter includes a basic introduction to text formatting with **nroff**.

The Three Modes of vi

The **vi** editor has three distinct modes of operation. While you are editing a file, **vi** is in either *insert mode, escape mode,* or *last line mode.*

Insert mode is the mode in which you do your typing. The **vi** editor functions much like a typewriter in insert mode. Each character you type appears on the screen as you type it. You can backspace over text you have already typed to correct mistakes, but you can't move around on a line or jump between lines in insert mode.

Pressing the ESC key while you are in insert mode puts you in escape mode. In escape mode, ordinary characters (letters, numbers, and punctuation) have special functions; for example, the letter *x* deletes the character the cursor is on. Escape mode commands are unusual in that they do not appear on the screen as you type them, and they are executed immediately without you pressing RETURN. Once you get into escape mode, you can use ordinary keys to move around in a file, mark text to be moved or deleted, change text, and more. Then you simply press one of several keys to get back into insert mode and resume typing your text.

 NOTE In the SCO manuals escape mode is referred to as *command mode.* We use the term *escape mode* here to remind you that you activate this mode by pressing the ESC key.

Typing a : (colon) in escape mode puts **vi** in last line mode. A colon, and whatever command you type next, now appears on the special last line of the screen, called the *status line.* You can use last line commands to replace text, make global substitutions, write files or parts of files to the disk, read in other files, and execute shell commands without leaving **vi**.

Getting In and Out of vi

You begin using **vi** to edit a file by typing the **vi** command on the command line, followed by the name of the file that you want to edit. Once you have entered **vi**, you must use special commands to begin typing text, move around a file, and exit **vi**. This section acquaints you with the basic commands you will need to enter, use, and exit from the **vi** editor. Later sections discuss some of the more advanced **vi** commands.

The best way to learn the many **vi** commands is to create a practice file and try the commands as you read about them. The more you use **vi**, the easier it will be.

Starting vi

You can use **vi** to edit any ordinary text file that you own, whether or not it was originally created with **vi**. Make sure you are in a directory in which you have write permission, or you will not be able to create files in that directory. (See Chapter 4, "Files and Directories," for more information

about file and directory access permissions.) Type the **vi** command followed
by the name of a new or existing file. For example, to edit a file called
to.laura, you would use the command

```
$ vi to.laura
```

 REMEMBER   If you use **vi** to create a new file, the file name cannot be
more than 14 characters long, and must not contain any characters that have
a special meaning to the shell.

When you enter a file with **vi**, the screen will clear and the first part of
the file will be displayed, as shown in Figure 7-1.

 NOTE   Ordinarily, **vi** displays a full screen 23 lines long and 80 characters
wide. The screens that appear as figures in this chapter are slightly smaller
than this.

Figure 7-1.

```
Laura,

I just thought I'd fill you in on some of the changes that
have been going on around here in the past few months.
I'll tell you the most
surprising news first: Marina left the company last month,
quite suddenly. She said she "needed to find herself," and
the rumor is that she's gone up to that town in Oregon.

Sven's wife is about to have a baby, and he's pushing for
a few months paternity leave, but you can guess how well
that's going over with the board.


~
~
~
"to.laura" 13 lines, 472 characters
```

A File Displayed by **vi***.*

The name of the file appears enclosed in quotes on the status line at the bottom of the screen, followed by the number of lines and characters in the file. If the file is new, the file name is followed by the message "[New file]." Notice that there is a ~ (tilde) at the beginning of some lines in Figure 7-1. This signifies that nothing has been typed on these lines yet. A line that begins with a tilde is *not* a blank line, but a *null* line. Actual blank lines in a file have no marker at the beginning.

Getting into Insert Mode—Typing Ordinary Text

When you enter a file with **vi**, you are in escape mode. Before you can begin typing text, you must type a command that puts you in insert mode. After you type one of these commands, you can proceed as you would on a typewriter, pressing RETURN at the end of each line. The same cursor that appears in the shell marks your place in **vi**. The line the cursor is on at any given time is called the *current line*. To correct mistakes on the current line, you can back up with whichever backspace key works for you (this will be the same backspace key that you use in the shell).

To add text to a file, you must type one of the following commands that put you in insert mode. Where the new text appears with respect to the cursor depends on which command you use.

- The **a** (for append) command appends text *after* the cursor.

- The **A** (also for append) command appends text at the *end* of the current line, no matter where on the line the cursor is when you type the command.

- The **i** (insert) command inserts text *before* the cursor.

- The **I** (insert) command inserts text at the *beginning* of the current line, no matter where on the line the cursor is when you type the command.

- The **o** (open) command opens a new line *below* the current line and places the cursor at the beginning of that line.

- The **O** (open) command opens a new line *above* the current line and places the cursor at the beginning of that line.

Try using one of these commands to type a few lines of text, making sure to press RETURN at the end of each line.

If there is already text in the file, you will need to position the cursor where you want to begin typing before you enter any of these commands. To move the cursor, use the arrow keys (described in the next section) or any of the commands discussed in the section "Moving Around in a File."

 NOTE   Like the shell, **vi** is sensitive to the case of commands. Therefore, the command **a** is different from **A**, **i** is different from **I**, and so on.

Getting out of Insert Mode—Executing Commands

While you are typing, you can use the backspace key set for your terminal (usually BACKSPACE or CTRL-h) to back up and correct mistakes on the current line. However, the backspace key works only on the current line; if you want to change a previous line, you have to go into escape mode, which allows you to move around in a file. To switch from insert mode back to escape mode, simply press the ESC key. Now you can return to the place where you made a mistake and correct it.

There are numerous keys you can use to move the cursor through a file; we'll mention just a few of them here. On many keyboards the arrow keys, labeled →, ←, ↑, and ↓ move the cursor right, left, up, and down, respectively. On *any* keyboard, the **vi** escape mode commands **h**, **j**, **k**, and **l**, control cursor movement as follows:

- The **l** key spaces forward, just as the SPACEBAR or RIGHT ARROW does.

- The **h** spaces backward on a line, just as BACKSPACE or LEFT ARROW does.

- The **j** moves the cursor down one line, just as the DOWN ARROW does.

- The **k** moves the cursor up one line, just as the UP ARROW does.

See the section, "Moving Around in a File," for more examples of cursor movement commands.

After you've typed a few lines in insert mode, try changing to escape mode and using these cursor movement keys to maneuver around. Then use one of the insert mode commands explained in the preceding section to add some text to one of the lines you've already typed. For example, to insert some text before the word *She* in the file shown in Figure 7-1, move the cursor to the letter *S* and type the command **i**, which puts you back in insert mode. Nothing will look different, but whatever you type next will appear on the screen instead of being executed as an escape mode command.

 REMEMBER   The **vi** editor does not automatically wrap text, so if you add something to a line that already fills up the screen, the line will extend beyond the edge of the screen. Extremely long lines can cause **vi** to malfunction, and they are also inconvenient for you. It is a good idea to break long lines by inserting a RETURN. Move to an appropriate spot on the line (such as the beginning of a word) while in escape mode; then type **a** or **i** and press RETURN.

Saving Your File and Exiting from vi

During an editing session with **vi**, any changes that you make do not affect the file itself; instead, they are stored in a *buffer,* which is a temporary copy of the file. When you are ready to make the changes from a particular editing session permanent, you must write, or save, the file to your hard disk. When you save a file to the disk, the buffer overwrites the original file. You should write the file to the disk often to avoid losing the changes you've made to a file. To write a file to the disk, activate escape mode, type the last line command

```
:w
```

When you exit **vi**, you must decide whether you want to save the changes you've made. If you have not made any changes to the file, you can exit with the last line **:q** command. To enter this command, first press ESC to enter escape mode, then type

:q

and press RETURN. If you have made changes since last writing the file to disk, **vi** will display the error message "No write since last change (:quit! overrides)." If you don't want to save your changes (that is, if you want to preserve the old version of the file), use the last line **:q!** command.

If you do want to save the changes you've made to the file, you must first write the file to the disk with the **:w** command, and then exit **vi** with the **:q** command. Another choice is to type the last line command **:wq**, which first writes the file to the disk and then quits **vi**. The escape mode command **ZZ** has the same effect as **:wq**.

Moving Around in a File

You have now learned to use the simple cursor movement commands **h**, **j**, **k**, and **l**; however, these commands are of limited use when you want to move rapidly. In this section you will learn some additional cursor movement commands that allow you to move with precision between characters, words, sentences, lines, and screens. Just a few examples of each type of cursor movement are given here—for a complete list see "A Quick Reference to **vi** Commands," later in this chapter.

Every cursor movement command can be preceded by a number to indicate the number of times the cursor movement should be repeated. For example, the command **3j** moves the cursor down three lines, and the command **12h** moves the cursor back twelve spaces.

Besides moving around in a file with these commands, you can use them as addresses for commands that make changes to the file. For example, if you want to change one word, you can follow the change command with a command that moves the cursor one word. Examples of editing commands followed by cursor movement addresses appear in the upcoming section, "Making Changes to a File."

All the cursor movement commands described in this section are escape mode commands. Make sure you are in escape mode before you try to move around in a file. Press ESC to get into escape mode; if you are already in escape mode, the error bell will ring.

Moving to a Particular Character

Besides spacing backward and forward on a line, you can use commands to reach specific characters. The **f** (for find) command moves the cursor to the next occurrence on the current line of the character you type after the command. For example, to move to the next *B* on the current line, use the command **fB**. If there is no *B* on the current line, the error bell will ring.

The **F** command works the same as **f**, except it moves the cursor *backward* on the line to the *previous* occurrence of the next character typed.

The **t** (for to) command moves the cursor to the character immediately *before* the next occurrence of the next character typed after the command. For example, the command **tC** moves the cursor to the character before the next occurrence of an uppercase *C*. This command is especially useful when you use it as an address for another command. (See the section "Making Changes to a File," for examples of this.)

Typing **0** (zero) moves the cursor to the beginning of the current line, even if the first character on the line is a space or a tab. The **^** (caret) command moves the cursor to the first *nonwhitespace* character (any character that is not a space or a tab) on the line. This command is useful when a line is indented. The **$** (dollar sign) command moves the cursor to the last character on the current line, even if the last character is a space or a tab.

Moving One Word at a Time

Moving One Word at a Time

To move to the beginning of the next word, type **w** (for word). A word is a sequence of letters or numbers bounded either by whitespace characters (spaces, tabs, or newlines) or by punctuation marks. The sequence "half-life" is actually three words as far as the **w** command is concerned, *half, -,* and *life*. A sequence of punctuation marks also counts as a word.

To move swiftly over words that contain punctuation, use the **W** command instead of **w**. This command moves the cursor to the beginning of the next word just as **w** does, except **W** counts any sequence of characters (including punctuation marks) that is bounded by whitespace characters as a word.

To move backward on a line by words, use the **b** (for back) command. This command moves the cursor to the beginning of the preceding word, where a word is defined as it is by the **w** command. The **B** command works just like **b**, except it counts words as the **W** command does.

Moving a Sentence at a Time

The **(** (left parenthesis) moves the cursor to the beginning of the current sentence, or to the beginning of the previous sentence if the cursor is already at the beginning of a sentence. The **)** (right parenthesis) moves the cursor to the beginning of the next sentence. Both of these commands find the beginning of a sentence by searching for a period, an exclamation point, or a question mark followed by either two spaces or a newline.

Moving to a Different Line

You already know that **k** and **j** move the cursor up one line and down one line, respectively. You can precede these commands with numbers to move more than one line at a time. Because **vi** keeps track of the number of each line in a file, you can also move the cursor to a specific line in the file by using the **G** command. If you type **G** without a preceding number, the cursor the cursor to line 78, and the command **1G** moves the cursor to the beginning of the file. If you specify a number beyond the last line in the file, the error bell rings and the cursor does not move at all.

Making Changes to a File

You have learned how to use the escape mode commands **a**, **i**, and **o**, as well as their uppercase counterparts, to insert and append text. In this section you will learn commands that let you change, copy, move, and delete text that you have already typed. Some of these editing commands are escape mode commands, while others are last line commands. In some situations, you can use either an escape mode command or a last line command. Most escape mode editing commands operate on the current line by default, but some take addresses so you can specify a block of text on which to operate. Usually these addresses are cursor movements such as those discussed in the preceding section, and the command operates from the current line, or the current cursor position on the line, to the position specified by the cursor movement key that follows the command. Editing commands that take addresses are indicated in the text and listed in the section "A Quick Reference to **vi** Commands." Like cursor movement commands, most editing commands can be preceded by a number that determines how many times the command will be repeated.

Last line editing commands are generally used less often than escape mode commands. Escape mode commands are more efficient for changing just a few words or lines of text, while last line commands are better for manipulating large blocks of text. In the following sections, both escape mode commands and last line commands are presented for each task; you can choose the method you prefer.

The format for last line editing commands is

[address1[,address2]] command

The addresses can be either regular expressions enclosed in slashes, line numbers, or marked lines (see the next section, "Marking Text"). One

The addresses can be either regular expressions enclosed in slashes, line numbers, or marked lines (see the next section, "Marking Text"). One address specifies one line, while two addresses separated by commas specify a range of lines. For example, the address **/Grace/** specifies the next line that contains the word *Grace*, and the addresses **1,10** specify lines 1 through 10. When no address is specified, last line editing commands operate on the current line—the line the cursor was on before you typed the colon.

Marking Text

To move, copy, or delete a line or a block of text, first mark the text with the escape mode command **m** (for mark). You designate a block of text not by highlighting the text, as you do with some word processors, but by marking the beginning and end of the block. To mark a block of text, move the cursor to the first line of the block and type **m**x, where x is any lowercase letter. Then move to the end of the block and do the same thing, this time choosing a different letter.

 NOTE   If the text is only one line long, you need only mark that line. You may also want to mark a line to serve as a reference point when you are moving around in a file.

Once you've marked a line, you can move to that line from anywhere in the file by typing a **'** (single quote) followed by the letter you choose to mark the line. For example, if you mark a line with the letter *a* by typing the command **ma**, you can then move to that line from anywhere in the file by typing the command **'a** in escape mode. You can also use this address with any editing command that takes an address. See the following sections for examples of marked text used as addresses to editing commands. After you've marked the beginning and end of a block of text, the block can be identified with the addresses **'**x,**'** y, where x is the letter you assigned to the first line in the block and y is the letter you assigned to the last line in the block. You can use these addresses with last line editing commands such as **:d**, which deletes the lines you specify. For example, to delete a block of text that begins with the line marked *a* and ends with the line marked *b,* you would use the last line command **:' a,' b d**. See the following section for more information about the **:d** command.

Deleting Text

Both escape mode and last line editing commands will delete text from your file. To delete one or a few characters at a time, use the escape mode command **x**. Without a preceding number, **x** deletes the character the cursor is on. Preceded by a number, **x** deletes that number of characters, starting with the one the cursor is on.

To delete more than one character at a time, you can use either the escape mode commands **d** and **D** or the last line command **:d**. Use the escape mode commands to delete a partial line or just a few lines. Use **:d** when you want to delete a large block of text.

The escape mode **D** command operates only on the current line, deleting text from the current cursor position to the end of the line. The **d** command must take a following address. To delete the current line, type **dd**. Like most editing commands, **d** can be preceded with a number. The command **2dd** deletes two lines, the current line and the line below it.

If you follow the **d** command with a cursor movement command, you tell **vi** to delete everything from the current cursor position to the position specified by the cursor movement command. The following examples illustrate how a cursor movement address works with the **d** command.

- The command **dw** deletes everything up to the beginning of the next word; that is, it deletes the word the cursor is on.

- The command **dt.** deletes everything from the cursor to the next period on the current line. This is a good way to delete words from the end of a sentence without deleting the period. You can also substitute any character you like for the period.

- The command **d' a** deletes everything from the current line to the line marked *a* (see the previous section for instructions on marking text). If the current line comes after line *a* in the file, all text from line *a* to the current line will be deleted.

- The command **d(** deletes everything from the cursor to the beginning of the next sentence. After moving the cursor to the beginning of a sentence, you can use this command to quickly delete that sentence.

- The command **dG** deletes everything from the cursor to the end of the file. For example, **d89G** deletes everything from the current line to line 89. If the current line number is greater than 89, this command will delete backward to the specified line. Similarly, the command **d1G** deletes backward from the current line to the first line of the file.

 NOTE When the address after the **d** command is an intraline command (such as **f** or **t**), the deletion starts from the position of the cursor on the current line and leaves the text that precedes the cursor intact. If the address specifies a whole line (such as **G**), the deletion affects the entire current line.

To delete more than a few lines, use the last line **:d** command. The cursor need not be at the beginning or end of the block to be deleted because the **:d** command allows you to specify two addresses, which delimit the block. For example, you could delete lines 50 through 75 with the last line command

```
:50,75 d
```

The following command deletes a block of text whose first line is marked *a* and whose last line is marked *b*.

```
:'a,'b d
```

See the previous section, "Marking Text," for more information about marked blocks of text.

With no addresses, the **:d** command deletes the current line. With one address, **:d** deletes the line that has that address. For example, the following command deletes the next line containing the word *Question*.

```
:/Question/ d
```

to recover something that was not the last thing you deleted, you can usually do so. See the section "Retrieving Text" later in this chapter for more information.

Copying Text

There are two ways to copy text to another location. With the escape mode **y** command, you first make a copy of the original text in a special delete buffer, and then copy that text to a new location. To copy, or *yank,* text to a delete buffer, use the escape mode **y** (for yank) command, which takes a following address. Once you have yanked the text, move the cursor to the location to which you want to copy it, and type the escape mode **p** or **P** command. The **p** command places the yanked text *below* the cursor, while **P** places it *above* the cursor.

Just as the command **dd** deletes one line, the command **yy** copies one line. The **y** command can also take any cursor movement command as an address and can be preceded by a number. Some examples of **y** commands follow.

- The command **5yy** copies, or yanks, five lines to a delete buffer, beginning with the current line.

- The command **yw** copies the word the cursor is on.

- The command **y(** copies everything from the cursor to the beginning of the next sentence. If the cursor is at the beginning of a sentence, this command copies the entire sentence.

- The command **y1G** copies everything from the beginning of the file to the current line. Since any line in the file is certain to be below the first line, this command copies backward from the cursor to line 1.

The last line command **:co** allows you to copy text in one step instead of two, but you must know the addresses both of the lines to be copied and of the destination of the copy. You specify the addresses of the lines to be copied before the command, and the address of the destination after the of the destination of the copy. You specify the addresses of the lines to be copied before the command, and the address of the destination after the command. For example, to place a copy of lines 1 through 5 just below line 20, you would use the command

```
:1,5 co 20
```

To copy a block of text delimited by the line marked *a* and the line marked *b* to just below the current line, you would use the command

```
:'a,'b co .
```

(See the section "Marking Text" for information about marking lines.) You can also copy just one line by specifying a single address before the command. Most people use the escape mode **y** and **p** commands to copy a few lines or less, and the last line mode **:co** command to copy large blocks of text.

Moving Text

To move text with escape mode commands, you must first delete the text with the **d** command, and then place it where you want it with the **p** command, explained in the previous section. For example, if you want to move a line down five lines, you delete the line with the **dd** command, move the cursor down five lines, and then use the **p** command to insert the just-deleted line below the cursor. You can do the same thing with a word. First, you delete the word with the **dw** command; then you move to the place where you want the word to appear and use the **p** command to insert it after the cursor.

With the last line command **:m**, you can move a piece of text in one step. Specify the addresses of the lines to be moved before the command, and the destination of the text after the command. For example, to move lines 1 through 5 to just below line 15, you would use the command

```
:1,5 m 15
```

To move a block of text delimited by line *b* and line *e* to just below line *h*, you would use the command

```
:'b,'e m 'h
```

(See the section "Marking Text" for information about marking lines.)

Changing Text

One way you can change existing text into new text is by simply deleting the old text and then inserting the new, but several escape mode commands allow you to change text in one step. You can change anything from one character to many lines at a time.

To replace just one character, use the **r** (for replace) command. When you type **r** in escape mode, the character the cursor is on is replaced by the character you type next. For example, if you type **rF**, the character the cursor is on will be replaced with an *F*. Then you will be returned to escape mode so you can move to a different spot in the file.

To replace one character with an unlimited number of new characters, use the **s** (for substitute) command. Typing **s** in escape mode temporarily replaces the character the cursor is on with a **$** (dollar sign) and puts you in insert mode. The **$** is just a place marker, and it disappears as soon as you start typing. Whatever you type next replaces the original character. Since only one character is replaced, whatever came after that character on the line is pushed along head of the replacement text. When you are finished typing the new text, press ESC to get back into escape mode. If you precede **s** with a number, you replace that number of characters with whatever text you type next.

To change more than one character at a time, you can use the **c** command, which takes a following address. As soon as you type the **c** command and an address, you are placed in insert mode, and whatever you type next replaces the original text. When you are done typing the new text, press ESC to return to escape mode. Following the same pattern as the **d** command, **cc** changes the current line to the text you type next. Like **d**, **c** can be followed by any cursor movement key as an address. Here are a few examples:

- The command **3cc** changes the current line plus two more lines.

- The command **cw** changes the word the cursor is on.

- The command **cf**, changes everything from the cursor through the next comma on the line.

- The command **c′ a** changes everything from the cursor to the line you marked with an *a*. If no line has been marked with this letter, the error bell rings and nothing changes. If the current line is below the line marked *a* in the file, the current line is the last line changed instead of the first.

When the text to be changed is entirely on the current line, the last character to be changed is replaced with a **$** place marker that disappears as soon as you press ESC. If the text to be changed is more than one line long, that text disappears from the screen, and the cursor is positioned at the beginning of a new blank line.

The (uppercase) **C** command replaces all characters from the cursor to the end of the current line with the text that you type next.

Retrieving Text

The **vi** program retains copies of text you delete in special buffers called *delete buffers*. These buffers allow you to retrieve the last 9 pieces of text that you deleted, copied, or changed. Each time you delete, copy, or change a line or more of text, that text is placed on the top of a stack of delete buffers numbered 1 through 9. When a new piece of text is saved in buffer 1, what was in buffer 1 moves to buffer 2, what was in buffer 2 moves to buffer 3, and so on.

By referring to the delete buffer in which the text you want is saved, you can retrieve the text in that buffer. To refer to a numbered buffer, precede the number of the buffer with " (double quotes). For example, use **"4** to refer to buffer number 4. To return the text from a delete buffer to the file, first make sure you are in escape mode, and then move to the place where you want the text to go. Type the name of the buffer (the buffer number preceded by double quotes) followed by the **p** command. For example, you would use the command **"3p** to retrieve the text from buffer number 3.

Text that is less than one line long is not placed in the numbered buffers; however, the most recently deleted text of any length (even one character) is also placed in a special buffer, which can be accessed without a number. To retrieve the text you deleted most recently move to the place where you want to insert it, and type the escape mode **p** command with no preceding number or quotes.

 NOTE   If you delete something accidentally and typing **u** does not restore it, try restoring text from the numbered buffers. Without realizing it, you may have deleted something else, in which case that text would have replaced the text that you want in the first buffer.

Repeating Commands

You can repeat any escape mode editing command by typing the escape mode command **.** (period) as the next command. If the cursor position has changed since the last editing command was executed, **.** will cause the command to be executed relative to the new cursor position. Here are some examples of what the **.** command does in different situations:

- If you delete a word with the **dw** command, the cursor jumps to the beginning of the next word. If you then type a period, the new word the cursor is on is deleted.

- If you insert some text with the **I** command, get back into escape mode, and then move the cursor to another line, typing **.** inserts the same text you just inserted at the beginning of the new current line.

- If you change two lines of text with the command **2cc**, and then get back into escape mode and move to another line, typing **.** replaces two more lines with the same text that you typed in place of the previous two lines.

 REMEMBER   The **.** command repeats only escape mode editing commands, not cursor movement commands or last line commands.

The only case in which **.** does not repeat the last command executed is when the last command replaced one of the numbered buffers. If you replace one of the numbered buffers with the **p** or **P** command, typing **.** will replace each subsequent buffer until the last buffer on the stack is replaced.

Undoing Changes

You can undo most changes with the escape mode command **u** or the last line command **:u** (both for undo). For **u** or **:u** to work, they must be typed immediately after the change you want to undo; that is, they undo only the *last* command typed. Both the escape mode and last line commands undo changes made with either last line or escape mode commands. For example, if you delete three lines with the escape mode command **3dd**, you can restore them with the last line command **:u** *or* with the escape mode **u**.

 NOTE   You can undo the latest change even if you have moved elsewhere in the file since executing that command. For example, suppose you deleted a word, moved down two lines, and then decided you didn't want to delete the word after all. Typing **u** or **:u** would move the cursor back to the place where the word was deleted and restore it.

The escape mode command **U** (also for undo) undoes all of the changes made to the current line, no matter how many times you have changed it since moving to it; that is, **U** restores the line to its unedited state. You can only use the **U** command while the cursor is still on the line that you want to restore. If you have moved to another line, the **U** command will have no effect.

Searching

You can search for a word or phrase with the last line commands **/** (slash) and **?** (question mark). These commands are unique in that you do not have to type them after a colon; that is, the command **:/** is the same as **/** alone. By search began. If you prefer to have a search stop when it reaches the beginning or end of the file, you can set the environment option **nowrapscan**. See the upcoming section "Environment Options" for instructions on setting this variable.

Searching Forward

The / command scans forward in a file. For example, to search forward for the next occurrence of the words *the merger*, you would simply type

```
/the merger
```

Then, when you pressed RETURN, **vi** would search for that pattern in the file and move the cursor to it. Although the pattern used in this example is a simple regular expression that does not include any special symbols, you can also use very complex regular expressions with the search command. (For a discussion of regular expressions, see Chapter 5, "Command Line Fundamentals.")

Searching Backward

The **?** command searches backward in a file. To search backward for the previous occurrence of *the merger*, you would type

```
?the merger
```

and press RETURN.

Repeating a Search

Once you've searched for a particular pattern, that pattern is stored in memory, so the next time you want to search for the same pattern, all you have to do is type the escape mode command **n** (for next), and **vi** will search for the next occurrence of the pattern. When you type **n**, a / appears at the have to do is type the escape mode command **n** (for next), and **vi** will search for the next occurrence of the pattern. When you type **n**, a **/** appears at the bottom of the screen to show you that a search is underway. If you initiate a search with **?**, typing **n** continues the search backward, and a **?** prints at the bottom of the screen to show that a backward search is being carried out. To reverse the direction of either a forward or a backward search, type **N** instead of **n**. If your last search was initiated with **/**, typing **N** will search *backward* for the same pattern, and a **?** will appear at the bottom of the screen to indicate the direction of the search.

Substitution

Instead of moving to a word or line that you want to change and editing it, you can use the last line command **:s** to do substitutions. This command is most useful for doing *global substitutions*—replacing every occurrence of a word or group of words in a file. The syntax of this command is

:[*addresses*] s/*pattern1*/*pattern2*/

where *pattern1* is the regular expression you want to replace, and pattern2 is the regular expression you want to replace it with. The *addresses* specify the line or lines on which the substitution is to be made. If no addresses are specified, the substitution is made on the current line.

The following example changes the word *merchandise* to *product* on lines 1 through 10.

```
:1,10 s/merchandise/product/
```

Ordinarily, the **:s** command replaces only the first occurrence of a word on a given line. To replace *all* occurrences of a word on the addressed lines, follow the final slash with a **g**. For example, to replace every occurrence of the word *merchandise* on lines 1 through 10 with the word *product*, you would use the command

```
:1,10 s/merchandise/product/g
```

Suppose you want to replace a word or phrase not just on certain lines, but everywhere that it occurs in a file. This is a global substitution. The easiest way to do a global substitution is to put **%** (percent sign) before the **s** command in place of the addresses. The **%** represents all lines of the current file. To perform the substitution shown in the previous examples on every line in the file using the **%**, you would use the command

`:%s/merchandise/product/g`

Again, the **g** after the final slash is necessary only if you want to replace every occurrence of *merchandise* on every line. If you want to replace only the first occurrence on each line, leave the **g** off.

 NOTE   There must not be a space between the **%** and the **s** command.

If you are not sure that you want to change *every* occurrence of a pattern with a global substitution, you can have the substitute command ask you to confirm each replacement. To do this, follow the **s** command with the **c** (for confirm) flag, as in this example:

`:%s/merchandise/product/gc`

Now **vi** will point to each place where the substitution would occur and wait for you to type **y** to confirm. If you type **n** or simply press RETURN, that particular occurrence of the pattern will not be replaced. Global substitutions are among the most useful last line commands, especially when they are combined with the power of regular expressions. If you plan to use **vi** frequently, you should definitely become familiar with these helpful features.

Writing Files and Partial Files to the Disk

You have already learned how to write a file to the disk with the **:w** command. You can also write the buffer to a different file so both the original and the changed versions of a file are saved. It is also possible to write only part of a file to the disk, either as a replacement for the original file or as a different file.

To save both the original file and the buffer copy, you need only write the buffer to a file that has a different name from the original. To do this, type the last line **:w** command followed by the new name from you want to give the changed version of the file. For example, if the original file is called **raise**, and you want the new file to be called **raise.new**, type

```
:w raise.new
```

All the changes you have made to the buffer will appear in **raise.new**. Then, if you quit **vi** without writing the buffer to the original file with the **:q!** command, the original file will be preserved as it was before you made any changes.

To save certain lines of the current file to a different file, specify those lines as addresses before the **:w** command. For example, to write lines 1 through 12 to a file called **jargon**, type

```
:1,12 w jargon
```

 NOTE   When you write lines from a file to the disk, these lines are not removed from the buffer. To remove them from the buffer, you must delete them.

If you do not follow the the **:w** command with a new file name, the specified lines will overwrite the current file. The **vi** editor will not let this happen unless you follow the **w** with an **!** (exclamation point). The following example would write only lines 1 through 100 to the disk, overwriting the entire original file.

```
:1,100 w!
```

The **!** is necessary to tell **vi** that you really want to replace the original file. Whenever you want to write to a file that already exists, you need to use **:w!** instead of just **:w**. If you omit the **!**, you will get an error message.

You can also append the current file or certain lines of the current file to another file by using the redirection symbol **>>**. For example, to append the current file to a file called **insurance**, you would type

```
:w >> insurance
```

To append lines 150 through 200 of the current file to the file **insurance**, you would use the command

```
:150,200 w >> insurance
```

Reading in Other Files

You can integrate another file into the file you are editing with the last line **:r** command. This is called *reading* one file into another. This command always inserts the new file just below the current line. It doesn't matter where the cursor is on the current line; the line will not be broken. To read a file called **premium** into the current file below the current line, you would type

```
:r premium
```

After a file has been read in, its length in lines and characters is displayed on the last line. Like most last line commands, the **:r** command can be undone with the escape mode command **u**. If you read in a file and then change your mind, simply type **u**; remember, though, this only works if you have not typed another escape mode or last line command (except cursor movements) since you read in the file.

Modifying Your Environment

There are several parameters of **vi** that you can adjust to make the editor operate somewhat differently. By setting *environment options*, you can determine how many lines of text appear on the screen, use abbreviations to represent longer words or phrases, assign frequently used commands to a single key, and much more.

Environment Options

The numerous **vi** environment options control many aspects of the program's behavior, from the size of the window **vi** uses to whether or not lines wrap when they reach the right margin. You can set environment options in your **.exrc** file (see "The .exrc File" later in this section) or by using the last line command **:set**.

Each option is assigned an initial value, and you only need to set a value for an option if you want to change it; otherwise, you can leave the options as they are. To see a list of all the option values, type the last line command

```
:set all
```

A list showing the current value of each option will appear on the screen.

Many of the environment options are toggles that you switch on and off. For example, the **wrapscan** option (mentioned earlier in this chapter) has the values **wrapscan** (when the option is turned on) and **nowrapscan** (when the option is turned off). This pattern applies to all options that have binary values—the on value is the name of the option, and the off value is *no* plus the name of the option. Other options have numerical values that you can change to any appropriate number. When an option takes a numerical value, you can set its value with a command that has the syntax

> **:set** *option=x*

where *option* is the name of the option whose value you want to set, and *x* is the numerical value you want the option to have.

 NOTE   The option, equal sign, and number must not be separated by spaces.

When you set an option, its new value is valid only for the current editing session. If you exit **vi** and return to a file later, the options will have returned to their old values. To maintain your option settings between **vi** sessions, you must set them in your **.exrc** file. See the upcoming section "Your .exrc File" for more information on this topic.

Some of the more useful **vi** environment options are discussed in the following sections. For descriptions of all of the options, see the *SCO UNIX User's Reference* or the on-line **man** pages.

wrapmargin   Ordinarily **vi** is like the shell in that a line does not automatically break when it reaches the right edge of the screen; you must press RETURN when you want a line broken. You can make lines wrap automatically by setting the **wrapmargin** option. Initially, the value of this option is set to 0, so that text does not wrap at all. If you set the value to a different number, **wrapmargin** will insert a newline as soon as the text you type is one character away from the right edge of the screen. To set the margin at 5 characters, you would type

```
:set wrapmargin=5
```

The larger the number you type, the wider the margin and the shorter the lines.

 REMEMBER   Setting the **wrapmargin** variable does *not* mean that your text will be right justified. It only means you don't have to press RETURN at the end of each line.

number   When the **number** option is set, line numbers appear to the left of each line on the screen while you are editing a file. These numbers do not appear when you print the file or when you view it with any other utility. Initially this option is not set (that is, **nonumber** is set). To see the line numbers, type

```
:set number
```

You unset the **number** option by typing

```
:set nonumber
```

Some people use line numbers to keep track of where they are in a file. Whether or not you decide to display line numbers, remember that lines are automatically numbered. Even though the numbers may not appear on the screen, you can still use line-number addresses.

wrapscan   This option determines whether a file is treated as a continuous loop or recognized as having a beginning and an end for the purpose of searches. This option is initially on. To turn it off, type

```
:set nowrapscan
```

report   The value of this option determines how many lines you can delete, copy, change, or replace before the operation is reported on the last line of the screen. Initially, the value of this option is set to 5. Try yanking 10 lines, and the message "10 lines yanked" should appear at the bottom of the screen.

Abbreviations

Typing the same word over and over again can be tedious. With the last line command **ab** (abbreviate), you can designate abbreviations for long words or phrases. Then, when you type the abbreviation, it will automatically expand to the designated word or phrase. For the abbreviation to expand, it must be a word by itself; that is, it must be bounded on both ends by whitespace or punctuation.

To designate an abbreviation for a word or phrase, type

:ab *abbreviation word*

where *abbreviation* is any abbreviation you choose, and *word* is the word or phrase it should expand to. For example, to designate the abbreviation *de* for the phrase "deductible expense," you would type

```
:ab de deductible expense
```

 NOTE   The abbreviation you choose need not be a real abbreviation for the word or phrase it expands to, or even have any letters in common with the word. For example, you could have the number 6 expand to the phrase "deductible expense" if you wanted to. It is important, however, to choose abbreviations that are not real words you might want to use in another context. For example, *a* is not a good abbreviation, because every time you typed the word *a*, it would expand, whether you wanted it to or not.

Abbreviations can be designated either on the last line for a particular editing session or in your **.exrc** file. If you decide you no longer want an abbreviation to apply, you can use the **unab** command. For example, to unabbreviate the sequence *de,* you would type

```
:unab de
```

As you type this command, **de** will still expand, but for the last time. The next time you type **de**, it will not expand. If an abbreviation is designated in your **.exrc** file, all you have to do to cancel it is delete that line from the **.exrc** file.

Mapping

As you use **vi** more and more, you will probably find that you type certain sequences of escape mode or last line commands over and over again. A convenient last line command called **:map** allows you to designate one key to stand for a whole sequence of commands. Just as a designated abbreviation can expand to a longer piece of text, a short command of your choice can be mapped to a sequence of commands, so that when you are in escape or last line mode, you can type the short command to execute all the commands in the long sequence. Again, this can be done either on the last line in a particular editing session or in your **.exrc** file.

Any ordinary key (letter, number, or punctuation) can be mapped to a sequence of commands. Even if that key already functions as an escape mode command, your mapping will override its original function. For this reason, it is best to choose either keys that have no escape mode function or keys that you will not need. For example, **v** does not function as an escape mode command, so it would be a good key to map. Uppercase **S** is an escape mode command, but it is identical in function to **cc**, so you could map it to some other sequence of functions.

The **:map** command causes mapping to work only in escape mode, while the **:map!** (with an exclamation point) command causes it to work in insert mode. Here are some sample **:map** commands:

- The command **:map g $** makes **g** function like the cursor movement command **$**, which moves the cursor to the end of the current line. This maps a key to only one command, but since **g** is handier to type than **$**, it does make this command more convenient to use.

- The command **:map v d)o** maps v to two commands. The first, **d)**, deletes everything from the current cursor postion to the beginning of the next sentence. The second, **o**, opens a new line below the cursor. Now just typing **v** while in escape mode will execute both of these commands.

- The command **:map S ct.** maps S to the **ct.** command, which changes everything from the current cursor position to the next period on the line.

- The command **:map S ISTOP** maps the character *S* to the command **I**, which inserts text at the beginning of the current line. Since **I** puts you in insert mode, the remaining characters in the mapping are simply typed as text. Thus the command **S** will now insert the word *STOP* at the beginning of the current line.

- The command **:map V xp** maps V to two commands. The first, **x**, deletes the character the cursor is on. The second, **p**, inserts the last deleted text—the character you just deleted—after the cursor, which has moved forward one character. As a result, the original two characters now appear in reverse order.

Remember, these are just sample mappings. You can use different characters to map these same sequences of commands, or you can use the same characters to map any other command sequences that you might find useful. As you become proficient with **vi** escape mode commands, you will certainly discover sequences of commands that you want to map.

When you no longer need a particular mapping, you can use the **:unmap** command to take away the special meaning of a mapped sequence. For example, to unmap the letter *S,* you would type

`:unmap S`

If the mapping is set in your **.exrc** file, all you have to do to unmap it is remove that line from the file. To unmap a sequence mapped with the **:map!** command, use the **:unmap!** command.

The .exrc File

An **.exrc** file is a file in your home directory in which you can place commands that you want to be executed each time you start **vi**. These commands can include **ab** (with which you designate abbreviations for frequently used words), **map** (with which you create macros for long command sequences), and **set** (with which you specify command and option settings). Although the last line commands **set**, **ab**, and **map** can be executed by placing them in your **.exrc** file, last line editing commands and shell escapes cannot be executed in this way.

There will probably not be an **.exrc** file in your account when you first log in, so if you want to have one you will have to create it. You can use **vi** to create an **.exrc** file in your home directory. If you want a certain option value, macro, or abbreviation to be set every time you use **vi**, it is most efficient to set it in the **.exrc** file. Commands in an **.exrc** file look just like last line commands, but without the preceding **:** (colon). Figure 7-2 shows the contents of a typical **.exrc** file as viewed with **vi**.

Executing Shell Commands from Within vi

While you are editing a file with **vi**, you still have access to all the UNIX shell commands. In addition, you can put the results of a shell command into the file you are editing. You can even use a shell filter to change all or part of the file you are editing, replacing the original lines with the output of the filter.

Figure 7-2.

```
set wrapmargin=10
set nowarn
ab lbg LeBlond Group
ab di directory
ab co command
map g $
map S ISTOP
map # ct.
~
~
~
~
~
~
~
".exrc" 8 lines, 110 characters
```

A Sample .exrc File.

Shell Escapes

You can execute shell commands while in the middle of editing a file by using shell escapes, special **vi** commands that give you access to a shell. With shell escapes you don't have to save your file, exit **vi**, and then return to **vi** and find your place again each time you want to execute a shell command. To execute a shell command from within **vi**, type

   :!*command*

where *command* is the name of the command you want to execute. For example, to execute the **date** command, type

`:!date`

The date as displayed by the **date** command will appear on the last line of the screen, and you will be instructed to press RETURN to continue. Unless the shell command you type mentions the file you are editing, no shell command that you execute with this type of shell escape will affect the buffer you are editing. That is, the results of the command will not appear in the buffer or change it in any way.

Unless you set the **nowarn** option, **vi** warns you each time you execute a shell escape if you've made changes since last writing the current file; it still executes the command, but it pauses first. This warning is intended to protect your work, but it can be annoying. If you use shell escapes often, you may want to turn off the warning message with the command

```
:set nowarn
```

You can also set this option in your **.exrc** file, as shown in Figure 7-2.

Placing the Results of a Shell Commmand in the File

When you execute a shell command with the last line **:!** command, the results of that command are displayed on the screen but do not become part of the file. A different type of shell escape places the results of the command in the file. In escape mode, type **!!** (no colon) followed by a shell command, and the results of that command will replace the current line. For example, to put the date and time on the current line, you would type

```
!!date
```

 NOTE   If you don't want to overwrite the current line, be sure the cursor is on a blank line when you execute the **!!** command. Since the output of the command is placed in the file, only commands that produce output can be used in this way.

Filtering All or Part of a File

You can also use the last line **:!** command to filter all or part of a file through a shell command. The command must be a filter—a command that takes the standard input and produces the standard output. See Chapter 6 for more information about filters. To run an entire file through a filter, precede the **!** with a **%**, which represents the current file. For example, to run a whole file through the **sort** program, you would type

`:%!sort`

 NOTE There should be no space between the **%** and the **!**.

To filter part of a file, specify the lines to be filtered as addresses before the **!**. For example, to run lines 1 through 10 through the **sort** program, you would type

`:1,10!sort`

Command Line Options

Suppose you are in the midst of editing a file and want to get out of **vi** for a moment to do something else. When you return to **vi**, you have to move the cursor back to the place where you were editing. You can do this with cursor movement commands or by searching with **/**; however, there are also convenient command line options that cause **vi** to start at a place other than the beginning of the file. The command **vi +***filename* causes **vi** to start with the window at the end of the file. If you specify a number after the **+**, **vi** will start with the cursor on the specified line, and with that line in the center of the window.

Finally, if you specify a search pattern after the **+**, **vi** will start with the cursor on the first line that contains that pattern. The format for specifying a search pattern is

vi +/*expression file*

where *expression* is the regular expression you want **vi** to start at, and *file* is the file you want to edit. For example, to start **vi** at the first line that contains the word *regret* in a file called **responses**, type

```
$ vi +/regret responses
```

The only way the shell can tell where the regular expression ends and the file name begins is that they are separated by a space. Therefore, if you include any spaces in the regular expression, you must precede each one with a \ (backslash) to tell the shell that these are not real spaces, but part of the regular expression. For example, if you wanted to start **vi** at the first line containing the phrase "unable to comply" in a file called **responses**, you would type

```
$ vi +/unable\ to\ comply forms
```

The last space, the one between *comply* and *forms,* is not preceded by a \ because this is the real space that separates the regular expression from the file name.

TIP   One way to take advantage of this command line option is to always insert the same word (for example, the word *STOP*) on a line just before you exit the editor. That way, even if you don't remember where you were editing last you can simply type **vi +/STOP** to find your place in the file. (Don't forget to delete the identifying word from the file.)

Notice that the / used in the **+/***expression* option looks just like the / used in searches and, in fact, it is the same character. When you use this command line option, a search is initiated as soon as you enter **vi**. If you then type the escape mode **n** command, the cursor moves to the next occurrence of the regular expression.

A Quick Reference to vi Commands

Table 7-1 is a quick reference that you can use once you have read at least the first few sections of this chapter, and are familiar with the basic escape mode and last line commands. The following points will help you use the table quickly and efficiently.

- The commands are grouped by function and listed alphabetically within each section.

- Unless otherwise stated, all escape mode cursor movement and editing commands can be preceded by a number specifying how many times the command should be repeated. Only when a preceding number does something other than repeat the command is the preceding number explained and indicated in the command's syntax.

- The variable *n* is used to indicate a number as part of a command. Where this variable is enclosed in parentheses, it represents an optional number argument. For example, (*n*)CTRL-d indicates that the CTRL-d command may or may not be preceded by a number.

- Unless otherwise stated, any escape mode cursor movement can be used as the address for any escape mode editing command that takes a following address.

Table 7-1.

Exiting **vi**	
:w	Writes the editing buffer to disk; if a following file name is specified, writes the buffer to a file with that name
:q	Exits **vi** without writing to disk
:wq	Writes the file to disk, and then quits
:x	Writes the buffer to disk only if changes have been made since the last **write**, and then quits
ZZ	Same as **:x**
Q	Puts you in **ex** command mode; use the **ex** command **vi** to return to visual mode

A Summary of **vi** *Commands*

Table 7-1.

Moving to a Different Character

f	Moves to next occurrence on the current line of the character you type next
F	Moves to the previous occurrence on the current line of the character you type next
h	Moves back one space
l	Moves forward one space
t	Moves to the space before the next occurrence of the character you type next
T	Same as **t,** but scans backward on the current line
$	Moves to the last character of the current line
^	Moves to the first nonwhitespace character on the current line

Moving to a Different Word

b	Moves back one word (bounded by punctuation or whitespace)
B	Moves back one word (bounded by whitespace characters)
e	Moves to the end of the current or next word
E	Moves to the end of the word (bounded by whitespace characters)
w	Moves to the beginning of the next word (bounded by punctuation or whitespace)
W	Moves to the beginning of the next word (bounded by whitespace)

Moving to a Different Line

j	Moves down one line
k	Moves up one line
(*n*)G	Moves to the last line of the file or to line number *n*
(*n*)L	Moves to the bottom of the screen or *n* lines from the bottom
M	Moves to the beginning of the middle line on the screen
%	Moves to),], or } matching the next occurrence of (, [, or {, respectively
'*x*	Moves to the line marked *x* with the **m** command
+	Moves up one line
–	Moves down one line

A Summary of **vi** *Commands (continued)*

Table 7-1.

Moving to a Different Sentence

(	Moves to the beginning of the current or previous sentence
)	Moves to the beginning of the next sentence

Repeating Commands

. (period)	Repeats the last escape mode editing command (deletion, insertion, and so on)
, (comma)	Repeats the last search with **f**, **F**, **t**, or **T**, but reverses direction
&	Repeats the last substitution (executed with the last line command **:s**) on the current line (the pattern must be matched)

Scrolling (These commands cannot be used as cursor movement addresses.)

CTRL-f	Pages forward one screenful
CTRL-b	Pages backward one screenful
(n)CTRL-d	Scrolls down half a screen or n lines
(n)CTRL-u	Scrolls up half a screen or n lines

Redrawing the Screen

CTRL-r or CTRL-l	Redraws the screen when it has been scrambled by a system message, a message from another user, or some other interruption
(n)z$size$	Redraws the screen with the current line or line n at the top of the screen; if a following *size* is specified, the screen is redrawn with that number of lines
(n)z$size$.	Redraws the screen with the current line or line n at the middle of the screen; if a following *size* is specified, the screen is redrawn with that number of lines
(n)z$size$–	Redraws the screen with the current line or line n at the bottom of the screen; if a following *size* is specified, the screen is redrawn with that number of lines

A Summary of vi Commands (continued)

Table 7-1.

Appending and Inserting New Text

a	Appends text *after* the cursor
A	Appends text at end of the current line
i	Inserts text before the cursor
I	Inserts text at beginning of the current line
o	Opens a new line below the current line
O	Opens a new line above the current line

Replacing Existing Text

cc	Changes one line to the next text typed
cx	Changes text from cursor position to address specified by x to the next text typed
C	Changes current line from cursor position through end to the next text typed
r	Replaces the character the cursor is on with the next character typed
R	Replaces existing characters one-for-one with the characters typed next
s	Substitutes the text typed next for the character the cursor is on
S	Changes the current line (identical to **cc**)
:*x,y* **s/***re1***/***re2***/(g)(c)**	Replaces the regular expression *re1* with regular expression *re2* on the lines specified by addresses x through y: *if* **g** is set, substitutes for every occurrence of *re1* on specified lines; if **c** is set, asks you to confirm each substitution
:%s/*re1***/***re2***/(g)(c)**	Same as above, but makes the substitution on every line in the file containing *re1*

Deleting Text

x	Deletes the character the cursor is on
X	Deletes the character before the cursor
dd	Deletes one line
dx	Deletes from the cursor to the address specified by x
D	Deletes from the cursor to the end of the current line
x,y **d**	Deletes lines with addresses x through y

A Summary of **vi** *Commands (continued)*

Table 7-1.

Copying Text

yy	Copies the current line
y*x*	Copies from the current cursor position to position *x*
Y	Copies the current line (identical to **yy**)
p	Places text copied with **y** or **Y** after the cursor
P	Places text copied with **y** or **Y** before the cursor
:*x,y* **co** z	Copies lines with addresses *x* through *y* to below the line with address *z*

Moving Text

:*x,y,* **m** z	Moves lines with addresses *x* through *y* to below the line with address *z*

Miscellaneous Editing Commands

J	Joins the current line and the next line
m*x*	Marks the current line (and the current cursor position) with the letter *x*
p	Replaces the last deleted, copied, or changed text after the cursor
"*n***p**	Places the text in delete buffer number *n* after the cursor
"*x***p**	Places the text in named delete buffer *x* after the cursor
P	Replaces the last deleted, copied, or changed text before the cursor
"*n***P**	Places the text in delete buffer number *n* before the cursor
"*x***P**	Places the text in named delete buffer *x* before the cursor
u	Undoes the last editing command
U	Undoes all editing changes to the current line
"*x***yy**	Copies the current line into named delete buffer *x*
~	Changes the case of the letter the cursor is on (upper- to lowercase and vice versa); cannot be preceded by a number
(*n*)>	Shifts *n* lines right by the value of the shiftwidth option
(*n*)<	Shifts *n* lines left by the value of the shiftwidth option

A Summary of vi Commands (continued)

Table 7-1.

Searching

/expression	Searches for the next occurrence of *expression* (any regular expression) in the file
?expression	Searches backward for the previous occurrence of *expression* (any regular expression) in the file
n	Repeats the last search with **/** or **?**
N	Repeats the last search with **/** or **?**, but reverses the direction of the search

Miscellaneous Escape Mode Commands

"*x*	Used to name delete buffers; puts the next deleted, changed, or copied text in named buffer *x*
CTRL-g	Displays the current line number and information about the length of the file at the bottom of the screen
m*x*	Marks the current line (and current cursor position) with the letter *x*

Miscellaneous Last Line Commands

=	Displays the current line number
ab *str1 str2*	Designates *str1* as an abbreviation that will expand to *str2* (any word or phrase) when typed in insert mode
unab *str1*	Unabbreviates (removes the special significance of) *str*, a string abbreviated with the **ab** command
map *str1 str2*	Maps *str1*, where *str1* is any sequence of characters, so *str1* will expand to *str2* when typed in escape mode
unmap *str*	Unmaps *str*, a string mapped with the **map** command
(*x,y*) **w** (*file*)	Writes lines with addresses *x* through *y* to a file called *file*
(*address*) **r** *file*	Reads the file *file* into the current file below the current line; if an *address* is specified, reads the file in below the specified line

*A Summary of **vi** Commands (continued)*

Text Formatting with the nroff Formatter

The **nroff** text formatter is part of the SCO XENIX document preparation system designed to help you produce high-quality formatted documents. Unfortunately, the **nroff** formatter is not currently available for SCO UNIX directly from SCO. However, similar text formatters, such as **eroff**, are available from other vendors. Macro packages, such as the **mm** and **ms** macros, add commands that simplify formatting to **nroff**. Macros let you concentrate on your text rather than focusing on complex formatting commands. The **nroff** formatter and the macros offer features such as right-margin justification, automatic hyphenation, numbering, footnotes, and environments for quotations, displays, and figures. Although they are simple to use, it does take time to get used to them.

 TIP The word *nroff* has two syllables, *n-roff,* and is pronounced "en rawf." The roff family of typesetters originated from an older program named **roff**, which stood for runoff; however, the *n* in **nroff** is a mystery.

The **nroff** formatter looks at a file in which you have interspersed lines of text with lines of format control information. Determine the format of your documents by including **nroff** commands directly in the text. You can enter both text and **nroff** commands with an editor, such as **vi**, discussed earlier. When you finish editing your text and inserting formatting instructions, you ask **nroff** to format it for you. When the formatting is done, you have two files: your original text file (the "raw" or "uncooked" version) and a new file that contains the formatted (or "cooked") version.

Most **nroff** commands begin with a period and must be entered at the beginning of a line. For example, to turn right justification off, use

```
.na
```

Some commands take *arguments,* values listed after the command that specify how much or how many times the command should take effect. Arguments can also specify text to be used by the command. For example, this command indents the following line one inch:

```
.ti li
```

Some **nroff** commands begin with a backslash (\) and can appear anywhere within the text. For example, the \f command indicates a font change. The commands \fI and \fR, which change the font to italic and Roman, respectively, are illustrated in this example:

```
I just want to emphasize \fIsomething\fR.
```

Macros

A macro package is a set of ready-made functions designed to simplify complex procedures. Macros allow you to do in a few steps what would take a good deal of effort with regular **nroff** commands. Macros can handle elements such as paragraphs, headers and footers, and displays.

There are many macro packages that serve special purposes. The **mm** macros (memorandum macros) produce business letters and memos. The **ms** macros (macros for science) are used in engineering and computer science. The **me** macros (macros for education) package is used in universities for technical writing. Only the **mm** macro package is discussed here, because it is especially suited for business communication.

 NOTE   In many ways, **nroff** resembles a computer language: It is powerful and flexible, but requires many operations to be specified at a level of detail and complexity too difficult for most people to use effectively. For this reason, you should use a macro package instead of direct **nroff** commands whenever possible.

All macro commands start with a period at the beginning of a line. Macro commands are usually all uppercase and one or two letters long. For example, to indicate the start of a paragraph, you use

```
.P
```

TIP   You may be tempted to think of macro commands and **nroff** commands as the same, but they are different. Be careful when you mix the two, because some direct **nroff** commands may interfere with macro commands.

Fill and Justification

The ability to *fill* and *justify* lines is one of the most important features of a formatter, because these processes give the output text its finished appearance.

When the formatter is in fill mode, it scrunches all the input lines together in the output. The format of the output text does not depend on the format of the input file. To the formatter, the input file is only a stream of words. To produce filled text, the formatter takes words from the input, regardless of the original line length, and adds them to the output line until the line reaches the right margin. If the formatter can hyphenate and include part of a word on the line, it does. When the formatter comes across a blank line or a paragraph command in the input, it stops filling the current paragraph. With the **mm** macros, your text is automatically filled. If you want to turn fill off, use the **.nf** (no fill) command. To turn fill on again use the **.fi** (fill) command. The following example shows raw **nroff** input that uses both commands.

```
.nf
In truth, our village has become a butt
For one of those fleet railroad shafts, and o'er
Our peaceful plain its soothing sound is --
 Concord

.fi
The Fitchburg Railroad touches the pond about a hundred rods
south of where I dwell.
I usually go to the village along its causeway, and am, as
it were, related to society by this link.

Henry David Thoreau
```

The resulting cooked output demonstrates both filled and unfilled text.

```
In truth, our village has become a butt
For one of those fleet railroad shafts, and o'er
Our peaceful plain its soothing sound is --
 Concord

The Fitchburg Railroad touches the pond about a hundred
rods south of where I dwell. I usually go to the village
along its causeway, and am, as it were, related to society
by this link.

Henry David Thoreau
```

 TIP   When you type your text in **vi** (or another editor), you don't have to be concerned with the length of the lines you enter. The formatter ignores your line length and fills the text to fit within the specified margins.

When the formatter is in justify mode, all the lines of the justified output are flush with the right margin. An exception is the last line of a paragraph, which is never justified. Filled but unjustified text is said to have a *ragged* right margin, while justified text has a *flush* right margin. A line must be filled before it can be justified; justification won't work if fill is turned off.

The **ms** macros automatically justify your text, while the **mm** macros do not. To turn justification off, use the **.na** (no adjustment) command. To turn it on, use the **.ad** (adjustment) command. This raw unfilled input

```
.na
   If the injustice is part of the necessary friction of the
machine of government, let it go:  Perchance it will wear
smooth--certainly the machine will wear out.

.ad
   There will never be a really free and enlightened State
until the State comes to recognize the individual as a
higher and independent power, from which all its own power
and authority are derived, and treats him accordingly.
```

results in the following filled and justified output.

```
     If the injustice is part of the necessary friction of the
machine of government, let it go:  Perchance it will wear
smooth--certainly the machine will wear out.
     There will never be a really free and enlightened State
until the State comes to recognize the individual as a higher
and independent power, from which all its own power and
authority are derived, and treats him accordingly.
```

 NOTE   The fill and justify commands are direct **nroff** commands. Although it is generally not a good idea to mix **nroff** and macro commands, the **nroff** fill and justify commands will always work properly with macro commands.

Paragraphs

Paragraphs are one of the basic building blocks of a document. A paragraph usually begins with a paragraph command and ends with a blank line or another paragraph command. You can create two types of paragraphs with the **mm** macros: left block and standard indented paragraphs. It is also possible to format a paragraph manually. With the **mm** macros, the formatter fills, but does not justify, the lines of a paragraph unless you direct it to do otherwise.

The **mm** paragraph command is **.P**. To produce a left block paragraph, use **.P 0**. To produce a standard indented paragraph use **.P 1**. The following input file produces a standard indented paragraph.

```
.P 1
If the injustice is part of the necessary friction of the
machine of government, let it go:  Perchance it will wear
smooth--certainly the machine will wear out.
```

Here is the resulting output:

```
     If the injustice is part of the necessary friction of
the machine of government, let it go:  Perchance it will
wear smooth--certainly the machine will wear out.
```

As mentioned, you can also format paragraphs manually in **nroff**. As long as you separate paragraphs with blank lines, the formatter will treat your paragraphs as integral blocks of text. However, since your paragraph is only a block of text to the formatter (without the **.P** command, **nroff** does not really see it as a paragraph), it cannot be indented automatically. Of course, you can indent your paragraphs manually by inserting spaces or tabs in the first line, or you can leave them flush with the left margin. Manual formatting is fine for small jobs, but for long documents it lacks the flexibility of the **.P** command.

Section Headings

A *heading* is a title within the text that sets apart parts of the document such as chapters, sections, and subsections. There are two types of headings: unnumbered and numbered.

The **.H** (heading) command creates a numbered heading. You must specify the *heading level* and the text of the heading. The heading level describes the depth of the section heading. By convention, first-level titles are all uppercase letters while subsequent levels are entered in lowercase. The following example demonstrates the first three heading levels.

 NOTE If the heading text includes any spaces, you must enclose it in double or single quotes.

```
.H 1 "THE HIKE"
The hiking party will depart from Observation Point at 7am and
will arrive at Jenner's Pass near 4pm.
.H 2 "Items To Bring"
The three categories of items to bring are clothing, food, and
camping equipment.
.H 3 "Clothing"
The weather is likely to be sunny, but prepare for the worst.
Hurricanes are not unheard of in these parts.
```

Here is the resulting output.

```
4. The Hike

    The hiking party will depart from Observation Point at
7am and will arrive at Jenner's Pass near 4pm.

4.1 Items To Bring

    The three categories of items to bring are clothing,
food, and camping equipment.

4.1.1 Clothing The weather is likely to be sunny, but
prepare for the worst. Hurricanes are not unheard of in
these parts.
```

The **.HU** command creates an unnumbered heading. Unnumbered headings can be especially useful in setting up appendixes and other sections that may not fit the numbering scheme of your document. You must specify the text of each section heading. Unless the formatter is told otherwise, all unnumbered headings are second-level headings. The following example demonstrates a second level unnumbered heading.

```
.H 1 "UNDER PRESSURE"
In this rush rush business, there often does not seem to be
enough time to get everything done.
.HU "Making a Deadline"
When up against a deadline, if you first muddle through what
must be done, then plan to do what should be done, saving
for last what would be fun to do, you will seldom get
further than the first category.
However, do those same things in reverse order, and somehow
they will all get done, often with time to spare.
```

The output looks like this:

```
8. UNDER PRESSURE
In this rush rush business, there often does not seem to be
enough time to get everything done.

Making a Deadline

When up against a deadline, if you first muddle through
what must be done, then plan to do what should be done,
saving for last what would be fun to do, you will seldom
get further than the first category.
```

```
However, do those same things in reverse order, and somehow
they will all get done, often with time to spare.
```

 NOTE   Numbered and unnumbered headings can be intermixed. Unnumbered headings are often used in place of the lowest-level numbered heading.

Unless you tell the formatter otherwise, unnumbered headings exist at only one level: the level specified by the **Hu** (unnumbered heading) register. Initially, the **Hu** register has a value of 2, causing **.HU** commands to yield second-level unnumbered headings. You can change the value of the **Hu** register to 3 and the level of subsequent unnumbered headings with a command such as this:

```
.nr Hu 3
```

Lists

Each item in a list is preceded by some sort of mark, such as a number, a dash, a word, or a phrase. You can make automatically numbered and alphabetized lists, bulleted lists, dashed lists, and lists that have your own marks or start with your own words or phrases.

All lists are composed of the following parts:

- A list initialization command, such as **.AL**, **.BL**, or **.DL**, which controls the appearance of the list

- One or more **.LI** (list item) commands, each followed by the actual text of the list item

- An **.LE** (list end) command that terminates the list

Lists can be nested (put one inside another) up to five levels deep. All of the list initialization commands can be followed by two optional arguments: a number that specifies how far each item in the list will be indented, and a number that controls blank lines around items in the list. If you omit the latter or give it a value of 0, a blank line will separate each item. If you give it a value of 1, blank lines will not separate the items.

You should explicitly set an argument to null if you need a placeholder. To set an argument to null, use a pair of double quotes. For example, you might use a null argument as follows if you want to prevent blank lines from separating items, but do not want to reset the indentation.

```
.AL A "" 1
```

An *automatic list* is a sequentially numbered or alphabetized list. The automatic list command **.AL** generates lists in a variety of styles. You specify the type of list after the **.AL** command using one of the following values:

1	Arabic numbers
A	uppercase letters
a	Lowercase letters
I	Uppercase Roman numerals
i	Lowercase Roman numerals

If the type of list is omitted or null, the formatter will use Arabic numbers to label the list. The following example produces an automatic list.

```
Rules for driving in New York:
.AL 1 "" 1
.LI
Anything done while honking your horn is legal.
.LI
You may park anywhere if you turn your four-way flashers on.
.LI
A red light means the next six cars may go through the
intersection.
.LE
```

Here is the resulting output:

```
Rules for driving in New York:

1. Anything done while honking your horn is legal.
```

```
2. You may park anywhere if you turn your four-way
   flashers on.
3. A red light means the next six cars may go through the
   intersection.
```

Each item in a *bulleted list* is preceded by a bullet and a single space. The **mm** list initialization command for a bulleted list is **.BL**, as shown in this example:

```
Business Communication
.BL "" 1
.LI
If you call in the morning rather than the afternoon, you
are far more likely to get what you called for.
.LI
Usually a telephone caller makes three points. The third
one is the real reason for the call.
.LI
If you think that something goes without saying, it is
probably in the best interest of everyone involved to say
it.
.LE
```

This input produces the following list.

```
Business Communication

⊕        If you call in the morning rather than the afternoon,
         you are far more likely to get what you called for.
⊕        Usually a telephone caller makes three points. The
         third one is the real reason for the call.
⊕        If you think that something goes without saying, it
         is probably in the best interest of everyone involved
         to say it.
```

 TIP   The **nroff** bullet resembles a pair of cross hairs (⊕). You may find that a marked list with a well-chosen mark, such as an asterisk or a lowercase *o*, suits you better.

Each item in a *dashed list* is preceded by a dash and a single space. The dashed list command is identical to the bulleted list command, except that

it inserts a dash instead of a bullet. The **mm** list initialization command for
a dashed list is **.DL**. Here is an example of a dashed list:

```
Famous last words:

  - We won't need reservations.
  - What happens if you touch these two wires tog--
  - It's always sunny there this time of year.
  - Don't worry, it's not loaded.
```

Each item in a marked list is preceded by an arbitrary mark, which may
consist of more than one character. The **mm** list initialization command for
a marked list is **.ML**. It is followed by an argument that specifies the element
that is to appear before each item in the list. The mark cannot include
ordinary spaces; any spaces in the mark must be preceded by a backslash
(\). The following example creates a marked list.

```
A Few Tips for Business Writers
.ML "Writing tip:" 16
.LI
Use the active voice.
.LI
Put statements in positive form.
.LI
Use definite, specific, concrete language.
.LI
Omit needless words.
.LE
```

This example results in the output,

```
A Few Tips for Business Writers
   Writing tip: Use the active voice.
   Writing tip: Put statements in positive form.
   Writing tip: Use definite, specific, concrete language.
   Writing tip: Omit needless words.
```

NOTE   Notice the double quotes around the mark argument. Marks that
contain spaces must be enclosed in double quotes, or each space within the
mark must be preceded by a backslash.

A *variable-item list* allows you to put a different mark before each item in the list. This type of list is typically used to display definitions of terms or phrases. The text that serves as the mark for a particular item is specified in each list item command. The **mm** command for a variable-item list is **.VL**. For example, here is an input file that creates a variable-item list:

```
Day Two
.VL 1i 2
.LI "12:30 pm"
Lunch in the Pheasant Room
.LI "1:30 pm"
Seminar: "Sales Management", R. R. Hopkins.
A sales management perspective from the executive offices.
.LI "3:00 pm"
Nap
.LI "4:00 pm"
Lecture: "In Search of Mediocrity", J. Stanton.
A search for honest, nonexcellence-oriented business.
A fair product at a good price, America's lost
commodity.
.LI "5:30 pm"
Dinner at the Flying Eel Banquet Room
.LE
```

This file produces the following output:

```
Day Two

12:30 pm      Lunch in the Pheasant Room
 1:30 pm      Seminar: "Sales Management", R. R. Hopkins.
              A sales management perspective from the
              executive offices.
 3:00 pm      Nap
 4:00 pm      Lecture: "In Search of Mediocrity", J. Stanton.
              A search for honest, nonexcellence-oriented
              business. A fair product at a good price,
              America's lost commodity.
 5:30 pm      Dinner at the Flying Eel Banquet Room
```

Displays

A *display* is a block of text that the formatter treats as an integral unit; it is kept together rather than split across a page break. A display can be a chart, a table, or a paragraph that must remain intact. Displays are not filled or indented in the output text; the formatter preserves the spacing and formatting of the text from the input file. The **mm** macros provide two styles of displays: a static style and a floating style. The text of the display is preceded either by a static-display command **.DS** or a floating-display command **.DF**, and is followed by the display-end command **.DE**.

An optional argument can follow a display command to specify how the formatter positions the display. You can use one of the following values:

L   (Left)   Positions the display flush against the left margin

I   (Indent)   Indents the display by the value of the **Si** (static-indent) register, initially set to five

C   (Center)   Centers each line between the left and right margins

CB   (Center block) Centers the entire display as a block of text (a single unit), using the longest line for positioning

If you do not specify a position or if you use null, the formatter positions the display flush with the left margin. Another optional argument follows the position argument and controls whether or not the text in the display is filled. If you omit this argument, specify it as **N** (nofill), or use null, the formatter does not fill the text. If you use **F** (fill), the formatter fills the text. A final optional argument follows the fill argument, and specifies the number of spaces the right margin is to be indented. This value has no effect when the display is not being filled.

A *static display* stays exactly where you put it. It appears in the same relative position in the output text as it does in the input file. When you specify a block of text in the input file as a static display, the formatter places the display on the current page only if there is room for the entire block. If the display does not fit in the space that remains on the page, it is shifted to the top of the next page. Of course, this may result in blank space at the bottom of some pages. The **mm** static-display **.DS** command begins a static display, as shown here:

```
.DS
Ingredients:
1/2 c      flour
1/8 tsp    baking powder
1 tsp      sugar
1/2 tsp    salt
1/2 T      shortening
2-3 tbsp   milk
.DE
```

A *floating display* is similar to a static display; it is a block of text that the formatter keeps on one page. However, a floating display will not leave a blank space at the bottom of a page. If there is not enough room for a floating display on the current page, the formatter sets aside the display and finishes filling the page with the text that follows the display. When the page is full, the formatter places the display at the top of the next page, and then continues with the text from the previous page. A floating display is useful if you are displaying a table or chart whose exact placement is flexible and you do not want blank space at the bottom of a page. The **mm** floating-display **.DF** command begins a floating display.

```
.DF
A note about frybread:
    This frybread is often called Navajo frybread and comes
from the American Indians of the southwest. It was
originally made from staples and used powdered milk and
lard.
.DE
```

Headers and Footers

Headers and footers are running titles that appear at the top and bottom of the page. A title that occurs at the top of the page is known as a *header*. A title printed at the bottom of the page is a *footer*. You can have headers printed on all pages, on all odd-numbered pages, or on all even-numbered pages. Headers that print on odd-numbered pages are often called *odd headers*, and headers that print on even-numbered pages are called *even headers*. Headers that print on *every* page are simply called *page headers*.

 NOTE   Since each kind of header is distinct, you can use all three types at once—page headers, even headers, and odd headers.

The same choices are available for footers as for headers; you can use odd footers, even footers, and page footers.

All running titles work in the same way and have the same format. The **mm** macros provide three-part titles for headers and footers. For example, the **mm** page header command

```
.PH "'left'center'right'"
```

would place the text *left* against the left margin at the top of each page. Similarly, *center* would be centered at the top of each page and *right* would be placed against the right margin.

The header and footer commands and their meanings are as follows:

.PH	Page header
.EH	Even header
.OH	Odd header
.PF	Page footer
.EF	Even footer
.OF	Odd footer

Remember, headers print at the top of the page, and footers print at the bottom. Page headers and page footers print on every page. Even and odd running titles print on even- and odd-numbered pages, respectively.

Initially, with the **mm** macros, the formatter prints the page number at the top of each page. To remove the page number, change the value of the center portion of the page header to null, as follows:

```
.PH ""
```

You can put the page number somewhere else on the page by including the **P** (page number) register in a title. The sequence **\\\\nP** tells the formatter to include the page number in a header or footer. You can also place the date in a header or footer. The date is stored in the **DT** (date) string and is accessed with the sequence ***(DT**. For example, to include both the page number and the date in a footer, use

```
.PF "'Page \\\\nP''\\\\*(DT'"
```

Page Formatting

For the most part, the **mm** macros take care of page formatting for you. They automatically set top, bottom, left, and right margins, spacing, and tab settings. These can be changed from their initial values with direct **nroff** commands. As mentioned, it is generally good practice to avoid mixing direct **nroff** commands with **mm** macros in your document, because some direct **nroff** commands interfere with **mm** macros. However, a few handy **nroff** commands are safe to use with the **mm** macros. The following sections describe these commands.

Line Breaks

When it is in fill mode, unless you specify otherwise, the formatter joins one input line to another until it encounters a blank line that signals the end of a paragraph. As you'll recall, the last line of a paragraph is broken, and is never filled or justified. There are two other ways to break a line that is not to be filled: with the **nroff** break command and with spaces at the beginning of a line.

The **nroff** break command is **.br**. When you insert the break command, the line that is currently being filled ends. After the break, the text continues on a new line flush against the left margin.

If a line in the input file begins with a whitespace character (a space or a tab), the line that is currently being filled ends. The next line begins with the whitespace characters against the left margin.

Spacing

You can double- or triple-space your document by changing the line spacing in the output. Use the **nroff** line spacing command **.ls**. The following command creates double-spaced output:

```
.ls 2
```

Use **.ls 1** to restore single-spacing, and **.ls 3** to set triple-spacing.

Centering

You can center one or more lines with the **nroff** center command **.ce**. To center one line, precede it with

```
.ce
```

To center five lines, use

```
.ce 5
```

 NOTE To create a centered display use the display command **.DS C**.

Temporary Indent

If you want to indent a single line, use the **nroff** temporary indent command **.ti**. For example, to indent a single line eight characters, use

```
.ti 8
```

 NOTE For indented displays, use the display command **.DS I**.

You can also use the temporary indent with a negative argument to produce a one-line "reverse indent," sometimes used in bibliographies.

Fonts

The standard Roman font may be changed to italic or underlined for emphasis in your document. Line printers and letter-quality printers, which cannot change fonts, represent italic as underlined text.

There are at least two ways to produce italic and underlining when you are using the **mm** macros. The first method is with the **mm** italic command **.I**. This, like other **mm** commands, is placed at the beginning of a line by itself. A **.R** command restores the text to Roman. The second method is with the **nroff** in-line escape commands, **\fI** and **\fR**. These are placed in the text within a line or word.

Again, the **.I** command changes the font to italic, and the italic text continues until the **.R** command restores the Roman font. For example, the following paragraph would appear in emphasized text.

```
.I
You'll spend less time getting answers from people if you go
to their offices to ask them questions.
That way, you control when the conversation ends.
.R
```

If only one word is to be italicized, it can be entered alone on a line after an **.I** command, as shown here:

```
.I word
```

In this case, no **.R** command is required to restore the previous font. The previous font automatically resumes on the next line. Here is an example:

```
I am not surprised what was done, but that
.I you
were the one who did it.
```

The result would look like this:

```
I am not surprised what was done, but that
you were the one who did it.
```

You can also change fonts within a line or word with the in-line **nroff** command \f. To produce italics, precede the text to be italicized with the sequence \fI and follow it with \fR. For example,

```
We are charmed to receive the newest volume of \fITrouncer
Tales\fR and look forward to meeting you at the reading.
```

produces

```
We are charmed to receive the newest volume of Trouncer
Tales and look forward to meeting you at the reading.
```

Running nroff

After you have created your input file, you are ready to format it with **nroff**. The **nroff** formatter can be used to print on a line printer or a letter-quality printer. To format a file named **report** using **nroff** and the **mm** macros, type

```
$ nroff -mm report > report.n
```

at the UNIX shell prompt. This creates a new file **report.n**, which you will then send to the printer.

 TIP   When you format your file with **nroff** give the formatted version a **.n** extension so that you'll know what kind of file it is when you see it in your directory.

You can preview the **nroff** formatted file **report.n** with the following command.

```
$ more report.n
```

Printing Your Formatted File

Now that you have created a formatted file, you are ready to print it. To print the **nroff** formatted file **report.n**, type

```
$ lp report.n
```

For more information about printing, see Chapter 8.

The **vi** editor is a powerful and flexible text editor. UNIX professionals use the **vi** editor to create not only ordinary text files, but also shell scripts and programs. Though at first it is somewhat difficult to learn, you will find **vi** an indispensable UNIX tool.

If it is available on your system, the **nroff** formatter, along with the **mm** macros, provides you with powerful tools for producing professional-quality documents. With its complexities, subtleties, and idiosyncrasies, **nroff** can be quite a challenge. Although mastering **nroff** may take some time, it is well worth the effort.

8

Printing

SCO UNIX makes printing both simple and powerful. A single command, **lp**, prints your files. You can print on any one of many printers you may have connected to your system. This chapter covers the primary tools that make up the SCO UNIX printer spooling system: the commands **lp, lpstat, cancel**, and **lprint**. Additionally, it discusses how to send files through filters or formatters before they are printed.

The Printer Spooling System

The SCO UNIX printer spooling system, or print service, is a collection of commands that allow you to use the printers attached to your system. A request to print a file is *spooled,* or queued up, behind other print requests that have been sent to the printer. Each print request is processed and waits its turn to be printed. If there are no printers attached to your system, it is unlikely that the printer spooling system is running.

The print spooler handles the following functions behind the scenes:

- Receives the files users want printed
- Filters the files properly
- Sends print requests to the printer
- Schedules all the printers on the system
- Keeps track of the status of print requests
- Keeps track of the type of paper in each printer
- Keeps track of which fonts are available on each printer
- Notifies users of job status of print problems

Print Requests

A *print request* is a request to print using the system printers. Your print request can contain a lot of information: the printer destination, the pages to be printed, and the number of copies to be printed. When you submit a print request, the system either accepts or rejects the request. If it accepts the request, it tells you your print request's unique identification and places the request in line behind any other requests that are waiting to be printed. When your request gets to the head of the line, it is printed.

Printer Destination

The *printer destination* is the printer to which your print request is sent. Each printer on the system has a unique name. When you send the print service a print request, you can specify by name the printer to which you want your request sent. If you do not specify a destination, your request is sent to the system's default printer destination. In the examples you'll see in this chapter, the default printer is **laserjet**.

 NOTE   A printer may have more than one name. For example, **lazport** and **lazland** may both refer to a laser printer, in portrait and landscape mode, respectively.

Printer Classes

The printers on the system can be organized into classes. Printers with similar characteristics are grouped together. For instance, line printers, laser printers, and daisy-wheel printers can be grouped into individual classes. If you send a print request to a class of printers, the request will be printed on the first available printer of that class.

Printer Forms

On UNIX, you can print using different types of paper or forms, such as letterhead, labels, and blank checks. Forms may also be used to select bins on sheet feeders. The print service and the system administrator manage the forms loaded on the system. The system administrator can place special forms in the printer's auxilary paper bins or load them in place of the regular printer paper. When you send a print request, you can specify the form you want your print request to use. When you request a special form, you can specify a destination, or the print spooler can send the request to a printer on which that form is mounted. If the printer destination supports the form, but it is not mounted, the system administrator is notified. If the form is not recognized or not supported on the printer destination you have specified, your request will be rejected.

 NOTE   Forms can be difficult for the system administrator to manage. Often, small systems do not have forms implemented at all.

XENIX   XENIX does not support forms. Different types of paper must be loaded manually before printing.

Print Wheels

On UNIX, you can print using different print wheels. Depending on the type of printer, a *print wheel* may be a character set, a font cartridge (as on the HP LaserJet), or literally a wheel (as on daisy-wheel printers). The print service and the system administrator manage the print wheels mounted on the system. When you send a print request, you can specify the print wheel you want your print request to use. When you send a request requiring a special print wheel, you can specify the destination or the print spooler can send the request to whatever printer has that print wheel available. If the printer destination supports the print wheel but it is not mounted, the system administrator is notified. If the print wheel is not recognized or not supported on the printer destination you have specified, your request will be rejected.

 NOTE   Print wheels, like forms, can be difficult for the system administrator to manage. Small systems often do not have print wheels implemented.

Forms and print wheels are intimately connected, because a form may require a particular character set. Thus, some forms may require both form and print wheel changes. Any form and print wheel conflicts will cause your request to be rejected.

XENIX   XENIX does not support print wheels. Different character sets must be loaded manually before you print.

Sending a Print Request—lp

The **lp** command requests a file, or group of files, to be printed. The files are spooled, or queued up, behind other files that are waiting to be printed. For example, the following command prints the file **average.grf**.

```
$ lp average.grf
request id is laserjet-534 (1 file)
```

To print more than one file at once, merely supply **lp** with a list of the files to be printed. The following command prints three files.

```
$ lp guest.list announce invite
request id is laserjet-535 (3 files)
```

 NOTE   If you need to stop a print request, use the **cancel** command described later in this chapter.

XENIX   A similar command **lpr** is supplied with XENIX. It works identically to **lp**, and is supplied to maintain compatibility with previous versions of UNIX, which used **lpr** instead of **lp**. It is normally not used.

The Request ID

The **lp** command responds to your print request with a *request ID*. This consists of the name of the printer on which the file is to be printed and a unique number identifying the file. The print request in a previous example, returned

```
request id is laserjet-534 (1 file)
```

The request ID is **laserjet-534**. This is request number 534 made to printer **laserjet**.

NOTE   If you forget the ID of a print request you've sent to be printed, you can list all your current requests with the **lpstat** command, described later in this chapter.

To modify a request that you've already sent, use the request ID and the **-i** option. For example, to modify the request from the previous example, you would use the request ID **laserjet-534**. To request three copies of the file already sent to the printer, you would type

```
$ lp -i laserjet-534 -n3
```

The options you can use to change your print request are described in the next section. If the request has already finished printing, your change will be rejected. If your request is already printing, it will be stopped and restarted from the beginning, unless the **-P** (page list) option is specified.

XENIX   XENIX does not provide the **-i** option. You cannot modify requests already sent to the print spooler in XENIX.

Later in this chapter, you will learn to use the request ID to cancel a print request.

Print Options

In addition to the name of the file you want printed, you can supply **lp** with one or more print options that change the way a file is printed. All of the **lp** options are described in the following sections. For example, the following request,

```
$ lp -n3 rugby.txt
```

uses the **-n** (number) option to print three copies of the file **rugby.txt**. Options appear between the **lp** command and the file or files to be printed, as in the example above. The single exception to this rule is the **-d** option, which follows the files to be printed. It is covered in the following section.

XENIX   In XENIX, no space is allowed between an **lp** option and its argument. The following UNIX command

```
$ lp letter -d xerox
```

would look like this in XENIX:

```
$ lp letter -dxerox
```

The -d Option   To send a print request to a specific printer, use the **-d** option, followed by the name of the printer. If the printer is unavailable, the print request will be rejected. Without the **-d** option, print requests are sent to the default printer destination. For example, to send a file **advent.memo** to a printer named **xerox**, you would use this command:

```
$ lp advent.memo -d xerox
request id is xerox-178 (1 file)
```

Notice that the **-d** option *follows* the file name.

The -c Option   With the **-c** option, **lp** copies the files to be printed when the request is received, and the files are ultimately printed from the copies. Without the **-c** option, files are not copied, but are printed directly from the file. Normally, if a file is deleted or changed after a print request is made, but before the file is printed, the changes are reflected in your print request. Use **-c** to prevent this.

The -f Option   Only available on UNIX, the **-f** option prints the print request on a special preprinted form, instead of on standard paper. Follow the **-f** option with a form name. The print service and the system administrator make sure the form is available on the printer destination. Forms may be used to select paper in an auxilary paper bin or to select paper size. If the printer destination supports the form, but it is not mounted, the system administrator is notified. If the form is not recognized or not supported on the printer destination you have specified, or if you are not allowed to use the form, your request will be rejected. The **-d any** option causes a request to be printed on any printer that has the desired form mounted.

NOTE You can use the **lpstat -f** command, introduced later in this chapter, to find out which forms your system supports.

The -H Option Available only on UNIX, the **-H** option provides special handling of print requests. It is followed by one of the following values, which determine the special handling of your request.

hold	Holds the request until further notice. This will stop a request that is already printing or suspend a request that is in the queue. Other requests lined up at the printer will print ahead of your held request until it is resumed.
resume	Resumes a held print request. The request continues printing or resumes its place in the queue.
immediate	Moves a request to the front of the queue. If another request is already printing, you may place that printing request on hold. This option is only available to administrators.

For example, to place print request **ibm-40** on hold, you would type

```
$ lp -i ibm-40 -H hold
```

You would resume the print request with

```
$ lp -i ibm-40 -H resume
```

The -m and -w Options With the **-m** option, mail is sent to you when your request has finished printing.

The **-w** option writes a message to your terminal after your request has been printed. If you are no longer logged in, you are sent mail. The following example demonstrates the **-w** option.

```
$ lp -w news
request id is laserjet-536
$
lp: printer request laserjet-536 has been printed on laserjet
```

The -n Option   The **-n** option must be followed by a number that specifies the number of copies to print. For example, to print five copies of a file called **handout**, type

```
$ lp -n5 handout
```

The -o Option   Available only on UNIX, **-o** provides special options for your print request. These options are in the spooler script (the program that prints your request) and may be changed by the system administrator. The system administrator may have modified the script to include additional options or may have changed them altogether. In fact, options may vary depending on the type of printers connected to the system; an HP LaserJet may use one set of options, while a Tandy printer uses another set. The **-o** option is followed by a value that determines the special options for your print request. Here, for example, are the special options provided with the "standard" spooler script:

nobanner	Does not print a banner page before the request
nofilebreak	Does not insert a form feed between each file in the print request
length=*scale*	Prints a page length given by *scale*
width=*scale*	Prints a page width given by *scale*
lpi=*pitch*	Prints with a line pitch set to *pitch* lines per inch
cpi=*pitch*	Prints with a character pitch set to *pitch* characters per inch; the value of *pitch* can also be **pica**, **elite**, or **compressed**

For example, to print two files, **report.txt** and **stats.liz**, with no page break between them, you would use the command

```
$ lp -o nofilebreak report.txt stats.liz
```

 NOTE   You can collect several special options by specifying **-o** more than once on the command line.

The -P Option   Available only on UNIX, the **-P** option prints the pages specified after the option. Ranges of numbers, individual page numbers, or both may be specified. This option works only if there is a filter available to handle it. If there is not, the request is rejected. For example, to print pages 1 through 10, 12, and 15 of a file named **catalog.txt,** depending on the filter, you might use the command,

```
$ lp -P1.10,12,15 catalog.txt
```

The -s Option   The -s option suppresses messages from **lp,** such as error messages and the request ID message. This is useful in shell scripts, which are discussed in Chapters 10 and 11.

The -S Option   Available only on UNIX, the **-S** option prints your request using the print wheel specified after the option. If the print wheel is available, but not mounted, the system administrator is notified. If the print wheel is unrecognized or not supported by the destination, your print request is rejected.

 NOTE   The term *print wheel* originally referred to the print wheel on a daisy-wheel printer. But SCO UNIX also uses the print wheel feature to manage font cartridges and character sets on laser printers.

If the **-d any** option is used, the request is printed on any printer where the desired print wheel is mounted. For example, to print a file **pueblo** with character set **spanish,** on any printer that has the required print wheel mounted, use the command,

```
$ lp -S spanish pueblo -d any
```

 NOTE   You can use the **lpstat -S** command, introduced later in this chapter, to find out which print wheels your system supports.

The -t Option   The -t option prints a title on the banner page of the output. Follow this option with the text of the title in double quotation marks.

Canceling a Print Request—cancel

To cancel a print request, use the **cancel** command and the ID assigned when the request was sent. For example, if **lp** returned the following request ID, the subsequent **cancel** command would cancel the request.

```
$ lp file.n -d star
request id is star-24
$ cancel star-24
request "star-24" canceled
```

If a request is already printing, a **cancel** command will stop the request. Most small systems print quickly, so a **cancel** command must be used promptly to have the desired effect.

If you specify only a printer name after the **cancel** command, only the request that is currently printing on that printer is canceled. For example, if request **xerox-178** were currently printing, this command would cancel it:

```
$ cancel xerox
request "xerox-178" canceled
```

Reporting the Status of a Printer—lpstat

You can determine the status of a print request with the **lpstat** command. This command can tell you the status of a particular print request, the mounted forms or print wheels, or the status of the entire print service. With no options, **lpstat** only prints the status of requests you have made to **lp**, as in the following example,

```
$ lpstat
xerox-179        petra     784  Feb 1  14:41 on xerox
laserjet-537     petra   12120  Feb 1  14:39 on laserjet
laserjet-538     petra    4054  Feb 1  14:42
```

Status Options

Like the **lp** command, **lpstat** can take a number of options. These options determine what information is printed. For example, the **-d** option prints the system's default printer destination with the command:

```
$ lpstat -d
```

Many of the **lpstat** options must be followed by a list. For instance, the **-p** option prints the status of each printer in a list of printers, and the **-u** option prints the status requests made by a list of users. The **-u** option is followed by a list of login names, as in the following command:

```
$ lpstat -u laurak,kenya
```

The list of items must be separated by commas, as in the previous example.

XENIX   Remember, in XENIX, no space may appear between an option and its argument.

If you omit the list after an option that takes a list, all information relevant to that option will be printed. Typing the word **all** in place of a list accomplishes the same thing. For example, the command

```
$ lpstat -o
```

and the command

```
$ lpstat -o all
```

would both print the status of all output requests.

XENIX   Since the XENIX **lpstat** command does not recognize the word **all** after its options, use the first method to print all relevant information in XENIX.

The -u Option   This option, followed by a list of users, gives the status of print requests by those users. Without a list of users, this option gives the status of print requests by all users. Without any options, the **lpstat** command reports the status of only your own print requests. The following command illustrates the **-u** option.

```
$ lpstat -u howard,mollym
star-25         howard        8815      Feb 4 13:41 on star
laser2-340      howard       26301      Feb 4 13:42 on laser2
laser2-341      howard         577      Feb 4 13:55
xerox-178       mollym        1301      Feb 4 13:42 on xerox
```

The -o Option   The **-o** option, followed by a list, gives the status of print requests for a list of intermixed printers, class names, and request IDs. This option prints the status of the listed requests and of requests sent to the listed printers and classes, as well. Without a list of requests, this option reports the status of all output requests. The **-l** option (only available on UNIX), gives the status in more detail. The following example prints the status of requests sent to printer **xerox** and to printers in the class **linep**.

```
$ lpstat -o xerox,linep
xerox-201       darby       10015      Feb 12 16:21 on xerox
xerox-202       meirion       701      Feb 12 16:30
ibm-108         meirion       815      Feb 12 16:24 on ibm
```

The -f Option   Only available on UNIX, the **-f** option lists the forms recognized by the system. The **-l** option adds a description of each form. For example, the following command gives the description of the recognized forms.

```
$ lpstat -f -l
```

The -S Option   Available only on UNIX, the **-S** option verifies that the listed print wheels are recognized by **lp**, and shows whether the listed print wheels are mounted. Without a list, this option lists all the recognized print wheels. The **-l** option adds a description of each print wheel. For example, the following command gives the description of all of the recognized print wheels.

```
$ lpstat -S -l
```

The -d Option   With the **-d** option, the **lpstat** command reports the default printer destination for **lp**, as in the following example:

```
$ lpstat -d
system default destination: laserjet
```

The -s Option   The -s option provides a status summary. The summary includes the default printer destination, a list of class names and their members, a list of printers, a list of forms, and a list of all print wheels. The following example demonstrates this option.

```
$ lpstat -s
scheduler is running
system default destination: laserjet
members of class lasers:
     xerox
     laserjet
     laser2
members of class linep:
     ibm
     star
device for xerox: /dev/ttyi1a
device for laserjet: /dev/lp1
device for laser2: /dev/ttyi1c
device for ibm: /dev/ttyi1d
device for star: /dev/ttyi1e
device for daisy: /dev/ttyi1f
```

The -t Option   With this option, **lpstat** prints all status information, including all the information in the -s status summary and then some. The information provided includes the scheduler status, system default destination, class members, printer device names, printer status, class status, mounted forms, mounted print wheels, and a list of spooled print jobs. The following example illustrates the -t option.

```
$ lpstat -t
scheduler is running
system default destination: laserjet
members of class lasers:
     xerox
     laserjet
     laser2
members of class linep:
     ibm
     star
device for xerox: /dev/ttyi1a
```

```
device for laserjet: /dev/lp1
device for laser2: /dev/ttyi1c
device for ibm: /dev/ttyi1d
device for star: /dev/ttyi1e
device for daisy: /dev/ttyi1f
xerox accepting requests since Jan 6 12:12
laserjet accepting requests since Jan 6 12:14
laser2 accepting requests since Jan 21 16:04
ibm accepting requests since Dec 5 17:15
star accepting requests since Dec 19 12:04
daisy not accepting requests since Dec 17 11:15 -
     daisy wheel disconnected indefinitely
printer xerox now printing xerox-186. enabled since Jan 6 12:12
printer laserjet now printing laserjet-540. enabled since Jan 6 12:14
printer laser2 is idle. enabled since Jan 21 16:04
printer ibm is idle. enabled since Dec 5 17:15
printer star is idle. enabled since Dec 19 12:04
xerox-186      petra     824       Feb 1 14:20 on xerox
laserjet-540   darby    1140       Feb 1 14:30
```

Printing at Your Terminal—lprint

If your terminal has local printing capabilities, you can attach a printer directly to the printer port of your terminal to print locally. For example, to print a file **dogma.list** at a local printer attached to the printer port of your terminal, you would type

```
$ lprint dogma.list
```

To make **lprint** use the standard input for printing, use the **-** option. For example, the following command uses the **pr** filter to print a file.

```
$ pr dogma.list | lprint -
```

Only certain terminals have the local printing capability defined on the system. You may get an error message when using **lprint**, as in the following example:

```
$ lprint jargon
lprint: terminal does not support local print
```

If your terminal is not supported, the system administrator must modify the file **/etc/termcap** to include your terminal. Entries for **PN** (start printing) and **PS** (end printing) must be added with the appropriate control or escape characters for your terminal. This procedure is described in the *SCO UNIX System Administrator's Reference*.

Printing with the pr Filter

The **pr** filter breaks your text neatly into pages, single- or double-spacing it, and adding a header that may contain the file name, page numbers, or any text you specify. As with many SCO UNIX commands, the **pr** command can be followed by a number of options that determine how the command treats your text.

 NOTE Although **pr** paginates your text and adds a header, it does not format the text. Use the **nroff** text formatter, described later in this chapter, if it is installed on your system, to format your files.

Without any options, **pr** paginates your text, printing the date and time, the file name, and the page number at the top of every page. The following example shows only the first several lines of a file printed with **pr**.

```
$ pr report.txt

Sep 2 14:10 1989 report.txt Page 1

This report attempts to explain the declining state of the
nation's savings and loan institutions. The report published
last week by the Secretary of the Treasury explains a great
deal, as you may see from the following quote:
```

The **pr** command displays the specified files on the standard output; it does not automatically send them to the printer. To send the output of **pr** to the printer, you can redirect it to a file and then print the file, or you can simply pipe it to the **lp** command, as in the following example:

```
$ pr report.txt | lp
request id is laserjet-539 (standard output)
```

The **-d** option double-spaces the output. The following command prints a double-spaced file with **pr** and sends a request to the printer.

```
$ pr -d report.txt | lp
```

The *-k* option produces output with *k* equally spaced columns. This option is great for condensing lists of words or names that would otherwise require lots of paper to print. It can, in fact, be used for printing text in newspaper-style columns if the text is properly formatted (that is, if the line length does not exceed the width of a column). The following command prints a file **name.list** in four equally spaced columns per page and sends a request to the printer spooler.

```
$ pr -4 name.list | lp
```

The *+k* option begins printing with page *k*. The following command prints a file with **pr**, starting at the tenth page and spooling the file to the printer.

```
$ pr +10 report.txt | lp
```

The **-o***k* option offsets the text *k* spaces to the right of the paper's left edge. This option is extremely useful because it adds a left margin to text that would otherwise print on the left edge of the paper. The following command provides a left margin of five spaces.

```
$ pr -o5 report.txt | lp
```

The **-l***k* option sets the page length to *k* lines per page. This is useful if your printed text tends to suffer from "drift," caused by incorrect pagination. The default page length is 66 lines per page, but if your printer prints only 60 lines per page, more and more of each page will drift to the top of the next page. The following command uses **pr** to paginate and print a file at 60 lines per page.

```
$ pr -l60 report.txt | lp
```

The final option, **-h**, changes the header printed by **pr**. Normally, the header prints the time, date, file name, and page number at the top of every page. You can enclose an argument in double quotes after the **-h** option to specify text to replace the file name in the **pr** header. The following command replaces the file name in the standard **pr** header with new text, and sends the result to the printer.

```
$ pr -h "The Future of Savings and Loans" report.txt | lp

Sep 2 14:10 1989 The Future of Savings and Loans Page 1

This report attempts to explain the declining state of the
nation's savings and loan institutions. The report published
last week by the Secretary of the Treasury explains a great
deal, as you may see from the following quote:
```

XENIX   Remember that XENIX does not allow spaces to appear between an option and its argument.

Printing with nroff

The **nroff** text formatter is part of the document preparation system only available on XENIX. It formats your text files and prepares them for printing. You determine the format of a file by including **nroff** commands directly within the text of the file. The **nroff** text formatter and the commands required to prepare a file for **nroff** are described in detail in Chapter 7, "Editing and Text Processing."

When you have created a text file complete with **nroff** commands, two steps remain: you must format the file through **nroff**, and you must print it. If you format the file separately with **nroff**, creating a new formatted file, you may print the new file directly with the **lp** command. In the following example, the unformatted text file **letter.txt** is formatted with **nroff**, creating a new formatted version **letter.n**. This new file is then printed directly with **lp**.

```
$ nroff -mm letter.txt > letter.n
$ lp letter.n
request id is laserjet-538 (1 file)
```

You can also format the file with **nroff** and print the formatted version with **lp** all in one command. In the following example, the file **letter.txt** is formatted with **nroff** and piped to the **lp** command.

```
$ nroff -mm letter.txt | lp
request id is laserjet-539 (standard input)
```

In SCO UNIX, the printer spooling system handles the printing of files. The primary tools that make up the printer spooling system are the commands **lp, lpstat, cancel,** and **lprint**. The **lp** command sends a print request to the printer spooling system. It offers great flexibility in the number and variety of options to the command. The **lpstat** command prints information about many aspects of the printer spooler system. Again, many options provide great flexibility. The **cancel** command removes a print request from the print spooler. If the request is currently printing, the request is stopped. The **lprint** command sends a file to a local printer directly attached to your terminal.

Files can be sent through filters, such as **pr,** or formatted with **nroff** before they are sent to the printer. Using pipes, commands can be filtered or formatted, and then printed in one action.

CHAPTER

9

Sending and Receiving Mail

One of the most convenient and fun features of SCO UNIX is its ability to send and receive electronic mail quickly and easily using the **mail** program. The UNIX mail system is sometimes called a *mailbox* system. Each user on the system has a "mailbox" to which other users can send mail. In reality, these mailboxes are files in the directory **/usr/spool/mail**. There is a file in this directory corresponding to each account on the system.

Using a mail program is similar to sending mail through the post office. When you send a letter, the mail program, like your letter carrier, delivers your letter directly to the mailbox of the recipient. Sending mail to a user really means sending mail to that user's mailbox. To read your own mail you simply look in your own mailbox on the system.

The **mail** program provides you with tools for sending and receiving mail. This chapter describes these tools and summarizes the most useful **mail** features. The first part of the chapter covers sending mail, and the second part discusses receiving mail. This chapter also tells you how you can customize your mail environment.

To differentiate between incoming mail and outgoing mail, we'll call mail that you receive, *messages,* and mail that you send, *letters.* This distinction is arbitrary, but it helps avoid confusion in discussions of incoming and outgoing mail.

Variations on a Theme

Numerous versions of the mail program are available, from very simple programs to quite complex ones. They all have different features and functions, and sometimes different names. The various mail tools often differ in subtle ways. SCO UNIX and SCO XENIX each have their own versions of **mail**. XENIX **mail** has few fancy features. UNIX **mail** offers more enhancements and convenience features. The programs differ in the commands they use, the responses they give, and their prompts. For example, the UNIX mail prompt is a question mark (**?**), and the XENIX mail prompt is an underscore (_).

Although we point out instances where XENIX **mail** differs, the examples in this chapter use the UNIX **mail** program. The commands and responses are from SCO UNIX **mail**, and the prompt appears as a question mark.

Modes and Commands of mail

Before you plunge into the operation of **mail**, you should be aware of a few important details. The **mail** program has two modes: sending and receiving. Sending mail is a simple matter; you just type your letter and send it. As you enter your letter, you can edit, review, and modify it. Reading mail is more involved; you can enter commands at the mail prompt to manipulate the messages in your mailbox. There are commands to help you save, delete, and respond to your messages.

When you are sending mail, you'll use some important commands called the *tilde escape codes*. These mail commands consist of a tilde (~) followed by a single-character code on a line by itself, sometimes followed by an argument. Tilde escape codes are typed at the beginning of a line in the body of a letter. For example, an important tilde escape is tilde-v (~v), which allows you to make changes to your letter with the visual editor.

 NOTE   Tilde-v means type a tilde, then a v. Do not type both keys at the same time as you would with CTRL-C.

When you are reading mail, you enter commands on a line by themselves at the mail prompt. Some commands can be followed by arguments separated by spaces.

 TIP   You need not type entire **mail** commands. You can abbreviate most commands to one or two letters. For example, you can enter **t** instead of the whole **type** command and **ho** instead of the entire **hold** command. This chapter gives the abbreviation in parentheses after the name of each command.

Sending Mail

The **mail** program is both remarkably powerful and extremely easy to use. From the shell prompt, you can send electronic mail at any time to anyone on the network, almost anywhere in the world. It is easy to send mail to someone, whether they are across the room or across the nation. To send mail to someone on the network, you must know that person's *account name* (sometimes referred to as *login name, user name,* or simply *login*). It is important to differentiate between someone's real name and their account name. You may also need to know that person's *system address* or *network* *address.* To send mail to someone on your own system, you do not need a system address, but to send mail to someone on another system—perhaps in another part of the world—you need to know their system address. In **mail**, an account name and system address make up the complete mailing address, just as a person's name and street address make up the postal address of a letter.

Sending a Letter to One Person or Many People

You use the command **mail** to send a letter. Every name you type after the **mail** command is an account to which you want to send mail. In UNIX-speak, the **mail** command takes one or more arguments that specify the user or users to whom mail is to be sent. For example, to send a letter to account **kenya** from the shell prompt, you would type

```
$ mail kenya
```

You can mail identical copies of a letter to several users simultaneously. For example, to send a letter to two accounts at once—say to accounts **lawton** and **book**—you would type

```
$ mail lawton book
```

This command tells **mail** that you are sending the same letter to both accounts.

Whether you are sending your letter to one person or many, **mail** usually asks you to specify the subject of the letter, as follows:

```
Subject:
```

In response, type a one-line summary and press RETURN. When the recipient checks her mail, the subject line will tell her what your letter is about before she reads it.

Now, type the body of your letter, pressing RETURN at the end of each line, as in the following example.

```
$ mail kenya
subject: buckeye and rds

Evan:
     Both buckeye and rds are alive and well. Ma Bell pulled the
plug on everyone in the Willamette Valley that didn't pay their
bill by Mar 1 when they changed over to the new ESS5 system.
               Laura Kingston
```

You can only correct mistakes in the current line with the BACKSPACE key. If you make a mistake and press RETURN before you've corrected it, it is too late. To correct mistakes in previous lines or make editing changes, you need to use a text editor such as **vi**, which is covered in the section "Writing a Letter Using an Editor."

When your letter is ready to send, press CTRL-d on a line by itself (that is, CTRL and d simultaneously) to end your letter and send it. The **mail** program responds **EOT** for "End Of Transmission." For example, CTRL-d ends the following letter.

```
$ mail kenya
subject: buckeye and rds

Evan:
     Both buckeye and rds are alive and well. Ma Bell pulled the
plug on everyone in the Willamette Valley that didn't pay their
bill by Mar 1 when they changed over to the new ESS5 system.
               Laura Kingston
EOT
$
```

XENIX   When you complete a letter in XENIX, it responds (**end of message**).

If CTRL-d doesn't work, you can end your letter with a tilde escape code, tilde-dot (~.). Type ~. (a tilde followed by a dot) at the beginning of a line at the end of your letter.

 CAUTION   Once a letter is sent there is no way to "unsend" it, so be careful what you send. It's a good idea to write your letters with an editor, so you can make any necessary changes before you send them.

After you've sent a letter, the **mail** program tells you if something has gone wrong. If SCO UNIX does nothing after a command, everything is okay. If mail cannot be delivered to the user and address you specified, you are notified by a message or via return mail. The **mail** program, like your letter carrier, attempts to return the mail to you. Your undeliverable mail will resurface as returned mail in your mailbox or will be saved in a file named **dead.letter** in your home directory. In UNIX, undeliverable mail is usually returned to your mailbox, and does not generate an error message. XENIX places undeliverable mail in your **dead.letter** file and produces an error message, such as

```
No local user named "roberts"
Letter saved in "/usr/laurak/dead.letter" [Appended] 6/98
```

 NOTE If you are sending mail to another system and your letter is undeliverable, it will be returned via return mail, whether you are on UNIX or XENIX. The returned letter will be in your system mailbox when you check your mail.

Killing a Letter

At some point, you may want to kill a letter, perhaps to start the whole thing over. The easiest way to do this is with the interrupt key, usually CTRL-c or DEL. You can press the interrupt key at any point in a letter. The **mail** program will respond with a message acknowledging your interrupt. Press the interrupt key again to confirm that you really want to kill the letter or continue typing if you do not. For example, if interrupt is set to DEL, you would kill a letter by pressing DEL twice, as indicated here:

```
$ mail lawton
Subject: deadline

Chris, Friday I was supposed to see the final of your
report. I have not even seen a draft (which was due me the
Friday before last). What happened? Are you
(Interrupt — one more to kill letter)
$
```

If the interrupt key doesn't seem to work, there is another way to kill a letter. You can kill a letter by typing the tilde escape code tilde-q (**~q**) at the beginning of a line in the body of your letter. The *q* stands for "quit."

 NOTE   With either method of killing a letter, a copy of your letter (or everything you typed up to the point you killed it) is usually saved in a file called **dead.letter** in your home directory. UNIX does not tell you this, but XENIX issues a message such as

```
Letter saved in "/usr/laurak/dead.letter" [Appended] 5/75
```

Reviewing Your Letter

As you write your letter, you may want to see what it looks like so far. To have **mail** show you your letter, type tilde-p (**~p**) at the beginning of a line in the body of your letter. In this case, the *p* stands for "print." The following example demonstrates this:

```
$ mail book
Subject: report

Larry:
    My report was supposed to be on your desk late last
week. The report itself was placed in limbo (as per Heidi's
orders), after the system crash.
~p
------
Message contains:
To: book
Subject: report

Larry:
    My report was supposed to be on your desk late last
week. The report itself was placed in limbo (as per Heidi's
orders), after the system crash.
(continue)
```

The **mail** program prints **(continue)** to tell you that you may continue writing your letter. Or, if your letter is finished, you can press CTRL-d to send it.

Enclosing a File in Your Letter

Perhaps you want to include a report or table in a letter you are writing. It is useful to be able to insert the contents of a file into your letter. Use tilde-r (**~r**) to read in a file. To add the file **report** to your letter, you would type

```
~r report
```

in the body of your letter. Of course, if the specified file does not exist, **mail** will complain.

The following example encloses the file **report.data** in a letter, and then uses tilde-p to view the result.

```
$ mail book
Subject: report data

Larry:
    Here is some of the most critical data from the report:
~r report.data
"report.data" 4/140
~p
------
Message contains:
To: book
Subject: report

Larry:
     Here is some of the most critical data from the report:
Item    Code #   Whls   Rtl    Qty
Dutch   C04442   4.60   6.30   124
Whole   C46724   2.30   3.25   200
French  C47423   2.50   3.60   110
(continue)
```

Sending a File with mail

Sometimes you may want to send a file that has been prepared with another program. The **mail** program can send any text file. You already know how to include a file in a letter with tilde-r. You can also send a file from the command line without even entering the **mail** program by simply redirecting the standard input. For example, to send a file called **invite** to account **kenya**, you would type the following line at the shell prompt.

```
$ mail kenya < invite
```

The < character is the redirection symbol. It tells **mail** to look in **invite** for its input instead of asking you to type your letter. (For more information about redirection, review Chapter 5, "Command Line Fundamentals.")

 CAUTION   Be careful when using redirection with **mail**. If you accidentally use the output redirection symbol (>) instead of the input redirection symbol (<), you will overwrite the file, destroying its contents.

After you have sent a file, SCO UNIX doesn't issue a message if the transmission has been successful; it only tells you if something has gone wrong. As always with UNIX, no news is good news.

Another way to send a text file is to pipe the output of a command to **mail**. This is useful if you want to send the text through a filter, such as **sort** or **pr**, before it is mailed. For example, to place a file in two columns with **pr** before sending it with **mail**, you would use the command

```
$ pr -2 news | mail heidi
```

When you send a file using redirection or piping, **mail** does not ask you for a subject. If you want the mail to have a subject line, you must use the **-s** option when you call **mail** from the command line. The text immediately following **-s** on the command line is the subject of the mail. If the subject contains spaces, you must surround it with double quotes. For example, this command

```
$ mail -s "Thirtieth Birthday" kenya < invite
```

would mail the file **invite** to account **kenya** with a subject line that reads "Thirtieth Birthday."

Writing a Letter Using an Editor

You can use an editor, such as **vi**, to write or edit your letters. This is useful for correcting mistakes that you missed on previous lines or for letters that require more than simple formatting. However, this requires some knowledge of the editor. You may find a text editor helpful because it allows you to make editing changes in letters sent by **mail**, but it is not essential. You might get along fine without ever editing your letters, but for long letters it is certainly a good idea to do so. If you do not know how to use an editor, you can skip this section. To find out more about the SCO UNIX editors, see Chapter 7, "Editing and Text Processing."

 REMEMBER   If you make a serious mistake but don't know how to use a text editor to correct it, you can always kill the letter and start again.

You may edit your letter with **vi** by entering the tilde escape code tilde-v (**~v**) at the beginning of a line in the body of your letter. The *v* stands for "visual editor." For example, to edit a typo on a previous line with **vi**, you would enter the tilde escape code as follows:

```
$ mail laurak
Subject:

Laura, I am not a great tyoinst, but I will write you al
letter anyway. I just got my UNIX account and I am learning
how to use the amail progam. How do you edit these things
andyway?
~v
```

The **vi** editor will display your letter as illustrated in Figure 9-1. The letter may now be edited with **vi**.

Figure 9-1.

```
Laura, I am not a great tyoinst, but I will write you al
letter anyway. I just got my UNIX account and I am learning
how to use the amail progam. How do you edit these things
andyway?
~
~
~
~
~
~
~
~
~
~
"/tmp/Re02234" 3 lines, 186 characters
```

Editing a Letter with **vi**.

When you finish editing, you must exit **vi** and return to **mail**. To exit **vi**, type **:wq** and press RETURN. Now **mail** will respond

```
(continue)
```

You can continue writing your letter using **mail**, or, if your letter is finished, you can press CTRL-d to send it.

 NOTE   If you prefer a line editor to the visual editor, you can edit your letter with **ed** by typing tilde-e (**~e**) instead of tilde-v.

Sending Mail to Other Computers

Networks connect computer systems through network cables, phone lines, and satellite links. Many networks connect UNIX systems, such as Micnet, the UUCP network, Internet, and BITNET. If your system is part of a network, you can send mail to and receive mail from users on other systems. To find out what networks—if any—your system is connected to, ask your system administrator. This section presents an overview of network addressing and sending mail to other systems. Chapter 13, "Communicating Using the UUCP System," discusses the details of setting up the most common SCO UNIX network, the UUCP network.

In many cases, sending mail to accounts on other systems is simply a matter of adding the name of the recipient's system to the account name, much as you would add the recipient's country to the address of an international letter. If the recipient's system is not directly connected to yours over the network, you have to specify a series of systems through which your mail will travel to reach its destination. The difficulty arises in determining the proper form of address for the network you are using.

A Micnet network is used to establish a network of computers that are in the same office or building. The network is supplied with both UNIX and XENIX. It consists of computers directly connected by serial communication lines in one of a variety of configurations. To send mail to a user over the Micnet network, you follow the user's account name with the name of the user's remote system, separating the account name and the system name with an at sign (@). For example, to send mail to **karri** at system **marigold** connected over the Micnet network, you would type

```
$ mail karri@marigold
```

After entering this command, you could continue with your letter just as if you were sending mail to a local user. The **mail** program would pass your letter to the computer **marigold** through the Micnet network, which would deliver it to **karri**. Of course, your computer must recognize **marigold** or the mail would not be delivered.

XENIX   Micnet addressing on XENIX is a little different, because XENIX does not support at sign addressing. The system name comes first, followed by a colon and a user name, as shown here:

```
$ mail marigold:karri
```

REMEMBER   For the Micnet network the addressing format is *User-at-System* or *User-colon-System*.

The UUCP network (often called USENET) is used primarily over phone lines to connect remote machines, but it can connect two local systems using a serial connection. To send mail to a user over the UUCP network, you need to precede the user's account name with the name of the user's remote system (the reverse of Micnet addressing). In this case, the account name and system name are separated by an exclamation point (!), which is referred to as a *bang*. For example, to send mail to **keithj** at system **boulder**, you would type

```
$ mail boulder!keithj
```

The **mail** program would hand the mail over to system **boulder** through the UUCP network, which would in turn deliver the mail to account **keithj**.

 TIP   To find out which UUCP sites your system can communicate with, use the **uuname** command covered in Chapter 13, "Communicating Using the UUCP System."

To send mail to an account on a system that is not directly connected to your system on the UUCP network, you may have to go through another system. The other system acts as an intermediary, passing the mail along to its ultimate destination. In fact, your mail can go through a series of systems that are connected to each other in the network. This is known as *routing* mail or *multihop* mail; each intermediate step along the way is another hop and you are allowed up to 20 hops. For instance, to route mail to account **graham** through several systems in the network, you might use this command:

```
$ mail helm!orion!abs!graham
```

The mail would pass in turn through systems **helm**, **orion**, and **abs**. It would go from one machine to the next one specified in the path, finally ending on the **abs** system where account **graham** resides. Each intervening machine must know about the next machine in the path. If either the path through the network or the user is incorrect, the mail system will attempt to return your mail. Some machines will not return mail, so your mail may occasionally disappear. If you're sending something important, be sure to save a copy until you are certain it has reached its destination.

 REMEMBER   For the UUCP network the addressing format is *System1-bang-System2-bang-User.*

 NOTE   If you use the C shell, you must "escape" exclamation marks with a backslash (\). That is, the exclamation point in UUCP network addresses must be preceded by a backslash, as shown here:

```
% mail boulder\!keithj
```

The Internet is a government sponsored, world-wide network of UNIX systems. If your machine is directly or indirectly connected to the Internet, you can send mail to anyone else on the Internet, anywhere in the world. The Internet is organized into a series of *domains:* government, commercial, educational, and so on. Each domain is further divided into a series of *subdomains,* and, in turn, these subdomains are divided into individual machine names, or *hosts.* Some Internet addresses are divided still further. Each system on the Internet has a unique network address, comprised of its domain, subdomain, and host name. Each part of the address is separated by a dot (.). This style addressing is called *domain addressing.* Here are two examples:

```
$ mail sorrel.redwood.COM!kenya
```

and

```
$ mail kenya@sorrel.redwood.COM
```

XENIX   XENIX users would use the former example of the bang addressing format, because XENIX does not support at sign addressing.

In the above examples, **COM** is the domain, **redwood** is the subnet, and **sorrel** is the host machine. **COM** indicates the commercial domain, while **GOV, MIL,** and **EDU** stand for the government, military, and educational domains, respectively. **UUCP** is the domain for the UUCP network.

NOTE   While it is common to capitalize the domain and subdomain of an address, domain addressing is not case specific. That is, the **mail** program does not care whether the Internet address is in upper- or lowercase. The account name is still case sensitive.

If you were indirectly connected to the Internet through another computer, you would specify a path through the network by separating each hop with a bang. For example, the following command would send mail through **chia**, which is connected to the Internet.

```
$ mail chia!sorrel.redwood.COM!kenya
```

 REMEMBER   Domain addressing, whether combined with at sign or bang addressing, has the format *Host-dot-Subnet-dot-Domain.*

The UNIX **mail** program is more intelligent than the XENIX **mail** program. You can specify an address with the bang format or the at format and the UNIX **mail** program will sort out the details and convert it to the proper format before sending the message. For instance, you can specify UUCP addresses with the at sign format as well as with the bang format. The account name is separated from the computer name by an at sign, and successive hops are separated by dots (.). This is similar in format to domain addressing. Using the bang format, you could use the following command to send mail to **sebast** at system **abs**.

```
$ mail helm!orion!abs!sebast
```

On UNIX, using the at sign, you could use this command instead:

```
$ mail sebast@abs.orion.helm
```

The UNIX **mail** program would decode the command and convert it to a form suitable for the network being used.

 REMEMBER   Routed mail using an at sign has the format *User-at-System2-dot-System1*.

 CAUTION   You cannot combine bang and at sign formatting. The bang and at sign should not appear in the same mail address.

On UNIX only, an intelligent router is available. You can send mail to a network and let the network figure out what format to use. For example, the following command would send a letter to **sheila** and let the **uunet** network figure out how to get the mail to system **smokey.**

```
$ mail sheila%smokey@uunet
```

There are various conventions for the many different networks. If your system is connected to another network, such as BITNET or CSNET, you may have to use a completely different format for addressing remote mail. Sometimes it may be necessary to go through one network to use another network, which requires creative and experimental mail addressing. If you have questions about remote mail on your system, ask your system administrator.

 TIP   If you are not certain of your own system address, ask your system administrator, who should know the most reliable path through the network. Others need to know your system address to send you mail from other systems.

Getting Help While Sending Mail

If you need help while sending mail, there are two ways you can get information. If you need help using the **mail** command to send mail, you can use the UNIX on-line manual. If you need help using the tilde escape codes while you are typing a letter, you can display a summary of all the tilde escapes.

To find out more about the **mail** command, its variations, and its options, type

```
$ man mail
```

at the shell prompt. If the UNIX on-line manual pages are installed on your system, **man** will give you a concise summary of all the **mail** functions and options available on your system. A good reference for all the UNIX commands, including **mail**, is the *SCO UNIX User's Guide* or the *SCO UNIX User's Reference*.

To find out more about the tilde escape codes while you are typing a letter in **mail**, type tilde-question mark (**~?**) from within the body of your letter. For example, from within the following letter, typed in UNIX, a tilde-question mark displays the available tilde escape codes.

```
$ mail kenya
Subject: experiment
Evan, I am doing a little experimentation here with mail.
I want to learn the tilde escape codes.
~?
----------------------- ~ ESCAPES -----------------------
~~              Quote a single tilde
~a,~A           Autograph (insert 'sign' variable)
~b users        Add users to Bcc list
~c users        Add users to Cc list
~d              Read in dead.letter file
~e              Edit the message buffer
~f messages     Read in messages, do not right-shift
~h              Prompt for To list, Subject and Cc list
~i string       Insert string into message (~a := ~i sign)
~m messages     Read in messages, right-shifted by a tab
~M messages     Read in messages, do not right-shift
~p              Print the message buffer
~q,~Q           Quit, save letter in $HOME/dead.letter
~r file         Read a file into the message buffer
~s subject      Set subject
~t users        Add users to To list
~v              Invoke display editor on message
~w file         Write message onto file
~x              Quit, do not save letter
~<file          Read a file into the message buffer
~.              End of input
~!command       Run a shell command
~|command       Pipe the message through the command
~^command       Pipe the message through the command
~:command       Execute regular mailx command
~_command       Execute regular mailx command
----------------------------------------------------------
(continue)
```

Receiving Mail

Mail that is sent to you is collected and placed in your mailbox in the system post office. If you have mail, as soon as you log in SCO UNIX displays the message

```
You have mail.
```

You use the **mail** command both to send mail to other users and to retrieve mail sent to you. You can also save, manage, and reply to your incoming mail when you retrieve it. To retrieve your mail from the system post office, type

```
$ mail
```

at the shell prompt.

When you first enter the **mail** program, **mail** shows you a list of the messages you have in your mailbox and allows you to read them in any order you wish. The list of messages might look like this:

```
$ mail
SCO System V Mail (version 3.2) Type ? for help.
"/user/spool/mail/laurak": 3 messages 3 new
 N 3 kenya@redwood.UUCP Tue May 9 01:02 12/343 Hiya. Biya.
 N 2 erich@boulder.UUCP Mon May 8 13:23 12/407 buckeye and rds
>N 1 kenya@redwood.UUCP Mon May 8 12:18 12/360 This is it. Period.
?
```

The **mail** program shows you the sender, date and time sent, size, and subject of each message you have received. The section "Listing Your Messages" later in this chapter tells you more about the message list.

An important concept in **mail** is that of the current message. The *current message* is either the first new message in your mailbox or the last message read. UNIX **mail** marks the current message with a greater-than sign (>), as in the previous example. XENIX **mail**, on the other hand, does not mark the current message. However, in either mail program, if you type an equal sign (=) at the mail prompt, the current message number will be printed. When you use a read, reply, save, or delete command (all described in the following sections) without a message list, your command refers to the current message. For example, if you type a lone **d** (for "delete") and press RETURN while in **mail**, the program will delete the current message.

If you have no messages, **mail** tells you when you check your mailbox, as in the following example.

```
$ mail
No mail in /usr/spool/mail/laurak
$
```

After listing your messages, **mail** displays a prompt. The mail prompt (like the shell prompt) indicates that **mail** is waiting for a command from you. The XENIX mail prompt is an underscore (_), and the UNIX mail prompt is a question mark (?).

Reading Your Messages

There are several ways to read your messages once you are in **mail**. The easiest way is simply to press RETURN after the mail prompt; the next message (or the first new one) in your mailbox will be displayed. To read your messages one by one, continue pressing RETURN after each message until the last message has been displayed. If you press RETURN when you have reached the end of the messages, **mail** responds

```
Can't go beyond last message.
```

This just means **mail** could not find any more messages in your mailbox.

 TIP   By default, messages are not displayed a page at a time. In fact, long messages often scroll off the screen faster than you can read them. Since **mail** does not paginate messages, you will have to freeze the screen to read a long message. You can press CTRL-s to freeze the screen and CTRL-q to release it. You can have UNIX **mail** paginate your messages by setting the **crt** variable in your **.mailrc** file (see "Modifying Your Environment" later in this chapter).

With the dot command (.), you can read the current message. This is especially useful after you delete a message since simply pressing RETURN tends to skip a message.

Another way to read your messages is to type the actual message number at the mail prompt. When **mail** lists your messages it numbers them sequentially, giving the earliest mail the lowest number. Look back at the example message list in the previous section, and observe that the messages are numbered in a column on the left side of the list. To read a message, type its message number at the mail prompt and press RETURN. For example, to read message 1, type **1**, to read message 2, type **2**, and so on.

 NOTE   Typing a message number is a shorthand way to access the **print** command (**p**). For instance, instead of typing **2** at the mail prompt, you might have typed **p 2** and **mail** would have displayed message number 2 in the same way.

Figure 9-2 illustrates several methods of displaying mail.

After reading a message, most likely you will either leave the message in your mailbox, save it in a file, reply to it, or delete it. These **mail** operations are described in the following sections.

The mail Message

Here is a sample of a message received through **mail**:

```
? 2
Message 2:
>From boulder!erich Mon May 8 22:23:25
Received: from boulder by redwood.UUCP id aa00385; Thu, 8 Mar 90
To: laurak@redwood.UUCP
Subject: buckeye and rds
Date: Mon May 8 13:23:19 1990
From: erich@boulder
Message-ID: <9005082223.aa00385@boulder.UUCP>
Status: R

I just got my uunet bill. $35. Forget what I said about
expensive uunet transfers. It's cheap! (as long as go thru
Compuserve).
?
```

Figure 9-2.

```
$ mail
SCO System V Mail (version 3.2) Type ? for help.
"/user/spool/mail/laurak": 3 messages 3 new
 N 3 kenya@redwood.UUCP Tue May 9 01:02 12/343 Hiya. Biya.
 N 2 erich@boulder.UUCP Mon May 8 13:23 12/407 buckeye and rds
>N 1 kenya@redwood.UUCP Mon May 8 12:18 12/360 This is it. Period.
?
Message 1:
From kenya Mon May 8 21:18:59 1990
From: kenya@redwood.UUCP (Evan Fuller)
X-Mailer: SCO System V Mail (version 3.2)
To: laurak
Subject: This is it. Period.
Date: Mon, 8 May 90 12:18:55 PST
Message-ID: <9005082118.aa01301@redwood.UUCP>
Status: R

Laura, I thought you were coming to work today. I am leaving
now. I have to get home early. See you tomorrow.
                Evan
? 3
Message 3:
From kenya Tue May 9 09:02:32 1990
From: kenya@redwood.UUCP (Evan Fuller)
X-Mailer: SCO System V Mail (version 3.2)
To: laurak
Subject: Hiya. Biya.
Date: Tue, 9 May 90 01:02:25 PST
Message-ID: <9005090902.aa03523@redwood.UUCP>
Status: R

I just popped in, but I'm popping back out again. How about
lunch Wednesday? Somewhere cheap.
                Evan
?
Can't go beyond last message.
?
```

Various Ways to Read Mail.

The top two lines of the message (beginning with **From**) are the *postmark*, which is added by the **mail** program. If the message were from a user on the same machine, the message would have a one-line postmark. Since the message was forwarded from a user on another machine, the postmark contains one line for each step the message took on its way to its destination. Material from the postmark to the blank line is called the *message header* and is also created by the **mail** program. The message header contains information such as **To:**, **From:**, **Subject:**, **Date:**, and more. It can be from a few lines to several pages long, depending on the system and the number of steps it takes to reach you. Following the message header is the actual body of the message.

Exiting mail

Eventually, you will want to leave the **mail** program. There are two commands for doing so: **quit (q)** and **exit (x)**.

The **quit** command does two things: First, it removes the messages you have read and saves them in a file called **mbox** in your home directory. Second, it takes you out of the **mail** program. This is the usual way to quit **mail**. Because **quit** removes all the messages you have looked at, leaving **mail** in this way prevents your system mailbox from becoming too cluttered. The following example quits mail, removes two messages from your mailbox, and returns you to the shell prompt.

```
? q
Saved 2 messages in /u/laurak/mbox
Held 0 messages in /usr/spool/mail/laurak.
$
```

If you have held messages in your system mailbox (see the upcoming section "Holding Messages"), **mail** tells you how many. The following example quits mail, leaves two messages in your mailbox, and returns you to the shell prompt.

```
? q
Saved 0 messages in /u/laurak/mbox
Held 2 messages in /usr/spool/mail/laurak.
$
```

XENIX In contrast to UNIX, by default XENIX **mail** does not automatically remove mail from your system mailbox. To prevent excess mail from accumulating, delete messages you have already read with the **d** command (covered later in this chapter in the section "Deleting Messages"), or move them to your **mbox** with the **mbox** command. To make XENIX automatically move the messages you have read to your **mbox** when you quit **mail**, set the environment variable **nohold** in your **.mailrc** file (see "Modifying Your Environment" later in this chapter).

The **exit** command leaves the **mail** program without much ado. It doesn't tidy up your mailbox, and it doesn't move or remove any of your messages. If you often exit **mail** this way and do not delete your messages, your mailbox may become cluttered with old messages that just take up space. The **exit** command is a hasty way to exit **mail**, useful if you want to take care of your mail at a later date. For example, the following example exits **mail** without touching any of the messages, and returns you to the shell prompt.

```
? x
$
```

Listing Your Messages

After you have read a few messages, you may want to see the list of messages in your system mailbox again. The **header** command (**h**) tells **mail** to list your messages as it did when you first entered the program. For example, the list of message headers may look something like this:

```
? h
  N 6 chrisd@azalea Tue May 9 05:44 22/937 clearance
 >P 5 keithj@boulder.UUCP Fri May 19 13:23 46/2012 Using UNIX
  U 4 graham@abs.UUCP Tue May 9 02:18 19/634 Internet stuff
  * 3 kenya@redwood.UUCP Tue May 9 01:02 12/343 Hiya. Biya.
    1 kenya@redwood.UUCP Mon May 8 12:18 12/360 This is it. Period.
?
```

The message list includes a lot of information. The message headers tell you the number, sender, date, time, size, and subject of your messages. They also tell you whether your mail is new, unread, held, saved, or replied to. The code to the left of each message number shows that message's status. The code **N** indicates new messages, and **U** means unread messages. An asterisk (∗) indicates messages that have been saved with a **save** or **write** command. An **M** stands for messages saved in your **mbox**, and **P** marks messages held in your system mailbox with the **hold** or **preserve** command. Messages with no code have already been read. Deleted messages do not appear on the message list.

Again, the greater-than sign (>) marks the current message. The current message is either the first new message in your mailbox or the last message you read.

XENIX   The XENIX **mail** program offers limited status codes, and does not mark the current message. It marks saved messages with an ∗, messages to be put in your **mbox** with an **M**, and held messages with an **H**.

 TIP   If you have a lot of messages in your mailbox, the message list may not show all of your messages at once. Instead, it will show them one screenful at a time. You can display the next screenful of messages with an **h +**, or the previous screenful of messages with **h −**.

Message Lists

Many **mail** commands take a list of messages as an argument. A *message list* is a list of message identifiers, ranges, users, search strings, or message types separated by spaces. If no messsage list is provided, commands that take a message list as an argument use the current message.

Message identifiers can be either message numbers, or one of four special characters. The caret (^), dot (.), and dollar sign ($) specify the first, current, and last messages respectively. The asterisk (∗) specifies all messages.

A *range* of messages is specified with two message identifiers separated by a hyphen. For example, to print all of the messages from the current message to the last message, you would use the command

```
? p .-$
```

A user name in a message list specifies the messages sent by a particular user. For example, to hold the messages from user **kenya**, you would use the command

```
? ho kenya
```

Message lists can include combinations of numbers, ranges, and names. For example, to delete all messages up to message 3 and also messages 8 and 9, you would use the command

```
? d ^-3 8 9
```

Replying to Messages

As you read your messages, **mail** allows you to send a reply to the originator of a message without using a new **mail** command. The **reply** command (**r**) sends mail to the sender of a message. The subject line of the reply automatically holds the subject of the original message. To reply to the current message, type

```
? r
```

at the mail prompt. To reply to a specific message or more than one message, follow the **reply** command with a message list. For the most part, replying to mail is much like sending mail. The only difference is that **mail** does not ask for a subject when it is replying (unless no subject appeared in the original message). The following example uses the **reply** command to reply to a message.

```
Message 1:
From lawton Wed Mar  8 05:32:40 1990
From: lawton@redwood.UUCP (Chris Lawton)
```

```
X-Mailer: SCO System V Mail (version 3.2)
To: book
Subject: report
Date: Wed, 7 Mar 90 21:32:35 PST
Message-ID: <9003080532.aa01301@redwood.UUCP>

Larry:
    My report was supposed to be on your desk late last week.
The report itself was placed in limbo (as per Heidi's orders),
after the system crash.
                    Chris
? r
To: lawton
Subject: report
```

**Chris, don't worry too much. I was going to write you a nasty
note, but I talked to Heidi this morning. Finish your current
project, then work on the report. Thanks.**
                    Larry Book
```
EOT
```

 NOTE A similar command, **Reply (R)**, sends a reply to a specified message, including all recipients of the original message. This command must be used with care; it sends your reply to the sender, as well as every account that received the original message.

Originating Mail from Within mail

You can send a letter from within **mail** with the **m** command. Using **m** from the mail prompt is similar to using the **mail** command at the command line, except that you cannot use redirection or command line options. Follow the **m** command on the same line with one or more accounts to which you want to send mail. For example, to send a letter to two people simultaneously from inside the **mail** program, you might use the command

? **m lawton heidi**

When you send mail from within the **mail** program, you type the subject and the body of your letter, followed by a CTRL-d, just as you do when you are using **mail** from the command line.

```
? m heidi
Subject: Lawton report

Heidi, I sent mail to Chris Lawton this morning about the
report. I think everything is cleared up now. Sorry for being
impatient. I am looking forward to seeing the results of the
new project.
                Larry Book
EOT
```

Deleting Messages

After you have read or replied to your messages, you may want to delete them. In UNIX, unless you indicate otherwise, each message you read is automatically moved to a file named **mbox** in your home directory when you leave mail with **quit**. Often, however, you will not want to keep a record of messages you have received. In this case, you can use the **delete** command (**d**) to delete messages. To delete the message you have just read—that is, the current message—type

```
? d
```

at the mail prompt. You can delete a specific message or delete more than one message by following the **delete** command with a message list.

 REMEMBER   Use the dot command (.) to print the next message after one you have deleted. If you just press RETURN, you will skip one message.

XENIX   Note that in XENIX, by default, messages you have read are not automatically moved to your **mbox** when you leave **mail** with **quit**.

Messages that are deleted are not actually removed from your mailbox, but are placed in limbo until you use the **quit** command to leave **mail**. You can bring them back to the land of the living with the **undelete** command (**u**), as long as you have not used **quit** to leave **mail**. When you use **undelete**, you specify messages that you have previously deleted. Once you have exited with **quit**, though, you can no longer undelete previously deleted messages; they have been permanently removed.

Holding Messages

If you wish to prevent your messages from being removed from your mailbox when you use **quit** to leave **mail**, you can use the **hold** command (**ho**) to hold your messages in your mailbox. To hold a message you have just read, type

```
? ho
```

at the mail prompt. To hold a specific message or more than one message, follow **hold** with a message list.

In the message list, held messages are indicated with a **P** (for "preserved") in UNIX and an **H** (for "held") in XENIX (see the section "Listing Your Messages" earlier in this chapter). When you **quit**, if you have held messages in your system mailbox, **mail** will remind you. For example:

```
Held 2 messages in /usr/spool/mail/laurak.
```

Saving Messages

Occasionally, you may want to save a message as a file for future reference. Perhaps you want to edit or print the file separately. Or someone may have sent you a program that you want to compile. Use the **save** command (**s**) to save a message to a file. To save the message you have just read (the current message) to a file called **report**, you would type

```
? s report
```

at the mail prompt. If **report** already existed, the message would be appended to the bottom of the file. You can follow the **save** command with a message list to specify a certain file or a group of files to be saved under one name. For example, to save messages 2, 4, 5, and 6 in a file called **letters.home**, you would type

```
? s 2 4-6 letters.home
```

Another way to save a message to a file is with the **write** command (**w**), which is virtually identical to **save**, except it does not include the postmark or the message header (the block of text that identifies the sender, recipient, subject, and so on) in the file. This command is useful for saving files in which the header is a bother, such as programs and scripts.

Messages saved with either **save** or **write** are marked in the message list with an asterisk (∗). If you leave **mail** with the **quit** command, saved messages are deleted from your mailbox.

 NOTE   To keep a saved message in your mailbox, use the **hold** command described previously in the section "Holding Messages."

Getting Help While Reading Mail

You can get a brief summary of the important **mail** commands by asking **mail** for help. This is useful when you've forgotten which command does what or how a particular command works. Type the **help** command at the mail prompt to get help. For example, from within UNIX **mail help** produces the following list:

```
? help
              mailx commands
type [msglist]          print messages
next                    goto and type next message
edit [msglist]          edit messages
from [msglist]          give header lines of messages
delete [msglist]        delete messages
undelete [msglist]      restore deleted messages
save [msglist] file     append messages to file
reply [message]         reply to message, including all recipients
Reply [msglist]         reply to the authors of the messages
preserve [msglist]      preserve messages in mailbox
mail user               mail to specific user
```

```
quit                    quit, preserving unread messages
xit                     quit, preserving all messages
header                  print page of active messageheaders
!                       shell escape
cd [directory]          chdir to directory or home if none given
list                    list all commands (no explanations)
top [msglist]           print top 5 lines of messages
z [-]                   display next [last] page of 10 headers
[msglist] is optional and specifies messages by number, author,
subject or type. The default is the current message.
```

You can get a comprehensive list of the **mail** commands by typing **list** at the mail prompt. Unfortunately, no explanations for the commands are provided with this list. For example, typing **list** from within UNIX **mail** provides the following list:

```
? list
Commands are:
next, print, alias, type, Type, Print, visual, top, touch, preserve,
delete, dp, dt, undelete, unset, mail, Mail, mbox, !, copy, Copy,
chdir, cd, save, Save, source, set, shell, version, group, write,
forward, Forward, from, file, folder, folders, ?, z, headers, help, =,
Reply, Respond, reply, respond, edit, echo, quit, lpr, list, xit, exit,
size, hold, if, else, endif, alternates, ignore, discard, #, pipe, |
```

For further help in using **mail** see the *SCO UNIX User's Guide* or the *SCO UNIX User's Reference*.

Modifying Your Environment

In this section, you will learn how to customize your mail environment by modifying a special file known as the **.mailrc** file. You will learn how to use the **alias** command to create mailing lists and abbreviate long mailing addresses. You will also learn how to **set** and **unset** environment variables to change your mail environment.

Modifying Your .mailrc File

Every time you start **mail**, it executes the commands contained in the personal startup file, **.mailrc**, located in your home directory. The most common use of the **.mailrc** file is to set up display options and alias lists, which are described in the following sections. An error in the **.mailrc** file will cause the remaining lines in the file to be ignored. Aliases and environment variables are especially useful in your **.mailrc** file. The following example shows a typical **.mailrc** file on a UNIX system. Lines that begin with pound signs (#) are comments.

```
$ cat .mailrc
# alias for mailing to myself
alias me        laurak
# alias to simplify Graham's mailing address
alias graham    helm!orion!abs!graham
# alias for others in project
alias project   lawton book heidi
# do not ignore interrupts while entering messages
unset ignore
# askcc: prompt for "carbon copy" list after message is entered.
# asksub: prompt for subject if not specified on command line
# chron: list messages in chronological order
set askcc asksub chron
# append: puts messages at end of mbox instead of beginning
# keepsave: keeps saved messages instead of deleting them
set append keepsave
# cause long messages to be paginated
set crt=23
# signature inserted into text with ~a command
set sign="=\nLaura Kingston"
```

The next example shows a typical **.mailrc** file on a XENIX system.

```
$ cat .mailrc
# alias for mailing to myself
alias me        laurak
# alias to simplify Graham's mailing address
alias graham    helm!orion!abs!graham
# alias for others in project
alias project   lawton book heidi
# do not ignore interrupts while entering messages
unset ignore
```

```
# askcc: prompt for "carbon copy" list after message is entered.
# asksubject: prompt for subject if not specified on command line
# chron: list messages in chronological order
# autombox: messages that have been read are put in the mbox file
set askcc asksubject chron autombox
# cause long messages to be paginated
set page=23
```

 NOTE Similar to the **.mailrc** file, the optional system-wide mail startup file **/usr/lib/mail/mailrc** is executed before the **.mailrc** file. It sets initial parameters for all the users on the system.

Aliases

With the **alias** command you can create personal mailing lists or abbreviate long mailing addresses. For example, to create an alias for a list of people involved in a project, you might include the line

```
alias project   lawton book heidi
```

in your **.mailrc** file. The alias **project** could then be used in place of the user names **lawton, book,** and **heidi.** To send a letter to all the people that make up the alias, you would simply type

$ **mail project**

at the shell prompt.

To abbreviate a long mailing address, you might use the line

```
alias graham    helm!orion!abs!graham
```

in your **.mailrc** file. Then, instead of typing the long mailing address, you could simply type

$ **mail graham**

Environment Variables

You can customize your **mail** environment with the **set** and **unset** commands. Environment variables are of two types: switch and string. A *switch* variable is either on or off (set or unset). A *string* variable takes a value that is a pathname, a number, or a single character. The following line in your **.mailrc** file would set a switch variable.

```
set chron
```

Including this line in your **.mailrc** file would set a string variable:

```
set VISUAL=/bin/vi
```

The environment variables are listed in detail in the UNIX on-line manual and in the *SCO UNIX User's Reference*.

The **mail** command is used from the shell prompt to both send and receive mail. The command followed by one or more account names sends mail. When you are sending a letter, the tilde escape codes allow you to print your letter up to any point, make changes with the visual editor, and much more. The **mail** command alone retrieves your mail from the system post office. When retrieving your mail, you may read, save, manage, and reply to your messages from the mail prompt.

The **mail** program offers simplicity, speed, and relative dependability. Neither rain, nor sleet, nor dead of night will keep **mail** from its appointed rounds.

The Bourne Shell

When you log in to an SCO UNIX system, you communicate with one of several command interpreters. This chapter discusses the Bourne shell command interpreter, **sh.** The shell is a UNIX program that supports a powerful command language. The shell reads and executes commands from its standard input. It can function as a user interface, translating and executing your commands one by one as you enter them at the command line, or it can function as a programming language, reading commands from a file and executing them one after another.

The Bourne shell gives you the capabilities of a high-level programming language through shell scripts. What would take several lines with a traditional programming language takes only a few lines in a shell script. With the shell, commands can be combined, passed parameters, added or renamed, executed within loops or executed conditionally, and executed in the background. You can redirect command input from any source and redirect command output to a file, terminal, printer, or to another command.

Shells, Commands, and Scripts

When you log in to SCO UNIX, you are assigned a shell from which you operate. This shell is your *login shell*. It is your own copy of the command interpreter, and it reads your commands from the keyboard. When you type a command, your login shell starts a new process to execute the command. The new process is a *child* of your login shell. Conversely, the shell is the *parent* of the new process. A child of the login shell can start a new process, which, in turn, can start another new process, and so on. At any moment, you may have several processes running: your login shell, and also its many levels of descendants.

You can even start a new copy of the command interpreter while you are logged in. This new copy of the shell is called a *subshell*. You can terminate a subshell and return to the parent process by typing **exit** or simply pressing CTRL-d at the command line. You terminate your login shell by typing either **exit** or **logout**.

When you type a command at the keyboard, the shell assumes the command is the name of an executable file (along with its arguments). If the command is a compiled program, the shell creates a child process that immediately executes that program. If the file is executable, but is not a compiled program, it is assumed to be a shell script. When the shell executes a shell script, it creates a subshell to read the file and execute the commands inside it.

A *shell script* is nothing more than an executable text file containing shell commands. When you execute a shell script, you create a subshell that gets its input from a file, instead of from the keyboard. Any command that you can type interactively at the keyboard is valid in a shell script, including UNIX utilities, compiled programs, or other shell scripts. As with other commands you give interactively, a command in a shell script can include wildcard file references, input and output redirection, command substitution, and piping. Redirection and piping can also be used with the input and output of the shell script itself, allowing you to use scripts as filters.

 NOTE   Though both the Bourne shell and the C shell support shell scripts, it is often preferable to use Bourne shell scripts. A Bourne shell script will run properly whether it is executed from the Bourne or the C shell, while a C shell script will only run from the C shell. Furthermore, it is important to learn about Bourne shell scripts, because most of the scripts you come across will be written for the Bourne shell.

When you execute a shell script, a new subshell is created to read the commands inside the script. Changes made within the shell script do not affect the parent shell. With the dot (.) command, you can have the current shell read and execute a shell script, without creating a new subshell. Thus, all the changes made by the shell script remain in effect after the script finishes. You would commonly use the dot command to reinitialize your login shell by reading the **.profile** file in your home directory with the command

```
$ . .profile
```

To run another command in place of the current shell, use the **exec** command. This does not create a new process, but replaces the current shell with the new command. For example, to begin the C shell in place of the current shell, you would type

```
$ exec csh
```

Shell Variables

A *variable* is a name that may be assigned a value. The value may be any string of characters: a number, a word, or a line. The shell has variables that you create and assign values, as well as variables that are set by the shell itself. *User variables,* which are created and assigned values by the user, allow you to store and manipulate values for later use. *Environment vari-*

ables are maintained by the shell, but can be reset by the user. These variables have special meanings to the shell. *Positional parameters* are set by the shell when a shell script is invoked. They are taken directly from the command line. *Special variables* are set by the shell and cannot be changed. These allow you to access information about the shell, such as the number of parameters, process numbers, and exit status. The following sections describe the shell variables in detail and introduce several commands that help you manage them.

User Variables

A user variable assignment has the form

NAME=string

A variable name can be any sequence of letters, digits, or underscores that begins with a letter. Conventionally, user variables in the Bourne shell are all capital letters. No spaces can appear before or after the equal sign. Once a variable is assigned, a dollar sign references the variable. After the previous variable assignment, *$NAME* would yield the value *string* in a command line. In the following example, the variable **CITY** is assigned the value **Opelousas.**

```
$ CITY=Opelousas
```

The contents of the variable can be displayed with the **echo** command, as shown in the following example. Notice that without the dollar sign, the shell does not recognize the variable name as a variable.

```
$ echo $CITY
Opelousas
$ echo CITY
CITY
```

Because of the leading dollar sign, the shell recognizes **$CITY** as a variable reference. Whenever the shell encounters a reference to a variable, it immediately substitutes the value of the variable and passes this value along to be executed.

 CAUTION Be careful not to confuse the Bourne shell dollar sign prompt in the examples with the dollar sign that precedes a variable reference.

You can put more than one assignment on a single line. For example, the following command sets three variables at once.

```
$ CITY=Keeler  COUNTY=Inyo  STATE=California
```

When you assign a variable, you must put double quotation marks around values that contain spaces or tabs. Without double quotes, the shell will assume that the first word is the variable's value and that succeeding words are commands. You must also put double quotes around variable references that might contain multiple spaces or tabs to preserve their spacing. If no quotes are present, multiple spaces or tabs are treated as single spaces. The following example demonstrates both of these situations. In each case, omitting the quotes produces undesirable effects.

```
$ CITY=Pine Mountain
Mountain: not found
$ CITY="Pine Mountain"
$ echo $CITY
Pine Mountain

$ COUNTY="Chattahoochee        County"
$ echo $COUNTY
Chattahoochee County
$ echo "$COUNTY"
Chattahoochee        County
```

 NOTE Another way to deal with values that contain spaces or tabs is to escape individual spaces and tabs by preceding each with a backslash (\).

 TIP Characters that have special meanings to the shell, such as $ * ? and ( ) must be quoted with single quotes or escaped with a backslash. Because the shell always interprets a dollar sign as a variable reference, and because asterisks, question marks, and square brackets are used as wildcard characters in the shell, difficulties often arise in displaying these characters. To prevent variable and wildcard substitution, use a backslash (\) to escape special characters, or surround the text with single quotes ('). Other characters that may give surprising results unless quoted are quotes themselves, the newline, space, and tab characters, and the symbols **; & () | ^ <>.**

With the **read** command, your script can prompt the user for information and store the input in a user variable. The **read** command reads one line from standard input and assigns it to one or more variables. The next example reads one line of user input with the **read** command, and then displays the results with **echo**.

```
$ read CITY STATE
Laconia New Hampshire
$ echo $STATE
New Hampshire
$ echo $CITY
Laconia
```

You can read words into one or more variables by supplying the **read** command with a series of variable names. The **read** command assigns one word to each variable. If you have more words than variables, the last variable is assigned the remaining words. If you have more variables than words, the extra variables are left unassigned.

Environment Variables

When a new process is created, the *environment* is the collection of variables and their contents that is passed to the new child process. The environment contains information that is used by commands you execute, such as your home directory, your login name, or your terminal type. The variables usually contained in the environment are the *environment variables*.

Most of the environment variables are either inherited from a parent process or assigned by your login shell when it is started. The environment variables are initially set in your **.profile** file, which is executed when you first log in. The **.profile** file is discussed later, in the section "Modifying

Your Environment." The following list explains many of the important environment variables.

HOME   This variable stores the location of your home directory, in which many of your important files and subdirectories are kept. It is preferable to use this variable in your shell scripts, rather than the actual path to your home directory, so that your scripts can be used by others without modification. The **cd** command without arguments defaults to the **$HOME** directory.

PATH   This variable specifies the search path that the shell uses to find commands specified on the command line. The *search path* is an ordered list of directory pathnames separated by colons. The shell searches the directories of this list one after another when it looks for a command. The following line in your **.profile** sets your search path (the final dot specifies the current directory as part of the path).

```
PATH=/bin:/usr/bin:/u/bin:$HOME/bin:.
```

MAIL   The **MAIL** variable specifies the name of the file to check for new mail. If this variable is set, the shell tells you if new mail has arrived when you return to the command line. **MAIL** is not set automatically and should be set in your **.profile**. The following line in your **.profile** specifies your mail file.

```
MAIL=/usr/spool/mail/$LOGNAME
```

MAILPATH   This extension of the **MAIL** variable specifies files in which to check for new mail and the messages to print if new mail has arrived. If **MAILPATH** is set, the shell will tell you if mail has arrived in any of the specified files when you return to the command line. The variable contains a list of files separated by colons. Placing a percent sign and a message after a file name specifies the message the shell will print if that file is modified. If no message is specified, the default is "you have mail." The following line in your **.profile** specifies your mail file and the notification message.

```
MAILPATH=$MAIL%"Mail call!!"
```

MAILCHECK   This variable specifies how often (in seconds) the shell checks for the arrival of mail in the files specified by **MAIL** and **MAIL-PATH**. The default is 600 seconds, or 10 minutes.

SHELL   This variable specifies the default shell in your environment. It is used by many commands, such as **tset**.

TERM   This variable identifies your terminal type. You must set this variable if you are editing with the **vi** editor and before you configure your terminal with **tset**. **TERM** is usually set within your **.profile** file.

LOGNAME   This variable holds your account name, or login name. It is always preferable to use this variable in your shell scripts instead of your actual account name, so that your scripts can be used by others without modification. In XENIX, it is not automatically set and should be set in your **.profile** using the **logname** command.

PS1   This variable specifies the Bourne shell prompt, the string that appears on the command line when the shell is interactive. The default value for the Bourne shell prompt is a dollar sign and a space.

PS2   This variable defines the secondary prompt. When the shell expects more input after you press RETURN, it prompts with this string. The default value for the secondary prompt is a greater-than sign and a space.

CDPATH   This variable specifies the search path of the **cd** command, and provides the command with a list of directories in which to look one after another for the specified subdirectory. Each directory in the list is separated by a colon.

You can access the contents of any variable in the environment from the command line or from a shell script. However, if changes are made to the content of a variable, these changes are not reflected in the environment; they only affect the current shell or shell script. For the changes to be placed in the environment that the shell passes to its child processes, the variables must be named as arguments to the **export** command. The following lines in a shell script would change the contents of the **SHELL** environment variable and place it in the environment of the shell script.

```
SHELL=/bin/sh
export SHELL
```

You can **export** several environment variables at once, as the following line demonstrates.

```
export HOME PATH MAIL MAILCHECK PS1 SHELL
```

You can also print a list of all the variables in the current environment with the **env** command, as in the following example.

```
$ env
HOME=/u/laurak
PATH=/bin:/usr/bin:/u/bin:/u/laurak/bin:.
LOGNAME=laurak
TERM=wy50vb
HZ=100
TZ=PST8PDT
MAIL=/usr/spool/mail/laurak
MAILCHECK=1
NAME=Laura Kingston
SHELL=/bin/sh
```

XENIX   With XENIX, you use **printenv** instead of **env** to print a list of the variables in the current environment.

Positional Parameters

When a shell script is invoked, the shell stores each word of the command line in variables **$0** to **$9**. Since these variables specify the position of the words on the command line, they are called *positional parameters*. The variable **$0** typically holds the name of the calling program, because it is usually the first word of the command line. Variables **$1** through **$9** hold up to nine arguments of the calling program. The following lines from a shell script display the calling program and the first three arguments to the command.

```
echo "Calling program: $0"
echo "Argument 1: $1"
echo "Argument 2: $2"
echo "Argument 3: $3"
```

The **shift** command shifts each of the command line arguments one position to the left. Argument one is lost, argument two becomes argument one, and so on. This command can also be used to access arguments in positions numbered higher than nine. The following lines from a shell script use the **shift** command to remove the **-h** command line option and its argument.

```
if test "$1" = "-h"   # test if first argument is -h
then                   # if it is a -h
   HEADER=$2 ; shift ; shift  # set HEADER=2nd arg, lose 1 & 2
else                   # if its not -h
   HEADER="Report"     # set variable HEADER to "Report"
fi
pr -h "$HEADER" $*     # display all the files w/header using pr
```

 NOTE   Text to the right of a pound sign (#) is a comment and is ignored by the shell.

The **$*** parameter gives all of the command line arguments, not just the first nine. Its best use is to pass the parameters of a shell script on to another command, as in the previous example.

The **set** command allows you to force the values of the positional parameters. The arguments that follow the **set** command are used to set the command line argument variables (**$1** to **$9**). The line

```
set Mendocino California
```

sets the positional parameters **$1** and **$2** to **Mendocino** and **California**, respectively. The parameter **$0** may not be given a value with **set**. A useful application of **set** is to extract information displayed in columnar form, using backquote substitution. For example, the following lines from a shell script extract the second column from the output of **who**.

```
set `who | grep $USER`
TERMINAL=$2
```

Special Variables

Special variables are set by the shell and cannot be changed. These variables give you information about the shell, such as the number of parameters, process numbers, and exit status.

Closely related to the positional parameters, the $# variable gives the number of parameters on the command line (not including parameter $0). The following line from a shell script uses the $# variable.

```
echo "$# files to view"
```

The $$ variable holds the process identification number of the current process. The $$ variable is often used to generate unique names for temporary files. Using the process number as part of a file name ensures that there will be no file name conflicts. If you place your temporary files in the **/tmp** directory, the system will automatically remove them when they are no longer needed.

The $! variable holds the process identification number of the last process you ran in the background using the ampersand. It is useful if you want a shell script to automatically kill or report on a process placed in the background. The following example uses the $! variable to kill a sort executed as a background process.

```
$ sort bigfile > sorted &
4610
$ kill -9 $!
4610 Killed
```

The $? variable holds the exit status of the last command executed. When a process stops, naturally or otherwise, it returns an *exit status*, sometimes called *a condition code* or a *return code*, to the parent process. A nonzero exit code indicates that the command failed. A zero indicates that the command succeeded.

NOTE   Your shell scripts can return an exit status with the **exit** command.

Shell Programming

The following sections tell you how to create and execute shell scripts. Additionally, they cover commenting and programming style. Any command or variable that can be used at the command line can also be used in a shell script; thus, all of the sections in this chapter will help you become a better shell programmer.

Shell Scripts

To make a shell script, you have to create the text file and reset the permissions to make the file executable. To create the text file, you can use a text editor such as **vi** (discussed in Chapter 7). The text file you create will not have execute permission set, so you must use the **chmod** command (see Chapter 4) to change the access permissions of your shell script.

For example, you can create a shell script called **mkremind**, that will maintain a hidden file, **.reminder**, in your home directory in which you can compile one-line notes to yourself. Then, you can create another shell script that retrieves these notes. After you create the text file with **vi**, you can display it with the **cat** command, as in the following example:)

```
$ cat mkremind
:
# @(#)mkremind -- Enter a one-line reminder
#    Created: Karri Modes      28 Apr 90
#
echo "Enter reminder (one line):"
line >> $HOME/.reminder
```

NOTE It is conventional to begin Bourne shell scripts with a single colon (:) on a line by itself. This represents a *null* ("do nothing") command, which makes it obvious that the script is to be interpreted by the Bourne shell.

NOTE The symbol @(#) allows you or another user to get a summary of the script using the **what** command. If you supply the script file name as argument to the **what** command, all the lines in the script containing **@(#)** will be displayed. To see what an unknown script does, you might use the command

```
% what mkremind
```

Next, you must set the proper permissions to make the shell script executable. If you tried to execute the script now, the shell would not recognize **mkremind** as an executable file and would display an error message, such as

```
$ mkremind
mkremind: execute permission denied
```

Use the **chmod** command to give yourself, the owner, execute permission. The **ls** command with the **-l** option lists the access privileges for the **mkremind** file before and after the **chmod** command, as shown here:

```
$ ls -l mkremind
-rw-r--r--   1 modes    group       69 Aug 19 13:46 mkremind
$ chmod u+x mkremind
$ ls -l mkremind
-rwxr--r--   1 modes    group       69 Aug 19 13:46 mkremind
```

At this point, the file **mkremind** is executable.

To run a shell script, simply type its file name at the command line. The shell executes all the commands in the script, one after another. Returning to the previous example, you can run the **mkremind** script by typing **mkremind** at the command line, and then type a one-line note to yourself, as shown here:

```
$ mkremind
Enter reminder (one line):
Don't forget to turn off the coffee pot!
```

As promised, you can create another useful shell script to retrieve the reminders from the **.reminder** file. You already have the script **mkremind**, which allows you to enter a reminder. This new script will be called **remind**, and will allow you to see the notes you have entered. The following example creates the text file **remind**, sets the proper permissions, and runs the shell script.

```
$ cat remind
:
# @(#) remind - Display hidden reminder file
#   created: Karri Modes      28 Apr 90
#
echo "Notes:"
more -10 $HOME/.reminder

$ chmod u+x remind
$ remind
Notes:
Don't forget to turn off the coffee pot!
```

Comments and Programming Style

It is important to write your shell scripts so that others can read them and understand what they do. You can make your scripts easier to understand with comments and formatting. The pound sign (#) allows you to enter a comment in your shell script. If you put the pound sign at the beginning of a line, the shell will ignore the line. If you put it after a command, the shell will ignore the remainder of the line. The following example demonstrates a well-commented shell script.

```
$ cat remind
:
# @(#) remind -- Display hidden reminder file
#   created:  Karri Modes           28 Apr 88
#   modified: Katherine Williams  28 Mar 89
#   modified: Sebastian Graham    12 Jun 90
#
FILE="$HOME/.reminder"                # create variable
if [ ! -r $FILE ]                     # is file readable?
then                                  # if not readable
   echo "remind: Cannot open $FILE"   # print error message
   exit 1                             # exit with error code
else                                  # if readable
   echo "Notes:"                      # print heading
   more -10 $FILE                     # display file a bit at a time
fi
```

This simple script may not need such elaborate documentation; however, as a script grows in size and complexity, it becomes more and more important to know who created it, who has modified it, what the script does, and how it works. Comments are essential to good programming. Scripts that you write will often be modified and maintained by other people, who will need your comments to understand them. Good commenting saves time and money.

You can make your shell scripts easier to read by formatting them carefully. Indent each level of a conditional command, and the body of a looping command. Indentation does not affect the execution of your script; the shell ignores initial spaces and tabs. In the previous example, the **then** and **else** part of the conditional command are indented, clearly showing the control structures in the script. In addition to indenting, you can use white space in the form of blank lines or empty comment lines to set off parts of a script.

Supporting Commands

The following sections discuss commands that are useful at the command line and in shell scripts. These commands are most useful when combined with other commands, such as the control commands discussed later in this chapter.

Conditional Evaluation: test

The **test** command tests certain conditions and returns the results in the form of an exit status. If the condition is true, the **test** command returns a zero exit status. If the condition is false, it returns a nonzero value. The **test** command is used to evalutate conditional expressions for control commands, such as **if, while,** and **until.** In the following example, which tests the equality of two strings, the $? variable returns the status of the comparison.

```
$ test "one" = "two"
$ echo $?
1
```

Here is a list of **test** command options and their meanings:

Parentheses

( )   group or change the order of operation

Logical Operators

!   negation

-a   AND

-o   OR

Strings

-z *s1*   true if the length of string *s1* is zero

-n *s1*   true if the length of string *s1* is nonzero

s1 = *s2*   true if strings *s1* and *s2* are identical

s1 != *s2*   true if strings *s1* and *s2* are *not* identical

Numbers

n1 **-eq** *n2*   true if the integers *n1* and *n2* are algebraically equal

                        The following operators may be substituted for **-eq**

n1 **-ne** *n2*   not equal

n1 **-gt** *n2*   greater than

n1 **-ge** *n2*   greater than or equal

n1 **-lt** *n2*   less than

n1 **-le** *n2*   less than or equal

Files

-r *file*	true if *file* exists and is readable
-w *file*	true if *file* exists and is writable
-x *file*	true if *file* exists and is executable
-f *file*	true if *file* exists and is a regular file
-d *file*	true if *file* exists and is a directory
-s *file*	true if *file* exists and is not empty

 NOTE All of the operators and flags are separate arguments to **test**, and must be separated by spaces. Because parentheses are meaningful to the shell, they must be escaped with the backslash (\).

The following lines from a shell script demonstrate a more complicated example of the **test** command.

```
if
    test \( ! -z $FILE \) -a \( -r $FILE \)
then
    echo "Readable: $FILE"
fi
```

You can abbreviate the **test** command with square brackets ([ ]). Simply place square brackets around what would be the options or arguments to the command. For example, the following line from a shell script

```
if test -s .reminder
```

could also be written

```
if [ -s .reminder ]
```

You must leave spaces between the arguments and the brackets or **test** will not work.

Control Commands

The *control commands* change the order of execution of the commands in your shell script. The following sections discuss conditional commands, looping commands, and the termination command. A *conditional command* executes a set of commands only if certain conditions are met. A *looping command* executes a set of commands several times. The **exit** command ends a shell script or interactive shell session.

Conditional Commands: if

One form of the **if** command is the **if..then** construction, which works like this: *If some condition is met, then execute the following commands.* The **if..then** construction has the following format:

```
if
    test-command
then
    commands
fi
```

The **if** and **then** statements must appear on separate lines. The **fi** (*if* spelled backward) statement marks the end of the **if..then** construction. The shell will execute the commands following **then** only if the last command following **if** returns a true, or nonzero, exit status.

 REMEMBER   You can use the **test** command with any **if** construction to return an exit status based on the result of a test. Remember, you can employ square brackets ([ ]) as a synonym for the **test** command, but each bracket must be preceded and followed by a space.

The following shell script illustrates the **if..then** construction used with **test** (implied by square brackets) to check that an argument was specified.

```
$ cat pformat
:
# @(#)pformat -- format a file with pr
#
if [ -z $1 ]      # is argument specified?
then              # if no argument specified
   echo "pformat: No filename specified."
   echo "Usage: pformat file"
fi
pr -d -o5 -f $*  # pr w/spacing=2,offset=5,form feeds
```

Another form of the **if** command is the **if..then..else** construction. The idea is simply this: *If some condition is met, then execute one set of commands, or else, if the condition is not met, execute another set of commands.* The format for the command is as follows:

> **if**
> > *test-command*
>
> **then**
> > *commands*
>
> **else**
> > *commands*
>
> **fi**

As you can see, the **fi** statement also ends the **if..then..else** construction.

The following shell script illustrates the **if..then..else** construction, using **test** to check the user's system mailbox for mail.

```
$ cat mailchk
:
# @(#)mailchk -- check if mail has arrived
#
# -s option true if file not empty
if [ -s "$MAIL" ]
then
   echo "You have mail, and here it is!"
   mail
else
   echo "So sorry, maybe later we'll have something for you."
   exit 1
fi
```

The final form of the **if** command is the **if..then..elif** construction. It is like **if..then..else**, but combines the **else** and another **if..then** into one statement: *If some condition is met, then execute one set of commands, or else, if the condition is not met, consider another if statement with another condition.* The **elif** statement is a combination of **else** and **if**. This structure allows you to create a set of nested **if..then..else** constructions. It has the following format:

> **if**
> > *test-command*
>
> **then**
> > *commands*
>
> **elif**
> > *test-commands*
>
> **then**
> > *commands*
>
> **fi**

The shell script **copy** demonstrates the **if..then..elif** instructions.

```
$ cat zcopy
:
# @(#)zcopy -- copy a file to directory
#
if [ ! -f $1 ]          # is first argument a regular file?
then                    # if not a regular file
   echo "zcopy: $1 is not a regular file."
elif [ ! -d $2 ]        # is second argument a directory?
then                    # if not a directory
   echo "zcopy: $2 is not a directory."
else                    # if args are file and directory
   cp $1 $2             # copy file to directory
fi
```

The Multiple Choice Command: case

The **case** construction has a multiple choice format that matches one of several patterns and executes a corresponding set of commands. It has the format

```
case word in
  pattern1)
    commands ;;
  pattern2)
    commands ;;
  pattern3)
    commands ;;
  *)
    commands ;;
esac
```

Word is often a variable or command substitution. The ;; symbol marks the end of a set of commands for a particular branch of the **case**. The **esac** statement marks the end of the **case** construction (*esac* is *case* spelled backward).

As a pattern, the asterisk (∗) matches any string of characters. It is often used as the last pattern in the **case** construction to match input that does not match any other pattern, thus providing a useful way to detect erroneous or unexpected input.

Other patterns you can specify are the characters ?, [ ], and |. The question mark matches any single character. The square brackets match any single character contained within the brackets. A hyphen between two characters within the brackets specifies a range of characters. The vertical bar separates alternate choices of the **case** construction. The input may match either of the patterns separated by the vertical bar.

The following shell script **hint** illustrates the **case** construction and the available patterns.

```
$ cat hint
:
# @(#)hint -- Print a hint on directory command usage
#
case $1 in
    pwd|PWD)        # is the first argument "pwd"
        echo "pwd - Print Working Directory Name"
        echo "usage: pwd" ;;
    cd|CD)          # is the first argument "cd"
        echo "cd - Change Directory"
        echo "usage: cd [directory]" ;;
    *)              # otherwise
```

```
        echo "hint - Explain a directory command"
        echo "Usage: hint [command]" ;;
esac
```

Looping Commands: *for*

The **for..in** loop executes a set of commands once for each member of a list.
It has the format

> **for** *variable*
>   **in** *argument-list*
> **do**
>   *commands*
> **done**

For each repetition of the loop, the next member of the list is assigned to
the variable given after the **for** statement. This variable can be used within
the commands of the loop, as in the following example.

```
$ cat receipts
:
# @(#) receipts -- record day's cash receipts in 3 databases
#
echo "Input today's cash totals:"
read CASH                  # read in variable CASH
for DATABASE               # DATABASE set to each file in turn
   in general.db cash.db revenue.db
do                         # place text in each file
   echo `date +"%a %d %h"` "total: $CASH" >> $DATABASE
done
```

Another form of the **for** loop executes a set of commands once for each
argument of the command line. It has the format

> **for** *variable*
> **do**
>   *commands*
> **done**

For each repetition of the loop, the next argument of the command line is assigned to the variable after the **for** statement. This variable can be used anywhere within the commands of the loop. The following example shows the use of the **for** loop.

```
$ cat grab
:
# @(#)grab -- copy files from a directory to current
#    created: Greg Porter          1 Jun 90
# if [ -z "$2" ]            # is there a 1st and 2nd argument?
then                        # if arguments missing
    echo "Usage: grab dir file1 [file2] [file3]..."
    exit 1
fi
DIR=$1                      # first arg is directory
shift                       # remove directory from arg list
for FILE                    # FILE set to each arg in turn
do
    cp $DIR/$FILE .         # copy file to current directory
done
```

Conditional Looping: while and until

Another looping command, the **while** loop, repeatedly executes a set of commands while some particular condition is met. It has the following format:

> **while**
>   *test-command*
> **do**
>   *commands*
> **done**

The shell will execute the commands following **do** as long as the last command following **while** returns a true, or nonzero, exit status.

 REMEMBER The **test** command can be used with the **while** loop to return an exit status based on the result of a test. As before, the square brackets ([ ]) can be used as a synonym for the **test** command (again, each bracket must be surrounded by spaces). The **test** command was discussed earlier, in the section "Supporting Commands."

The following shell script illustrates the **while** loop using **test** (implicitly specified with the square brackets) to check the user's input for empty lines.

```
$ cat addendum
:
# @(#)addendum -- Add text to a file
#
echo "Enter addendum (end with empty line):"
INPUT="anything"
while [ -n "$INPUT" ]                  # is input blank?
do                                     # if input is not blank
    read INPUT                         # read a line
    echo $INPUT >> $1                  # append to file
done
```

The **until** and **while** loops are very similar. Whereas the **while** loop repeats its commands *while* some particular condition is met, the **until** loop repeats its commands *until* some particular condition is met. The difference lies in what causes **until** and **while** loops to stop looping. The conditions specified in a **while** loop indicate the conditions under which the loop is to repeat. The conditions specified in an **until** loop indicate the conditions that will cause the loop to stop. The **until** loop has the following format:

> **until**
>   *test-command*
> **do**
>   *commands*
> **done**

The shell will execute the commands following **do** until the last command following **until** returns a true, or nonzero, exit status.

The following shell script illustrates the **until** loop.

```
$ cat lsd
:
# @(#)lsd -- list directories back to root
#
CURRDIR=`pwd`                # get current directory
until [ $CURRDIR = "/" ]     # repeat until current dir is root
do
```

```
      CURRDIR=`pwd`          # get new current directory
      ls -ld $CURRDIR        # list directory
      cd ..                  # go back one directory
done
```

Controlling Loops: break and continue

You can interrupt a **for**, **while**, or **until** loop with a **break** or **continue** command. The **break** command exits the loop completely, transferring control to the command that follows the **done** statement. The **continue** command immediately begins the next execution of the loop, transferring control to the **done** statement, which continues the loop.

You can use the **break** to exit a loop when something comes up that was not originally in the loop condition. For example, if you've created a loop that repeats a number of times, you may want to exit the loop prematurely if certain input is received (a script that asks for a password, perhaps). In this case, you can exit the loop prematurely with **break**.

The **continue** is useful for skipping to the top of a loop when you do not want the remainder of the loop executed. If, for example, you've created a loop that repeatedly executes a set of commands, there may be an exceptional case in which you do not want the rest of the loop to execute. In this event, you can use **continue** to immediately skip to the top of the loop.

Getting Out: exit

You can use the **exit** command in two ways: to terminate a shell session or to terminate a shell script before the end of the file. With the **exit** command you can also make your shell scripts return an exit status.

When you type **exit** at the command line, the current shell is terminated. If the current shell is your login shell, you are also logged off the system. When the shell encounters an **exit** command in a shell script, the script is terminated.

Most commands return an exit status to the shell when they finish. It tells the shell whether the command failed or succeeded. A nonzero exit status indicates that the command failed. A zero indicates that the command was successful.

Normally, a shell script returns the exit status of the last command executed in the script. When the **exit** command appears in a shell script followed by a number, the shell script is terminated and the number is returned as the exit status.

 TIP   The **exit** command is useful with **if** constructions. The **if** construction can be used in a script to check that vital conditions are met (that mandatory arguments are supplied or certain options selected, for example). If the conditions are not met, the **exit** command can terminate the script and return an unsuccessful exit code, as in the **grab** shell script presented earlier in this chapter.

The Here Document

A *here document* allows you to redirect the input of a command in a shell script to lines that you place within the shell script itself. Thus, you can provide input to a command without having to use a separate file. It is called a here document because the input is *here,* within the shell script, not *there,* in another file.

A here document begins with the redirection symbol (<<) followed by a delimiter. The delimiter can be one or more characters, and these tell the shell where the here document begins and ends. Following the text of the here document, the delimiter is repeated on a line by itself. The following shell script redirects the here document to the **grep** command. This example uses **end** as the delimiter.

```
$ cat phone
:
# @(#)phone -- Lookup phone number
#
grep -i "$1" <<EOF
```

```
Dave Crockett      342 4379
Pacific Data       425 3821   contact: Bill West
Ross Olivera       425 4379
Mike Chon          448 2455   until April
Garage Barbecue    458 4003   hours: 10-8 M-F 10-12 F-S
Jessica Sedois     338 4647   or 338 2432
EOF

$ phone jess
Jessica Sedois     338 4647 or 338 2432
```

Modifying Your Environment

If the Bourne shell is your login shell, a shell script called **.profile** in your home directory runs each time you log in. The **.profile** file is responsible for setting much of your environment, such as your terminal type, home directory, and search path. You can modify your **.profile** to customize your environment or alter the actions that occur when you log in.

Modifying Your .profile

Because **.profile** is a regular shell script (that is, a text file) it can be changed with an editor such as **vi** (discussed in Chapter 7, "Editing and Text Processing"). On some systems you can edit this file yourself; on others, the system administrator must do it for you. Since the **.profile** is a dot file, it does not ordinarily appear when you type **ls**. To move to your home directory and see **.profile** listed there, type

```
$ cd
$ ls -l .profile
```

For example, you might like your **.profile** to print a list of personal reminders (see the shell scripts **mkremind** and **remind**, presented earlier in this chapter). If the personal reminders were kept in a file named

.reminder in your home directory, you could accomplish this by adding the following lines to the end of your .profile:

```
# check for .reminder file and display it if there.
if [ -s $HOME/.reminder ]
then
    more $HOME/.reminder
fi
```

 CAUTION Before you make any changes to your .profile, make a copy of the file for safekeeping.

Environment Variables in Your .profile

The environment variables, which determine your environment, are often set in your **.profile** file. (Environment variables were discussed in detail earlier in this chapter.)

You can change various aspects of your environment by editing the values assigned to them in the **.profile** file. The following example shows a stripped down version of the **.profile** in which various environment variables are set.

```
$ cat .profile
:
# @.profile
# Set environment variables
#
SHELL=/bin/sh
PATH=/bin:/usr/bin:/u/bin:$HOME/bin:.
MAIL=/usr/spool/mail/$LOGNAME
MAILPATH=$MAIL%"Mail call!!"
MAILCHECK=1
TERM=wy50
export SHELL PATH MAILCHECK MAILPATH NAME TERM
eval `tset -S`
```

With an editor, these environment variables can be changed.

Setting Terminal Options

To use a full-screen program, such as the **vi** editor, you must let the system know what type of terminal you are using. Since this must be done every time you log in, you should specify your terminal type in your **.profile** where it will be set automatically.

For example, the following lines in your **.profile** will automatically set your terminal type each time you log in.

```
SHELL=/bin/sh
TERM=wy50
export SHELL TERM
eval `tset -S`
```

Of course, in place of **wy50**, you would set the **TERM** variable to the code for your terminal.

 NOTE   The **tset** command uses the values of the **SHELL** and **TERM** variables. Make sure these values are set before you execute the **tset** command.

If you regularly log in from several different types of terminals, the following lines in your **.profile** will display a message that allows you to confirm your terminal type.

```
SHELL=/bin/sh
export SHELL
TERMSTAT=1
while
   [ $TERMSTAT != 0 ]
do
   eval `tset -S -m:?wy50vb`
   TERMSTAT=$?
done
unset TERMSTAT
export TERM
```

When you log in, the shell will display the following:

```
term=(wy50)
```

You may press RETURN to accept the default terminal type, or type another code for your terminal and then press RETURN. If the system does not recognize the terminal code you type, it will prompt you again.

The Bourne shell provides both a user interface and a programming language. As a user interface, the shell executes your commands as you type them on the command line. As a programming language, the shell executes commands from a file called a shell script. As well as executing the usual command line commands, shell scripts allow you to alter the flow of control with conditional and looping constructions. Several types of variables are available to the shell script programmer: user variables, environment variables, and read-only shell variables. By setting the environment variables and modifying the **.profile** file, shell programmers can alter the environment.

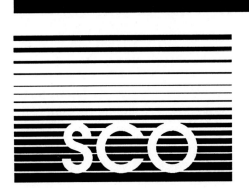

11

The C Shell

Whenever you log in to an SCO UNIX system, you communicate with a command interpreter. This chapter discusses the C shell command interpreter, **csh**. In many respects, the C shell is like the Bourne shell, which was covered in the previous chapter. Since much about the two shells is identical, text that would be redundant has been omitted from this chapter. Even if you only plan to use the C shell, you may find it helpful to read Chapter 10, the Bourne shell chapter, for general information about shells and shell scripts.

Like the Bourne shell, the C shell is a UNIX program that contains a powerful command language. It reads commands from the standard input, translating and executing them one at a time. It can function as a user interface, reading commands from the command line, or as a programming language, reading commands from a file.

Shells, Commands, and Scripts

When you log in to SCO UNIX, the shell you are assigned is called your *login shell*. It is your copy of the command interpreter and reads your commands from the keyboard. Typing a command creates a new process to execute the command. The new process is a *child* of your login shell and the login shell is the *parent* of the new process. The children of your login shell can in turn start new processes.

Each new copy of the shell is a *subshell*. As in the Bourne shell, you can terminate a subshell and return to the parent process by typing **exit** or pressing CTRL-d at the command line. You can terminate your login shell with either **exit** or **logout**.

Commands that you type at the keyboard must be executable files. To execute a compiled program, the shell starts a new process to execute the program. If the file is executable but is not a compiled program, it is assumed to be a shell script. A *shell script* is an executable text file that contains standard shell commands. To execute a shell script, the shell starts a new subshell to read the file and execute the commands within it.

 NOTE Bourne shell scripts run properly from both the Bourne shell and the C shell, while C shell scripts run properly only from the C shell; therefore, it is often preferable to write Bourne shell scripts instead of C shell scripts since they are more flexible. However, if you will primarily be using the C shell, it is useful to learn about C shell scripts, because the C shell has many advanced features that are missing from the Bourne shell.

Since it is a new subshell, not the parent shell, that reads and executes the commands in the script file, changes made from within a shell script have no effect on the parent shell. With the **source** command, you can have the current shell read and execute a shell script without creating a new subshell. Thus, any changes made by the shell script will remain in effect after the script finishes. For example, the **source** command is commonly used to reinitiate your login shell by reading the **.login** and **.cshrc** files in your home directory, as follows:

```
% source .login
% source .cshrc
```

To run another command in place of the current shell, including your login shell, use the **exec** command. This simply replaces the current shell with the new process. For example, to execute the Bourne shell in place of the current shell, type

```
% exec sh
```

The History List

From the moment you first log in, the C shell automatically keeps a list of the commands you type. The history feature allows you to recall and manipulate the commands in this list. You can use the history list to recall previous commands, to make minor changes to similar commands, to correct command line mistakes, or just to keep a record of what you have done.

The shell assigns a number to each command you give. The first command you give when you enter a shell is number one, the second command is number two, and so on. A command in the history list is called an *event*, and the number associated with each event is called the *event number*. Each subshell you start has its own history list; therefore, you can only recall commands that you've typed in the current shell.

If you type **history** on the command line, the shell will display all the commands in the history list. For example:

```
% history
    24   time
    25   cat /u/bin/dates
    26   deadline
    27   vi .login
    28   c 11
    29   pwd
    30   ls -l
```

```
31   c 10
32   ch 10
33   prep -x c10 &
34   kill 28617
35   ps
36   ls
37   rm c10*
38   prep -x ch10 &
39   c 11
40   vi outline
41   cd
42   vi .exrc
43   history
```

By default, the history list has a length of 20 events. The history list will only hold the number of commands specified by the **history** environment variable. As more commands are executed and added to the history list, the earliest commands are removed from the list and lost. By changing the value in the **history** variable, you can change the number of commands saved in the history list. However, if the history list becomes too long, your shell may run out of memory. Setting the history list to a length of 50 is a reasonable choice, because the list gives you a nice, long record of your commands, yet doesn't use too much memory. You can do this with the following command.

```
% set history = 50
```

 TIP   You can place the previous command in your **.cshrc** file to automatically set the size of the history list every time you enter a shell. This procedure is covered later in this chapter, in the section "Modifying Your Environment."

Recalling a Previous Command

There are three ways to recall a command from the history list: you can recall the previous command; you can recall a command by its event number (absolutely or relatively); or, you can recall a command by the text it begins with. History substitutions always begin with the ! (exclamation mark, or bang character), and they may begin *anywhere* on the input line. Any line that contains a history substitution is echoed to your terminal before it is executed to show the result of the full substitution.

 NOTE If you want to use the ! in another context, you must escape it with a \ (backslash). Preceding the ! with a \ tells the shell not to perform a history substitution for the !. This is important to remember, because it comes up frequently and is often overlooked.

You can recall the previous command with:

```
% !!
```

The shell substitutes every occurrence of !! on the command line with the text of the previous command, as the following example demonstrates.

```
% cat .reminder
Don't forget to turn off the coffee pot.
% !!
cat .reminder
Don't forget to turn off the coffee pot.
```

Though you will often use !! alone simply to recall the previous command, remember that a history substitution can appear anywhere on the input line. The following command uses !! with additional text on the command line.

```
% who | sort
laurak      ttyi1a        May   8 10:44
petra       ttyi1c        May   7 17:29
root        tty01         May   6 09:20
% !! > users
who | sort > users
```

You can recall a command deep in the history list with an ! followed by an event number. If the event is in the history list, the shell places the event on the command line. In the following example, a command several events back in the history list is recalled.

```
% history
    49  vi remind
    50  who | sort
    51  remind &
    52  ps
    53  history
% !50
who | sort
laurak      ttyi1a      May  8 10:44
petra       ttyi1c      May  7 17:29
root        tty01       May  6 09:20
```

If the event isn't in the history list, you will get an error message such as shown here:

```
% !12
12: Event not found.
```

You can recall an event relatively by using an **!** and a negative number. The number specifies the event's relative position in the history list, that is, how far back it is. The following example recalls a command four events back in the history list.

```
% history
    55  /u/bin/randcall
    56  ps
    57  randcall
    58  csh -v remind
    59  history
% !-4
ps
  PID TTY  TIME COMMAND
29850 i1a  0:11 csh
30758 i1a  0:00 ps
```

You recall an event by the text it begins with by typing the pattern to be found after the **!**. The shell searches for the most recent event that *begins* with the pattern you've specified, as shown here:

```
% history
    63  rmdir library
    62  cat > sample2
```

```
    61  rm sample
    64  report
    65  history
% !rm sample2
rm sample sample2
```

You can also use the **?** (question mark) as a search character in history substitution. It works much like the search command in **vi**. Place a **?** in front of a search pattern to recall the most recent event that contains that pattern. This lets you avoid retyping a long command. If text will immediately follow the recalled command, place a **?** after the search pattern as well. The following example demonstrates both forms.

```
% history
    67  prep tables | mail kenya
    68  vi tables figure
    69  l reports
    70  prep tables
    71  history
% !?ken
prep tables | mail kenya
% !?fig?.txt
vi tables figure.txt
```

Recalling Parts of a Previous Command

You can reference the individual arguments of a command line stored in the history list. Again, this saves you typing if you are dealing with long commands or file names. The arguments are numbered sequentially, with the first command on the line numbered zero. To recall a particular argument in the command, follow the event specification with a colon and the number of the argument in the command. You can recall the first argument of a previous command with a ^ (caret) and the last argument by a $ (dollar sign). All the arguments (excluding argument number zero) can be recalled with an * (asterisk). It's also possible to recall a range of words by separating two numbers with a hyphen. The following example recalls the last argument of event number 73 and sends the file to the printer.

```
% history
    73   more Hopi.txt.f Pueblo.txt.f
    74   ls
    75   pr -h "People of the Southwest" Pueblo.txt.f | lp
    76   mail kenya < Pueblo.txt.f
    77   history
% lp !73:$
lp Pueblo.txt.f
```

The next example recalls the second argument (not counting the initial command, which is numbered zero) of event 75 in the history list. Notice that text within single or double quotes is treated as one argument.

```
% mktitle !75:2
mktitle "People of the Southwest"
```

You can specify individual arguments using any of the various ways to recall a command: by event number, by text within the event, or by specifying the previous command. For instance, you can recall the second argument in the previous command with **!!** followed by a colon and the argument number, as in

```
% sort !!:2
```

You can recall just the arguments in the last command that starts with the pattern **mor** by issuing the command

```
% lp !mor:*
lp Hopi.txt.f Pueblo.txt.f
```

Modifying a Previous Command

Using another aspect of the history mechanism, you can modify a previous command. Should you make a mistake in a complex command, it is easier to correct the mistake than to type the whole command over. Also, if you are executing a series of commands, each with only minor differences, it is easier to modify a few parameters than to type similar commands repeatedly.

You can fix a typo in the previous command by typing a ^(caret), the mistyped text, another ^, and then the replacement text. The following example corrects a mistake in the previous command.

```
% moer outline lab7.n sample2
moer: Command not found.
% ^moer^more
more outline lab7.n sample2
```

If the substitution has spaces in it, you need to place a third ^ at the end of the line. The ^ notation is actually a convenient shorthand; here is a more general way to write the preceding event modification:

```
% !!:s/moer/more/
```

The **s** is a modifier that stands for substitute. You can modify any command by following an event specification with a colon and one of the following modifiers.

r	Root, remove the file name extension of a file name
h	Head, remove the last element of a pathname
t	Tail, remove all but the last element of a pathname
p	Print, but do not execute, the event
q	Quote this part of the event to prevent it from being further modified
s/old**/**new**/**	Substitute *new* for *old*
gs/old**/**new**/**	Globally substitute *new* for *old* wherever it occurs within the command

As with the **vi** substitution command, an **&** (ampersand) in the *new* string of a history substitution is replaced with the *old* string. If the *old* string of a history substitution is null (as in s//**new**/), the previous *old* string is used.

These event modifications can be used in combination; simply place colons between them, and each new modifier will act on the result returned by the previous one. Furthermore, you can combine these event modifications with any event specification including the specification of particular words. This flexibility makes the history feature tremendously powerful.

Aliases

With the C shell, you can create a whole set of simple commands. These new commands are called *aliases* because they allow you to rename and group existing commands. For each new alias, you must define a command or a set of commands the alias will perform. The shell maintains a list of your new aliases. When you type one of the words to which you have assigned an alias on the command line, the shell substitutes and executes the full alias. Thus, the alias function is useful for simplifying complex new commands as well as for redefining existing ones.

Creating an Alias

An alias is assigned with the **alias** command. You must supply the **alias** command with the word to which you want to assign the alias and with the commands the alias is to execute. The following example creates an alias **bye** that is simply a synonym for **logout**.

```
% alias bye logout
% bye

Welcome to SCO System V

redwood!login:
```

 NOTE   The first argument of the **alias** command is always the word to which you are assigning the alias. Any subsequent arguments are assumed to be commands the alias is to execute.

It is quite possible to replace a standard UNIX command by creating an alias that uses a command name. In fact, using **alias,** you can change the behavior of any command. This is useful for potentially damaging commands, such as **rm.** In the following example, the **-i** option is made the new default for the **rm** command, so that **rm** asks for verification before it removes any file.

```
% alias rm rm -i
% rm questions
questions: ?
```

Now, whenever you type **rm,** the **rm -i** command will be executed.

Though it can be helpful to make simple changes to UNIX commands, you shouldn't change their functions extensively. C shell scripts that expect commands to perform a certain way may malfunction if the commands they use are altered too drastically.

If you use a command whose meaning or function has been changed by an alias, you can temporarily prevent the alias substitution either by surrounding the command with single quotation marks or by preceding it with a \, as in the following example.

```
% alias ls ls -CFq
% ls p*
phone*   port
% \ls bank
phone
port
% 'ls' bank
phone
port
```

It may be necessary to use the \ or single quotes within an alias assignment. The following example creates an alias named **pwd** that, in turn, contains the command **pwd.** When you type **pwd,** the shell substitutes and attempts to execute the alias commands, but when it gets to the command **pwd** in the alias, it attempts another alias substitution. Around and around it goes, trapped in an *alias loop*. Escaping the **pwd** command with a \ to prevent alias substitution solves this problem.

```
% alias pwd 'echo "Current directory:" ; pwd'
% pwd
Alias loop.

% alias pwd 'echo "Current directory:" ; \pwd'
% pwd
Current directory:
/u/laurak/bin
```

 NOTE   If your alias uses multiple commands, separate the commands with semicolons and enclose the entire command part of the alias in single or double quotes. If you use double quotes, any variable or command substitution will be done immediately when the alias is created. If you use single quotes, variable or command substitution will be suppressed until the alias is used. If a complicated alias does not work as you had expected, look carefully at the placement of single and double quotes in it.

Displaying Aliases

Without any arguments, the **alias** command displays a list of the current aliases previously assigned with the **alias** command, as shown here:

```
% alias
bye       logout
lp        lp -o nobanner
ls        (ls -CFq)
note      echo "Enter note (end w/CTRL-d):" ; cat >> $home/.note
notes     more -10 $home/.note
pwd       echo "Current directory:" ; \pwd
rm        (rm -i)
sos       cu scobbs -s 2400
```

 NOTE   The commands in the alias list may look a little different than they did when you defined them. First, neither single nor double quotes appear around the command portion of the alias, even if your alias was defined with them. Second, parentheses are placed around the command portion of multiword aliases defined without quotes. Third, if your alias was defined without single quotes and involved variable, history, or command substitution, the substitutions were immediately performed when the alias was created.

With one argument, the **alias** command displays the alias for that argument, as in this example:

```
% alias note
echo "Enter note (end w/CTRL-d):" ; cat >> $home/.note
```

The **unalias** command removes an alias from the list of aliases, as shown here:

```
% unalias note
% note
note: Command not found.
```

Argument Substitution Within an Alias

You can use command line arguments within your aliases. In the same way that the history mechanism handles command line arguments, the **alias** command uses the ! followed by a : and a modifier. The modifiers are the same as those used by the history function. With the **alias** command, you must precede the ! with a \ so the shell does not immediately perform a history substitution.

The following example creates two aliases that use argument substitution. The first **alias** grabs the full pathname of a specified file in the current directory. The second releases, or copies, the grabbed file to the current directory. These aliases use command and variable substitution as well.

```
% alias grab 'set grabfile = `pwd`/\!:1'
% alias grab
set grabfile `pwd`/!:1

% alias release 'cp $grabfile ./\!:*'
% alias release
cp $grabfile ./!:*
```

```
% ls
bill        rosso       sheila3     modes
% grab bill modes
% cd ~/letters
% release
% ls
bill        modes
```

 NOTE   The command portions of the previous **alias** commands are surrounded by single quotes so that variable and command substitution will be suppressed until the aliases are used. A \ is used to escape each **!** preventing history substitution.

Shell Variables

Variables operate in the C shell much as they do in the Bourne shell. A *variable* is a name that can be assigned a value. The value may be a number, a word, or a line. The shell has variables that you create and assign values, as well as variables that are set by the shell itself. Unlike the Bourne shell, the C shell has numeric variables that you can treat as numbers and variable arrays to which you can assign multiple values. *User variables*, which can be created and assigned values by the user, allow you to store and manipulate values for later use. These include string variables, string arrays, numeric variables, and numeric arrays. *Environment variables* are maintained by the shell, yet can be reset by the user. They have a special meaning to the shell, and help determine how your shell will act. There are environment variables that can be assigned values and environment variables that can only be turned off and on like switches. *Positional parameters* are set by the shell when a shell script is invoked. They are taken directly from the command line. *Special variables*, which are set by the shell and cannot be changed, allow you to access information about the shell, such as the number of parameters, process numbers, and exit status. The following sections describe the shell variables, as well as several commands to help you manage them.

User Variables

You can create user variables from any sequence of letters and digits, as long as the first character is a letter. Three commands declare and manipulate user variables: **set**, **@**, and **setenv**. The **set** command is used to declare nonnumeric string variables, while the **@** command only works with numeric variables. The **setenv** command is used to set environment variables. The **set** and **@** commands declare a local variable, one that is available only within the shell in which it was created. The **setenv** command declares a variable and places it in the current environment, which makes it available to all child processes (this is similar to using the **export** command in the Bourne shell).

String Variables   In the C shell, string variables are declared with the **set** command. A string variable assignment has the form

> set *name* = *string*

The spacing around the equal sign is unimportant. Once you've assigned a variable, a $ references it. Thereafter, within the same shell or shell script, **$***name* will be replaced by *string* wherever it occurs. In the following example, the variable **wine** is assigned the value **Chardonnay**.

```
% set wine = Chardonnay
```

You can display the value of the variable with the **echo** command, as in the following example. Notice that without the $, the shell does not recognize the variable name as a variable.

```
% echo $wine
Chardonnay
% echo wine
wine
```

Because of the leading **$**, the shell recognizes **$wine** as a variable. Whenever the shell finds a reference to a variable, it immediately substitutes it with the variable's value.

NOTE   If you want a $ *not* to be interpreted as a reference to a variable, you can precede it with a \ or surround the text with single quotes to prevent variable substitution.

You can put more than one assignment on a single line. For example, the following command sets two variables at once.

```
% set white=Chardonnay red=Burgundy
```

When you assign a variable, put double quotes around values that contain spaces or tabs. Without double quotes, the shell will assume that only the first word is the variable's value. Furthermore, put double quotes around references to variables that might contain multiple spaces or tabs to preserve their spacing. Without quotes, multiple spaces or tabs are treated as single spaces. Here is an example:

```
% set label = Rene Junot
% echo $label
Rene
% set label = "Rene Junot"
% echo $label
Rene Junot

% set label = "Pahrump      Cellars"
% echo $label
Pahrump Cellars
% echo "$label"
Pahrump      Cellars
```

 NOTE   Another way to deal with values that contain spaces or tabs is to escape individual spaces and tabs by preceding each one with a \.

 TIP   Characters that have special meaning to the shell, such as $ * ? [ ] ( ) and ~ must be quoted with single quotes or escaped with a \.

You can make your script prompt the user for information and store the input in a user variable; however, the C shell does not have a command equivalent to the Bourne shell's **read** command, so you must improvise. You can use command substitution and the **line** command to read a line of user input. The **line** command reads a single line of text from the standard input (even if it is a file) and backquotes assign it to a variable, as the following example makes clear.

```
% set quantity = `line`
ten cases
% echo $quantity
ten cases
```

Naturally, this is most useful inside a shell script. Unlike **read,** this method cannot assign individual words to multiple variables. If you need to break the input into words, use an array instead of a standard variable. In this case, you would put parentheses around the part of the command that reads `line`. Arrays are discussed in the next section.

NOTE If you enclose the `line` portion of the command in double quotes, the spacing in the line the user types will be preserved, even if the line contains multiple spaces or tabs.

String Arrays A *string array* is a list of nonnumeric values referenced by a single variable name. A number specifies which element of the array is to be referenced. The string array is declared a little differently than a regular string variable: You use the **set** command and the equal sign, but the values of the variable are enclosed in parentheses. The following example declares an array of the variable **reds**. The parentheses tell the shell that **reds** is an array.

```
% set reds = (Bordeaux Burgundy Beaujolais)
% echo $reds
Bordeaux Burgundy Beaujolais
```

NOTE To specify an element that contains spaces, enclose the text of the element in double quotes.

Elements of the array are referenced by following the name of the string array with an index number enclosed in square brackets. The index number specifies which element of the array you are referencing. Two numbers separated by a hyphen within the square brackets specify a range of elements in the array. An * within the square brackets specifies all the elements of the array. For example:

```
% set reds = (Bordeaux Burgundy "Johannesburg Riesling")
% echo $reds[*]
Bordeaux Burgundy Johannesburg Riesling
% echo $reds[1]
Bordeaux
% echo $reds[3]
Johannesburg Riesling
% echo $reds[1-2]
Bordeaux Burgundy
```

To assign a value to an individual element in an array, use the variable name and the index number enclosed in square brackets, as you would with an ordinary string variable.

```
% set reds[3] = Rhine
% echo $reds[*]
Bordeaux Burgundy Rhine
```

The number of elements in an array is determined by the number of elements specified when the array is first declared. Sometimes you may not know what values an array will contain when it is declared, but you may still wish to declare an array of a certain size. In this case, you can specify the necessary number of null elements, as shown here:

```
% set labels = ("Rene Junot" "" "" "" "")
% echo $labels
Rene Junot
% set labels[2] = "Chateau-Avignon"
% echo $labels
Rene Junot Chateau-Avignon
```

You can determine the number of elements in an array after it has been declared with a special form of the user variable. If you precede the array name with a $ and a #, the shell will give the number of elements in the specified array. For example:

```
% set whites = (Chardonnay Chablis "Sauvignon Blanc" Grenache)
% echo $#whites
4
```

Numeric Variables   You use the @ command to declare numeric variables. Unlike the **set** command, which only assigns a constant value to a variable, the @ command can assign the results of a complex mathematical expression to a variable. The expressions the @ command can evaluate and the operations it performs are derived from the C programming language—the UNIX system programming language. The @ command has the following format:

> *@# variable operator expression*

The *variable* is the variable to which you are assigning a value or expression. The name of a variable assigned with the @ command cannot contain numeric characters. The *operator* is one of these C assignment operators:

=	Assigns the value of the expression to the variable
++	Increments the variable
– –	Decrements the variable
+=	Adds the expression to the variable and assigns the result to the variable
–=	Subtracts the expression from the variable and assigns the result to the variable
*=	Multiplies the expression by the variable and assigns the result to the variable
/=	Divides the variable by the expression and assigns the result to the variable
%=	Takes the remainder, after dividing the variable by the expression, and assigns the result to the variable

The *expression* is a mathematical expression that may contain constants, other variables, or C operators. Arithmetic and logical operators are commonly used in expressions with the @ command. Expressions, which are also used by the **if** and **while** commands, are covered later in this chapter. The following examples illustrate the @ command and some of its operators and expressions.

```
@ cases = 4
@ lastnum = ($#argv - 1)
@ hour = `date +%H`
@ root = `random 255` * `random 255`
@ num = `cat $filename | wc -l`
@ rand = ( $root % $num ) + 1
```

The ability to handle numbers and perform arithmetic makes the C shell a powerful tool that allows you to perform complex tasks without having to learn a full programming language.

Numeric Arrays   Before you can use @ to assign values to the elements of a numeric array, you must declare the array with the **set** command. Using **set,** you can assign any values to the elements of a numeric array including zeros, other numbers, and null strings. The way you use the **set** command is similar to the way you declare string arrays. For example:

```
% set quarterly = (0 0 0 0)
```

You can assign values to the individual elements of an array with the @ command by placing the index number of the array element in square brackets after the variable name. The index number can be a constant or another variable, as shown here:

```
% set shipment = (0 0 0 0 0)
% @ shipment[1] = 75
% @ shipment[3] = 125
% @ shipment[4] = 120
% echo $shipment[1]
75
% echo $shipment
75 0 125 120 0 0
```

Environment Variables

In the Bourne shell, variables that are inherited with the environment are called environment variables; however, unlike the environment variables in the Bourne shell, the environment variables in the C shell are less than straightforward. Some C shell environment variables are passed with the environment, while others are not. Some variables are uppercase, such as **TERM**, while others are lowercase, such as **prompt**. Some have both an uppercase and a lowercase form that have different meanings, such as **HOME** and **home**, or **MAIL** and **mail**. Many of these variables do not take values, but are set on or off, like a switch, such as **ignoreeof**. In the C shell, an *environment variable* can be any variable that affects the way your shell operates.

In spite of the many types of environment variables available in the C shell, there are a few general guidelines that can help you keep them straight. Uppercase variables should be placed in the environment. If they are not set automatically, you can assign them with the **setenv** command. If you want them to be set automatically, you can assign them in your **.login** file, as discussed later in this chapter, under "Modifying Your Environment."

Lowercase variables should not be placed in the environment. If they are not set automatically, you can assign them with the **set** command. If you want them to be set automatically, you can assign them in your **.cshrc** file. Putting them in **.cshrc**, which is executed every time you enter a subshell, ensures that these variables will affect every subshell you enter (see "Modifying Your Environment").

Some of the environment variables have an upper- and a lowercase form with different meanings. For some variables, both forms are set automatically. For other variables, setting the uppercase form with the **setenv** command automatically sets both the uppercase and the lowercase variables. Finally, for some variables, although the uppercase form is set automatically, you can choose to set the lowercase variable yourself.

The following sections explain many of the important environment variables.

HOME   The C shell **HOME** variable works the same as the **HOME** variable in the Bourne shell. It specifies your home directory, the directory you are in when you first log in. Your home directory is assigned from the directory entry in **/etc/passwd**, which was set when your account was created. The **cd** command without arguments puts you in the directory named by the **HOME** variable. This variable is automatically assigned and placed in the environment. Since you cannot very well change your home directory, there is no need to change the **HOME** variable. This variable is related to the **home** variable described below.

home   The **home** variable is identical to the **HOME** variable. It is automatically assigned when you enter a shell.

PATH   The **PATH** variable works the same as **PATH** in the Bourne shell. It specifies the search path the shell uses to find a file or command you have specified on the command line. The search path is a list of directories in which the shell will search one by one in an attempt to find your command. The **PATH** variable is automatically assigned with a default value and placed in the environment. The default value usually includes the directories **/bin** and **/usr/bin**, because these directories hold most of the UNIX utilities.

The **PATH** variable is assigned with the **setenv** command. If you want it to be set automatically, assign the variable in your **.login** file. The search path is specified as a list of directories separated by colons. The variable **$HOME** specifies your home directory. A single dot, which should appear at the end of the list, specifies the current directory. The following line is from a **.login** file.

```
setenv PATH /bin:/usr/bin:$HOME/bin:$HOME/lib:.
```

PATH variable is closely related to the **path**, described below. If you reset the **PATH** variable, **path** is automatically reset, and vice versa. Thus, there are two ways to reset your search path. The previous example demonstrated one way, and the next example under **path** will demonstrate another. The two methods are roughly equivalent.

Whenever you reset the path from the command line, type **rehash** to rebuild the shell's table of command locations. If you forget to do this, the shell may not be able to find commands that are located along the new path.

path   The **path** variable is almost identical to **PATH**. It is automatically given a default value every time you enter a shell. You can reassign **path** with the **set** command. If you want it to be set automatically, assign the variable in your **.cshrc** file. The search path is specified as a string array, so it appears as a list of directories delimited by spaces, and enclosed in parentheses. The following line is from a **.cshrc** file.

```
set path = (/bin /usr/bin $HOME/bin $HOME/lib .)
```

This example is equivalent to that given for the **PATH** variable. You need only set one of the two variables, because resetting one of them automatically resets the other.

MAIL   The **MAIL** variable specifies your system mailbox. This variable has no effect on the C shell, because the C shell uses the **mail** variable, instead of **MAIL**. However, **MAIL** is useful if you use the Bourne shell frequently. If you set this variable, you are notified when mail arrives while you are using the Bourne shell. **MAIL** is not assigned automatically, so you must assign it and place it in the environment. To do so, place this line in your **.login** file:

```
setenv MAIL /usr/spool/mail/$LOGNAME
```

mail   The C shell **mail** variable is much like a combination of the Bourne shell's **MAIL**, **MAILCHECK**, and **MAILPATH** variables. It can specify your system mailbox, a mail check interval, and the name of auxiliary mailboxes. When you specify a single file with **mail**, the shell will notify you whenever mail arrives in that file by displaying the message "You have new mail." If the first word of **mail** is a number and the second word is a file, the number specifies the interval in seconds at which the shell checks to see whether mail has arrived in the specified file. The default interval is 600 seconds, or 10 minutes. If multiple files are specified, the shell notifies you with the message "New mail in *filename*," when mail arrives in the file *filename*. This variable is not automatically assigned, so if you want the C shell to notify you of new mail, you must assign it.

You can assign the **mail** variable with the **set** command. If you want it to be assigned automatically when you enter a shell, assign it in your **.cshrc** file. The following line from a **.cshrc** file specifies a mail check interval of one minute and a system mailbox at **/usr/spool/mail/$LOGNAME**.

```
set mail = (60 /usr/spool/mail/$LOGNAME)
```

SHELL   The **SHELL** variable specifies the default shell in your environment. It is used by some programs, such as **vi** and **mail**, to choose a subshell and to determine the format of output, such as **tset**. Your shell is assigned from the login shell entry in **/etc/passwd**, which is set when your account is created. The **SHELL** variable is automatically assigned and placed in the environment. If you need to change your default shell, reassign the variable with the **setenv** command. Give the full pathname of the new shell, as in

```
% setenv SHELL /bin/sh
```

The **SHELL** variable is closely related to **shell**.

shell   Like the **SHELL** variable, **shell** specifies the default shell in your environment. It is used to choose a shell when you are creating a subshell to read shell scripts. This variable is set from the **SHELL** variable every time you enter the C shell. Since setting **SHELL** sets both variables, you can use the command in the previous example to change the default shell.

LOGNAME   The **LOGNAME** variable contains your account name, or login name. You can use this variable in place of your actual login name in your shell scripts, so that they can be used by anyone. In UNIX, this variable is automatically assigned and placed in the environment.

XENIX   In XENIX, you must assign the **LOGNAME** variable with the **setenv** and **logname** commands. If you use the **LOGNAME** variable in your **.cshrc** file (as mentioned earlier with the **mail** variable), you must assign it near the top of the file before you use it. If you do not use

LOGNAME in your **.cshrc** file, assign it in your **.login** file. The following line from a **.cshrc** file sets the **LOGNAME** variable.

```
setenv LOGNAME `logname`
```

TERM   The **TERM** variable identifies your terminal type. It is used by full-screen programs, such as **vi**, and by **tset** to configure your terminal. This variable is not set automatically so you must assign it. You should assign **TERM** with the **setenv** command in your **.login** file. Setting the **TERM** and **TERMCAP** variables is discussed later in this chapter under "Modifying Your Environment."

TERMCAP   The **TERMCAP** variable contains information about your terminal. It is usually set with **TERM** by **tset** in your **.login** file.

prompt   The **prompt** variable, which is similar to the **PS1** variable in the Bourne shell, specifies the C shell prompt. When you change the value of this variable, the appearance of the prompt changes. You can use the prompt to tell you the history event number, who you are logged in as, or what machine you're on. The **prompt** variable is automatically assigned a default value when you enter a shell. By default, it is initially set to a **%** (percent sign) followed by a space.

The **prompt** variable is assigned with the **set** command. If you want it to be set automatically, assign the variable in your **.cshrc** file. For example, if you regularly use the C shell history function, you can have the prompt display the current event number. Then, as you look over your screen, you will see the event numbers of the most recent commands. An **!** in a prompt string is substituted with the current event number. Note that you have to escape the **!** with a ****. The following example makes the current event number appear in the prompt.

```
% set prompt = '\!% '
23%
```

If you are working on more than one machine from the same terminal, it is sometimes difficult to recall which machine you are currently logged in to. You can change the prompt so that it indicates the machine you are currently using. For example, to change the prompt to the machine name **sparta**, you would use the command:

```
% setenv prompt = "sparta% "
sparta%
```

history   The **history** variable contains a number that specifies the size of the history list. This variable was discussed earlier under "The History List." By default, it has a value of zero, so to activate the history list you need to reassign the **history** variable with the **set** command. If you want it to be assigned automatically when you enter a shell, assign it in your **.cshrc** file. The following line from **.cshrc** sets the history list to a length of 50.

```
set history = 50
```

histchars   The **histchars** variable specifies the two characters used to trigger history substitution. If you change the value, the first character is used in place of the ! history character, and the second in place of the ^ history character. This is a great opportunity, because it is often tedious to escape every ! on the command line with a \. You can reassign the **histchars** variable with the **set** command. If you want the variable to be assigned automatically, put the appropriate command in your **.cshrc** file. The following line from **.cshrc** changes the history characters to the # and the @.

```
set histchars="#@"
```

cdpath   The **cdpath** variable specifies the search path of the **cd** command. The search path is a list of directories in which **cd** will search one by one for the directory you have specified. The **cdpath** is not automatically assigned, so you must assign it if you want **cd** to use a search path. You can assign this variable with the **set** command. If you want it to be set automatically, assign it in your **.cshrc** file. The search path is specified as a string array, so it appears as a list of directories delimited by spaces, and enclosed in parentheses. The following line is from a **.cshrc** file.

```
set cdpath = (.. $HOME $HOME/text / /usr /lib)
```

cdspell   When it is set, the switch variable **cdspell** causes the shell to check the spelling of the directories specified with **cd**. If you change directories using **cd** and misspell the directory name, the shell responds with an alternative spelling of an existing directory. If you then enter **y** to indicate that the suggested directory is correct, the **cd** command changes to that directory.

echo   When it is set, the **echo** switch variable causes each command and its argument to be echoed just before it is executed.

ignoreeof   When set, the **ignoreeof** switch variable prevents a shell from being terminated accidentally with a CTRL-d. If **ignoreeof** is set, you must use **exit** or **logout** to leave the shell. It is not set by default.

noclobber   When set, the **noclobber** switch variable ensures that files are not accidentally destroyed with output redirection, and that >> redirections refer to existing files. Use the redirection symbols **>!** and **>>!** to override **noclobber**. By default, this variable is not set.

noglob   When set, the **noglob** switch variable inhibits file name expansion. It does not interpret the symbols *, ?, ~, and [ ] as ambiguous file names. This is sometimes useful within shell scripts that do not deal with file names, but make use of these symbols in other contexts. This variable is not set initially.

nonomatch   When it is set, the **nonomatch** switch variable causes ambiguous file names without matching files to be passed to their commands without file name expansion. By default, when **nonomatch** is not set, an ambiguous file reference with no matching files causes an error.

verbose   When set, the **verbose** switch variable causes the shell to display each command after a history substitution. This variable is set by default.

Positional Parameters

The shell stores each word of the command line in a string array variable **argv**. The words on the command line are stored in **argv[1]**, **argv[2]**, and so on. A reference to an element of the **argv** array that has a higher index number than the actual number of command line arguments produces an error. The variable **argv[*]** or **argv** alone gives all the command line arguments. In the following example, lines from a shell script print the command line arguments.

```
echo "Arguments: $argv[*]"
echo "Argument 1: $argv[1]"
echo "Argument 2: $argv[2]"
echo "Calling program: $0"
```

 NOTE   The variable **argv[1]** can be abbreviated to **$1**, **argv[2]** to **$2**, and so on. The variable **argv[*]** can be abbreviated **$***. The variable **$0** holds the name of the calling program, because it is usually the "zeroth" word on the command line.

Unlike command line arguments in the Bourne shell, command line arguments in the C shell can be reset individually. You can use the **set** command to change any element of the **argv** array, as shown here:

```
set argv[1] = "-o"
set argv[2] = "1-12"
```

Special Variables

Special variables are set by the shell and cannot be changed. These variables provide useful information about the shell.

Closely related to **argv** is the **$#argv** variable (abbreviated **$#**), which gives the number of arguments on the command line. The following line in a shell script reports the number of arguments to the shell script.

```
echo "There are $#argv arguments"
```

The **$$** variable holds the process identification number of the current shell. It is often used by shell scripts to create unique temporary file names. If you place the temporary files in the directory **/tmp**, they will automatically be removed by the system's clean-up program. The following lines from a shell script use a **tmp** file to store information temporarily.

```
mktitle init.a > /tmp/tmp$$
cat header /tmp/tmp$$ | pr
```

The **child** variable holds the process identification number of the last process you ran in the background. It is identical to the Bourne shell **$!** variable. The following example runs **nroff** as a background process, prints the process number, and kills the process using the **child** variable.

```
% prep bigreport &
12153
% kill -9 $child
12153 Killed
```

The **status** variable holds the exit status of the last command executed. It is identical to the Bourne shell's **$?** variable. When a process stops for any reason, it returns an *exit status,* sometimes called a *condition code* or a *return code,* to the parent process. A nonzero exit code indicates that the command has failed. A zero indicates that the command has been executed successfully.

 NOTE   You can return the exit status of your choice from your shell scripts with the **exit** command.

Shell Programming

The following sections tell you how to create and execute shell scripts. Additionally, they cover commenting and programming style. Turn to the section on shell programming in the previous chapter for more complete information about shell scripts. Any command or variable that can be used on the command line can be used in a shell script. Thus, this whole chapter will help you become a better shell programmer.

Shell Scripts

Shell scripts are simply executable text files that contain shell commands. Creating a shell script involves two simple steps: making the text file and setting the permissions to make the file executable. You can create the text file with an editor such as **vi**, as discussed in Chapter 7, "Editing and Text Processing." The text file that you create will not have execute permission set automatically, so you must use the **chmod** command to change the access permissions of your shell script. For example, you can create a shell script called **search** that uses **grep** and **find** to search the current directory (and deeper) for files containing text that matches a specified pattern, as in this example:

```
% cat search
#
# @(#) search -- Search current directory for pattern
#  created:    Corey Ostman    23 Dec 88
#
grep -l "$1" `find $2 -print` # find supplies grep w/file
                              # through command substitution
```

 NOTE You must begin a C shell script with a single # (pound sign) on the first line. This tells the shell that the script is a C shell script. Even if you are running the script from the C shell, the # is essential, because the C shell assumes that any script without it is a Bourne shell script. A C shell script cannot be run directly from the Bourne shell because the Bourne shell assumes all scripts are Bourne shell scripts (even scripts that begin with the #).

 NOTE The symbols **@(#)** allow you or another user to get a summary of the script using the **what** command. To see what an unknown script does, you might use the command

% **what search**

You cannot execute the script yet, because the shell would not recognize **search** as an executable file. The proper execute permissions have not been set, so the shell would give you an error message such as this:

```
% search
search: Permission denied.
```

Use the **chmod** command to give yourself, the owner, execute permission. The **ls** command with the - l option lists the access privileges for the **search** file before and after the **chmod** command, as shown here:

```
% ls -l search
-rw-r--r--   1 laurak    group          112 Sep 19 16:18 search
% chmod u+x search
% !ls
ls -l search
-rwxr--r--   1 laurak    group          112 Sep 19 16:18 search
```

At this point, the file **search** is executable.

As with Bourne shell scripts, you execute C shell scripts simply by typing their file name on the command line. The shell then executes all the commands in the script, one by one. You can run the script created in the previous section by typing the command **search** at the command line and supplying a pattern to search for, as in

```
% search avenue
```

 NOTE If you add a shell script to a directory in your search path after you have started the C shell, the script will not necessarily be found when you try to execute it. If you wish to use a command that was added after you have logged in, first use the following command to make the shell recompute its table of command locations and find the new command.

```
% rehash
```

The many ways you can use shell scripts—to establish supporting commands and flow control commands, for example—are discussed later in this chapter.

Comments and Programming Style

It is important to write your shell scripts so that others can read them and understand what they do. Good commenting and formatting can make your scripts easy to read. Comments in C shell scripts are entered in the same way as comments in Bourne shell scripts—with the # (pound sign). If you put a # at the beginning of a line, the shell will ignore that line. If you put a # after a command, the shell will ignore the remainder of the line. The following example demonstrates good commenting style.

```
% cat search
#
# @(#) search -- search current directory for pattern
#   created:      Corey Ostman      23 Dec 88
#   modified:     Eddy Large        10 Apr 86
#
if ("$2" == "") then               # are both arguments supplied?
   echo "search: no pattern given"  # if arguments missing
   echo "usage: search pattern"
   exit 1                          # return unsuccessful exit status
endif
grep -l "$1" `find $2 -print`      # find supplies grep with filenames
                                   #    through command substitution
```

You should document even simple scripts thoroughly. As a script grows in size and complexity, it becomes increasingly important to know who created it, who modified it, what the script does, and how it works. Comments are essential to good programming and are especially important if a script is going to be shared with other users.

Careful formatting is another way to make your scripts easy to read. Indent each level of conditional commands and the bodies of looping commands. Indentation does not affect the execution of your script, because initial spaces and tabs are ignored by the shell. In addition, you can use blank lines or empty comment lines to separate logical components of the script.

Notice that the previous shell script checks to see if arguments are supplied and returns an appropriate exit status. Even if the script is given bad arguments, it exits gracefully, which makes the script much heartier. Be sure that your shell scripts take the unexpected into account. This not only makes them more user friendly, but it can prevent unexpected and potentially damaging results.

Supporting Commands

This section covers commands that you can use on the command line and in shell scripts. These commmands are most useful when combined with others, such as the control commands, discussed later in this chapter.

Expressions

Expressions were discussed briefly under numeric variables and the @ command. Expressions are also used with the **if** and **while** commands, which are covered later in this chapter. An *expression* is an arithmetic construction that can contain constants, variables, and C operators. It computes a value and returns the results to the @, **if**, or **while** command. The following example sets the variable **bottles** to the value of **$case** multiplied by 12.

```
@ bottles = $case * 12
```

Here are the most useful C operators that can be used in expressions:

Parentheses

( )   Change the order of evaluation

Arithmetic operators

+   Add

–   Subtract

*   Multiply

/   Divide

%   Remainder

–   Unary minus

Relational operators

>	Greater than
<	Less than
>=	Greater than or equal to
<=	Less than or equal to
!=	Not equal to (used for strings)
==	Equal to (used for strings)

Logical operators

&&	AND
||	OR
!	Logical negation

The == and != operators compare their arguments as strings; all others operate on numbers. Null or missing arguments have a value of 0. The results of all expressions are strings, which represent decimal numbers. Each element of an expression must be surrounded by spaces.

The following operations, which deal with files and directories, may also appear in expressions. Each must be followed by a file name or a directory name.

–r *file*	True if *file* exists and is readable
-w *file*	True if *file* exists and is writable
-x *file*	True if *file* exists and is executable
-e *file*	True if *file* exists
-o *file*	True if *file* exists and is owned by the user
-z *file*	True if *file* exists and has a size of zero
-f *file*	True if *file* exists and is an ordinary file
-d *file*	True if *file* exists and is a directory

The following lines from a shell script show how expressions can be used with conditional commands.

```
if (( -r "$FILE" ) && ( "$1" != "" )) then
    vi $1
endif
```

Another form of expression tests whether a command terminates successfully. The command surrounded by {} (curly braces) appears in a conditional statement. If the command is successful (with an exit status of zero), this form returns one. If the command is unsuccessful (with a nonzero exit status), it returns zero. The following lines from a shell script use curly braces and the **if** command to perform a test with **grep**. If **grep** finds **$WORD** in any of the files in the current directory, the script prints those file names in a three-column list.

```
if { grep $WORD * } then
    grep -l $WORD * | pr -3
else
    echo "$WORD : not found"
endif
```

Repeating Commands: repeat

The **repeat** command is used to repeat a command several times. Follow the command with the number of times to repeat and the commands to be repeated. For example, the following command prints five copies of a file.

```
% repeat 5 print annual
```

Control Commands

The *control commands* change the order of execution of the commands in your shell script. The following sections discuss conditional commands, looping commands, and the **exit** command.

Conditional Commands: if

The simplest form of the **if** command works on one line, like this: *if some condition is met, execute a single command.* It has the following format.

> **if** (*expression*) *command*

The **if**, *expression*, and *command* must all appear on the same line. If *expression* evaluates to true (zero), *command* is executed. If *expression* evaluates to false (nonzero), *command* will not execute and the shell will continue execution with the command that follows the **if**. This construction is useful when you have a simple expression and a single command to execute conditionally, as in this example:

```
% cat day
#
# @(#) day -- print the day and date
#
date +"%a %h %d, 19%y"
set day = `date +%a`
if ($day == Sat || $day == Sun) echo "Happy Weekend"
```

The **if..then** construction is similar to the **if** construction, and works like this: *if some condition is met, then execute the following commands.* The format for the **if..then** construction is as follows:

if *(expression)* **then**
   commands
endif

The **if**, *expression*, and **then** must be on the same line, and the **endif** must be on a line by itself. The **endif** statement marks the end of the **if..then** construction. If *expression* evaluates to true (zero), the *commands* following **then** are executed. If *expression* evaluates to false (nonzero), the *commands* following **then** are *not* executed and the shell continues execution with the commands that follow **endif**. This shell script illustrates the use of **if..then**:

```
% cat view
#
# @(#) view --  view a file on the terminal screen
#
if ("$1" == "") then
    echo "view: No arguments"
    exit 1
endif
pr -122 $* | more
```

The idea behind the **if.. then.. else** construction is this: *if some condition is met, then execute one set of commands, or else, if the condition is not met, execute another set of commands.* This construction has the format;

if *(expression)* **then**
   commands
else
   commands
endif

Again, the **if**, *expression,* and **then** must be on the same line; **else** and **endif** must be on lines by themselves. If *expression* evaluates to true (zero), the *commands* between the **then** and **else** are executed, after which control is passed to the commands that follow **endif**. If *expression* evaluates to false (nonzero), the *commands* following the **else** are executed. The following shell script shows an example of the **if..then..else** construction.

```
% cat remind
#
# @(#) remind -- print a reminder file (if it exists)
#
if (-e ~/.reminder) then
    echo "remind: .reminder does not exist."
else
    more ~/.reminder
endif
```

Multiple Choice Commands: switch

The **switch** construction is similar to the Bourne shell's **case..esac**. It has a multiple choice format that matches one of several patterns and executes a corresponding set of commands. The format for **switch** is as follows:

> **switch** (*input*)
>   **case** *pattern*:
>   *commands*
>   **breaksw**
>   **case** *pattern*:
>   *commands*
>   **breaksw**
>   **default:**
>   *commands*
>   **breaksw**
>   *endsw*

The *input* is typically a variable or a command substitution. The **switch** tests to see if the *input* matches one of the patterns in the **switch** construction. If the *input* matches a pattern, the *commands* following the matching **case** statement are executed. The **breaksw** marks the end of a set of commands for a particular branch of the **switch** structure. When the shell reaches a **breaksw**, control shifts to the commands that follow the **endsw**.

You can use a **default** statement in place of a **case** to match input that does not match any other pattern. This provides a useful way to detect erroneous or unexpected input. The **default** statement is optional.

Patterns can contain variables, as well as the metacharacters *, ?, and [ ]. The * matches any sequence of characters, the ? matches any single character, and the [ ] match any single character enclosed within them.

The following shell script illustrates the use of the **switch** construction.

```
% cat report
#
# @(#) report -- Manage administrative reports
#
echo "[r]ead report, [w]rite report, [f]ile report"
echo "command: \c"
set command = `line`
switch $command
  case [Rr]:
    more $1
    breaksw
  case [Ww]:
    vi $1
    breaksw
  case [Ff]:
    mail admin < $1
    breaksw
  default:
    echo "Command not found."
endsw
```

Looping Commands: foreach

The **foreach** loop is similar to the **for..in** loop in the Bourne shell; it executes a set of commands once for each member of a list. The **foreach** loop has the format:

    foreach *variable (argument-list)*
      commands
    end

For each repetition of the loop, the next member of the *argument list* is assigned to the *variable* given after the **foreach** statement. This variable can be used within the *commands* of the loop, as in the following example.

```
% cat protect
#
# @(#) protect -- protect files with given extension
#
foreach file ('ls *.$1')
   cp $file protect/$file
end
```

 NOTE   Using the variable **$argv** for the argument list in the **foreach** loop accomplishes the same thing as the **for** loop does in the Bourne shell. The loop executes once for each element on the command line, the element being assigned, one at a time, to the variable after the **foreach** statement.

Conditional Looping: while

Another looping command, **while**, causes the shell to execute a set of commands repeatedly while some particular condition is met. It has the following format.

> **while** *(expression)*
>   *commands*
> **end**

The shell will execute the *commands* between the **while** and the **end** as long as *expression* evaluates to true (zero). When the expression evaluates to false (nonzero), control passes to the commands that follow the **end** statement. The following shell script illustrates the **while** loop.

```
% cat getinput
#
# @(#) getinput -- gets input from terminal, end with dot
#
set input = ""
```

```
while ($input != ".")
    set input = `line`
    echo $input
end
```

Controlling Loops: break and continue

The **break** and **continue** commands are designed to interrupt a **foreach** or **while** loop. The former exits the loop, and the latter jumps to the top of the loop. These commands always occur within a loop.

The **break** command exits a loop completely, transferring control to the command after the **end** statement. It can be used to exit a loop when some event happens that is not in the loop condition. For example, if you create a loop that executes once for each file in an argument list, you may want to exit the loop prematurely if any one of the files is not found. You can use the **break** command for this purpose.

The **continue** command immediately begins the next execution of a loop by transferring control to the **end** statement, which continues the loop. It is useful to skip to the top of a loop when you do not want the remainder of the loop to be executed. If, for example, you had a loop that executed once for each file in an argument list and one of the files in the list was not found, you would not want to execute the remainder of the loop for a nonexistent file. In this situation, you could use **continue** to immediately skip to the top of the loop.

Unconditional Jump: goto

The **goto** command is an unconditional jump to a specified location in the shell script. It may occur inside or outside a loop.

The **goto** statement immediately transfers control to the commands following a specified label. The label names a particular line in the shell script. The **goto** command is most often used in combination with the **if** and **if..then** statements. The following shell script illustrates the use of **goto**.

```
% cat toc
#
# @(#) toc -- table of contents
#
if ("$1" == "-q") then
    shift
    goto quiet
endif
echo "Making a table of contents for $1"
quiet:
grep '^([1-9])' $1 | sed -f toc.sed >! $1.toc
```

The label must be a single word on a line by itself, and must be followed by a colon.

 NOTE In general, the use of **goto** is considered bad programming practice, because it makes code harder to follow. Nonetheless, **goto** may be useful for debugging or as a temporary shortcut.

Getting Out: exit

You can use the **exit** command in two ways: to terminate a shell script before the end, and to make your shell scripts return an exit status.

When you type **exit** at the command line, the current shell terminates. If it is your login shell, you are logged off the system. When the shell encounters an **exit** command in a shell script, the script is terminated.

Normally, a shell script returns the exit status of the last command executed in the script. When the **exit** command followed by a number occurs in a shell script, the shell script is terminated and the number is returned as the exit status. The exit status of a command or shell script is available to the parent process through the **status** variable, described earlier in this chapter.

 NOTE The **exit** command and the **status** variable are especially useful with **if** constructions. The **if** can be used in a script to check that certain vital conditions are met before the rest of the script is executed. If the conditions are not met, the **exit** command can terminate the script and return an unsuccessful exit code.

The Here Document

A *here document* allows you to redirect the input of a command in a shell script to lines that you place within the shell script itself. Thus, you can provide input to a command without having to use a separate file. The name *here document* indicates that the input is *here,* within the shell script, not *there*, in another file.

The C shell's here document works exactly like the Bourne shell's here document. The beginning of a here document consists of the redirection symbol << followed by a delimiter. The delimiter can be one or more characters, and tells the shell where the here document begins and ends. The text of the here document is followed by the delimiter repeated on a line by itself. The following shell script uses the here document and the **cat** command to catenate a standard header to the top of a memo. This example uses **EOF** as the delimiter.

```
% cat memo
#
# @(#) memo -- prepare and attach a header to a memo
#
cat - $1 <<EOF
MEMORANDUM

Date: `date +"%d %h %y"`
From: Gerard McDowell
Director, Internal Affairs
EOF
```

Modifying Your Environment

Every time you enter a C shell (either your login shell or a subshell) a shell script in your home directory called **.cshrc** is run. Furthermore, if the C shell is your login shell, a shell script in your home directory called **.login** is also run when you log in. The **.login** file is similar to the Bourne shell's **.profile**. The **.login** and **.cshrc** files set much of your environment. You can modify either of these files to customize your environment or alter the actions that occur when you log in.

Because **.login** and **.cshrc** are regular shell scripts, you can edit them with an editor such as **vi** (covered in Chapter 7). Since both files are hidden dot files, they do not ordinarily appear when you type **ls**. Use **ls –a** to list all the files in your home directory, including dot files.

Modifying Your .cshrc

The **.cshrc** file runs each time you enter a new shell; thus, it runs each time you log in, each time you enter a subshell, and each time you run a shell script. It is most often used to set C shell aliases; user variables, and shell variables that must be available to other shells. You can use **.cshrc** to set your **prompt**, **path**, and **mail** variables, as well as other environment variables, and to create new commands and abbreviations with the **alias** command. For example, the following lines from a **.cshrc** file set several important variables and define some useful commands.

```
#
# @(#) .cshrc
#    Modified:  19 Jun 89  by  Wes Modes
#
# .cshrc file for C-Shell account.
# Commands here are executed each time csh starts up.
#
# set prompt string to reflect history event number
set prompt = "% "
# set path
set path = (/bin /usr/bin /usr/$LOGNAME/bin .)
# set mail and mail interval
set mail = (60 /usr/spool/mail/$LOGNAME)
# set history
set history=50

# aliases
alias ls        'ls -CFq'
alias bye       logout
alias rm        'rm -i'
alias lp        'lp -o nobanner'
alias pwd       'echo "Current directory:" ; \pwd'
alias note      'echo "Enter note:" ; cat >> $home/.note'
alias notes     'more -10 $home/.note'
alias grab      'set grabfile = `pwd`/\!:1'
```

```
alias release 'cp $grabfile ./\!:*'
alias sos      cu scobbs -s 2400
```

Modifying Your .login

The **.login** shell script is run only once when you log in. It is typically used to set environment variables that are passed to other shells through the environment or to perform actions that need be executed only once per session. You can use **.login** to configure your terminal, check your mail, or print a welcome message. For example, to automatically check your mail when you log in you may want to add the following lines to the end of your **.login** file.

```
if (! -z $MAIL) then
    /bin/echo -n "You have mail, wanna read it now? "
    set query = `line`
    if ("$query" == "y") mail
else
    echo "So sorry, no mail now. Try later."
endif
```

 TIP   Before you make any changes to your **.login** file, make a copy of the file for safekeeping.

Setting Terminal Options

If you want to use a full-screen program, such as the **vi** editor, the system must know what type of terminal you are using. Since this information must be provided every time you log in, you should include your terminal type in your **.login** file, so that it will be set automatically. For example, you might place the following lines in **.login**.

```
set SHELL = /bin/csh
set TERM = ansi
eval `tset -s`
```

Of course, in place of **ansi,** you would substitute your own terminal code.

NOTE   The **tset** command uses the values of the **SHELL** and **TERM** variables. Make sure these variables are set before you issue the **tset** command.

If you regularly log in from several different terminals, place the following lines in your **.login** file instead of those shown previously.

```
#
# set terminal parameters
set noglob
set termstat = 1
while $termstat
    set term = (`tset -h -m unknown:?ansi -r -S -Q`)
    set termstat = $status
end
setenv TERM "$term"
setenv TERMCAP /etc/termcap
unset term noglob
```

When you log in, if your terminal has not already been configured, the shell will display the following:

```
term=(ansi)
```

You can then press RETURN to accept the default terminal type, or you can type in the code for another terminal and press RETURN. The **while** loop causes your **.login** file to request your terminal type again if you supply a terminal code it does not recognize.

NOTE   To find out more about **tset,** refer to the *SCO UNIX User's Reference.*

The C shell is like the Bourne shell in many ways: it is a user interface and a programming language. But the C shell provides additional features— such as history substitution, aliases, and job control—that make it tremendously powerful. Like the Bourne shell, the C shell uses variables, but the C shell offers arrays of both string and numeric variables. The C shell programming language is designed to resemble its namesake, the C language, and is therefore much like an advanced high-level programming language. Furthermore, by modifying your **.login** and **.cshrc** files you can customize your environment.

CHAPTER

12

System Administration

Many of the tasks involved in administering an SCO UNIX system are taken care of automatically by the system itself; however, someone must set up the unique components of an SCO UNIX system, such as user accounts and any special software. Because SCO UNIX is a multiuser system, each user's activity must be authorized and, to some extent, controlled. Although in theory an SCO UNIX system could run forever without human intervention, certain tasks that help to keep the system running more smoothly and efficiently must be performed by a human being.

Although SCO UNIX may at times seem to be a mysterious "black box," it is important to keep in mind that you can control almost all aspects of system operation. Using the *SCO UNIX System Administrator's Reference* and this book, you should be able to set up your system to meet your needs, and take care of any problems that arise thereafter. If you are a new system administrator, this chapter will help you understand some of the tasks you must carry out, including how to solve some common system problems. Although this chapter is primarily addressed to system administrators, it may also interest ordinary users.

Who Is the System Administrator?

The system administrator on an SCO UNIX system is the person (or people) who performs the administrative tasks that must be done by a human being. The system administrator is usually someone who is knowledgeable about all aspects of the system. Most system administrators have an account on the system to which users can send electronic mail if they have any questions or problems. If you don't know who the administrator of your SCO UNIX system is, ask the person who assigned you your account name and password. Chances are, he or she either is the system administrator or knows who is.

The system administrator usually logs in to the SCO UNIX system as **root**, a user whose home directory is /. A person logged in as **root** is called the *superuser* because this person has read and write permission on all files in the system, and execute permission on all executable files. On some systems, there may be several system administrators, each of whom carries out specific duties from her or his own account, which has specific superuser powers. Only the superuser can execute most of the commands that are used for system administration.

A Few Words of Caution

The superuser has unlimited power over the system. There is no file or program that cannot be accessed—and damaged by—a person logged in as **root**; therefore, you must use extreme caution whenever you do anything as **root**. If you follow a few simple guidelines, you will reduce the risk of damaging files.

- Avoid creating files in any of the directories used for system files, including /, **/bin**, **/usr** and its subdirectories, and **/lib**, unless there is a specific reason for the file to be located there. You may be unaware of an already-existing file that has the same name as one you want to create. Also, certain directories are searched and the files in them automatically executed at given times. If you must create files as **root**, create them either in the **/tmp** directory, the **/u/bin** or **/u/lib** directory, or in the home directory of your non-superuser account.

- Avoid removing system files, even if you don't think you need them. If you want to remove a utility from the system, it is much safer to use **custom** than to remove the executable file yourself. As for system files that are not executable, do not remove them at all. They may be required by a utility, and it would be hard to restore them later.

- Avoid making changes to system text files or shell scripts unless you are specifically directed to do so by this book or by one of the SCO UNIX manuals. If you do make a change, retain the original lines in the file as comments by preceding them with a # symbol, or save a copy of the original file with a slightly different name. This way, you will always have a way to restore the file to its original state in case you make a change that turns out to be incorrect.

- Avoid using commands that you don't understand. When you are in doubt about what a command does, consult the *SCO UNIX System Administrator's Reference* or the *SCO UNIX User's Reference*. Many administrative commands affect a number of files and can wreak havoc if used improperly.

The System Administration Shell—sysadmsh

The system administration shell **sysadmsh** is a menu-based shell designed to make administering your system easier. The **sysadmsh** allows you to run many system administration commands without having to enter these commands—sometimes with numerous options—on the command line.

This saves you not only the time it takes to enter the commands, but the effort of memorizing the commands and options that accomplish each task. One drawback of using the **sysadmsh** is that the menu options it provides are often more limited than those for the equivalent command on the command line. On the command line, you can choose any option or set of options you like, but when you use **sysadmsh**, you are limited to the particular set of options that **sysadmsh** provides. If you want to issue these commands with different options, you must do so from the command line.

Chapter 2, in the *SCO UNIX System Administrator's Reference,* "sysadmsh: Using the System Administration Shell," explains how to use the **sysadmsh** interface and includes a list of administrative commands and their corresponding **sysadmsh** menu options. This list refers you to other sections of the UNIX documentation that contain detailed information on each command. Throughout this book, as in the *SCO UNIX System Administrator's Reference,* menu selections are indicated with the → symbol. For example, the sequence

Backups→Create

indicates the following procedure:

1. Enter the system administration shell with the command

   # **sysadmsh**

 NOTE   The # is the shell prompt when you are logged in as the system administrator.

2. Select the **Backups** option from the main **sysadmsh** menu. To select a menu option, either highlight the option by moving to it with the arrow keys or type the first letter of the option. For example, to select the **Backups** option, you would type **B**.

3. From the menu that appears, select the **Create** option.

 NOTE   To enter most of the **sysadmsh** command sequences, you must be logged in as **root**, or have certain superuser powers.

When the selection of an option requires you to enter a name or number before proceeding, that necessity is indicated by a colon. For example, the sequence **Accounts→User→Examine:Password** indicates the following actions:

1. Enter the system administration shell.

2. Select the **Accounts** option.

3. Select the **User** option from the new menu that appears.

4. Select the **Examine** option. At this point, a form will appear.

5. On the form, fill in the name of the user whose account you want to examine.

6. After filling in the form, select the **Password** option.

Because using **sysadmsh** is generally a safer way to perform most system administration tasks, you should use it as often as you can. A good rule of thumb is: use the **sysadmsh** unless you need to use commands or options that are not available through it. This lessens your chance of making an error. If, on the other hand, you are familiar with the command you want to use, or you want to use particular command line options, go ahead and use the UNIX command from the command line. The examples in this chapter use **sysadmsh** commands whenever possible. Though most **sysadmsh** commands correspond to actual SCO UNIX commands that can be entered from the command line, some tasks—creating user accounts—can *only* be done with **sysadmsh**. Whenever the action of a **sysadmsh** menu option is the same as that of an ordinary UNIX command, **sysadmsh** displays the name of that command at the far left of the highlighted status line.

One advantage of using **sysadmsh** is that if you are ever stuck without any manuals and don't remember what command you need, you can use the built-in Help menu to find out what the various menu options do. To access the Help menu, press F1, the first function key. You can then choose a topic, search for particular words or topics, and even print out the information that the Help program provides. Once you've entered the Help menu, you can also get information about using the Help menu itself.

Ordinary users can use **sysadmsh,** but not all of the commands accessed through **sysadmsh** are available to them. Of the **sysadmsh** options that are available to ordinary users, perhaps the most useful are those that involve formatting and copying files to and from floppy disks. The **Media** command gives you a list of other options that you can use to list a floppy's contents, and copy files to and from floppy archives, and copy entire disks. If a particular option is not available to a user, **sysadmsh** prints an error message and returns the user to the previous menu.

Installing the System Software

The first task of the system administrator is to install the SCO UNIX system software on the computer. During installation, the administrator supplies information about the type of hardware the system has and sets up any special file systems that need to be reserved for user accounts. The system administrator also decides which parts of the SCO UNIX software to install. These and other topics are discussed in detail in Chapter 2, "Installing the System."

Starting and Stopping the System

Most SCO UNIX systems remain on and running 24 hours a day. This is recommended for several reasons.

- It reduces the stress on the hard disk and other hardware components that results from being warmed and cooled and from the heads landing on the media surfaces.

- It saves time because you do not have to boot up the system every day. If ordinary users do not have access to the console, they will not be able to boot the system.

- It allows the administrator to execute time-consuming jobs at times when there are few or no users on the system. Depending on the level of security enabled on your system, ordinary users may also be able to schedule jobs for less busy times. You can schedule specific tasks for **cron** to run at specific times with the **at** and **crontabs** utilities.

- It allows you to send and receive electronic mail from other computers your system is connected to at any hour of the day. This is especially important if you have a high volume of electronic mail or if you exchange mail with systems in other time zones. When your system is not on, mail coming to you from other systems may be delayed or even returned to the sender.

A system that is always on will at times need to be shut down and restarted for maintenance, installation of new software, or installation of new hardware components, such as a hard disk. The next three subsections explain what is involved in turning an SCO UNIX system on and off.

Starting Up the System

A UNIX system is *booted,* or started up, from the system console. Since the SCO UNIX operating system software resides on a hard disk, the first step in starting up the system is often simply turning on the computer. Before the operating system starts up, or boots, most computers run a self-check to make sure everything is operating properly. Then the screen clears and you see this prompt:

```
Boot
  :
```

Pressing RETURN at this prompt loads the default SCO UNIX kernel program, which is determined by an entry in the file **/etc/default/boot** that begins with the word **DEFBOOTSTR**. You can change this entry if your system has special hardware configurations that require a different program to be used.

There are several possible levels of operation, each one assigned a number. These levels are called *init levels*. The two most common levels are **init** level 1, also called system maintenance or single user mode, and **init** level 2, also called multiuser mode. When you see the prompt

```
Type CONTROL-d to continue with normal startup,
(or give the root password for system maintenance):
```

you must decide whether to stay in single user (system maintenance) mode or to bring the system up in multiuser (normal) mode. In single user mode, only **root** can be logged in. You use this mode to repair damaged files, install new system software, or do any other work on the system that requires no users to be logged in.

If you elect to continue in system maintenance mode, parts of the boot process that are only necessary for multiuser operation will not be executed. For example, if you have a /**u** filesystem for user accounts, it will not be mounted. Similarly, a multiport board, designed to support several user terminals, will not be set up for use, and the terminals connected to it will not be available for logins.

If you tell the computer to enter multiuser mode, you are prompted to supply a new time and date. The clock on your system is usually updated by the computer's built-in clock, so the time displayed at this prompt will probably be correct, but if it is not, you can reset it. Some information now appears on the screen, telling you what processes are being started. If you have a multiport board, information about that board is also displayed. Then, an ordinary login prompt appears on the console screen and on each of the enabled terminals, indicating that the system is ready for normal use.

Shutting Down the System

To ensure that no data is lost or scrambled when a system goes down, it must be shut down with special commands that make sure everything is in order and all processes are properly terminated. The superuser is the only person authorized to use these commands. Unplugging or turning off the computer is a dangerous way to shut a system down. Even if no users are logged on to the system, any background or system processes that are running when the system is shut down improperly will be instantly terminated, resulting in possible loss or scrambling of data. The situation becomes even worse if users *are* logged on and running their own processes.

The safest way to shut down your system is with the **/etc/shutdown** command. With no arguments or options the **shutdown** command does the following things:

1. It broadcasts a message that has the following format to all terminals where users are logged in.

```
Broadcast message from root (tty01) on Fri Apr 6 19:44:09 PDT 1990
THE SYSTEM IS BEING SHUT DOWN NOW! ! !
Log off now or risk your files being damaged.
```

2. It waits 60 seconds (or another interval specified with the **-g** option) to give users a chance to log off.

3. It prompts you to confirm the shutdown, as follows:

```
Do you want to continue? (y or n):
```

4. It displays messages about the stages of the shutdown procedure, which may include the following:

```
The system is coming down. Please wait.

System services are now being stopped.

cron aborted: SIGTERM

!SIGTERM  Fri Apr 6 19:45:35 PDT 1990
!*******CRON ABORTED******* Fri Apr 6 19:46:15 PDT 1990
Print services stopped.
The system is down.
```

The **shutdown** command can be followed by several options that alter its behavior.

    -y   This option runs the **shutdown** command without prompting you for confirmation.

-g[*hh*:]*mm*   This option specifies the number of hours and minutes before shutdown. You can use it to specify an interval different from the default if you want to shut the system down when you are not around, or if you want to give users more warning. Note that if you use the **-g** option to shut down the system when you are not there, you must also use the **-y** option so the **shutdown** program does not wait for you to confirm.

-i*level*   This option specifies the level of operation you want to bring the system to. As mentioned at the beginning of this section, **init** level 1 is single user, or system maintenance mode, and level 2 is multiuser mode. The **init** levels you can select are 0, 1, 2, 5, 6, s, and S. See the **init** section in the *SCO UNIX System Administrator's Reference* for more information about the **init** levels.

XENIX   The XENIX **shutdown** command behaves differently from the UNIX command and has a different command line syntax. XENIX does not have a default shutdown time, so you must specify the time until shutdown. Follow the **shutdown** command with a number in the format [*hh*:]*mm*, where *hh* is the optional number of hours and *mm* is the number of minutes. If you follow the **shutdown** command with the argument **su**, instead of a number, the system will go into system maintenance mode (**init** level 1).

The messages printed by the XENIX **shutdown** command also differ from those printed by UNIX. The XENIX shutdown does not prompt you to confirm, but does tell you when all users have logged off. Also, instead of itemizing the processes that have been stopped, the XENIX **shutdown** command prints the process numbers of the processes that have been killed.

 CAUTION   Once you have invoked the **shutdown** command on either UNIX or XENIX, do not attempt to interrupt its execution by pressing the BREAK key or the interrupt key. If you change your mind about shutting down the system, you will have to wait for the system to complete the shutdown procedure and then reboot. See the *SCO UNIX System Administrator's Reference* or *SCO XENIX System Maintenance* for more information about the **shutdown** command.

If you are not the system administrator, remember that a message from **root** telling you that the system is going down in a few minutes is the signal to quickly finish what you are doing and log out. If the shutdown is scheduled for more than a few minutes away, you can keep working until just before the scheduled time. If you do not log out or if you leave background processes running, your processes will not be completed. You can either kill your processes yourself before logging out or let the system terminate them—the result is the same.

Accidental Shutdowns   Occasionally a UNIX system will be shut down accidentally by a power outage, hardware malfunction, or human error (such as someone tripping over the power cord). For the most part, UNIX stores data in files instead of in memory; therefore, system crashes usually result in very little lost data. For example, if you are editing a file, a copy of the buffer is usually saved so you can retrieve any changes you might have made since writing the file to disk. When this happens, mail is automatically sent from **root** upon reboot telling users how to recover the buffer of any files they were editing. In addition, SCO UNIX uses the **fsck** (for "filesystem check") utility to check and repair data after the system has been shut down improperly. Nonetheless, a system crash may result in some lost data.

Another type of crash, often more devastating than a system crash, is a *disk crash,* which occurs when the hard disk is damaged. Depending on the extent of the damage to the disk, some or all of the data stored on it may be lost. A system is usually unable to repair itself after a severe disk crash. With any luck, you will never experience a disk crash, but if there is a disk crash on your system, it is not the end of the world. As long as your system is backed up frequently, you should suffer minimal loss of data.

Backing Up the System

Some PCs do not have hard disks, but instead load both software and user files from floppy disks. SCO UNIX, on the other hand, does not rely heavily on floppy disks. Although it is possible to store data on floppy disks, all operating system software, as well as most user files, are stored permanently on a large hard disk. If users log in from terminals (rather than PCs emulating terminals), they may not even have access to a floppy disk drive. Because users cannot easily make backups of their own files, it is up to the system administrator to make regular backups of the system, not only to preserve the operating system in case of data loss or corruption, but also to save copies of user files. Thus system backups are very important to all users of a UNIX system. Even if your SCO UNIX system serves only as a platform for an application, such as a special accounting program for your business, that application will create and update files. These files are just as vulnerable to data loss or corruption as ordinary user files, and they must be backed up as well. The following sections and the *SCO UNIX System Administrator's Reference* (Chapter 6, "Backing Up Filesystems") explain how to create a backup schedule and perform and restore backups.

Frequency of Backups

If your SCO UNIX system is heavily used by a number of people, you will probably want to do a backup every day. Fortunately, the **sysadmsh** backup program provides different levels of backups that can save only those files modified since the last lower level backup. If you do these high-level backups frequently, you can reduce the number of low-level, or complete, backups needed.

If your system is not used often, or is only used by one or two people, you may not need to do daily backups. The way to determine whether daily backups are necessary is to consider the effect of losing a day's work on the system. If one user makes a few changes to one or two files, it may not be worth making a backup, but if ten users work all day on twenty new files, or if your system is running a large application that creates and accesses many files, losing a day's worth of data would be a major setback.

You must also decide how long you want to save your backups. The *SCO UNIX System Administrator's Reference* suggests that low-level backups be saved for one year. At first, this may seem unnecessarily long. Why would you need to save a backup for a year when the next backup probably saved all the same files and more? There are two reasons: First, if an important file, either a user file or a system file, is accidentally deleted, it may go unnoticed for a while. Saving backups for a year provides a way to retrieve files that may have been deleted months ago. Second, if you find that some of your files have become corrupted, there is no telling when they were damaged. You may need to restore a backup from several months back to find uncorrupted versions of the files. It is usually sufficient to save only low-level backups for one year. Files on higher level backups will probably be on one of the low-level backups. Still, you may want to save even high-level backups for one month or longer.

Creating a Backup Schedule

Once you've determined how frequently you need to make system backups, you can edit the file **/usr/lib/sysadmin/schedule** to create a backup schedule. (For the remainder of this section, this file will be referred to as *the schedule file*.) The schedule file determines what level of backups are to be performed on what days and what utility will be used to do the backups. The **sysadmsh** command sequence

Backups→Schedule

lets you edit this file. This section will probably be easier to understand if you look at this file as you read. If you do not choose to use the default schedule and type of media, you should make any changes that you want to this file. First, in the line "site mymachine," change the word *mymachine* to the name of your system. You should make this change even if you want to use the defaults for the rest of the information. The next lines of the file contain the names of different types of media and media devices, including different sizes of floppy disks on different drives, and different tape drives. Find the line with the backup device you will be using and make sure this is the only line that is not commented out (preceded by a **#** comment symbol). If this line is commented out, remove the **#** symbol. The original default backup device is floppy disk drive 0, a high-density drive that uses 96 tpi (tracks per inch), 5 1/4-inch disks. Drive 0 is the primary floppy drive. Be sure to comment out the original default line if you will be using another backup medium.

The Backup Descriptor Table, immediately below the media entries, determines the information that is used in instructing you how to label your volumes once a backup is complete. If you are using tapes as a backup medium, replace the dashes in this table with the size of the tape you will be using for each level of backup.

 NOTE The *System Administrator's Reference* supplied with the earlier releases of SCO UNIX says that the size of the tape specified in the Backup Descriptor Table should be the length of the tape in feet. The size should actually be the number of kilobytes the tape holds.

If you will be using floppy disks instead of tape, leave the dashes in the table as they are. The default backup schedule uses only four of the ten possible backup levels: 0, 1, 8, and 9. Consequently, the Backup Descriptor Table contains lines only for these levels. If you intend to use other backup levels, you will need to create entries in the table for them.

The schedule file already contains a sample backup schedule. If you have a **/u** filesystem, the sample schedule contains lines for both **root** and **/u**. In this case, the sample schedule creates a backup for the **/u** filesystem every day, and a backup for the **root** filesystem every other day. You may think you can back up the **root** filesystem less frequently, because it consists of files that you can recopy from the installation floppy disks; however, you frequently change system files in the **root** filesystem when configuring the system, so it is just as important to have backups of the **root** filesystem as of other filesystems. If you do not have a **/u** filesystem, there will only be an entry for **root** in the schedule file. In this case, the sample backup schedule will create a backup of the **root** filesystem every day. You can use this schedule if you want to or adjust it to your needs. Remember that if you do not have a /**u** filesystem, the root filesystem contains all of the user files as well as the system files, and must be backed up as often as suggested for the /**u** filesystem.

Tapes Versus Floppy Disks

The initial default backup device is the primary floppy disk drive. Since the operating system software comes on floppy disks that you have to install on your computer, every system must have at least one floppy disk drive. Thus the advantage of using floppy disks for system backups (perhaps the *only* advantage) is that they do not require any additional hardware. The disadvantages of floppy disk backups are that they require a large number of disks, and they also require someone to swap disks in and out of the machine during the entire procedure. Tape backups are superior to floppy disk drives in terms of speed, number of volumes required, and convenience. If you plan to back up your system frequently (as you should), it is highly recommended that you have a tape drive.

Performing a Backup

Using **sysadmsh** commands, you can easily perform either scheduled or unscheduled backups. If you do a scheduled backup, the schedule file automatically determines what level backup to do, what medium to use, and what files to back up. The **sysadmsh** command sequence

Backups→Create

is an interface with an ordinary SCO UNIX archiving utility. By default, **sysadmsh** uses the **cpio** utility to copy files between filesystems and backup media. The **cpio** utility works on any SCO UNIX or XENIX filesystem. You can edit the schedule file to make **sysadmsh** use the **xbackup** utility instead of **cpio**. Simply change the word *cpio* in the final column of the backup schedule to *xbackup*.

The **xbackup** utility is the same as the XENIX **backup** utility, but the name has been changed in SCO UNIX to make it clear that this utility is for XENIX filesystems. You may want to use **xbackup** instead of **cpio** to back up a XENIX filesystem for the purpose of transferring it to a system running XENIX. Since the XENIX **sysadmsh** uses the **backup** utility, it is easier to restore a backup made with this utility on a XENIX system. Keep in mind, however, that **xbackup** works *only* on XENIX filesystems, and a backup made with **xbackup** cannot be restored with **cpio**.

XENIX   To perform a backup on a XENIX system, you should log in as **backup**, which puts you directly in the Filesystem Maintenance menu. The reason for doing backups under the **backup** identity is to avoid accidentally damaging or removing important files that could be removed by the super-user. By default, the XENIX **sysadmsh** uses the **backup** utility to copy filesystems to and from backup media. See the section "Alternative Backup Methods" for backup commands that can be entered from the command line.

You should perform backups when few or no users are logged on so that you will be sure to have the most recent version of each user file. However, if your system has a **/u** filesystem or other user filesystems, you must make sure that these filesystems are mounted before you can create backups of them. If you have just booted the system in single user mode, filesystems besides the **root** will not be mounted. To mount them, you can either bring the system up in multiuser mode or use the **Filesystems** option of the **sysadmsh**.

Restoring Backups

To restore any backup to the hard disk, use the **sysadmsh** command sequence

Backups→Restore

You can then choose to restore either an entire filesystem (by selecting the **Full** option) or certain files or directories (by selecting the **Partial** option).

Next, you are presented with a form that you fill in to specify the filesystem, files, or directories you want to restore and the medium the backup is stored on. The **sysadmsh** backup program uses the schedule file to determine what backup method you use, and restores the backup to the hard disk with the appropriate utility. If your backups are made with **cpio**, **cpio** is used to restore the backup to the hard disk. If your backups are made with **xbackup**, they are restored with **xrestore**.

 CAUTION   When you use **xrestore** to restore an entire filesystem, the filesystem you are restoring to is overwritten. That is, the entire filesystem is replaced by the contents of the backup, and the newer files are removed. See the section "Alternative Backup Methods" for ways to backup and restore XENIX filesystems without incurring this risk.

You can restore an entire filesystem from a **cpio** backup without destroying any new files created after the backup was made. However, if one version of a file is on the backup, and a newer version is on the hard disk, the older version will overwrite the newer one; therefore, you must be careful when restoring from backups. Do not restore an entire filesystem, or even the contents of the last high-level backup if, for example, you just need to replace one user's lost files. Instead, restore just the files you are looking for. See the next section, "Alternative Backup Methods," for ways to restore particular files.

Alternative Backup Methods

If you want to make your system backups automatically with **cron**, instead of using **sysadmsh**, there are two SCO UNIX utilities you can use. One is **cpio**, the utility used when you select the **sysadmsh Backups** option. The other is **tar**. Both **cpio** and **tar** work on either XENIX or UNIX filesystems. Each of these two utilities has advantages and disadvantages.

The **tar** utility is easy to use because of its relatively simple command line options. It can split files between volumes if there is not room for a whole file at the end of a volume. Each volume (tape or floppy disk) of a **tar** backup is independent, and individual files can be recovered without starting at disk (or tape) number one. The disadvantage of **tar** is that it does not back up named pipes, nodes, device files, or empty directories. The **tar** utility is recommended for floppy backups, user file backups, multivolume tape backups, and full system tape backups.

The **cpio** utility creates portable backups because of its standard header format. It can split files between volumes and back up special files, including device files, pipes, and empty directories. Its command line options are versatile, though somewhat complex. The **cpio** utility also has some disadvantages. To restore a file from a **cpio** backup, the directory on the first volume of the backup must be read first, followed by every disk in sequence until the appropriate file is reached. If any of the volumes are corrupted or lost, you cannot restore any files from later volumes. The **cpio** utility is recommended for single volume tape backups and full system tape backups.

To do automatic backups, you must use a tape drive. (If the backup is made on floppy disks, someone has to swap the disks in and out of the drive.) The following set of examples illustrates how you can back up and restore whole or partial filesystems with **cpio** and **tar**. You can place any of these commands in a shell script and then run that script from the **crontab** file. See the next section, "Creating a Schedule of Jobs," for more information about executing commands from the **crontab** file. These examples assume that the backup volume is a 150 megabyte cartridge tape. For a nonerror correcting driver, replace *erct0* in the examples with *rct0*. For detailed information about the commands or options used in the examples, see the *SCO UNIX System Administrator's Reference*.

The first example shows how you would back up the entire system (including pipes, nodes, and empty directories) to an error correcting tape. The **cpio** utility is used to create the backup.

```
# find / -print | sort | cpio -ocB > /dev/erct0
```

The next command line uses **cpio** to back up just the **root** filesystem, and not the **/u** filesystem. The backslash is necessary to tell the shell that the commands are all part of the same line, even though they may not fit on one screen line.

```
# find / -print | egrep -v "^/u/" | sort | cpio -ocBv \
/dev/erct0
```

This example backs up the entire system (except for pipes, device files, nodes, and empty directories) using **tar**:

```
# tar cvf /dev/erct0 /
```

The next set of examples shows how to restore files and directories from backups made with **tar** and **cpio**. You would use this command line to get a listing of all the files and directories on a **cpio** archive tape:

```
# cpio -icBrt < /dev/erct0
```

The following example would restore just the file **/u/daleb/horseshoes** from a **cpio** archive tape.

```
# cpio -icBvdmlu /u/daleb/horseshoes < /dev/erct0
```

This example would restore just the directory **/u/sshadeed** (and all of its files and subdirectories) from a **cpio** archive tape:

```
# cpio -icBvdmlu /u/sshadeed < /dev/erct0
```

The next example would list, but not restore, the files and directories on a **tar** archive tape. This is useful for determining which volume of a multivolume backup contains the file or files you want.

```
# tar tvf /dev/erct0
```

The following example would extract one file, **/u/daleb/horseshoes**, and one directory **/u/carolb** from a **tar** archive tape.

```
# tar xvf /dev/erct0 /u/daleb/horseshoes /u/carolb
```

 NOTE   If you want to run a backup command from a shell script executed from a **crontab** file, you must include the following line in the script

```
PATH=/bin:/usr/bin:/etc
```

Without this line, **cron** will not know where to find the backup commands.

Creating a Schedule of Jobs

There are a number of routine tasks that should be performed on your system. The **crontab** utility provides a way for you to schedule these tasks to be run automatically by **cron**. The **cron** program starts up automatically whenever the system is booted in multiuser mode, and runs all scheduled jobs at the specified times. These include jobs scheduled for a later time with the **at** utility, jobs queued with the **batch** utility, and jobs scheduled for regular times in files in the **/usr/spool/cron/crontabs** directory. These files are referred to as *crontab files*. When the system is installed, three crontab files are automatically created in the **/usr/spool/cron/crontabs** directory, **root**, **adm**, and **uucp**. Each of these files is designed to handle particular kinds of administrative jobs. Unless you have parceled out the system administration tasks to several users, there is no need to have separate crontab files for different sets of administrative tasks. All of the administrative crontab files can be combined in the **root** crontab file. Use the **crontab** utility to create new crontab files in this directory. Some of the tasks you may want to have **cron** automatically perform include backing up the system and polling systems to which you are connected via **uucp**.

NOTE   If you want to back up the system automatically with a line in the **crontab** file, the **sysadmsh** cannot be used for backups. See the previous section, "Alternative Backup Methods," for examples of backup commands that can be entered from the command line.

Figure 12-1 shows a sample crontab file on a system with just one system administrator. The third line of the file (commented out by the preceding #) explains what the six fields in each line are. The first five fields determine the time at which the commands are executed. An asterisk (*) in any of the time fields indicates that the command is to be executed at every occurrence of that unit. For example, an asterisk in the hour field means that the command will be executed every hour at the minute specified. An asterisk in the month field means the command is to be executed every month on the specified day or days. See the *SCO UNIX System Administrator's Reference* for more information about any of the commands that appear in

Figure 12-1. To start running the commands in a new or changed crontab file, execute the **crontab** command. For example, if you make some changes to the **root** crontab file, type the command

```
# crontab < /usr/spool/cron/crontab/root
```

Figure 12-1.

```
# crontab for root
# Created by Jerrod Lompopo
# min    hour    day    month    DayOfWeek    command;command
#(0-59) (0-23)  (1-31)  (1-12)    (0-6) where 0=Sunday
# -----------------------------------------------------------------
#     update system clock from real time clock at 2:02am
02  2  *  *  *  cat -s /dev/clock >/dev/null 2>&1 || exit 0;\
/etc/setclock `date +mdHMy'
#     Update the calendars. Send mail to users from calendar files
00  2  *  *  *  /usr/bin/calendar -
#     Remove all core dumps
25  5  *  *  *  /bin/find / -name core -exec rm {} ;
#     Remove all nohup dumps
30  5  *  *  *  /bin/find / -name nohup.out -exec rm {} ;
#     Rebuild the news history files
45  4  *  *  *  /usr/lib/news/expire -r -I -e 999999 -E 999999
#     Backup some stuff to tape with  backup.tape  shell script
30  4  *  *  *  /u/bin/backup.tape
#     fsck. Forget it if someone is logged in. Takes < 90 sec max.
55  5  *  *  *  /etc/umount /dev/u;/bin/fsck "-y" >/dev/null 2>&1
#     Reboot at 6:00 even if fsck fails or hangs. No need to remount.
00  6  *  *  *  /bin/sync; /bin/sleep 10; /etc/reboot
#     Forced call to uunet once a day.
30  2  *  *  *  /usr/lib/uucp/uucico -r1 -Suunet
#     Forced call to sosco every hour.
25  *  *  *  *  /usr/lib/uucp/uucico -r1 -Ssosco
#     Clean out the uucp stuff on Sat at 6pm
00 18  6  *  *  ulimit 5000; /bin/su uucp -c "/usr/lib/uucp/uudemon.\
clean"
#     Office portfolio housekeeping
0 0 1 * *   op caltrim 30
0 0 * * 1-5 op cronsched
0 0 * * 1   op cronsched -w
```

A Sample crontab File.

Using Printers

An SCO UNIX system is capable of supporting a number of different kinds of printers, from dot matrix to laser. Once you install a printer on your system and get it working, the print spooler manages all print requests and checks that everything is in working order. The print spooler and other user-oriented aspects of printers are discussed in Chapter 9. This chapter and the *SCO UNIX System Administrator's Reference* (Chapter 15, "Using Printers") explain how to set up printers on the system and control the actions of the print spooler.

Installing Printers

SCO UNIX supports both serial and parallel printers. Which type of port you connect your printer to depends on the type of printer you have. A serial port can handle either login terminals or printers. To make sure the serial port you want to connect a serial printer to is not enabled for logins, you must disable the port before you connect the printer. If the port is enabled for logins, the **getty** program, which sends the login prompt to terminals and waits for a user response, will be running on the device, and you will not be able to print. To disable logins on a serial port for use with a printer, use the command

```
# disable ttynn
```

where *nn* is the number of the **tty** device associated with that port. Since parallel ports cannot be used for user terminals, you do not have to change the way a parallel port is set up before you install a parallel printer.

 NOTE If a login prompt prints out on the printer either when you first connect it or when you send a request to it, it is probably because the **getty** process associated with that terminal has refused to die. If this happens, try enabling the port and then disabling it again. As a last resort, you can shut the system down and reboot. Once you've rebooted, the **getty** process should no longer be running.

Configuring Printers

After connecting a printer and disabling the port to which it is connected, you must configure the printer for use. Use the **sysadmsh Printers** option to configure and enable printers. It is easy to configure a printer using **sysadmsh**. First use the **sysadmsh** command sequence

Printers→Configure→Add

A form appears on which you fill in some information about the new printer, beginning with its name. Many administrators choose to name the printer something descriptive, for example, "laser" if the printer is a laser printer or "daisy" if it is a daisy wheel; however, you can use any name up to fourteen characters long. If you want a name that has two words, use an underscore character to separate them, for example "daisy_wheel." Since users may have to type them frequently, it is best to keep printer names as short as possible.

The other information you enter about the printer includes the class the printer will be associated with, the name of the interface script used to communicate with the printer, the type of connection the printer will use, and the name of the device file associated with the printer port. The device name is the full pathname of the file, for example, **/dev/tty1a** or **/dev/lp0**.

XENIX The XENIX **sysadmsh** uses the command sequence

System→Add→Printer

to configure printers. Instead of a form, XENIX uses the **mkdev lp** command (an interactive question and answer program) for obtaining information about the printer.

After you've configured the printer, you must do two things to allow it to accept and print requests. First, use the **sysadmsh** command sequence

Printers→Schedule→Accept

and enter the name of the printer to make it begin accepting requests. Next, enable the printer for printing with the **sysadmsh** command sequence

Printers→Schedule→Enable

and enter the name of the printer to be enabled.

 NOTE   Enabling a printer is not the same as enabling the port the printer is connected to. Enabling the *printer* allows data to be sent to the printer, while enabling the *port* spawns a **getty** process that sends a login prompt to the device using the port (exactly what you don't want to do with a printer). Follow the **enable** command with *the name of the printer* to enable printing on the port, or with *the name of the device file associated with the port* to enable a login terminal.

Establishing Printer Classes

A class of printers is a group of printers to which users can send a request. You may want to group printers according to type (for example, all laser printers), or they may be similar in some other way. For example, they may all be in the same area or office.

Printers in a class are arranged in the order in which you add them to the class. When a user sends a request to a class of printers, the printers in the class are used in the order in which they were added. Therefore, if one printer in a class is faster than others or produces better output, that printer should be the first one you add.

Adding a printer to a class simply means specifying a class name in the form **sysadmsh** uses when you configure a printer or examine the values for the printer. If the class you specify does not exist, it is created. Once you have created one or more classes, you can list them by pressing F3 when you get to this section of the form. If you want to add a printer to a class after it has been configured, examine the configuration for the printer with the **sysadmsh** command sequence

Printers→Configure→Examine

and enter the name of the printer. The same form that is presented when you first add the printer will be displayed, and you can then enter the name of a class to which you want the printer added.

XENIX   To add a printer to a class, use the **sysadmsh** command sequence

System→Add→Printer

and then select the option **3. Reconfigure an existing printer** from the menu presented by **mkdev lp**.

Starting and Stopping the Print Service

Ordinarily, the print service is started every time the system boots and goes into multiuser mode. When the print service starts up, all printers that have been listed to accept requests begin accepting, and all enabled printers begin printing. If for some reason you need to shut down the print service, you can do so with the **sysadmsh** command sequence

Printers→Schedule→Stop

When you want to start the print service again, use the **sysadmsh** command sequence

Printers→Schedule→Begin

Administering User Accounts

Chapter 2 explains how to create user accounts on an SCO UNIX system. Once you have set up an account, you can monitor and control its activity. In fact, several system administration tasks have to be done for each account on your system from time to time. Many aspects of account administration are explained in detail in Chapter 10 of the *SCO UNIX System Administrator's Reference,* "Administering User Accounts." Much of what is involved in administering user accounts on SCO UNIX is intricately tied up in maintaining system security. This is not so much the case on XENIX, which does not conform to such a high level of security. Most of the information in this section does not apply to XENIX. For more information about administering XENIX accounts, see Chapter 10 in the *SCO XENIX System Administrator's Reference,* "Preparing XENIX for Users."

Changing Systemwide Defaults

Each time you create an account, you can choose to accept the default parameters for the account or to modify the defaults. If you find that you need to modify the defaults for every account you create, you may want to change the system defaults for certain parameters. For example, the default password expiration time is 42 days. If you select a longer expiration time for all or most users, you can change the default to a longer time. This allows you to select the default for the new accounts you create. Use the **sysadmsh** command sequence

Accounts→Defaults

to modify any of the system defaults. The menu displayed offers three choices, **Password, Logins,** and **Authorizations**.

   Selecting the **Logins** option, allows you to change the number of unsuccessful logins that can be tried before an account or terminal is locked.

The low default numbers in these categories are designed to keep un-authorized users from breaking into the system by repeatedly trying different account names or passwords.

The **Password** option lets you change the default expiration time, lifetime, and length of passwords for user accounts. It lets you determine whether users will be allowed to choose their own passwords. You can decide how vulnerable your system is to break-ins, and adjust the default password parameters accordingly. If no strangers have access to your computer or terminals, and if only a few people use your system, it is not as important to have users change their passwords frequently as it is on a large system where access to terminals is less controlled.

The **Authorizations** option lets you select which kernel and subsystem command authorizations will be available to ordinary users. Kernel authorizations pertain to processes and determine the permissions a user's process will have (these may be differ from the permissions the user has). Subsystem authorizations apply to users and give them permission to execute certain commands or sets of commands. If you press F3 for a list of subsystem authorizations, only a small subset of the available authorizations will be listed. In addition to those listed, you can select authorizations that give users limited superuser powers. Since these authorizations are generally assigned to only one user, you would not want to assign them as default authorizations. Instead, you would assign them individually to the appropriate accounts.

One group of command authorizations that is not assigned through the **Accounts** option of the **sysadmsh** is the set that includes the **crontab, at,** and **batch** utilities. These utilities allow users to initiate jobs to be performed on a regular schedule or at a later time. By default, ordinary users on SCO UNIX are not allowed to use any of these utilities. If you want to allow certain users or all users to use **at, batch,** and **crontab,** you can do so with the **sysadmsh** option **Jobs.** The following example shows the **sysadmsh** command sequence you would use to allow all users to run jobs at a later time with **at** and **batch.**

Jobs→Authorize→Delayed→Default→Allow

Initially, all users are denied permission to use **at** and **batch**. If you want to allow only certain users to use these commands while keeping **Deny** as the system default, you can use the following **sysadmsh** command sequence.

Jobs→Authorize→Delayed→User:Allow

After you select the **User** option, you are prompted to enter the name of the user whose permissions you want to alter.

XENIX   On XENIX, you can authorize all users to use the **at, batch,** and **crontab** commands simply by making sure the file **/usr/lib/cron/at.allow** does not exist. Then you can restrict certain users from using these commands by putting their login names in the file **/usr/lib/cron/at.deny**.

If you choose to give all or some users access to the **crontab, at,** and **batch** commands, you must also give those users the kernel authorization **chmodsugid**. You can assign this authorization as a system default or on a case-by-case basis.

Changing the Defaults for an Account

Whether or not you change any of the systemwide default settings for user accounts, you may want to change the settings for particular user accounts. For example, if you increase the number of unsuccessful logins allowed systemwide, you may want to make the number lower for the **root** account.

If you have a large system, you may want to have several system administrators instead of just one. Rather than letting all of the administrators log in to the **root** account, you can create different accounts, each with a limited number of administrative authorizations. To assign administrative authorizations to an account, thereby changing the default authorizations for that account, use the **sysadmsh** command sequence

Accounts→Userl→Examine

Then enter the name of the user to whom you want to assign the authorizations and select the **Privileges** option. You can then choose to modify either the kernel authorizations or the subsystem authorizations for that user. Certain subsystem authorizations determine administrative authorizations. They are as follows:

mem   This authorization allows access to "private" system data. A user who has this authorization can list all processes on the system.

terminal   A user with this authorization can write to any terminal with the **write** command.

lp   This authorization lets the user administer the print service.

backup   This authorization is necessary to make backups of the entire system.

auth   A user with this authorization can create and remove user accounts, change user passwords, and perform other tasks involved in administering user accounts.

audit   This authorization allows the user to run system audits and generate reports about system activity.

cron   This authorization lets the user deny and permit use of the **at**, **batch**, and **crontab** utilities.

sysadmin   This authorization lets the user use the **integrity** command, which checks the permissions of files listed in the File Control database.

The **root** account has all of the administrative authorizations. These authorizations can also be assigned to one or more administrative accounts. When you examine the permissions for a user (as described previously), the administrative authorizations are not listed with the other subsystem authorizations. You must type the name of each administrative authorization that you want to assign to an account.

Setting Up the /u Filesystem or Directory

If you have chosen to locate users' home directories in a **/u** filesystem or a **/u** directory, you may want to create some additional directories in **/u**. If you want to allow users to create shell scripts or C programs that will be accessible to other users, create a **/u/bin** directory in which to store them. User-created files should *not* be mixed with system files in system directories such as **/usr/bin** or **/bin**. If you want to allow users to place scripts in the **/u/bin** directory themselves, make the directory readable, writable, and executable by all users. Be sure to remind users to make any files they put in **/u/bin** executable by other users. If your system needs a high level of security, you can allow users to execute the files in **/u/bin** but not to put files there themselves. You may want to require users to submit their scripts to you for inspection, and then place them in **/u/bin** yourself. In this case, make the directory readable and executable but not writable by all users. If you have a **/u/bin** directory, remind users to put this directory in their execution search paths.

If your system will have a number of special data or text files that should be accessible to all users, you may also want to create a **/u/lib** directory. The same considerations apply to the permissions for this directory as to those for **/u/bin**.

Adding Hardware and Device Drivers

There are two basic steps involved in installing new hardware on your computer. One step is to install or set up a device driver for the hardware. A *device driver* is the software interface between the hardware device and the computer, and it controls data transmission between the two. Some device drivers are set up when you install your system. For example, the device drivers that drive the console display must be installed before you can use the console during the installation procedure. Other device drivers are present in the operating system but cannot be used until you set them up and tell them how the hardware will be connected to the computer.

Each hardware device on the system must have a corresponding file in the directory **/dev**. Files in this directory are called *device files* or *device nodes* and are used to access peripheral hardware devices including terminals, printers, modems, and disk drives. The system uses these special files to send data to and from the hardware devices.

Installing a Dial-Out Only Modem

SCO UNIX supports both dial-out and dial-in modems, and you can configure the same modem for both dial-in and dial-out. Each serial port is associated with two device nodes, one with modem control and one without. The port with modem control will be associated with a file in **/dev** whose name ends in an uppercase letter, such as **tty1A**, while the port without modem control will have a name ending in a lowercase letter, such as **tty1a**. Before you install a modem on your system, disable the serial port without modem control that you plan to connect the modem to. For example, if you are installing a modem on COM 1, type

```
# disable /dev/tty1a
```

This command disables the port without modem control. As long as your modem is only a dial-out modem, you can leave the port disabled. The file **/usr/lib/uucp/Devices** must contain correct entries for your modem. This file contains entries for many modem types. Find the line that corresponds to your modem and make sure that it is not preceded by a # comment symbol, which tells the shell to ignore that line in the file. The following lines configure a Hayes 2400-baud modem on COM 1.

```
Direct tty1a - 1200-2400 direct
ACU tty1A - 1200-2400 /usr/lib/uucp/dialHA24
```

If no line in the file looks correct for your modem, you can edit one of the existing lines. If you do this, don't forget to leave a copy of the original line (preceded by a #) in case you ever need it. Next, change the ownership of the device file for the modem port to **uucp**. For example, if your modem is on COM 1, type the command

```
# chown uucp /dev/tty1a
```

If you are using a different port, substitute the name of the device file for that port.

Installing a Dial-In Modem

To configure a modem for dial-in use, you must disable the non modem control port as you would for a dial-out modem, and then enable the modem control port to which the modem is connected. For example, if you are installing the modem on COM 1, type the following commands.

```
# disable tty1a
# enable tty1A
```

Then, check in the file **/etc/inittab** to make sure it includes a line like the following for the port you have just enabled.

```
t1A:2:respawn:/etc/getty tty1A 3
```

Depending on what port you install your modem on, the first number in this line may differ. The line in the previous example instructs the **getty** program to run on the device **tty1A**. If your modem is on COM 2, the first number will be **t2A**. If the modem is connected to one of the ports of a multiport board, other parts of this line will also be different. The last field on the line is the number of the gettydef string that **getty** uses when sending the login prompt to that terminal. A *gettydef string* is a line in the file **/etc/gettydefs** that contains the baud rate and various settings for the terminal. What is important is that the third field says **respawn**, and the fourth **/etc/getty**.

XENIX   On XENIX, enable the port with modem control as described for
UNIX, and then check the file **/etc/ttys** instead of **/etc/inittab** to find the
correct entry for a modem. If you have installed a modem on COM 1 and
enabled the modem control port, you should see the following line in this
/etc/ttys file.

```
12tty1A
```

The **1** in the first column indicates an enabled state for the terminal. The **2**
in the second column shows the **gettydef** string (from the file **/etc/gettydefs**)
that is used for the terminal. The rest of the line is the name of the device
file. This name will be different depending on what port your modem is
connected to.

On UNIX only, once you have enabled the modem control port connected to a modem, make sure there is an entry in the Terminal Database
for the modem control port on which you have just installed the modem. To
see whether there is an entry in the Terminal Database, use the **sysadmsh**
command sequence

Accounts→Terminal→Examine

and enter the name of the device node associated with the port. For example,
if the modem is on COM 1, enter **tty1A**. If there is already an entry for this
terminal, the current information about the terminal will be displayed. If
there is no entry, **sysadmsh** will tell you so. To create an entry, use the
sysadmsh command sequence

Accounts→Terminal→Add

and then enter the name of the device node of the port.

Once you have configured the modem port and made sure there is a
Terminal Database entry for it, have someone call your system. If the
modem is properly enabled, your system should display a login prompt on

the caller's terminal. If this does not happen, first make sure you are using the correct kind of cable, and then try disabling and reenabling the port.

Configuring a Modem for Both Dial-In and Dial-Out

To configure a modem for both dial-in and dial-out use, follow the steps for configuring dial-in modems and those for dial-out modems, as described in the previous sections and in Chapter 14 of the *SCO UNIX System Administrator's Reference,* "Installing Ports, Terminals, and Modems." Your modem should now work both for calling out with **cu** and for accepting calls from other systems. Test its two-way capability first by having someone call in, and then by calling out. If this works, the modem is ready for use.

It is possible that just configuring the modem for both dial-in and dial-out will not be enough. Initially, if you enable the modem control port with the **enable** command, the system tells the **getty** program to run on the device so users can log in normally when they call in. The problem with this is that when a user does call and log in from the modem, **getty** may keep running on the device, making the port unavailable for dial-out use. In this case, you would have to disable the modem port, change the ownership back to **uucp**, and reenable the port. To avoid this problem, you can change the program the system runs on the port. The **/usr/lib/uucp/uugetty** program is devised to relinquish control of a port as soon as a user calling in logs out.

To change the program running on a modem port, you must edit two files. Before you change the entry for a device in these files, disable the device as described in the previous sections. To change the state of a device immediately, edit the file **/etc/inittab**. Although this change takes effect immediately, it is undone the next time the system is booted. To make the change permanent, edit the file **/etc/conf/cf.d/init.base**. To change the program run on the port, find the line for your modem port in these two system files. As you may recall, the line will look something like this:

```
t1A:2:respawn:/etc/getty tty1A 3
```

Edit the line so that it reads

```
t1A:2:respawn:/usr/lib/uucp/uugetty tty1A 3
```

After editing these files, enable the modem control port again.

XENIX You should not have any trouble getting a modem to work for both dial-in and dial-out use on XENIX. Simply follow the instructions in the preceding subsections for installing both a dial-in and a dial-out modem.

Multiport Boards

Most multiport boards come with their own drivers on software that you can install with **custom**. You can access the **custom** utility by entering the command

```
# custom
```

from the command line or by using this **sysadmsh** command sequence:

System→Software

XENIX On XENIX, you can access the **custom** utility either from the command line or with the following **sysadmsh** command sequence.

System→Add→Software

After physically connecting the hardware, simply choose the **custom** option, **Install**, and then select **A New Product** from the list of choices that is displayed. Follow the instructions to install the software. This software will correctly configure the multiport board by linking it into a new kernel and will also set up its ports. After you've installed the software, you will be prompted to shut down the system and reboot the new kernel.

XENIX   The XENIX **custom** utility uses a different format from the UNIX **custom** utility. To install a multiport board on a XENIX system select the **custom** option,

```
4. Add a supported product
```

Some "dumb" multiport boards with SCO-supplied device drivers are installed in place of one of the COM ports on your system. Use the **sysadmsh** command sequence

System→Hardware→Card_Serial

to configure a dumb multiport board.

Terminals

Terminals are connected to the computer via RS-232 serial cables. Before you add a terminal to your system, make sure that model of terminal is supported by SCO UNIX. The supported terminals are listed in the terminals section of the *SCO UNIX User's Reference*.

The device node for a terminal has a name with the form **tty***nn* where *nn* is a code that consists of a number and a letter. For example, the device node for COM 1 is **tty1a**. Another node, **tty1A** (note the uppercase *A*), also represents COM 1, but this device node gives the port modem control. Programs that deal only with special device files or terminals usually allow you to specify just the base name of the node (for example, **tty1a**). However, if you want to write directly to, or modify the behavior of, a terminal, you must specify the full pathname of the device node (such as **/dev/tty1a**). The examples in this book show the correct format for specifying terminal device files with particular commands.

Terminals On Serial Ports   The SCO UNIX system is initially set up for two terminals running at 9600 baud on COM ports 1 and 2. If you add a terminal on one of these ports, you only have to enable it, and it will be ready for use. To enable a terminal on COM 1, use the command

```
# enable ttyla
```

Make sure that you use a lowercase *a*; an uppercase *A* will give the port modem control, and it will not function properly with a login terminal. To enable a terminal on COM 2, use the previous command, but replace the **1** with a **2**.

After you have enabled a terminal, check to see if it is working by pressing RETURN or CTRL-d a few times. If the login prompt appears on the terminal screen, the terminal is enabled and ready for use. If the prompt does not appear, test the connection by disabling the terminal and sending some output to it. For example, to disable terminal **ttyla** and send the date to it, use the following commands.

```
# disable ttyla
# date > /dev/ttyla
```

If the date prints out on the terminal, reenable it with the **enable** command. Sometimes all it takes to get a terminal working is to disable it and reenable it a couple of times. If the date does not print, there could be a problem either with the setup of your terminal or with the wiring. Chapter 14 of the *SCO UNIX System Administrator's Reference*, "Adding Ports, Terminals, and Modems" discusses possible causes and solutions for inoperative terminals.

Terminals on Multiport Boards   If you have installed a multiport board, the SCO UNIX security system requires that you add each of the terminals connected to the multiport board to the Terminal Database. You can do this with the **sysadmsh** command sequence

Accounts→Terminal→Add

Use the name of the special device file in the /**dev** directory to specify a terminal that you want to add to the Terminal Database. For example, to add the device associated with device file /**dev/ttyi1c**, you would specify **ttyi1c**. You must do this for each of the terminals connected to the multiport board. If there is no entry for a terminal in the Terminal Database, no one will be able to log in on that terminal. In addition to adding the terminals connected to a multiport board to the Terminal Database, you must enable each of the terminals separately, just as you would a terminal on a serial port. Finally, you have to test the terminals, just as you would test a terminal connected to a COM port. See the previous section for instructions on testing a terminal.

Fixing System Problems

Because UNIX is such a complex operating system, there is a lot of room for human error, both in system administration and ordinary use. Some common system problems include corrupted system files and errors caused by misinstalled or misconfigured hardware. Problems can also result from system crashes. Fortunately, there are also many ways to solve most of these problems. The *SCO UNIX System Administrator's Reference* (Chapter 19, "Solving System Problems") offers solutions to some common system problems. In this chapter, we address some of the problems that are not covered in the *SCO UNIX System Administrator's Reference*.

You will undoubtedly encounter problems with your system at some point that are not addressed either in this book or in the *SCO UNIX System Administrator's Reference*. The SCO support staff is available to answer questions that you have about particular problems on your system. Thirty days of free technical support are provided with every SCO UNIX or XENIX system sold. The thirty-day period begins when you make your first call to the SCO support staff to register your UNIX or XENIX system; therefore, you should plan to use your system extensively during the month following your first call to the SCO support staff so that you can take advantage of this free assistance. After that, you can purchase one of several levels of extended support for your system. If your business depends heavily on your UNIX system, it is probably wise for your company to purchase extended support. SCO also maintains an electronic bulletin board system called SOS, on which many common problems and their solutions are posted. By logging in to the bulletin board, you can search for topics and send mail to the support staff. A thirty-day trial login on the SOS bulletin board is provided free with each SCO UNIX or XENIX operating system. If you did not receive information about the SOS bulletin board with your operating system, contact SCO customer service. After the thirty-day trial period, you can purchase continued SOS support.

Listing System Problems with fixperm

You can use the **fixperm** command to report and repair problems. The **fixperm** utility reports on incorrect file permissions, missing system files, and other file-related problems.

 CAUTION   You must be logged in as **root** and in the **/** directory for **fixperm** to work correctly.

To see a list of problems, use the following commands

```
# cd /
# fixperm -n /etc/perms/* 2> /tmp/permlist
```

These commands check system files against entries in the files in the **/etc/perms** directory, which show the correct permissions for each file. The output of **fixperm** is not the standard output, but the standard error; therefore, you cannot pipe the output of **fixperm** to a filter. However, since **fixperm** usually prints a large number of messages, you will probably not be able to read them all. In the previous example, the messages (the standard error) are redirected to a file called **permlist** in the **/tmp** directory.

You can use **fixperm** to repair, as well as list, system problems. With no options, **fixperm** repairs all the problems that it would report with the **-n** option. Before you use **fixperm** to repair system problems, you should list the problems with **fixperm -n**, as in the previous example. There may be some files whose permissions you have deliberately changed, and **fixperm** will change these file permissions back to their original values; if you keep the list of problems **fixperm -n** finds, you can go back later and restore the correct permissions for these files. The **fixperm** utility has other options with which you can repair specific kinds of problems. For example, the **-c** option creates missing files and directories, but does not modify file permissions. See the *SCO UNIX System Administrator's Reference* for more details about the options available for the **fixperm** utility.

A Printer That Won't Print

If the printer does not respond, there may be a problem with the printer itself. Make sure that there is paper in the printer and that, if your printer displays error codes, no error code is currently displayed.

There could also be a problem with the interface script the printer uses. There are two ways to solve this problem. You can switch to a different interface for the printer. For example, if you have an HP LaserJet printer, and the **hpjet** interface does not seem to work for you, you can try using the **standard** interface. You can also create a new printer interface script. The original printer interface scripts are stored in the directory **/usr/spool/lp/model**. Do not change the original files so you will always have the original printer scripts should any problems arise with the scripts you create. To create a new script based on one of the model scripts, copy the script you want to a new file and edit that file. Be sure to change the description line at the beginning of the file. Any script you create will appear in the list of existing interfaces when you either modify the information for a printer or add a new printer. You can select that interface just as you would any of the model interfaces.

Lost or Corrupted Files

If a command no longer works or gives persistent error messages where it used to work, it may be because the executable file has been corrupted or accidentally removed from your system. If a file has become corrupted, you can restore it from a system backup as described in the "Restoring Backups" section earlier this chapter, or you can recover the original version of the file from the installation floppy disks. The latter is a safer way to restore a system file because the backup version you restore may already have been corrupted.

You can restore individual system files from the installation floppy disks with the **custom** program. To do this, you must first find out which operating system package contains the file you need to restore. The **/etc/perms** directory contains files that list information about the location of the files on the installation floppy disks. An entry for a system file found on the installation software shows the following information:

- The first field shows the name (in all uppercase letters) of the operating system package the file belongs to. This is the name you need to recover a file with **custom**.

- The second field contains a letter that tells whether the file is a directory (d), a readable file (f), or an executable binary (x), and a 3-digit number that represents the mode of the file (read, write, and execute permissions).

- The third field contains the user and group the file is assigned to when it is installed.

- The fourth field contains the number of links to the file.

- The fifth field contains the full pathname of the file. This can be helpful if you are not sure whether a file is installed or if you think it is not installed where it should be.

- The sixth field contains the installation floppy volume number on which the file is located. This is the volume you will need to restore the file.

Suppose, for example, that you needed to restore the **rmdir** command because the file had become corrupted. To find out which volume of the installation disks contained this file, you could simply search the files in the **/etc/perms** directory for **rmdir**, as in this example:

```
# grep 'rmdir' /etc/perms/*
/etc/perms/inst:RTS x4711 root/sys 1 ./bin/rmdir N03
```

This command uses the **grep** utility to search all the files in the directory **/etc/perms** for the pattern **rmdir**. The output of the command shows the file in which the pattern is found, **/etc/perms/inst**, as well as some information about the file. From this output you can tell that the file **/bin/rmdir** is part of the RTS (Runtime System) package and resides on volume N03 of the installation floppies. Now you can run the **custom** program to restore the file. First select the **Install** option, and then choose **The Operating System** from the list of software. Next select the **Files** option, and you will be prompted to select the package the file is in. A list of files is displayed; simply move the highlight bar to the file you want and press RETURN. The file should now be restored to its proper place in the root filesystem, overwriting the version of the file that was previously stored on the hard disk.

Restoring Lost or Dead User Passwords

If an ordinary user forgets his or her password, or if the password for an account dies, there are two ways you can restore the password to make the account usable again. The superuser has the power to change the password for any account by giving the login name as an argument to the **passwd** command. To change the password for a user whose login name is **carolb**, you would use the command

```
# passwd carolb
```

You would then be prompted to choose between picking the password yourself or having the **passwd** program generate a new password for you. Rather than assigning a password of the user's choice, you should assign a random password and have the user change it.

When you try to change a user's password, you may get the error message, "Password request denied.", followed by the reason for the denial. Here are the reasons for password request denial, accompanied by a brief discussion of how to circumvent them:

Minimum time between password changes.	The user's password has been changed either within the system minimum time allowed between password changes or within the minimum time set for that user.

To remedy this situation, set the minimum time between changes for that user only to 0. Use the **sysadmsh** command sequence

Accounts→User→Examine

Then enter the name of the user and select the **Expiration** option. This way, the user can change the password as soon as he or she logs in with the password you assign. Later, you can change the minimum time for that user back to its original setting.

\Password lifetime has passed.

The password for this user has expired and not been changed within the allowed amount of time. To remedy this problem, temporarily change the lifetime for that user's password to **inf** (for *infinite*). Use the **sysadmsh** command sequence

Accounts→User→Examine

Then enter the name of the user and select the **Expiration** option. Once the user has changed her or his password, you can change the password lifetime for the account back to a normal value.

Not allowed to execute password for the given user.

You are not logged in as **root**. Only the superuser has the power to change another user's password.

Restoring a Lost root Password

Depending on how important your system is and how many people rely on it, a lost **root** password can be a real disaster. You should not take the **root** password lightly. Many system administrators use a system whereby the root password is known only by one person, but is written down and kept in a special place accessible to another person in case of emergency. If no one can log in as **root**, backups cannot be made, system files cannot be modified, and the system cannot even be shut down properly.

In the event that you do forget or lose the **root** password, there is one way to recover it or change the password so that you can log in as **root** again. Because this procedure effectively destroys the security of your system, you must obtain the instructions directly from the SCO support personnel. When you contact SCO about a lost **root** password, they will explain the security procedure you must go through before you can receive the instructions for restoring a lost **root** password. Do not use this method as an alternative to always knowing the **root** password. It can take some time to get the information from the SCO support personnel, and in an emergency, any wait is too long.

This chapter has given the new system administrator the necessary information to perform basic system administration tasks and keep the SCO UNIX system running smoothly. You should now be able to perform system backups, add new hardware devices, maintain user accounts, keep track of system security, and more. For further information about system administration, refer to the *SCO UNIX System Administrator's Reference* provided with each set of SCO UNIX operating system software.

CHAPTER

13

Communicating Using the UUCP System

One of the strengths of UNIX is its built-in communications facilities. With the UUCP (UNIX-to-UNIX Copy Program) system, you can connect UNIX systems over ordinary phone lines to exchange files and electronic mail. The UUCP system requires some initial set up, but once configured, UUCP provides simple, reliable, and error-free file transfer between almost any UNIX systems. UUCP also allows you to execute commands remotely on other UNIX systems, communicate interactively with other UNIX and non-UNIX computers, and exchange electronic mail with other UNIX systems.

Basic File Transfer Using UUCP

The backbone of the UUCP communications facility is the **uucp** utility
itself. The **uucp** utility transfers UNIX files from one UNIX system to
another. Using **uucp** is really not much more complicated than using the
UNIX **cp** command. Like **cp**, **uucp** takes two command line arguments, a
source file, and a destination file. If both the source and destination files are
on the local machine, **uucp** behaves exactly like **cp**; however, usually one
of these files is on the local machine and the other is on another, remote,
computer. For example, to get the file **/usr/games/rogue** from a remote
computer named **uscopia**, and place it in the file **/u/rosso/games/rogue** on
the local machine, the **uucp** command would be

```
$ uucp uscopia!/usr/games/rogue /u/rosso/games/rogue
```

If a full pathname is not given, local files are assumed to be in the current
directory. Assuming your current working directory were **/u/rosso/games**,
the previous command could be shortened to

```
$ uucp uscopia!/usr/games/rogue rogue
```

You indicate a remote file by preceding the name of the file with the name
of the remote computer, and inserting an exclamation mark (!) between the
two names. As mentioned previously, the ! character is called a bang in
UNIX lingo.

 TIP   If you do not know the name of the remote computer to use, you can
execute the **uuname** command, which displays the names of all the remote
computers known to your system.

After the **uucp** command has been executed, another difference between
it and the **cp** command becomes apparent. Immediately after the **uucp**
command completes, the destination file—in this case, **rogue**—is not
created at once, as it would be by the **cp** command. The reason for this is
that UUCP transfers are done in batch mode, which means the **uucp**

command simply sends the request and exits, without waiting for the file transfer to finish, or even to begin. Depending on how the system administrator has configured the UUCP facilities, the transfer may begin immediately, it may be delayed until off-hours when phone rates are lower, or it may even be put off until another day.

Files can also be sent to a remote computer from the local system by giving the local file as the first argument, and the desired location of the file on the remote computer as the second argument, as shown here:

```
$ uucp mush.c duey!/u/rosso/src/mush.c
```

One drawback of using the **uucp** command to transfer a file to a remote computer is that you must specify exactly where on the remote filesystem to place the file. At times, you may not know the ultimate destination of the file you are sending. For example, if you are sending a spreadsheet file called **expense.wks** to your accountant's computer, you may not know where on his or her system to put it. In this situation, you can use the **uuto** utility. Like the **uucp** command, **uuto** transfers files from the local system to a remote computer; however, rather than specifying the full pathname of the destination file, you give only the login name of the person who is to receive the file, as follows:

```
$ uuto /u/rosso/expense.wks duey!waxler
```

In this example, the file **/u/rosso/expense.wks** would be transferred to the user **waxler** on the computer **duey**. When the file arrives on the destination system, the recipient is notified via electronic mail. The recipient can then use the **uupick** command to pick up the incoming file. The **uupick** utility is the only interactive utility in the UUCP system. It displays each file and prompts you for the action to take. You may move the file into a directory, print it, delete it, or leave it alone and go on to the next file. The following commands are recognized by **uupick**.

m *dir*   Moves the current file to the directory *dir*. If a directory name is not given, the file is moved to the current directory.

a *dir*	Moves the current file to the directory *dir*, along with all other files from the same system.
d	Deletes the current file.
p	Prints the contents of the file to the screen. Obviously, this command should only be used with text files. The displayed file remains the current file.
RETURN	Leaves the current file where it is and goes on to the next file.
q	Quits from **uupick**, leaving any remaining files alone. Pressing CTRL-d will also do this.
!*cmd*	Executes the UNIX command *cmd*, and then returns to the current file.
*	Prints a summary of the **uupick** commands.

If Mr. Waxler's clients have had a busy day, he may have many client files waiting. The following is a sample **uupick** session, with Mr. Waxler's responses shown in boldface type

```
$ uupick

from system huey: file expense.wks
?
m client/oliver

from system widgets: file tax.wks
?
m client/widgets

from system widgets: file sales.rpt
?
m client/widgets

from system compsvs: file shipping.log
?
d
```

More Advanced UUCP Operation

The **uucp** command can transfer multiple files to the same directory. If the specified destination is a directory, multiple source files can be given, and all will be transferred to that directory. For example, the command

```
$ uucp branch3!/usr/reports/jan.sales branch3!/usr/reports/feb.sales\
       branch3!/usr/reports/mar.sales /usr/branch3/sales
```

would transfer the files **jan.sales**, **feb.sales**, and **mar.sales** from the remote computer **branch3** to the directory **usr/branch3/sales** on the local machine. However, the command line is so long that it must be extended onto the next screen line with a backslash character at the end of the first line. To simplify this command, you can use wildcard characters just as you can with the UNIX command shells. The **uucp** will also expand the wildcard characters * and ? on the remote system, so the previous command could be reduced to

```
$ uucp "branch3!/usr/reports/*.sales" /usr/branch3/sales
```

Note that the argument containing the wildcard character is enclosed in quotation marks. This prevents the local shell from trying to expand the wildcards before executing the **uucp** command.

Since most UUCP transfers are not done until long after the **uucp** command itself completes, it is helpful to be notified when the transfer has taken place. The **-m** option instructs **uucp** to send you an electronic mail message when your request has been completed. Adding **-m** to the previous command, as follows, would cause **uucp** to send you mail when all the files had arrived:

```
$ uucp -m "branch3!/usr/reports/*.sales" /usr/branch3/sales
```

In addition to yourself, you may want to notify other users when a transfer completes. The **-n** option, followed by an electronic mail address, will do this. For example, if you wanted the sales manager as well as yourself to be notified, you could use this command:

```
$ uucp -n -nbranch3!salesmgr "branch3!/usr/reports/*.sales"\
        /usr/branch3/sales
```

If you are transferring files to a specific user, you need not know the full pathname to the user's home directory. The ~ (tilde) character followed by the user's login can be used to refer to the home directory. The **mush.c** file transfer example, used earlier and shown again here,

```
$ uucp mush.c duey!/u/rosso/src/mush.c
```

could also be written

```
$ uucp mush.c duey!~rosso/src/mush.c
```

If you use the ~ character alone (that is, without a user name), **uucp** will use the directory **/usr/spool/uucppublic.** For example,

```
$ uucp mush.c duey!~/mush.c
```

would transfer the file **mush.c** into the directory **/usr/spool/uucppublic.** This directory is provided on most UNIX systems as a general-purpose file transfer area. Like **/tmp,** the directory is usually publicly readable and writable. It is an appropriate place to send files when you don't know a permitted directory to send them to using **uucp,** or a login name to send them to using **uuto.**

Forcing a UUCP Connection

Normally, UUCP connections are made on a regular schedule established by the system administrator. If you need to force a UUCP connection immediately, you can use the **uutry** command. Since this utility resides in the **/usr/lib/uucp** directory, it will not be found in your normal command search path. To excute **uutry**, you must type its full pathname. One command line argument—the name of the remote system—is required, as shown here:

```
$ /usr/lib/uucp/uutry duey
```

This command would cause your system to call out to system **duey** and attempt to connect. The **uutry** utility outputs status and debugging information about the connection. If you do not want to see this information, you can press the DEL key to interrupt the display. This does not affect the UUCP connection, which continues in the background.

Listing Other Sites

Before you can transfer files to or from a remote computer, you must know that computer's name. The **uuname** command lists the names of all the remote systems your computer knows about. The names are listed one per line, so if the list is long, you may want to pipe the output to the UNIX **more** utility. The **uuname** utility has two command line options: **uuname -l** displays the UUCP name of your local system, and **uuname -c** displays a list of the remote system names that can be used in place of a telephone number with the **cu** utility, described later in this chapter.

Correcting Problems

You may encounter several problems when using UUCP file transfers. The most common one is for a UUCP utility to fail with the error message "event not found" when you are using the C shell. The cause of this error is that the C shell intercepts the ! character in the UUCP command, and attempts to use it as part of the shell's history substitution. This will happen even if the argument containing the ! character is enclosed in quotation marks. To avoid this problem, you must precede all ! characters in a UUCP command with a backslash (\) character. Thus, the previous example would be entered as follows:

```
% uucp mush.c duey\!~rosso/src/mush.c
```

Another common problem has to do with file permissions. For a file to be sent to a remote system, it must be readable by the user **uucp**. The destination directory (and file, if it already exists) must also be writable by **uucp** on the remote system. For a file to be received, the source file must be readable by **uucp** on the remote system, and the destination must be writable by **uucp** on your computer. If any of these requirements are not met, the file transfer will fail with the error "Permission denied" or "Access denied." Keep this in mind when you are transferring files to and from your home directory. The **uucp** utility does not usually have permission to write there.

Another type of permissions problem may occur if the system administrator of the remote computer has restricted UUCP access to certain directories. If you attempt to send or request a file from a directory that is not permitted, you will receive the error "Remote access denied by host." If you receive this error, contact the remote computer's system administrator to find out in what directories transfers are allowed. The directory **/usr/spool/uucppublic** is the most common location for access.

Executing Commands on Remote Systems

In addition to file transfer, the UUCP system can also be used to execute commands on a remote computer using the **uux** utility. Of course, the commands can't be interactive, but they can have input and return output to you. For example, the following command would list the files in **/usr/spool/uucppublic** on system **duey**, and store the list in the file **duey.ls** on your machine.

```
$ uux 'duey!ls /usr/spool/uucppublic > /tmp/duey.ls'
```

Neither the input files nor the output files need to be on the computer where the command will be executed. The **uux** command issues the necessary file transfer commands to get the input files to that system, and then transfers the output file to its final destination. For example, the following **uux** command would find the differences between the file **/usr/james/report.txt** on the **mit** computer, and the file **/usr/james/report.txt** on the **athena** machine using the UNIX **diff** command. The command would actually be executed on the **ucscc** machine, and the output would be returned to the local system.

```
$ uux 'ucscc!diff mit!/usr/james/report.txt athena!~james/report.txt \
  > !/tmp/diff.out'
```

To complete this operation, **uux** would transfer both input files to the **ucscc** computer, execute the command, and transfer the output file back to the local host. Notice that in the output file argument, there is no system name to the left of the ! character. If no system name is specified for a file or command, **uux** assumes the file is or will be on the local system, and the command is executed on the local system. Also, in the second data file, the ~ character stands for the home directory of the user **james**.

Keep in mind that **uux** commands must obey all the UUCP restrictions placed on the systems by the administrators: input and output files must be in accessible directories; input files must be readable and output files writable by **uucp** on their respective systems; and the commands to be executed must be permitted by UUCP.

The **uux** command will notify you by electronic mail if the command fails, that is, exits with a nonzero exit status. By default, no notification is sent for a successful operation. You can use the **-z** option to force **uux** to notifiy you when the command succeeds. Other useful options to **uux** include the following:

-	A - alone as an option tells **uux** to read its standard input and supply that data to the remote command as standard input.
-a*login*	This option sends notification to the user account *login,* rather than to the person who invoked the **uux** command.
-b	If the remote command returns a nonzero exit status, this flag tells **uux** to return the input of the command **uux** was supposed to execute. This option is helpful for debugging.

-c   This option prevents the local files from being copied to the
            UUCP spool directory. A file link is used instead. Because it
            conserves disk space, this option is useful if any files on your
            system that are used in the **uux** command are very large;
            however, it cannot be used if the local files are on a different
            filesystem than the UUCP spool directory, because links will
            not work across filesystems. This mode is also the default.

-C   This flag forces **uux** to copy local files to the UUCP spool
            directory. This flag should be used when a file will be altered
            or removed before the **uux** request is serviced, or when a file
            is on a different filesystem than the UUCP spool directory.

-j   This option prints the UUCP job ID, which can then be used
            to check the status of the request using **uustat**.

-n   This prevents electronic mail notification from being sent if
            the remote command fails.

-p   This is the same as the - option.

-z   This option sends notification of success. Normally, **uux** does
            not send any notification when your remote command com-
            pletes. This option tells **uux** to send an electronic mail mes-
            sage when your command completes and exits with a zero
            status.

Technically, **uux** can execute any command or program on a UNIX
sytem. However, on most systems, **uux** is only allowed to execute a
restricted set of commands. This helps maintain system security, and
prevents either accidental or intentional damage to files on the computer.
On many systems, **uux** can only execute **rmail**, the command to deliver
mail arriving via UUCP. Other systems may not be that restrictive, but most
will deny access to potentially harmful commands, such as **mkfs** or **rm**.

UUCP and Electronic Mail

Chapter 9 described the UNIX electronic mail system. In addition to sending and receiving mail from users on the same computer, you can use electronic mail to exchange messages with users and computers all over the world. UUCP is the underlying method of transport for mail between computers. When a mail message is sent from one UNIX computer to another, the mail program actually puts the message in a file, submits a **uucp** request to transfer the file to the destination computer, and then uses **uux** to deliver the message on the remote system. All of this activity is invisible to both the sender and the recipient.

Unlike UUCP file transfers, mail messages may not travel directly from the source to the destination computer. The messages may pass through any number of intermediate computers to reach their final destination. Two or three "hops" are not uncommon, and messages traveling between two sites—both in remote areas—may visit as many as a dozen computers on the way to their destination.

To get your mail to its destination, you must address it properly, just as you would a postal letter. However, if the intended destination of your mail is not a computer directly connected to yours, you must also tell the UNIX mail system the route, or *path,* to use to deliver the message. Mail paths are specified by listing each computer along the desired route, and separating them with a ! character. The mail path **ssc2!uunet!decwrl!okstate** tells the mail program to route a message from the local system to the computer **ssc2** and then to the computer **okstate** by passing through **uunet** and **decwrl**. Most mail paths require only two or three intermediate stops. However, mail sent to a particularly remote computer—especially one that is on another continent—may require a tortuous path extending over an entire 80-character line or more, and may take several days to travel to its final destination.

When your message must make several stopovers, there is the possibility that it may never reach its destination. If one of the intermediate systems is not working, or if a large number of messages create a traffic jam at one site, your message may be delayed or may not be delivered at all. If your message is delayed, you will probably receive a warning message, such as this:

```
From uucp Sat Feb 3 03:02:58 1990
To: jsb
Date: Sat Feb 3 03:37:57 1990

Subject: Warning From uucp
We have been unable to contact machine 'huey' since you queued your job.

     huey!mail sca    (Date 02/02)
The job will be deleted in several days if the problem is not corrected.
If you care to kill the job, execute the following command:

     uustat -khueyN5e9f

Sincerely,
duey!uucp
```

The previous example concerns a message that has not yet left your local computer. You might receive a similar message from an intermediate site, but that message would probably not include instructions on how to cancel the job.

After a certain amount of time, usually several days, a system will stop trying to deliver your message, and will return it to you with the following notation:

```
From uucp Sat Feb 10 22:51:31 1990
To: duey!jsb
Date: Sat Feb 10 22:51:31 1990

Subject: Undeliverable Mail
This mail message is undeliverable.

(Probably to or from system 'huey')
It was sent to you or by you.
Sorry for the inconvenience.

     Sincerely,
     duey!uucp
```

Your original message will also be included. Don't worry, there are almost always alternate routes you can use to send your message again. If you are having trouble with a particular remote site, you can send mail to the **postmaster** account on that machine to find out what might be causing the problem.

File Transfer Using Mail

UNIX electronic mail has the advantage over UUCP file transfer of being able to send mail messages to computers all over the world, even though those computers never communicate directly with yours. It would be useful to be able to transfer files in this way. However, most UNIX electronic mail systems can send only text in mail messages; spreadsheets, executable programs, database files, and the like can't be sent directly. The **uuencode** utility is provided to translate binary files into text files that can be handled by the mail systems. The **uuencode** command translates each three bytes of the file into four printable ASCII characters. In addition, **uuencode** adds linefeeds to the file so that each line is exactly 60 characters long. This ensures that the file can be processed by mail programs that may not be able to handle mail messages with extremely long lines. Because of the added characters, an encoded mail message will be approximately one-third larger than the original file.

The **uuencode** command accepts either one or two arguments. A single argument is interpreted as the file name that will be assigned at the destination. In this case, **uuencode** reads its input from the standard input. With two arguments, the first becomes the input file name, and the second becomes the destination file name. In either case, the encoded file is written to **uuencode**'s standard output, which can be redirected to a file or piped directly to the mail command. Here are the first ten lines of a file encoded by **uuencode**:

```
begin 755 worms
M_@!5B^R!![&@! !35U:#?0@!#XY& :!0 B &+10S_< 3H@@L (/$"(F%
M5/___X/X ^%& (M%&#/]P!.@O#O @\0$:@' HAPh (/$!(-"#_ 3_30CI
M"@ ,>5/___]0 B &#?0@!#X07 :!@ B 'HH@T (/$!&H"Z% * "#
MQ@ 3_M53____]J4(V%/___U#)U(H_ (/$#(/X ^&' &@T (@!:/0 B 'H
M/@P@/ (/$"H#@H@!0* "#Q@ !UA!FA$$A $@!!(!1%E@@@@(@E::/0 b #@@#($4%
M _O@@@# #_____0U:#?@@!#X07 B&U^03___]#Oz/ - "#Q@!"
M?8!.#XW? :^@-18!!Oz/@# "#Q@ B)@$# ^OO@/ \ #4B :%@
MB %HH] "( >B/"P g.@/H@/ (/$!(N% / ^% /___ 8 (U%@5#H
MU@@L (/$!(F%/%_/[ X.]/[ P /A2 "-18!:&@! B %H] "( Ah@"/
```

Again, the output of **uuencode** can be sent directly to the **mail** program, as shown in this example:

```
$ uuencode /usr/games/worms worms | mail -s "worms"\
uunet!era!james
```

Note that **uuencode** is given two arguments. The first is the name of the source file, and the second is the name **uudecode**, which will give the decoded file on the destination system. These names need not be the same. Remember, if **uuencode** is given only one argument, it uses that as the destination file name, and reads its standard input for the data to encode.

When the encoded mail message reaches its destination, the **uudecode** utility translates it back into its original form. Usually, the mail message is saved to a file by the user from within the **mail** program, as shown here:

```
SCO System V Mail (version 3.2) Type ? for help
3 messages:
>N 1 root          Fri Feb 09 07:45 15/429
 N 2 fred          Fri Feb 09 13:27 23/4605
 N 3 roscoe!rosso Sat Feb 10 21:13 749/45688 worms
s 3 mesg5
"mesg5" [New file] 749/45688
```

After you write the message to a file, you can use the **uudecode** utility as follows to translate it back into its original form.

```
$ uudecode mesg5
```

Note that there is no need to edit the saved mail message to remove the mail header or any text preceding the file data. The **uudecode** utility ignores any text before the line that marks the start of the uuencoded file.

Checking the Status of UUCP Requests

Because UUCP transfers are not performed immediately, you may need to check on the status of waiting UUCP jobs. The **uustat** utility performs this function. It can display the status of UUCP requests that are either currently executing, or waiting to be executed. You can also use the **uustat** utility to cancel transfers that have already been submitted. With no command line arguments, **uustat** displays the status of your own waiting UUCP requests, as follows:

```
$ uustat
dueyN1e76      02/03-22:04 S duey rosso 177 D.huey27780bf
               02/03-22:04 S duey rosso rmail jamesd
louieN2f62     02/03-22:07 S louie rosso 177 D.huey27780bf
               02/03-22:07 S louie rosso rmail jamesd
soscoN0bc7     02/03-23:09 R sosco rosso /usr/spool/uucppublic/info
```

The previous display shows two outgoing electronic mail messages—one to computer **duey** and one to **louie**—and one file transfer requesting the file **/usr/spool/uucppublic/info** from machine **sosco**. The far-left column of **uustat**'s output contains the UUCP job identification name. The next column shows the date and time the request was submitted. The letter *S* or *R* in the next column indicates whether the request is to send or receive a file. The next two columns contain the site name the request will go to, and the user name of the requester. The final column shows the file name if the request is a file transfer, or the command to be executed if the request is a **uux** command. In the previous example, the first and third lines show file transfer requests, and the second line displays a command to be executed on the remote system. An electronic mail message will consist of two separate entries: the transfer of the file containing the mail message, and an **rmail** command to deliver the message.

The **-a** option to **uustat** displays UUCP jobs for all users on your system. Adding **-a** to the **uustat** command above would reveal more waiting UUCP jobs, as shown here:

```
$ uustat -a
dueyN1e76      02/03-22:04 S duey rosso 177 D.huey27780bf
               02/03-22:04 S duey rosso rmail jamesd
dueyN1a48      02/03-17:19 S duey jharris 149 D.huey2779b3e
               02/03-17:19 S duey jharris rmail root
               02/03-23:31 R duey sca /tmp/prog.c
louieN2f62     02/03-22:07 S louie rosso 177 D.huey27780bf
               02/03-22:07 S louie rosso rmail jamesd
soscoN0bc7     02/03-23:09 R sosco rosso /usr/spool/uucppublic/info
```

This display shows another electronic mail message from **jharris** destined for the **duey** machine, and a request by user **sca** for the file **/tmp/prog.c** from that same computer.

You can see all the requests for a particular computer by using the **-s** option. To obtain a listing of all the jobs queued for machine **huey,** you would use this command:

```
$ uustat -sucsc
dueyN1e76       02/03-22:04 S duey rosso 177 D.huey27780bf
                02/03-22:04 S duey rosso rmail jamesd
dueyN1a48       02/03-17:19 S duey jharris 149 D.huey2779b3e
                02/03-17:19 S duey jharris rmail root
                02/03-23:31 R duey sca /tmp/prog.c
```

The **-u** option displays the jobs for a specific user, as shown here:

```
$ uustat -ujharris
dueyN1a48       02/03-17:19 S duey jharris 149 D.huey2779b3e
                02/03-17:19 S duey jharris rmail root
```

Checking the Status of UUCP Connections

The **uustat** command can tell you the status of all your computer's UUCP connections as well as of its requests. The **-m** option lists the results of the last attempt to connect to each remote site, as in this example:

```
$ uustat -m
duey        1C      02/11-17:27 WRONG TIME TO CALL
louie       5C(4)   02/01-03:15 EXECDIAL REMOTE FAILURE
sosco               02/09-15:02 SUCCESSFUL
doc                 02/11-17:50 SUCCESSFUL
```

The **uustat -m** command displays one line for each remote computer. The leftmost column contains the name of the computer. The next column contains the number of UUCP jobs queued for that system. If a number appears in parentheses after the number of jobs (as in the second line of the previous example), that number indicates the age in days of the oldest request. If the last attempt to reach that system was successful, this column should be empty. The final two columns display the date and time of the last attempt, and a message describing the result of the attempt. The possible messages are

SUCCESSFUL: Your computer has successfully connected to the remote system.

WRONG TIME TO CALL: The system administrator has limited attempts to contact that system to certain times of day, and the last UUCP request was not made during the allowed times. The request will be queued for the next allowed time.

DEVICE LOCKED: There were no outgoing UUCP devices available at the time of the attempt, or the particular device designated for this site was not available.

EXECDIAL REMOTE FAILURE: For some reason, your computer could not connect to the remote computer. This could mean that the remote computer's phone line was busy, or that its modem did not answer.

Locked TALKING: Your computer and that particular remote computer have an active connection and are exchanging information.

REMOTE DOES NOT KNOW ME: Your computer is not listed in the remote computer's configuration files. Contact the system administrator of the remote computer to have your computer added to the remote system's configuration.

Canceling a UUCP Request

The **uustat** command can also be used to cancel UUCP requests. To do this, you must know the UUCP job ID, which can be obtained with the **uustat** **-a** command. The example below would cancel the request for the file from the machine **sosco**.

```
$ uustat -urosso
dueyN1e76      02/03-22:04 S duey rosso 177 D.huey27780bf
               02/03-22:04 S duey rosso   rmail jamesd
louieN2f62     02/03-22:07 S louie rosso 177 D.huey27780bf
               02/03-22:07 S louie rosso   rmail jamesd
soscoN0bc7     02/03-23:09 R sosco rosso   /usr/spool/uucppublic/info
$ uustat -ksoscoN0bc7
```

If a job is canceled successfully, **uustat** does not display any message. As a normal user, you are allowed to cancel only your own UUCP requests; however, the superuser can cancel any job. If you attempt to remove someone else's UUCP request, **uustat** returns the error "Not owner or root - can't kill job." If you make a mistake or specify a job that does not exist, **uustat** reports, "Can't find Job; Not killed."

Keeping a UUCP Request from Expiring

It is possible for a UUCP request to be queued for a remote computer, with which a connection is never established. To keep the job from waiting around forever, the **uuclean** utility normally deletes UUCP requests when they reach a certain age (see the section "UUCP System Administration," later in this chapter). At times, however, you may want to prevent a job from being deleted. The **-r** option to **uustat** will "rejuvenate" a job—that is, update its age to the current date—so that **uuclean** does not delete it. The **-r** option is used in the same way as **-k**, as this example shows:

```
$ uustat -rlouieN2f62
```

Interactive Communications

In addition to file transfer, the UUCP facility also provides a utility for interactive communications. The **cu** (Call Unix) utility allows you to use a modem connected to your local computer to call other UNIX systems, or any other computer or on-line system.

Calling Another Computer

Calling another system using **cu** can be as simple as entering the command **cu** followed by the telephone number of the desired remote system. If the UUCP configuration files have been set up properly by the system administrator, **cu** will select the first available outgoing line, choose the proper baud rate and other communications parameters, and issue the necessary modem commands. For example, a command to call another local UNIX computer might look like this:

```
$ cu 555-2345
```

The **cu** utility would then find a communications line to use, issue the appropriate dialing commands to the modem, and wait for the connection to be established. Once the connection had been made, **cu** would display the message "Connected" on your screen, and ring the terminal bell. Once the connection is made, all of your keystrokes are transmitted to the remote system, and its responses are displayed on your screen.

You can also call systems with which you have a UUCP link by substituting the system name for the phone number, as shown here:

```
$ cu duey
```

To be able to use the name of the system, the name must be defined in the UUCP configuration file **/usr/lib/uucp/Systems**. If the system name is not known, **cu** will display the message "Connect failed: SYSTEM NOT IN Systems FILE." As mentioned earlier, you can use the **uuname** utility to display a list of the systems your computer recognizes.

NOTE   Only digits, the dash, and the = character are allowed in phone numbers to **cu**. If other characters, such as letters, commas, spaces, parentheses, or slashes, are included in a phone number string, **cu** will interpret the string as a system name, and will search for it in the UUCP configuration file.

As with most UNIX utilities, several command line options understood by **cu** can be used to modify the command's behavior. The most common is the **-s** option, which is used to set the baud rate of a connection. You would use the following command lines to specify 2400 baud in the two previous examples.

```
$ cu -s2400 4251314
$ cu -s2400 duey
```

If you do not use a **-s** flag, **cu** selects the highest baud rate allowed for the particular system or communications line. Valid baud rates are 150, 300, 600, 1200, 2400, 4800, 9600, 19200, and 38400. You can also specify a baud rate range, such as **-s1200-4800**. The **cu** utility will then use the highest baud rate available within that range.

By default, **cu** sets the serial data communications parameters to 8 data bits, 1 stop bit, no parity, and full duplex. However, many systems require different parameters. The **-h** option tells **cu** to use half duplex mode, which means that **cu** itself will echo to the screen the characters you type. This option is needed if the remote system does not echo your keystrokes back to the screen.

These options tell **cu** the number of data bits and the parity to use:

-o   7 data bits, odd parity

-e   7 data bits, even parity

-oe   7 data bits, send no parity bit to the remote computer and ignore the data bit sent by the remote computer

By default, **cu** selects the first available tty device when calling out (or the first available device set at the specified baud rate). However, you can choose the device yourself by using the **-l** option. The name of the special device file should follow **-l** on the command line. To select **/dev/tty1A** as the device, you would use this command:

```
$ cu -ltty1A 12125559738
```

Note that there is no space between the **-l** and the name of the device, and that only the final portion of the device name is used, rather than the the full pathname. To use the **-l** option, you must be logged in to the system administrator account, or have write permission on the **/usr/lib/uucp/Devices** file.

Tilde Commands

Once the connection is established, every character you type, even CTRL-d and DEL (or whatever your end-of-file and interrupt characters are) is sent to the remote computer. So, is it possible to send commands to **cu** while you are connected to the remote system? In fact, how is the connection broken? Actually, **cu** does watch for one command character, the ~ (tilde), but only at a particular place: the beginning of a line (that is, following a carriage return). When **cu** encounters this combination of characters, it displays the name of the local system in square braces—**[huey]**, for example—to confirm that the next characters you type will be interpreted as a **cu** command, and will not be sent to the remote computer.

You can execute local commands from within **cu** while still maintaining your remote connection. To do so, type ~! followed by the local command to execute, as shown here:

```
~[huey]!ls
```

This command would list files in the current directory on the local system. Note that the **[huey]** portion of the previous example is not typed by you, but displayed by **cu** after you type the ! character to indicate the start of a **cu** command. When the local command completes, **cu** prints the message "(continue)" and returns to your remote session.

You can also escape to a local interactive shell by typing ~! with no command. The **cu** utility then starts up a shell on the local computer, and suspends the communications session until the shell exits. Which shell **cu** gives you is determined by your **SHELL** environment variable. You return to your remote session when the shell exits, that is, when you either type CTRL-d or issue the command **exit**.

File Transfer Using cu

The **cu** command has limited file transfer capability. With it, you can exchange text files with other UNIX systems. The remote system must be a UNIX or similar system, because part of the file transfer process involves running UNIX utilities on the remote computer. However, no error checking is done on the file, so be careful in case the connection is not completely reliable.

To transfer a file from the remote to the local computer, use the **cu** command **~%take** followed by the name of the file to transfer, as shown here:

```
~[huey]%take outline.txt
```

The file is transferred to your local system, using the same file name. If you add a second file name to the **take** command, the second name is used for the destination file on your computer.

After you issue the **take** command, you will see the command line that **cu** transmits to the remote system. This command line causes the remote computer to send the requested file, which **cu** then captures. The file does not appear on the screen; however, **cu** shows you the progress of the file transfer by printing a digit for each 1024 characters received. After the transfer is complete, **cu** displays the total number of lines and characters received, such as "145 lines/5703 characters."

Transmitting a file is the inverse of receiving one. The **~%put** command sends a file from the local computer to the remote host, as in this example:

```
~[huey]%put chapter3.txt
```

The **cu** utility sends a command line to the remote system telling it to receive the file, and then send the file itself. Following the transmission, **cu** displays the lines and characters transmitted.

Another helpful tilde command to use with the **put** and **take** commands is **cd**, which changes directories on the local system. To move to the directory **/tmp** prior to a file transfer, you would use the command

```
~[huey]%cd /tmp
```

Because **cu** does not perform any error checking during file transfers, you may want to check a file's integrity after a transfer is completed. You can use the UNIX **sum** command for this purpose, by performing a checksum on the original file and the transferred copy. Here is a portion of a **cu** session showing a file transfer and a checksum operation:

```
$ ~[huey]%take chapter6.txt
246 lines/11200 characters
$ sum -r chapter6.txt
14870    22
$ ~[huey]!sum -r chapter6.txt
14870    22
(continue)
```

The first **sum** command is executed on the remote system, and shows the checksum of the original file. The two numbers displayed by **sum** are the checksum of the file and the size of the file in disk blocks. The second **sum** command computes the checksum of the received file. Since the two checksums match, you can be fairly certain the file has been transferred accurately.

At times, you may want the tilde character at the beginning of a line to be sent to the remote computer rather than interpreted as the start of a **cu** command. In this case, typing two ~ characters at the beginning of a line tells **cu** to send a single tilde. Remember that this is only necessary when the tilde is at the beginning of a line. Tilde characters in any other position are routinely passed on by **cu**.

Session Recording

Even though **cu** can only exchange files with other UNIX systems, it is possible to record your entire on-line session when you call any remote system. This can be useful when you connect to information services and bulletin boards. Session recording uses another of the UNIX utilities, **tee**. The output of **cu** is sent through a UNIX pipe to the **tee** utility. Here is an example of session recording:

```
$ cu -s2400 16195554672 | tee session.rec
```

This command calls the remote computer at 2400 baud and stores the session record in the file **session.rec**. Every character displayed on the screen is stored in the file. This includes any control characters, screen formatting, and escape sequences. Because these special characters may be terminal-specific, you may need to edit the record file before the data can be printed or displayed on a different terminal.

 NOTE   To end the **cu** session, log out of the remote system by pressing CTRL-d or typing **exit**. If the connection is still not broken, entering **~.** (tilde-dot) will force **cu** to break the connection at your end.

Error Messages

The **cu** command is somewhat cryptic when it comes to reporting failures. It may display several possible error messages for a failed connection. All the messages begin with "Connect Failed:," which can be followed by any one of these:

EXECDIAL LOCAL FAILURE: This message means that **cu** received an unexpected response from the modem. This could mean the UUCP configuration information is not correct, the modem is not working, or the modem is not connected properly. If you receive this error, contact your system administrator.

EXECDIAL REMOTE FAILURE: This is probably the most common error message. It means that for some reason, a connection could not be established with the remote system. This might be because the remote system's phone line was busy, the remote modem did not answer, the phone number dialed was incorrect, or the remote modem was not compatible with your modem. It is often necessary to dial the remote computer manually on a voice telephone to determine which of these possibilities is the culprit.

DEVICE LOCKED: This tells you that the communications device **cu** tried to use was already in use. If your system has more than one dial-out device, use the **-l** option to select another device.

NO DEVICES AVAILABLE: This message is slightly different than the DEVICE LOCKED message. It indicates that the device **cu** attempted to access has not been configured as a dial-out device. Contact your system administrator to resolve this problem.

SYSTEM NOT IN Systems FILE: This message indicates that the system name given in place of a phone number was not found in the **/usr/lib/uucp/Systems** file. Have your system administrator add the system, or use the phone number directly. If you specified a phone number rather than a system name on the command line, check the phone number string to be sure it contains only digits, dashes, or the - character.

Receiving Calls from Remote Systems

While **cu** is used by people to make outgoing connections, another utility allows the computer itself to originate calls. The **ct** utility calls other computers or terminals, and then presents the standard UNIX login prompt. This capability is useful when you are making a connection that is a toll call. You can call to the remote system, execute a **ct** command (which can include a delay), hang up, and wait for the computer to call and begin the longer session.

The **ct** command is also valuable for security. Allowing direct dialing into a computer always carries the risk of unauthorized access. To reduce this risk, a computer can be configured so that users who log in through dial-in lines can execute only the **ct** command. The user must provide a phone number for the computer to call back, and the number can then be logged so that any access to the computer can easily be traced. With a small amount of shell programming, computers can even be set up to dial only preauthorized phone numbers.

The **ct** command requires at least one argument: the phone number to call. It searches the defined dial-out devices for an available device. If one is not found, **ct** enters an interactive mode, as in the following example:

```
$ ct 4598672
The one 1200 baud dialer is busy
Do you want to wait for dialer? (y for yes): y
Time, in minutes? 10
Waiting for dialer
```

The **ct** command waits the specified time for a device to become available, checking once per minute. If a device does not become available in the allotted time, **ct** displays the message "*** TIMEOUT ***" and exits. However, this is not the most convenient method if you are already dialed in on a modem line. In this case, you can invoke **ct** in the background, and use the **-w** flag to specify the wait time, as follows:

```
$ ct -w10 4592436 > /dev/null &
```

The redirection of **ct**'s output prevents the message "The dialer is busy, waiting for 10 minutes" from being displayed on the screen. The **&** character runs the **ct** command in the background.

After you log out, **ct** uses the freed up device to call the number you specified. The **ct** command also accepts multiple phone numbers, dialing each one in turn until a connection is made.

UUCP System Administration

Before any of the UUCP communications programs can be used, some configuration information must be placed in the UUCP information files. These files describe what systems your computer connects to, the serial ports your modems are connected to, the kinds of modems used, and the files and commands that can be accessed by remote computers. The files can be viewed and changed using one of the UNIX text editors, the **uuinstall** utility, or through the **sysadmsh** utility.

Setting Up UUCP Devices

The first thing that must be configured in the UUCP system is the serial device that will be used by UUCP. The file **/usr/lib/uucp/Devices** contains this information. It contains one line for each serial device; thus, each line of the file defines a single communications connection. Here is an example line from the **Devices** file:

```
ACU tty2A - 300-2400 /usr/lib/uucp/dialHA24
```

There are five fields on each line in the file, each separated by one or more spaces. The fields contain the following information:

Whether the connection is hardwired or over a modem. If the connection is hardwired, the word **direct** is displayed. For a modem, **ACU** (for Automatic Call Unit) is placed in this field.

The tty line used for this device. The **/dev** prefix is omitted, so if the full pathname of the device were **/dev/tty6B**, this field would contain **tty6B**.

The third field is not used, and should contain a dash character.

The baud rate or range of baud rates allowed. If more than one baud rate is permitted, this field contains the lowest and highest possible baud rates, separated by a dash.

The dialer program to use for sending modem commands. If the connection is a direct wire serial connection (no modem is used), the word **direct** is placed in this field. Otherwise, the full pathname to the dialer program is given. Dialer programs are normally found in the **/usr/lib/uucp** directory.

Lines in the **Devices** file that begin with the # character are ignored, so these lines can be used for comments. Blank lines are also ignored.

If **cu** or **ct** is the only utility that will be used, the **Devices** file is the only configuration needed. The **Systems** and **Permissions** files are only used by the various UUCP file transfer utilities.

Defining Remote Computers

The **/usr/lib/uucp/Systems** file contains information that UUCP needs to connect to remote systems. The file lists the name of the remote system, the devices that can be used to connect to it, the days and times the connection can be attempted, and the actual login sequence, including the login name and password to use on the remote computer.

Like the **Devices** file, the **Systems** file contains one line per system. Each line of the file is divided into six fields: system name, call schedule, device type, speed, phone number, and login sequence. Here is an example Systems file entry:

```
sosco Any ACU 2400 425-3502 ogin:-@-ogin:-@-ogin: uusls
```

These fields contain the following information:

Name: This field contains the name of the remote computer, in this case, **sosco**.

Schedule: This field tells you the days and times when UUCP can attempt to establish a connection to this computer. This field does not apply to **cu** or **ct** connections. **Any** means that UUCP can connect at any time. **Never** means you should never attempt to make the connection automatically. This value is used when the remote computer always calls your computer, or your computer uses **uucico** to poll on a regular basis. The field can also specify certain days of the week and times of the day.

Device type: This field contains either **Direct** if the connection is a direct line from one computer's serial port to another, or **ACU** if a modem is being used.

Speed: This field tells you the baud rate to use when establishing the connection. As in the **Devices** file, the baud rate may be specified as a range.

Phone number: This field holds the phone number to dial to reach the remote computer.

Login sequence: This field describes the "conversation" that must take place between your computer and the remote computer for your computer to log in to the remote system.

Giving Access Permissions to Remote Systems

The final UUCP configuration file is the **/usr/lib/uucp/Permissions** file, which tells UUCP how much access to your computer to grant to other computers. It specifies whether other systems can send files to you or request files, what directories they can access, and what commands they can execute using **uux**.

Cleaning Up Outdated Files

In some cases, a UUCP request may be queued for a site that can not be reached for some reason. The **uuclean** utility is provided to monitor and delete old requests, and to notify the requestors that the system has been unable to service their requests. Normally, the **uuclean** utility is set up by the system administrator to be run periodically by **cron**—once per day for example. If a file transfer request or an electronic mail message cannot be processed within one day, **uuclean** will send a mail message to the submitter warning of the delay. If a request cannot be serviced within seven days, **uuclean** will delete the request and send another message to the submittor. If the request is an electronic mail message, the original message will also be returned. Both the warning time and the deletion time can be overridden by command line options. The options for **uuclean** are

-C*time*   This option deletes any work files that are older than a certain age. Here, *time* is an integer that specifies the age in days. Work files are stored in the UUCP spool directories. Their names always begin with C, and they contain a description of each UUCP request.

-D*time*   This option deletes any data files that are *time* days old or older. Data files' names begin with D, and these files contain the actual files destined for remote systems.

-X*time*   This option deletes any remote execution files that are *time* days old or older. These files contain the commands to be executed on remote systems. Their names begin with X.

-W*time*   This option sends a message via electronic mail to users who have UUCP requests that are *time* days old or older. The message informs the user of the delay in servicing his or her request. It includes the UUCP job identifier and (if the job was a mail message) the original message.

-m*message*   The string *message* is included with the message sent by the -W option. If *message* includes spaces, be sure to enclose it (along with the **-m** option) in quotation marks.

-s*system*   This option removes only files queued for the remote system named *system*.

The following is a typical **uuclean** command line:

```
$ /usr/lib/uucp/uuclean -C10 -D10 -X10 -W5 "-mCall x375 if you need help"
```

This command would delete UUCP jobs that were ten days old or older, and would send a message to the requestor after five days. The message would include "Call x375 if you need help." Note that the **-m** option and the message string are enclosed in a single set of quotation marks, as required when the message string contains spaces.

Displaying Recorded UUCP Activity

The UUCP system maintains a log of all activity between your computer and other systems. The log files are located in the directory **/usr/spool/uucp/.Log**. Within this directory are three subdirectories: **uucico** contains log files for **uucp** file transfer; **uux** contains logs of commands your system has executed on other computers; and **uuxqt** contains logs of commands remote computers have run on your system.

Within each of these subdirectories is a log file for each remote system. You can use the **uulog** utility to display these logs. With no arguments, **uulog** displays the complete log of all activity to and from all remote systems, which can be quite lengthy. If you are only interested in recent activity, you can use the **-** character followed by an integer on the **uulog** command line. The **uulog** utility will then display only that number of lines from the end of the log file for each remote system your computer talks to.

For example, if your computer regularly connects with six other systems, the command **uulog -5** would display the last 5 lines of activity for each system, a total of 30 lines. This is a good way to check on the last connection for each remote computer.

If you only want to see the activity for a specific remote system, you can use the **-s** option to limit **uulog**'s output to that system. You can also combine the number option with the **-s** option to display recent activity for a given system. For example, the following command displays the last 15 lines of log entries for the system **huey**.

```
$ uulog -15 -shuey
uucp huey (9/18-6:01:30,107,0) CONN FAILED (EXECDIAL REMOTE FAILURE)
uucp huey (9/19-22:24:22,698,0) CONN FAILED (WRONG TIME TO CALL)
uucp huey (9/20-6:00:47,727,0) SUCCEEDED (call to huey )
uucp huey (9/20-6:00:49,727,0) OK (startup)
guest huey hueyN5e98 (9/20-6:00:49,727,0) REQUEST (scc2!D.scc22648a99 -->
huey!D.scc22648a99 (rosso))
guest huey hueyN5e98 (9/20-6:01:09,727,1) REQUEST (scc2!D.huey5e98a99 -->
huey!X.hueyN5e98 (rosso))
sca huey hueyN5e98 (9/20-6:01:09,727,2) REQUEST (huey!~sca/outline -->
ssc2!/u/sca/outline (sca))
uucp huey (9/20-6:01:12,727,2) OK (conversation complete tty2A 72)
uucp huey (9/21-6:00:50,753,0) SUCCEEDED (call to huey )
uucp huey (9/21-6:00:52,753,0) OK (startup)
uucp huey (9/21-6:00:54,753,0) OK (conversation complete tty2A 54)
uucp huey (9/23-6:00:52,4349,0) SUCCEEDED (call to huey )
uucp huey (9/23-6:00:51,4349,0) REMOTE REQUESTED (huey!D.hueycBT7j2 -->
scc2!D.hueycST7j2 (daemon))
uucp huey (9/23-6:01:26,4349,1) REMOTE REQUESTED (huey!D.hueycXT7j0 -->
scc2!X.hueycCT7j3 (daemon))
uucp huey (9/23-6:02:17,4349,1) OK (conversation complete tty2A 137) -->
```

As you can see, the UUCP log is densely packed with information, and is therefore somewhat difficult to decipher at first glance. There is one line for each file transfer, in addition to various lines that show the progress of a connection. All lines begin with the login name and the remote machine name. For file transfer entries, the login name shown is the name of the requester. For other entries, the login name is the name used to log in to the remote computer. Following the remote name, enclosed in parentheses, are the date and time of the log entry, the process ID of the UUCP process, and a sequence number that is incremented by one for each successful transfer. The next entry on the line is the actual status message. The messages and their meanings are as follows:

SUCCEEDED (call to *site*): This means your computer has successfully called out to the computer named *site* and logged in. This is the first entry of a dial-out session.

OK (startup): This entry indicates a successful startup of a UUCP connection. The two connecting machines have recognized each other, and the UUCP protocol has begun. If your computer is calling out, an OK entry will immediately follow a SUCCEEDED entry. If another computer is calling yours, this will be the first entry for a UUCP session.

REQUEST: This is a file transfer request by your computer. The transfer may be to or from your system, but was initiated by your system. Following REQUEST will be the source and destination files, and the login of the user who made the request, all in parentheses. For example, (**roscoe!D.rosco25bfedf — brumby!D.rosco25bfedf (rosso)**) shows a transfer of the file **D.rosco25bfedf** from the machine **roscoe** to the machine **brumby** by the user **rosso**. If the transfer is successful, no other entries will be made in the log file for that request.

REMOTE REQUEST: This indicates a request that was initiated by a remote computer. It will also be followed by the file and user information described previously.

ACCESS (DENIED) or PERMISSION (DENIED): One of these two messages will follow a REQUEST or REMOTE REQUEST entry if a file transfer request was denied. This might have occurred because the requesting system did not have access to the requested directory, the user making the request did not have permission on the named file, or the source file did not exist.

OK (conversation complete tty2A 137): This entry marks the end of the UUCP session. All requests from either system have been processed. The **tty1A** shows the tty device on which the connection took place. The integer following the tty name is the number of seconds the connection lasted.

CONN FAILED (DEVICE LOCKED): This tells you a connection attempt failed because there were no UUCP devices available, or the particular device for that site was not available.

CONN FAILED (WRONG TIME TO CALL): This indicates a connection attempt was made at a time outside the day and time limits defined for the remote system.

CONN FAILED (EXECDIAL REMOTE FAILURE): This means the connection failed because the system could not connect to the remote system's modem. This could be because the remote system's modem line was busy, the modem was not answering, or the phone number was incorrect.

REMOTE DOES NOT KNOW ME: This tells you that your system is not known by the remote system.

BAD LOGIN/MACHINE COMBINATION: This means a remote computer called your system and used a login name and a machine name that are not in your UUCP configuration files, which could indicate an attempt at unauthorized access to your computer.

By default, **uulog** displays the logs of connection status information and file transfers. Remote command execution is logged separately, and can be viewed by adding the **-x** option to the **uulog** command line. The **-x** option can be used along with the - and **-s** options. Here is an example of a remote execution log entry:

```
uucp unix386 (2/8-18:03:57,644,0) network XQT (PATH=/bin:/usr/bin
LOGNAME=uucp UU_MACHINE=sco UU_USER=network export UU_MACHINE UU_USER
PATH; rmail sca)
```

The first portion of the line is the same as the file transfer portion of the UUCP log. The next portion, beginning with **network XQT**, shows what command was executed (**rmail** in this example), and the values of the environment variables PATH, LOGNAME, UU_MACHINE, and UU_USER. These variables are set automatically before the remote command is executed.

The UUCP system extends the power of UNIX by linking UNIX systems together, whether they are in the same office, or around the world. Unattended, error-free file transfer and electronic mail make exchanging information easy. Remote command execution extends computing power, and interactive communication allows you access to computer systems of all types. In addition, utilities are available to track and manage communications and traffic. Taken together, *all* the UUCP utilities allow you to connect your UNIX system to just a few other systems, or to hundreds of other systems, depending on your needs.

CHAPTER

14

Using MS-DOS Under UNIX

UNIX provides important connectivity between UNIX and MS-DOS systems. Utilities for accessing files and directories on MS-DOS filesystems are a standard part of UNIX. These utilities provide a quick and simple way to exchange data with MS-DOS systems. The VP/ix package extends this connectivity even further by allowing you to actually run MS-DOS programs under UNIX. Because VP/ix operates as a standard UNIX process, you can run more than one MS-DOS program under UNIX, or have more than one person using MS-DOS at the same time.

Utilities for Accessing MS-DOS Files

UNIX supplies several commands for accessing and manipulating files on MS-DOS diskettes and MS-DOS partitions of hard disks. There are utilities that allow you to copy and move files between MS-DOS and UNIX filesystems, list files in MS-DOS directories, create and remove MS-DOS directories, and format MS-DOS diskettes.

UNIX Device Files for MS-DOS Access

The UNIX special device files used to access MS-DOS diskettes are the same ones used for UNIX-formatted diskettes. The device you use depends on the type and capacity of the disk. For example, you use the **/dev/fd0135ds9** device to access a 3 1/2-inch, 720K MS-DOS diskette. The special device file **/dev/install** can also be used. Because this device automatically determines the diskette type, it will work for any kind of diskette. Access to the MS-DOS partition of the hard disk is through the UNIX special device **/dev/hd0d** for the first hard disk, and through the device **/dev/hd1d** for the second hard disk.

To eliminate the need to type the entire pathname of the special device file, UNIX provides a way to specify the device name with a single letter. The file **/etc/defaults/msdos** contains the mapping of the letters to the UNIX device names. Here are the contents of an **/etc/defaults/msdos** file for a system that maps a high-density (1.2 megabyte), 5 1/4-inch drive 0 to the letter **A**, a low-density (720K) drive 1 to the letter **B**, and an MS-DOS hard disk partition to the letter **C**:

```
$ cat /etc/default/tar
A=/dev/fd096ds15
B=/dev/fd1135ds9
C=/dev/hd0d
```

The **/etc/defaults/msdos** file must be set up by the system administrator.

Listing Files on MS-DOS Disks

There are two UNIX utilities available for listing files on MS-DOS diskettes and hard disk partitions. The **dosdir** utility displays an MS-DOS style directory listing, while **dosls** displays a UNIX style listing. Both these utilities require an argument indicating the device to use. For MS-DOS diskettes, any of the standard UNIX diskette device names can be used, as can the single-letter abbreviation as described above. If a single letter is used, it must be followed by a colon (for consistency, the colon may also be used after a UNIX device name, but it is not required). If the UNIX device file or letter is used alone, **dosdir** and **dosls** lists the files in the root directory of the MS-DOS disk. The drive name or letter can also be followed by a subdirectory, and the utility will then list the files in that subdirectory.

 NOTE   When giving UNIX file and directory names on the command line, you can use the wildcard characters * or ? to select groups of files; however, these characters will not work for MS-DOS files. The UNIX command interpreters expand these special characters for you, so they can be used to select only UNIX files. The wildcard characters cannot be used with **dosdir**, **dosls**, or any other MS-DOS utility.

Transferring MS-DOS Files

To transfer files from MS-DOS to UNIX or from UNIX to MS-DOS, you can use the **doscp** utility, which operates in the same way as the UNIX **cp** command. The **doscp** command accepts as command line arguments a source file and a destination file or directory. One of these must be a UNIX file or directory, and one must be MS-DOS. The following command copies the file **startrek.txt** from the MS-DOS hard disk partition to the UNIX file named **startrek.txt** in the current UNIX directory:

```
$ doscp /dev/hd0d:startrek.txt startrek.txt
```

If the previous file were in the MS-DOS subdirectory **scifi**, the command would be

```
$ doscp /dev/hd0d:/scifi/startrek.txt startrek.txt
```

The **doscp** command will copy UNIX files to MS-DOS filesystems as well. This command would copy the UNIX file **starwars.txt** into the **scifi** subdirectory on an MS-DOS diskette:

```
$ doscp starwars.txt /dev/fd048ds9:/scifi
```

If no subdirectory is given for an MS-DOS destination, the file is placed in the root directory of the MS-DOS filesystem.

Like the **dosdir** and **dosls** utilities, **doscp** can use the one-letter abbreviations for device files from the **/etc/defaults/msdos** file. If the letter C were assigned to **/dev/hd0d**, the command for copying **startrek.txt** from MS-DOS to UNIX could be simplified to

```
$ doscp C:/scifi/startrek.txt startrek.txt
```

Notice that, when specifying MS-DOS directories, you use the UNIX format and the **/** separator character rather than the **** used under MS-DOS.

Transferring Multiple Files

As mentioned previously, the **∗** and **?** wildcard characters cannot be used to access MS-DOS files using the UNIX MS-DOS utilities. However, you can use wildcard characters to select groups of UNIX files to copy to an MS-DOS destination. This command would copy all the UNIX files in the current directory that end in **.c** to an MS-DOS diskette:

```
$ doscp *.c a:
```


Other MS-DOS Operations

There are several other UNIX utilities you can use to access MS-DOS filesystems. The **doscat** utility works like the UNIX **cat** command. This command accepts the names of MS-DOS files and writes their contents to the standard output:

```
$ doscat a:autoexec.bat
ECHO OFF
PATH=C:\DOS;C:\BIN
PROMPT $p$G
```

The **dosrm** command deletes MS-DOS files. The **dosmkdir** command creates new MS-DOS directories, and **dosrmdir** removes them. A directory must be empty before it can be deleted. You can format blank diskettes for MS-DOS using the **dosformat** command.

Using VP/ix to Run MS-DOS Programs Under UNIX

VP/ix is a software application that allows you to run MS-DOS programs directly under UNIX on 80386- or 80486-based computers. VP/ix makes use of the Intel 80386's ability to emulate an 8086 processor and its complete environment from within an 80386 UNIX process. This allows you to run multiple MS-DOS programs under UNIX, right alongside UNIX processes. VP/ix provides all the necessary hardware emulation and interfacing so the MS-DOS programs see a complete, but simulated, IBM PC environment, including standard IBM PC peripherals. Using VP/ix, your UNIX system can support several users running MS-DOS programs simultaneously. You can even run multiple MS-DOS programs on the system console by running a VP/ix session on each console multiscreen.

VP/ix System Requirements

VP/ix will operate on the UNIX system console, and on selected terminals over an RS-232 serial connection. When run on a serial terminal, VP/ix presents a character-only, monochrome display adaptor to MS-DOS programs. No screen graphics (except graphics characters) are possible on serial terminals. Some terminals supported by VP/ix are the WYSE 50 and

60, DEC VT-100, and ANSI-compatible terminals. Check the VP/ix documentation for a complete list of terminals supported in your version. You can add other terminals by creating a configuration file that tells VP/ix how to display the IBM PC character set on the terminal, and how to translate the terminal's keystrokes into IBM PC keyboard keystrokes. This process is long and involved, and should be attempted only by people who are extremely familiar with both the operation of their terminal and the IBM PC display and keyboard.

Not only must you be using a supported terminal to run VP/ix, you must also be connected to the right kind of serial port. All the serial devices supported by the standard UNIX operating system will work with VP/ix. Other serial devices, especially intelligent devices with onboard processors, often use their own UNIX device drivers. These drivers must have been created to support VP/ix as well. If you plan to use VP/ix through one of these devices, check with the vendor to be sure the device drivers support VP/ix.

VP/ix requires a great deal of system memory. Since it must emulate the entire address space of the 8086 processor, it requires at least one megabyte of data space in addition to the space needed for the actual VP/ix instructions and related data. SCO recommends two megabytes of memory for the first VP/ix session, plus one megabyte for each additional VP/ix session that will run at the same time. If you plan to run three VP/ix sessions at once, you should have at least four megabytes of memory. This amount is in addition to the memory that is required to run any other UNIX application programs on your system.

Accessing IBM PC Hardware

To simulate an IBM PC environment, VP/ix emulates the following IBM PC devices and peripherals:

- A keyboard
- A console screen, either monochrome, CGA, EGA, or VGA, depending on what type of display device is installed in your UNIX system

- One or two floppy diskette drives

- One or two serial ports

- One or two parallel printer ports

- A serial or bus mouse

- CMOS configuration memory

- Speaker and sound circuits

- Lotus-Intel-Microsoft 3.2 expanded memory

VP/ix emulates these devices down to the register level, so even MS-DOS programs that access IBM PC hardware at the lowest level will run correctly under VP/ix. The hard disk drive C is also emulated, but only through the MS-DOS filesystem. MS-DOS programs cannot directly access the hard disk controller.

Adding Nonstandard Hardware

VP/ix can simulate all the hardware found in the basic IBM PC environment. You may want to add other special hardware devices that require their own MS-DOS device driver. You can use two methods to add new hardware to the VP/ix environment. The first, Direct Device Access (DDA), allows you to define a "window" that MS-DOS programs can use to gain direct access to the hardware device without going through any UNIX device driver. This method works best when the interface to the hardware is through I/O registers and memory. It is not suitable for devices that use Direct Memory Access (DMA) or interrupts. For devices of this type, you need to create a VP/ix Installable Emulation Module (IEM) and a UNIX device driver for the hardware. Both the DDA and IEM require detailed knowledge of the hardware device you wish to add. For a complete description of both methods, see the "VP/ix Software Developer's Guide" section of the VP/ix manual.

Starting VP/ix

There are several ways to enter the MS-DOS environment from UNIX. The most common is to issue the command **vpix** from your UNIX command shell prompt. Alternatively, you can set up a user to enter VP/ix directly upon logging in to UNIX. People who use such an account need not know anything about the UNIX environment except the login procedure. You can also issue MS-DOS commands and start MS-DOS programs from your UNIX command shell prompt.

The VP/ix Operating Environment

When you issue the **vpix** command at a UNIX prompt, your screen displays messages nearly identical to those you see when booting an IBM PC computer with MS-DOS. The first message displayed is the ROM BIOS message, followed by a VP/ix version number and copyright message, and then by the MS-DOS startup message. Next come any messages from commands in the **autoexec.bat** file of your C drive. After startup is complete, you see a standard MS-DOS command prompt. By default, the prompt is set to **VP/ix** followed by the current drive letter and directory.

In addition to all standard MS-DOS commands and operations, VP/ix has a few extra capabilities to assist in interfacing with the UNIX environment. Most of these are accessed through the VP/ix menu, which is brought to your screen with a special keypress or sequence of keypresses. On the system console, you can bring up the VP/ix menu by holding down the ALT and SHIFT keys, and then pressing the SYSREQ key. (For other terminals, see the VP/ix release notes.) The VP/ix menu shown in Figure 14-1 will then appear. The box on the right lists the devices you can currently access from VP/ix. The box on the left is the actual menu. You can make selections either by highlighting the desired item using the arrow keys and then pressing RETURN, or by pressing the first letter of the selection. The available selections are

Escape menu   This choice exits the VP/ix menu and returns control to MS-DOS or to your MS-DOS program.

Floppy release	This option releases control of the floppy drive (if there is one) allocated to your current VP/ix session. This allows other VP/ix sessions or users to use the drive without your having to exit from VP/ix.
Printer flush	Printers connected to MS-DOS computers normally receive print data immediately when it is sent from an MS-DOS program; however, VP/ix buffers data that is sent to the MS-DOS print device in preparation for sending it to the UNIX print spooler. The data is not sent until the MS-DOS program closes the MS-DOS printer device. If you want to force the data in the buffer to be printed before the device is closed, select this item. Any data waiting to be printed will immediately be sent to the UNIX print spooler.
Quit VP/ix	This selection exits VP/ix immediately.
Reset VP/ix	This selection is equivalent to pressing the reset button on an MS-DOS computer, or pressing the CTRL, ALT, and DEL keys simultaneously. It restarts VP/ix.
Sound is ON/OFF	This selection toggles on and off the sound-generating capability of VP/ix. Choosing this selection changes the sound capability to the state opposite that shown on the menu.

Figure 14-1.

```
╒═ SCO VP/ix 1.2 ═╕   ┌─Device ──Assignment──────────┐
│ (Esc)ape menu   │   │ A:       /dev/rfd096ds15      │
│ (F)loppy release│   │ C:       /usr/vpix/defaults/C:│
│ (P)rinter flush │   │ LPT1:    /usr/bin/lp -s       │
│ (Q)uit VP/ix    │   ├─Terminal─────────────────────┤
│ (R)eset VP/ix   │   │ ansi     /dev/tty02           │
│ (S)ound is ON   │   └──────────────────────────────┘
│ (E)xecute shell │
╘═════════════════╛
```

The VP/ix Menu.

Execute shell   This choice suspends the VP/ix session, and starts a UNIX command shell.

You can also access these functions from the MS-DOS command line by using the special VP/ix **vpixcmd** command. This command allows you to perform these functions without using any exotic keystrokes, and to include them in MS-DOS batch files. Entering **vpixcmd** without any arguments displays a list of valid arguments, as shown here:

```
VP/ix Z:\USR>vpixcmd

    serial [ acquire | release ]
        acquire or release serial ports

    floppy [ acquire | release ]
        acquire or release floppy disk drives

    printer
        flush the VP/ix printer buffer

    quit
        exit from VP/ix back to Xenix

    reboot
        stay in VP/ix but reboot MS-DOS

    shell
        fork a UNIX command shell

    sound [ on | off ]
        turn sound on or off
```

 NOTE If your VP/ix session is configured to use more than one floppy drive, you cannot acquire or release a single drive. The **floppy acquire** and **floppy release** commands acquire or release all the floppy drives configured for the VP/ix session.

You may have noticed there is no **Floppy Acquire** selection on the VP/ix menu. Although **vpixcmd** can be used to acquire the floppy device, it is not necessary. The floppy device is automatically acquired when you attempt to access it. If it is not available, you will receive a "Not ready reading drive" message.

Pseudo Disk Drives

VP/ix simulates an MS-DOS hard disk C drive by creating a single large UNIX file and establishing an entire MS-DOS disk and filesystem in it. This pseudo disk drive contains all the standard MS-DOS files and commands. You can also install other MS-DOS files and programs on this psuedo drive. However, since this drive appears as one large file to the UNIX system, UNIX utilities and programs cannot access files on it. The pseudo drive can hold a maximum 20MB of data.

 NOTE   Because the C pseudo drive does not shrink when files are removed, it should only be used for permanent files so as not to waste UNIX disk space.

One C drive, **/usr/vpix/defaults/C:**, can be shared by all the users on the system. However, this drive is normally read-only; only the superuser can add files to it or remove files from it. Alternatively, you may have your own copy of the C pseudo drive in your VP/ix configuration subdirectory **vpix**. This has even more disadvantages: If your C drive is read-write, you cannot share it with other users, at least not while you are using it. This type of device also consumes more UNIX disk space than using the default C drive, since all the MS-DOS files from the default C drive must be duplicated on your own copy of the C pseudo drive.

In addition to the simulated hard disk, you can also have a pseudo floppy disk drive, capable of storing up to 360K of data. This is extremely useful if you are using an MS-DOS program that requires two disk drives, but your UNIX system has only one.

Like the pseudo C hard disk drive, a pseudo floppy drive is really a single large UNIX file that has an MS-DOS filesystem and individual MS-DOS files stored in it. This UNIX file can be located anywhere, but most commonly it is placed in the **vpix** subdirectory of your home directory. Before you can use the pseudo floppy, you must format it using the MS-DOS **format** command, just as you would a regular floppy disk.

 NOTE   UNIX utilities cannot access files on a psuedo hard disk or a pseudo floppy drive. Also, psuedo drives consume the maximum amount of UNIX disk space regardless of how much data is stored in them. For these reasons, you should avoid pseudo drives unless they are required by an MS-DOS application.

UNIX File Name Conversion Under VP/ix

VP/ix can access all the UNIX files on your system as well as its own MS-DOS files. But not all UNIX file names fit the MS-DOS file name format. MS-DOS file names must have between one and eight characters, which may be followed by an optional extension consisting of a period and one to three more characters. Also, all the letters in an MS-DOS file name must be uppercase. On the other hand, UNIX file names can have up to 14 characters arranged in any format, and can contain both upper- and lower-case characters. To enable MS-DOS programs to access files that do not fit the MS-DOS file name format, VP/ix translates UNIX file names into acceptable MS-DOS file names, according to the following rules:

- Lowercase letters are translated into uppercase letters.

- Any characters that are not legal in MS-DOS file names are changed to tildes.

- If the file name has a legal MS-DOS extension (that is, one to three characters), it is preserved. Illegal extensions are deleted. If, for example, an extension has four characters, it is removed completely.

- The first five characters of the file name are preserved. If the name has fewer than five characters, tildes are added. A final tilde is always added as the sixth character.

- The seventh and eighth characters are the *conversion table index characters*. These are used to create unique file names from names that would otherwise be identical as a result of the previous translation rules. For example, the UNIX file names **unix.file** and **unix.file2** would both translate to **UNIX~~** without the index characters. By adding the index characters, VP/ix can map these file names to **UNIX~~AA** and **UNIX~~AB**.

NOTE The mapping index characters are assigned sequentially as needed, that is, **AA**, followed by **AB**, **AC**, and so on. The sequence starts over from the beginning at the start of each VP/ix session. So, the same UNIX file may have a different name from one VP/ix session to the next. The file **unix.file** may be named **UNIX~~BY** at one time, and **UNIX~~AX** at another. For this reason, files that will be accessed in ways that require you to know the file name in advance—such as files used in programs and batch files—should be named following the MS-DOS conventions.

To help you read UNIX file names from within MS-DOS, VP/ix provides a special utility, **xdir**, which displays both the mapped MS-DOS file names described above and the UNIX file names. The **xdir** utility also displays UNIX-specific file information such as each file's owner and group, and UNIX file permissions. Here is some sample output from **xdir**:

```
VP/ix Z:\>xdir
Volume of drive Z is Unix
Directory of \
.              <DIR>      3/15/90     9:01p [rwr-r-] <003, 003> .
..             <DIR>      3/15/90     9:01p [rwr-r-] <003, 003> ..
DEV            <DIR>      3/10/90     1:06a [rwr-r-] <003, 003> dev
BOOT           24524      6/21/88     3:34p [r-----] <003, 003> boot
MNT            <DIR>      9/09/88     4:19p [rwr-r-] <003, 003> mnt
TMP            <DIR>      4/01/90    11:06p [rwrwrw] <003, 003> tmp
BIN            <DIR>      3/09/89    11:47p [rwr-r-] <003, 003> bin
ETC            <DIR>      4/01/90     9:22p [rwr-r-] <003, 003> etc
USR            <DIR>      3/10/90    12:21a [rwr-r-] <003, 003> usr
SHLIB          <DIR>      9/09/88     4:23p [rwr-r-] <003, 003> shlib
DOS              577     11/03/87    11:25a [r-----] <003, 003> dos
~PROF~AB         478      6/20/89    10:08p [rw----] <000, 000> .profile
LIB            <DIR>      1/21/90    10:47p [rwr-r-] <003, 003> lib
LOST~~AC       <DIR>      2/15/90     9:33p [rwr-r-] <003, 003> lost+found
UNIX          539919      3/15/90     9:01p [rwr-r-] <000, 000> unix
ONCE           <DIR>      6/15/89     9:19p [rwrwrw] <000, 000> once
UNIX~AD       523227      2/12/89    12:58a [rwr-r-] <003, 003> unix.orig
        17 File(s)  17538560 bytes free
```

From left to right, the columns displayed by **xdir** are the MS-DOS file name, the size of the file in bytes (or **<DIR>** if the entry is a directory), the date and time the file was last modified, the UNIX file permissions, the UNIX owner and group (shown as numbers rather than names), and the

UNIX file name. If you use **xdir** to list files in a psuedo drive or on a real MS-DOS disk, no group, owner, or UNIX file name information is displayed.

Executing UNIX Commands from VP/ix

In addition to all the MS-DOS commands, you also have access to UNIX commands from VP/ix. If you issue a command at the MS-DOS prompt that is not found in the MS-DOS command search path, the UNIX directories **/bin** and **/usr/bin** are also searched. If the command is found there, VP/ix executes it and then returns you to the MS-DOS prompt. You can also execute UNIX commands from any MS-DOS program that can execute external MS-DOS commands.

If you want to be able to run UNIX programs that reside in directories other than **/bin** or **/usr/bin**, you can add those commands to the MS-DOS search path by using the VP/ix **addcmds** utility. Because **addcmds** resides in the **/usr/vpix** directory, it will not normally be found in your command search path, so you must type the full pathname of the command, as shown here:

```
$ /usr/vpix/addcmds
```

This utility creates a .COM file in the **$HOME/vpix/xenixbin** directory for each command in your command search path, as defined by your PATH environment variable.

Executing MS-DOS Programs from the UNIX Shell Prompt

When VP/ix is installed on your UNIX system, new versions of the UNIX command interpreters **/bin/sh** and **/bin/csh** are installed as well. These new interpreters allow you to execute MS-DOS commands directly from your UNIX shell prompt. If a command is not found in the directories listed in the PATH environment variable, the directories in the DOSPATH environment variable are also searched. The DOSPATH variable normally contains the directories **/usr/vpix/dosbin**, **$HOME/vpix/dosbin**, and **.** for the current directory. All the standard MS-DOS operating system commands are in **/usr/vpix/dosbin**. You can add your own MS-DOS commands to the directory **$HOME/vpix/dosbin**. These files can be copies, or, to conserve disk space, you can use the **ln** command to create links instead.

 NOTE   Because UNIX cannot access files in VP/ix pseudo drives such as the C drive, you will not be able to execute MS-DOS commands that reside on these drives from your UNIX command prompt.

Exchanging Data Between UNIX and MS-DOS Commands

You can send data between MS-DOS and UNIX commands using UNIX pipes. From the UNIX command line, you can invoke an MS-DOS command and send its output to a UNIX utility as standard input. For example, the following command uses the MS-DOS **dir** command and the UNIX **grep** command to list only directories.

```
VP/ix Z:\USR\ROSSO>dir | grep "<DIR>"
```

 NOTE   The output of UNIX commands cannot be piped to MS-DOS programs.

MS-DOS and UNIX Special Command Line Characters

There is a conflict between certain characters used on MS-DOS and UNIX command lines. UNIX uses the / character to separate elements of path-names, and precedes command line options with the - character. MS-DOS uses / to precede command line options (or command line *switches*), and the \ character to separate pathname elements. By default, VP/ix recog-nizes the MS-DOS syntax. Use the VP/ix utility **xpath** to switch VP/ix to the UNIX syntax. After executing **xpath**, you can use the following MS-DOS command to list a UNIX directory:

```
Z:\USR>dir /etc/perms
Invalid parameter
Z:\USR>xpath
Z:\USR>dir /etc/perms -w

 Volume in drive Z is UNIX
 Directory of Z:\ETC\PERMS
 .            ..              INST        DSMD        TPMD
RTS          EXT             SOFT        CGI         TEXT
VPIX
        11 File(s)  6990848 bytes free
```

The VP/ix utility **dospath** switches the command line syntax back to MS-DOS format.

Translating MS-DOS and UNIX Text Files

UNIX and MS-DOS handle text files slightly differently: MS-DOS places a carriage return and a newline character at the end of each text line, while UNIX uses only a newline character. VP/ix provides two utilities to translate from one format to the other. The **addcr** utility converts from UNIX to MS-DOS format by adding a carriage return to the end of each line. The **rmcr** utility removes carriage returns, thus translating from MS-DOS to UNIX format. Both utilities require two command line arguments: the name of the original text file and the name to use for the newly translated file. Here is a series of UNIX commands that translates the MS-DOS batch file **autoexec.bat** to UNIX format, edits the file with **vi**, and then translates the file back into MS-DOS format:

```
VP/ix C:\>rmcr autoexec.bat /tmp/autoexec.bat
VP/ix C:\>vi /tmp/autoexec.bat
VP/ix C:\>addcr /tmp/autoexec.bat autoexec.bat
```

 NOTE   Because **addcr** and **rmcr** are UNIX utilities, you must always use the UNIX command line syntax with them, whether you begin from a UNIX or an MS-DOS command prompt.

Redirected MS-DOS Disk Drives

To provide easy access to the potentially large UNIX filesystem from within MS-DOS, VP/ix redirects four MS-DOS drive letters to strategic places in the UNIX filesystem. The Z and U drives are redirected to the entire UNIX filesystem, with the current directory on both these drives set to the directory where you invoked VP/ix or the MS-DOS program. Drives H and Y are mapped so that their root directories are set to your home directory. The root directory is the current directory on these drives.

You can change these drive redirections, or add additional drives using the VP/ix **dosmount** utility. This utility adds new drives by simulating networked disk drives. The **dosmount** command with no arguments displays the current available drives, as shown here:

```
VP/ix Z:\USR\ROSSO>dosmount
Redirected drives:
     Drive 'H:\' prefix '\usr\rosso'
     Drive 'U:\USR\ROSSO'
     Drive 'Y:\' prefix '\usr\rosso'
     Drive 'Z:\USR\ROSSO'
4 redirected drives
```

This **dosmount** listing displays the default VP/ix drive mapping as described previously. The prefix (**'\usr\rosso'**) shown for drives H and Y is the UNIX directory where the root directory for those drives is located.

To add new drives, enter **dosmount** followed by the desired drive letter. This command would add a drive E to the current four redirected drives:

```
VP/ix Z:\USR\ROSSO>dosmount e
Redirected drives:
     Drive 'E:\'
     Drive 'H:\' prefix '\usr\rosso'
     Drive 'U:\USR\ROSSO'
     Drive 'Y:\' prefix '\usr\rosso'
     Drive 'Z:\USR\ROSSO'
5 redirected drives
```

You can delete drives by giving the drive name followed by **-** as an argument to **dosmount**. To delete the Y drive from the previous list, you would use this command:

```
VP/ix Z:\USR\ROSSO>dosmount y:-
Redirected drives:
     Drive 'E:\'
     Drive 'H:\' prefix '\usr\rosso'
     Drive 'U:\USR\ROSSO'
     Drive 'Z:\USR\ROSSO'
4 redirected drives
```

You can also add or change a drive prefix directory using **dosmount**. The next commands would add the prefix **' \usr\lib'** to drive E, and delete the prefix from drive H:

```
VP/ix Z:\USR\ROSSO>dosmount e:\usr\lib
Redirected drives:
     Drive 'E:\' prefix '\usr\lib'
     Drive 'H:\' prefix '\usr\rosso'
     Drive 'U:\USR\ROSSO'
     Drive 'Z:\USR\ROSSO'
4 redirected drives
VP/ix Z:\USR\ROSSO>dosmount h:\
Redirected drives:
     Drive 'E:\' prefix '\usr\lib'
     Drive 'H:\'
     Drive 'U:\USR\ROSSO'
     Drive 'Z:\USR\ROSSO'
4 redirected drives
```

You can place your **dosmount** commands in your **autoexec.bat** file if you want them to execute automatically when MS-DOS boots.

VP/ix and UNIX File Permissions

Although MS-DOS does not have the same notion of file permissions and ownership as UNIX does, MS-DOS programs run under VP/ix must still abide by the UNIX file permission restrictions. Since MS-DOS does not have error messages to describe permissions errors, it substitutes messages that indicate other types of errors. Here is an example of a VP/ix session in which a user attempts to remove, rename, and create a file in the root directory where that user does not have permission to do so:

```
VP/ix Z:\>dir unix*.*

Volume in drive Z is UNIX
Directory of Z:\

UNIX              525919        3-15-90        9:01a
UNIX      BAK     572480       11-14-89       11:05a
UNIX      OLD     554190        3-15-90        9:01a
        3    File(s) 10739712 bytes free

VP/ix Z:\>del unix.old
Access denied

VP/ix Z:\>ren unix.bak unix.bkp
Duplicate file name or File not found

VP/ix Z:\>copy unix.bak unix.bkp
File creation error
        0 File(s) copied
```

In the last command, the error from the MS-DOS **copy** command indicates that the user has read permission on the source file, but does not have write permission on the destination file. If the user did not have read permission, the results would be slightly different, as this example shows:

```
VP/ix Z:\>copy unix.bak unix.bkp
      0 File(s) copied
```

To view a file's permissions while running MS-DOS under VP/ix, use the **xdir** utility as described earlier.

Quick-Starting VP/ix

When VP/ix starts normally, a great deal of initialization goes on. Loading the ROM BIOS and booting the MS-DOS operating system can take several seconds. While this may not sound like a long time, the delay can be annoying when you are executing many short MS-DOS programs. VP/ix provides a way to store an image of the VP/ix session after initialization has been completed. The **-s** command line option saves a memory image of the VP/ix session to a file. This image can then be restored using the **-r** option for nearly instantaneous startup of VP/ix.

With no other arguments, the command **vpix -s** given at your shell prompt saves an image of your VP/ix session in the file **vpix.img** in your VP/ix configuration directory. This command does not actually put you in a VP/ix session; it just brings up VP/ix, saves the session, and exits. You can also specify a file name after the **-s** option, and the image will be saved to that file. Likewise, restoring a session with **-r** alone restores from the **vpix.img** file, while **-r** followed by a file name restores the session from that file.

You can use the save and restore options to manage multiple VP/ix environments. For example, if you were using VP/ix from a WYSE 60 terminal and a DEC VT-100 terminal, you could save a session for each environment in a separate file. From the WYSE 60 terminal, the command **vpix -s vpix.wy60** would save a VP/ix session configured for that terminal. The command **vpix -s vpix.vt100** from the VT-100 terminal would save a session for the VT-100 terminal. Thereafter, you could use **-r** to invoke VP/ix with the appropriate saved environment.

 NOTE If you use the **-s** option with no file name argument, the image file used is **vpix.img** in the **vpix** subdirectory of your home directory. If you specify a file name, the file is saved in the current directory. The **-r** option with a file name also expects to find the file in the current directory. If you want the VP/ix image file to be saved in some other directory, you must specify the full pathname of the file for both the **-s** and **-r** options.

Running MS-DOS Programs as Background Tasks

You can run MS-DOS programs as UNIX background tasks if their input and output can be redirected. For example, the following command executes the MS-DOS **dir** command in the background, sending its output to the **dirlist** file.

```
$ vpix -c dir > & dirlist &
```

This capability can be used to run database reports, print jobs, compile programs, or perform other tasks that do not require user interaction or screen output. If you are running VP/ix from the system console, VP/ix will automatically emulate a monochrome character display.

On the system console, if you switch screens away from your VP/ix session, execution is suspended until you return to the VP/ix screen. If, however, your VP/ix session is running in either CGA or monochrome display mode, the MS-DOS program will continue to run, and the screen will continue to be updated. You can force VP/ix to use monochrome mode on the system console by using the **-m mono** command line option.

Running VP/ix on Serial Terminals

VP/ix can emulate an IBM PC console on several kinds of serial terminals. On a serial terminal, VP/ix emulates an IBM PC computer with a monochrome, character-only display. No colors or graphics are supported on serial terminals. For VP/ix to emulate an IBM PC keyboard and console display, the terminal must have the following capabilities:

- A display screen with at least 24 lines and 80 columns

- A mode in which writing a character in the last column does not send the cursor to the next line

- Escape sequences for clearing the screen, inserting lines, and deleting lines

When operating on a terminal, VP/ix must translate the terminal's keystrokes into IBM PC keyboard scancodes. Some terminals, such as the WYSE 60, have the same keyboard and character set as the IBM PC computer. MS-DOS programs running under VP/ix on these terminals operate exactly as they would on an IBM PC. However, other terminals may not have all the same keys as an IBM PC. The DEC VT-100 terminal, for instance, does not have function keys. On terminals such as this, VP/ix allows key sequences to be mapped to the missing IBM PC keys. On a VT-100 terminal, you emulate the F1 key by pressing ESC followed by the

1 key. Many terminals do not have the ALT key. To send keystrokes such as ALT-X to an MS-DOS application on these terminals, you must enter a key sequence to emulate pressing the ALT key, followed by the x key, and then by another key sequence to emulate releasing the ALT key. On the VT-100 terminal, you emulate depressing the ALT key by pressing ESC, followed by the t key. Releasing ALT is emulated by pressing ESC followed by T. For a complete list of key maps, see the *SCO VP/ix System Administrator's Guide*.

Solving Common VP/ix Problems

Here are some of the most common problems you may encounter when you are using VP/ix:

Application attempted to enter Protected mode If you see this message, an MS-DOS program has attempted to execute an 80286 or 80386 instruction to put the CPU in protected mode. Since VP/ix can only emulate 8086 instructions, you cannot run this program under VP/ix.

Cannot set keyboard INTTYPE This message may occur when you are invoking VP/ix on a serial terminal. It indicates that the serial driver the terminal is using does not have the support needed for VP/ix. Most likely, what's missing is a port on an intelligent serial device with its own UNIX driver. Contact the vendor of the device to see if VP/ix support is available.

General protection fault, cannot emulate instruction This message indicates that an MS-DOS program has attempted to execute an 80286 or 80386 instruction. VP/ix emulates only 8086 instructions, so the program in question cannot be run under VP/ix.

Memory allocation error This message tells you that VP/ix could not allocate enough memory to operate properly, which usually means your system does not have enough RAM installed to run VP/ix. Check your UNIX boot screen to see how much memory your system has.

Error 16 encountered opening file /dev/rfd096ds15 as drive A   This message is displayed during VP/ix initialization. It indicates that the named device could not be accessed, meaning that VP/ix could not gain exclusive access to it. Possible reasons for this error are that the device is already in use by another UNIX or VP/ix user, or that file permissions do not permit you access to the device.

/usr/vpix/defaults/C: is currently open for read/write access Opening psuedo hard disk C: read only   This message, also displayed during VP/ix initialization, indicates that the pseudo hard disk configured in your VP/ix session is already open for reading and writing by another VP/ix session. In this case, your session will have read-only permission on the drive. The drive name in the error message may be different if you are using a C drive other than the system default.

VP/ix Configuration

To emulate the MS-DOS devices, VP/ix translates access to the IBM PC hardware into corresponding operations to UNIX devices. Mapping of IBM PC devices to UNIX devices is controlled by your **vpix.cnf** configuration file. This file is normally located in the **vpix** subdirectory of your home directory. The file contains one-line entries matching the names of the VP/ix devices and the corresponding UNIX devices. Lines that begin with a semicolon are considered comments, so you can place notes in the file, or remove alternate mappings without actually deleting the line. The valid **vpix.cnf** entries are

ROM	This entry points to the file that contains the data normally found in the IBM PC BIOS ROM. This entry should be set to **/usr/vpix/defaults/rom** for all users, and should not be changed.
CMOS	This entry points to the file that contains the data normally found in the IBM PC CMOS memory, which stores configuration information about the computer. This entry should be set to

	/usr/vpix/defaults/cmos for all users, and should not be changed.
BOOTIMAGE	This entry points to a file that contains a memory image of the 8086 process after MS-DOS and other configuration programs, such as device drivers, have been loaded. This memory image is used with the **-r** option to allow for faster startup of VP/ix, a process known as *quick booting*.
EGAROM	This entry points to a UNIX file that contains the data normally found in the ROM chips on an EGA display card. The default setting for this entry is /usr/vpix/defaults/romega. If this entry is not present, the data in the real EGA device is used.
A	This entry assigns the MS-DOS floppy drive A to either a UNIX diskette drive or to a pseudo drive. If a UNIX device is used, it need not be the first drive; any drive can be used.
B	This entry defines the second MS-DOS floppy drive, in the same way that **A** defines the first.
C	This entry points to the pseudo disk drive C used by VP/ix. This drive contains the MS-DOS operating system files. The entry can be set to /usr/vpix/defaults/C: to use the shared drive, or to a specific file in your VP/ix configuration directory.
D	This entry allows VP/ix to access the MS-DOS partition of the UNIX system's hard disk. The UNIX file name that must be used is /dev/hd0d. For this device to be shared among several VP/ix users at once, the permissions must be read-only. If they are read-write, only one user at a time is allowed access.
COM1 COM2	These two entries assign the MS-DOS serial devices. An assigned device can be any available UNIX serial device that is not already in use. For

	example, on a system with a multiport serial device, COM1 could be assigned to /**dev/tty1d** and COM2 could be assigned to /**dev/tty1c**. These devices must not be enabled for login.
LPT1	This entry redirects the MS-DOS printer device to the UNIX print spooler. This can be either a UNIX device such as /**dev/lp0**, or a UNIX command, such as /**usr/bin/lp -s**.
MOUSE	This entry assigns the UNIX bus mouse /**dev/mouse** to the VP/ix user. It should not be used for a serial mouse.
COM1MOUSE COM2MOUSE	These entries assign a UNIX serial mouse device to the VP/ix user. The COM1 and COM2 designation has significance only to MS-DOS. Any UNIX serial device can be assigned to be a VP/ix serial mouse. For example, if a UNIX serial mouse were on /**dev/tty6a**, it could be assigned to either COM1MOUSE or COM2MOUSE, and it would appear to MS-DOS as a serial mouse on COM1 or COM2, respectively.
OFFSCREEN	This entry allows VP/ix to continue execution of the MS-DOS program on the UNIX console even if you switch to another multiscreen. This option is available only on the system console, and only if the console display is a monochrome or CGA display device.
EXTENDED	This entry allows VP/ix to emulate an extended (that is, 102-key) keyboard. This kind of keyboard can be recognized by its 12 function keys and by cursor motion keys that are separate from the numeric keypad. By default, VP/ix emulates the 84-key keyboard, which has only ten function keys.
SWITCHKEY	This entry provides an alternate way to switch multiscreens. On the UNIX system console, the ALT-F1 through ALT-F12 keys are used to switch between

multiscreens, so these keys are normally not available to MS-DOS programs. Adding SWITCHKEY
to your **vpix.cnf** file makes the ALT-F*n* keys pass
through to the MS-DOS application. You then
switch screens by holding down both CTRL and
ALT, and pressing one of the function keys.

Here is an example of a **vpix.cnf** file:

```
$ cat vpix.cnf
C                 $HOME/vpix/C.drive
ROM               /usr/vpix/defaults/rom
CMOS              /usr/vpix/defaults/cmos
BOOTIMAGE         $HOME/vpix/vpix.img
EGAROM            /usr/vpix/defaults/romega
A                 /dev/fd196ds15
LPT1              /usr/bin/lp -s
D                 /dev/hd0d
```

Notice that the variable **$HOME,** which stands for your home directory, is
used on lines one and four. This variable can be used on any **vpix.cnf** line.

When you are assigning devices to VP/ix users, remember that VP/ix
requires exclusive use of devices. For example, if you assign
/dev/rfd096ds15 as drive A to two different users, only one of them will be
allowed to use that drive from VP/ix at any given time. If the second user
invokes VP/ix, VP/ix will display the message

```
Error 16 encountered opening file /dev/rfd096ds15 as drive A
Press Enter To Continue
```

The second user will be allowed to start VP/ix, but will not have access to
the floppy drive.

Setting Up Your VP/ix Configuration File

Your **vpix.cnf** file is first created by the system administrator using the
vpixadm utility. This utility provides for setting up the initial VP/ix

configuration for UNIX users, and for modifying existing configurations. You can also create your **vpix.cnf** file directly using one of the UNIX text editors.

If you do not have a **vpix.cnf** file, VP/ix will use the system-wide file **/usr/vpix/defaults/vpix.cnf**. This file can also be modified by the system administrator using the **vpixadm** command or a UNIX text editor.

UNIX can exchange files with MS-DOS and perform other operations on MS-DOS files and filesystems. The files may be in your UNIX filesystem, on MS-DOS diskettes, or on an MS-DOS partition of your system's hard disk. With the addition of VP/ix, your UNIX system can simulate an IBM PC environment to run the MS-DOS operating system, and MS-DOS applications programs under it. VP/ix acts as the intermediary between UNIX and MS-DOS programs, providing a complete virtual IBM PC environment within UNIX. This gives you access to the extensive base of MS-DOS programs as well as to UNIX applications.

CHAPTER

15

An Overview of SCO Business Software

This chapter provides an overview of the major products in the SCO business software series. The intent is to give you a general tour of the features available in these applications, not to provide detailed information on how to use each product. The following software packages are discussed:

SCO Manager   A desktop package that features centralized control of multiple applications. This product offers menus you can customize, multitasking, a clipboard, electronic mail, a calendar, an intercom, and a five-function calculator.

SCO Professional	A Lotus 1-2-3 work-alike spreadsheet that is capable of reading and writing DOS files. Professional also supports SQL calls to SCO Integra from worksheet cells.
SCO Lyrix	A word processing program that offers proportional printing, columnar tables with four-function math, hyphenation, and line drawing, plus a spelling checker and thesaurus.
SCO Statistician	A statistical package that includes a broad range of statistical and forecasting functions.
SCO Masterplan	A project scheduling and management package based on the Critical Path method.
SCO ImageBuilder	A graphics presentation package that allows you to create graphs, charts, diagrams, and slides.
SCO Integra	A SQL-based relational database management system.
SCO FoxBASE+	A relational database management system offering source language and data file compatibility with dBASE III PLUS.
Microsoft Word	A full-featured word processing package from Microsoft that is familiar to many DOS users. This product can read and write DOS files. It also offers built-in outlining, automatic document formatting, document preview, two-window editing, a spelling checker, style sheets, glossaries, and more. In the word processing arena, Word is far superior to Lyrix.

All of the items in the preceding list that begin with SCO, except SCO FoxBASE+, are included in the SCO Office Portfolio. Although these products can be purchased and installed separately, it is not uncommon to purchase the SCO Manager as a menu-driven interface for the system, and then add other Office Portfolio applications as the need arises. In fact, SCO bundles four of these applications, including SCO Manager, SCO Professional, SCO Lyrix, and SCO Integra, in a package called the SCO Office Portfolio Suite. The remaining products in the preceding list, including SCO FoxBASE+ and Microsoft Word are standalone products licensed from their respective vendors.

 NOTE Although almost every product discussed in this chapter should run on both XENIX and UNIX, a few may not. Make sure you check system compatibility with SCO or your dealer before you order a particular application.

The SCO Office Portfolio Suite

As mentioned, the SCO Office Portfolio Suite includes four products: SCO Manager, SCO Professional, SCO Lyrix, and SCO Integra. The appeal of the Office Portfolio Suite is that it offers the triad of spreadsheet (Professional), word processing (Lyrix), and database (Integra) running under a menu-driven system (Manager). To start a given application, you simply select its name from SCO Manager's Application menu. When you subsequently leave the application, you are returned to SCO Manager. Thus, multiple applications are centrally controlled through a menu-based system.

You can also configure the SCO Manager to start up automatically whenever a user logs on to the system. This gives users who don't know much about the SCO UNIX or XENIX operating environment access to reasonably powerful business applications.

Each of the products included in the SCO Office Portfolio Suite is discussed in the following sections.

SCO Manager

SCO Manager provides a menu-driven interface for the SCO Office Portfolio products. Once SCO Manager is installed, you can start it by simply typing **op** at the XENIX or UNIX system prompt. A moment later, the SCO Manager Desktop, shown in Figure 15-1, appears on your screen.

The SCO Manager Desktop can be used to unite several software packages under a single menu-driven user interface. From the Desktop you can activate application programs that are provided by SCO or by third-party vendors. Once an application starts running, the SCO Manager Desktop disappears from your screen and the application takes over. When you leave the application you are returned to the SCO Manager Desktop.

When you install SCO Manager, a copy of the Multiview run time system is installed as well. Multiview allows you to run up to four applications at once under SCO Manager, and to switch back and forth among them.

SCO Manager also allows you to share information between applications through the clipboard. The clipboard is an area of memory that is used to store information temporarily. You can copy information from one application to the clipboard, and then paste the information from the clipboard into another application. For example, if you are preparing a report, you might

Figure 15-1.

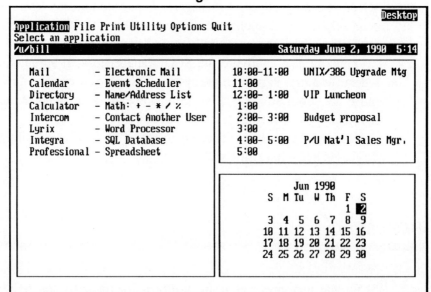

The SCO Manager Desktop.

prepare the numbers for the report in SCO Professional and then paste them into an SCO Lyrix document.

In addition, SCO Manager provides several convenient accessory programs including Mail, Calendar, Calculator, User Directory, and Intercom. These accessory programs are covered in the sections that follow.

To access the various features of SCO Manager, you must use its main menu. The available menu options are shown at the top of Figure 15-1. Briefly, these options perform the following functions:

Application	Runs an application or accessory program
File	Manages files and directories
Print	Controls printing
Utility	Accesses selected utilities
Options	Edits the application and utility lists and configures the SCO Manager Desktop
Quit	Exits the SCO Manager program

Running Applications

To run an application or an SCO Manager accessory program, select the Application option from the SCO Manager menu. SCO Manager activates the large window on the left of your screen, which contains the names of applications currently installed on the Manager Desktop. Use the arrow keys to move the highlight to the name of the application that you want to run and press RETURN. The Manager Desktop screen disappears, and is replaced after a moment by the application you've selected.

NOTE   You can add the XENIX or UNIX operating system to the list of applications as the System option. That way, you can run XENIX or UNIX under the Manager, as though the operating system itself were an application.

Switching Between Applications   You can also run multiple applications from the Manager Desktop and switch back and forth among them by using special *hot keys*. To do this, use Manager's Application menu option to start one application—SCO Professional for example. Then, press the special SHIFT-F1 hot key to activate the Manager again. When the Manager Desktop window reappears on your screen, select the Application option from Manager's menu and choose SCO Lyrix. The SCO Lyrix window appears on your screen. At this point, you have two applications running on the Manager Desktop. To switch from Lyrix to Professional, press the default hot key assigned to Professional, SHIFT-F8. To switch from Professional back to Lyrix, press SHIFT-F7.

The example in the previous paragraph is only one of many possible multitasking scenarios you can set up with SCO Manager. When you receive Manager, its hot keys are configured to activate the following applications by default:

Hot Key	Application
SHIFT-F1	SCO Manager
SHIFT-F2	Mail
SHIFT-F3	Calendar
SHIFT-F4	User Directory
SHIFT-F5	Calculator
SHIFT-F6	Intercom
SHIFT-F7	SCO Lyrix
SHIFT-F8	SCO Professional
SHIFT-F9	Displays a list of applications available from SCO Manager from which you can choose
SHIFT-F10	Displays a list of the applications that are currently running, so that you can select the one you want

Pressing SHIFT-F9 is the same as selecting Application from the Manager menu: it displays a box containing the list of available applications from which you can select the name of the application you want to start. Pressing SHIFT-F10, on the other hand, displays a box containing a list of applications that are already running, from which you can select the name of the application that you want to make active.

 NOTE   You can also configure SCO Manager's hot keys to run applications that you assign.

Using the Clipboard   As mentioned earlier, you can use the clipboard to share information between applications in the Office Portfolio. The clipboard is an area of memory that is used to store information temporarily. Each user has his or her own clipboard. You can copy information from an application to the clipboard, and then paste that information into another application. Again, if you are preparing a report, you might prepare the numbers for the report in Professional, and then paste them into a Lyrix document.

To copy and paste information to and from the clipboard, you use the Transfer command. Although this command is available in most applications that use the clipboard, the procedure for using it may vary slightly from one application to the next. Furthermore, the type of information that is copied to the clipboard may differ for each application. Consult the documentation for an individual application to determine the correct procedure for using its version of the Transfer command.

For example, to access the Transfer command in SCO Manager, you select the File command first and then the Transfer command. In Manager, the Transfer command is used to copy entire files to and from the clipboard. On the other hand, in SCO Professional and Lyrix, the Transfer command is directly available on the main menu. In the case of Professional, you can use Transfer to copy the data in a range of worksheet cells to the clipboard, and in the case of Lyrix, you can use it to copy a block of text.

In most cases, the Transfer command allows you to copy information both to and from the clipboard for the current application. For example, imagine that both SCO Professional and SCO Lyrix were currently running on the SCO Manager desktop. While in Professional, you would use the Transfer command to copy the information in a range of cells from the worksheet to the clipboard. Then, you would press the SHIFT-F7 hot key to switch to SCO Lyrix. Finally, you would use the Transfer command in Lyrix to paste the information on the clipboard to the appropriate spot in your Lyrix document.

Each time you copy information from an application to the clipboard, you are prompted to assign a file name to that information; thus, you can store an almost unlimited amount of data on the clipboard, segmented by file names. When you paste data from the clipboard to an application, you are prompted with a list of available file names, and you simply choose the one that represents the information you want to paste into the current application.

When you paste information from the clipboard to an application, the information is automatically translated into the receiving application's file format. The original information on the clipboard remains unchanged, with one exception: When you use the Transfer command to access the clipboard from within SCO Manager, you must copy an entire file from disk to the clipboard, and you must specify the file format for the file you are copying. You are prompted to select from the following formats:

- Text—Straight text file

- Lyrix—Lyrix (word processor) file format

- Professional—Professional (Lotus 1-2-3) file format

- Graphics—Graphics metafile

- DIF—Visicalc DIF format

- SYLK—Multiplan SYLK spreadsheet format

- ImageBuilder—Graphics file

- CSV—Comma separated values

- DBF—dBASE II file format

Conversely, when you paste information from the clipboard, you can only paste that information to a file on disk. However, you can change the format of the file to any of those in the preceding list.

 NOTE   You can also create direct links between applications that do not involve the clipboard. For example, you can create a link between a Microsoft Word document and a specific range of cells in an SCO Professional worksheet. Once you've created the link from within Word, the information from the range of cells in the Professional worksheet is copied to the Word document. If you subsequently change the data in the Professional worksheet, the Word document is updated automatically. Only certain applications support linking in this fashion, and those do so only in certain situations.

Managing Files

You can also use SCO Manager to perform routine file management tasks. To access Manager's file management facilities, select the File command from Manager's main menu. When you select this command, the screen in Figure 15-2 is displayed. Notice that the file names and subdirectories in your home directory now appear at the bottom of the screen. In addition, a new list of menu options appears at the top of the Manager screen. Briefly, these menu options perform the following functions:

View	Displays the contents of a file on your screen
Copy	Copies one or more files
Rename	Changes the name of one or more files, or moves one or more files to a new location
Erase	Erases one or more files
Directory	Changes the current directory, creates a new directory, or deletes a directory
Modes	Changes permissions for files
Wastebasket	Recovers a file that you have erased
Archive	Moves files to or from a floppy disk, lists the files already on a floppy disk, or formats a new floppy disk
Transfer	Copies files to or from the clipboard, removes files from the clipboard, or sends files to other users by electronic mail

When you select one of these options, Manager prompts you for a file name. At that point, you can either type the name of the file to which you want the command applied, or you can select the name of a file from the list of file names at the bottom of the screen.

Figure 15-2.

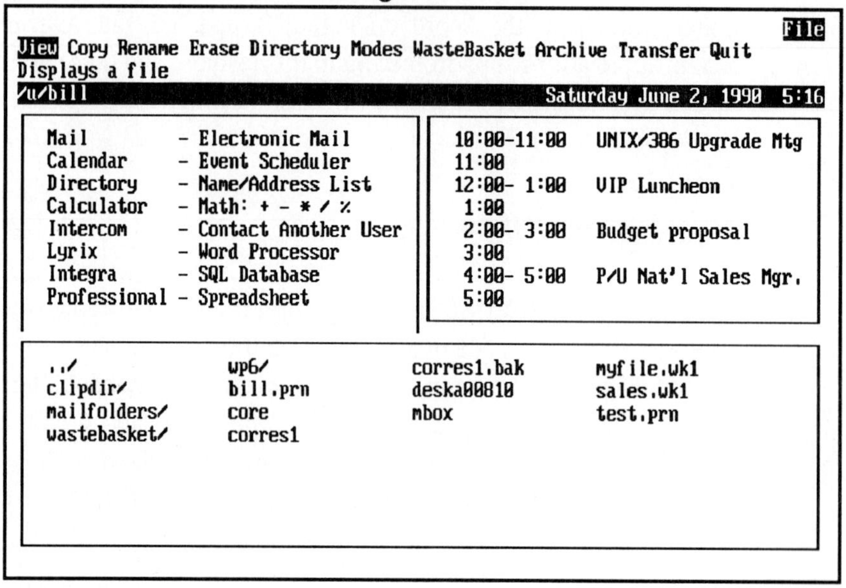

```
                                                                       File
View Copy Rename Erase Directory Modes WasteBasket Archive Transfer Quit
Displays a file
/u/bill                                        Saturday June 2, 1990  5:16

  Mail          - Electronic Mail      10:00-11:00  UNIX/386 Upgrade Mtg
  Calendar      - Event Scheduler      11:00
  Directory     - Name/Address List    12:00- 1:00  VIP Luncheon
  Calculator    - Math: + - * / %       1:00
  Intercom      - Contact Another User  2:00- 3:00  Budget proposal
  Lyrix         - Word Processor        3:00
  Integra       - SQL Database          4:00- 5:00  P/U Nat'l Sales Mgr.
  Professional  - Spreadsheet           5:00


  ../             wp6/            corres1.bak     myfile.wk1
  clipdir/        bill.prn        deska00810      sales.wk1
  mailfolders/    core            mbox            test.prn
  wastebasket/    corres1

```

The File Menu Options.

Printing

SCO Manager allows you to print the contents of any file you own. To print
from Manager, select the Print option from the main menu. When you select
this option, the screen in Figure 15-3 is displayed, and a list of files and
subdirectories in your home directory appears at the bottom of the Manager
screen. In addition, a new set of Print menu options becomes available.
Briefly, these options perform the following functions:

Go	Sends one or more files to the current printer
Select	Chooses a different printer
Printstatus	Checks the status of a print job
Cancel	Cancels a print job

Figure 15-3.

```
                    Current printer: laser.jet                Print
 Go Select PrintStatus Cancel Quit
Send file(s) to the current printer
/u/bill                                    Saturday June 2, 1990  5:17

   Mail         - Electronic Mail       10:00-11:00   UNIX/386 Upgrade Mtg
   Calendar     - Event Scheduler       11:00
   Directory    - Name/Address List     12:00- 1:00   VIP Luncheon
   Calculator   - Math: + - * / %        1:00
   Intercom     - Contact Another User   2:00- 3:00   Budget proposal
   Lyrix        - Word Processor         3:00
   Integra      - SQL Database           4:00- 5:00   P/U Nat'l Sales Mgr.
   Professional - Spreadsheet            5:00


   ../              wp6/           corres1.bak     myfile.wk1
   clipdir/         bill.prn       deska00810      sales.wk1
   mailfolders/     core           mbox            test.prn
   wastebasket/     corres1



```

The Print Menu Options.

If you select the Go option, a list of files in your current directory appears on your screen. You can then select the file you want to print.

If you choose the Select option, Manager displays a list of available printer drivers from which you can select the printer that you want to use.

If you select Printstatus, you'll see a box that contains listings for any jobs currently waiting to be printed. Each listing includes the login name of the person who sent the job, the number of characters in the file, and the date and time the job was sent.

Selecting Cancel displays a box that lists any print jobs you have sent to the current printer. You can then select the print job that you want to cancel.

Running Utilities

You can also run XENIX or UNIX utilities from within SCO Manager. To do this, select the Utility option from Manager's main menu. When you select this option, Manager displays the screen shown in Figure 15-4. To select a utility use the arrow keys to highlight its name, and then press RETURN.

You'll notice that many of the selections in the utilities list in Figure 15-4 correspond to standard XENIX and UNIX utilities discussed throughout this book. However, some of the utilities listed perform specialized processes that are specific to SCO Manager. For example, the last four entries in the list, which begin with Terminal, allow you to configure SCO Manager to suit your specific preferences.

Configuring the Manager Desktop

You can configure the Manager Desktop to suit your preferences. To do this, use the Options selection from Manager's main menu. When you select

Figure 15-4.

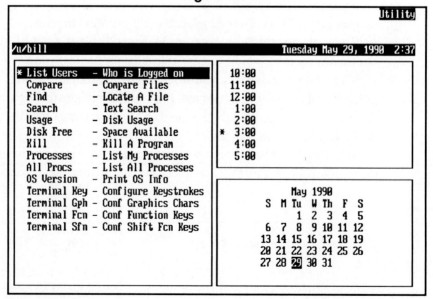

The Utility Screen.

this option, Manager displays the menu choices shown at the top of Figure 15-5. Briefly, these menu options perform the following functions:

Display   Configures the position of Manager's Application, Event, Calendar, and File windows

Reminders   Configures the display of mail and upcoming appointment reminders

Applist   Modifies or adds to the list of applications that are displayed for your selection, and configures the function keys for an application.

Utillist   Modifies the list of utilities displayed for your selection

Save   Saves the modifications you've made to the Manager Desktop configuration

Figure 15-5.

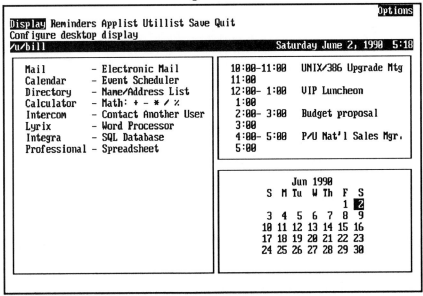

The Options Menu.

Mail

Manager's Mail accessory program makes sending, receiving, and managing electronic mail easy even for the novice user. To activate the Mail accessory program, select the Application option from Manager's main menu, and then select Mail. Manager displays the screen shown in Figure 15-6.

The Mail accessory program allows you to exchange mail with any of the users on your system. For example, you can send mail to another user, to several users at the same time, or to yourself as a reminder. You can also receive messages from others, forward messages, and insert a message you have received into a message that you are sending.

You can send just about anything with the Mail program; you can even attach the contents of an entire file to a message.

You can also use the Mail accessory program to manage your mail. For example, you can create aliases as automatic distribution lists for outgoing

Figure 15-6.

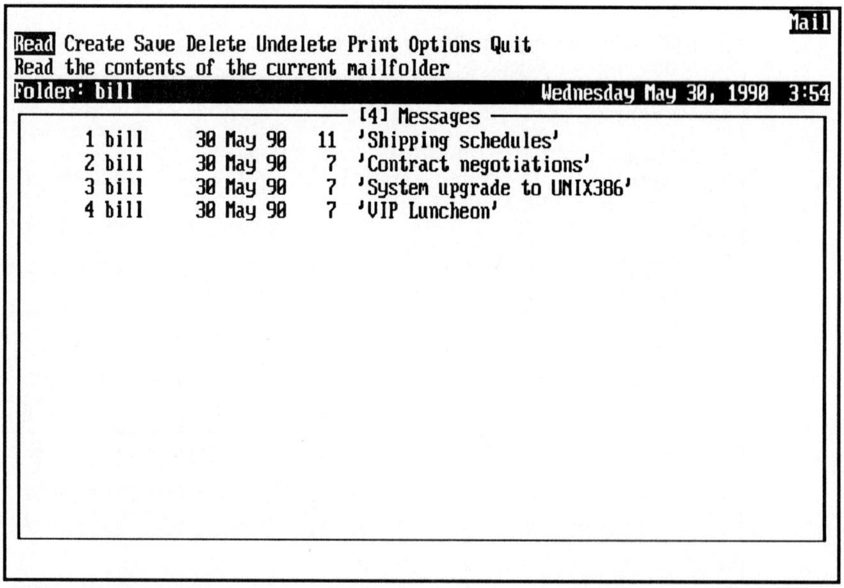

```
                                                                      Mail
Read Create Save Delete Undelete Print Options Quit
Read the contents of the current mailfolder
Folder: bill                               Wednesday May 30, 1990  3:54
                              ─── [4] Messages ───
        1 bill      30 May 90   11  'Shipping schedules'
        2 bill      30 May 90    7  'Contract negotiations'
        3 bill      30 May 90    7  'System upgrade to UNIX386'
        4 bill      30 May 90    7  'VIP Luncheon'
```

The Mail Screen.

mail. You can also save mail messages permanently either in separate files or in special files referred to as mail folders.

Briefly, the menu options listed at the top of the Mail screen in Figure 15-6 perform the following functions:

Read	Reads mail that has been sent to you
Create	Sends mail to others or to yourself
Save	Saves messages to a file or mail folder
Delete	Deletes messages from a mail folder
Undelete	Restores messages that you have deleted
Print	Sends mail messages to the current printer
Options	Configures Mail options, switches to another mail folder, or manages mail aliases

 NOTE   For an in-depth discussion of how to access and use Mail from the XENIX or UNIX system prompt, see Chapter 9, "Sending and Receiving Mail."

Calendar

The Calendar accessory program provides access to an on-line appointment book that lets you effectively manage your daily schedule. You can use it to schedule events days, weeks, and even months ahead. You can also configure Calendar to display your daily schedule of events and to remind you of events shortly before they occur.

In addition to organizing you own calendar, the Calendar program gives you access to the calendars of other users on the system. You can search those calendars for free time and make entries for meetings, events, and so on. Thus, providing everyone keeps their calendar up-to-date, you can avoid scheduling conflicts. You can also configure your calendar to control both who has access to it and what changes they are allowed to make.

Each user has his or her own calendar. By default, your calendar for the current day's events appears in the upper-right window of SCO Manager's Desktop screen. You can update your personal calendar, as well as the calendars of other users, by using the Calendar accessory program. To start this program, select the Application option from Manager's main menu, and then select Calendar. The Calendar window appears on your screen as shown in Figure 15-7.

When you start the Calendar program, your calendar for the current day is displayed on the screen. In addition, the following menu options are displayed:

Next	Moves to the next day
Back	Moves to the previous day
Goto	Displays a three month calendar; you can also select a particular day to display in the Calendar window
Add	Adds an event to the current calendar
Edit	Changes an event
Delete	Removes an event
View	Displays a week or a month of calendars
Print	Prints a calendar
Transfer	Uses the clipboard to transfer information from a calendar to a text file, from one place to another within the same calendar, or from one calendar to another
Options	Creates new calendars, switches to a new calendar, sets permissions for calendars, sets alias lists, and sets other calendar options

Intercom

The Intercom allows you to hold interactive conversations with other users who are logged on to the system. The conversation is private and occurs by means of typed messages. As you type a message, the other user receives that message on his or her screen and can respond to it immediately. To use the Intercom, select the Application option from Manager's main menu. When you select this option, the screen in Figure 15-8 appears.

Figure 15-7.

```
                                                                    Calendar
Next Back Goto Add Edit Delete View Print Transfer Options Quit
Move to the next day
Calendar: bill                                   Thursday May 31, 1990  9:49
                          Thursday May 31, 1990
  8:00- 9:00   Scheduling Meeting     Building 1
  9:00
 10:00-11:00   Meet with QC           Building 35
 11:00
 12:00- 1:00   Lunch with Jack        Shadowbrook
  1:00
  2:00- 3:00   Budget Proposal        VP Manufacturing
  3:00
  4:00- 5:00   Meet with Purchasing   Conference Room 3
  5:00
```

The Calendar Screen.

Figure 15-8.

```
                                                                    Intercom
Send Disable Quit
Call another user
Intercom for bill                                Thursday May 31, 1990 11:57

  ┌──────────────────────────────────────────────────────────────────┐
  │                                                                    │
  │                                                                    │
  │                                                                    │
  │                                                                    │
  │                                                                    │
  └──────────────────────────────────────────────────────────────────┘

  ┌──────────────────────────────────────────────────────────────────┐
  │                                                                    │
  │                                                                    │
  │                                                                    │
  └──────────────────────────────────────────────────────────────────┘
```

The Intercom Screen.

To call another user, select the Send menu option. Manager displays a list of users currently logged on to the system. Select the name of the user you want to contact. Manager displays a small message box on the other user's screen stating that you are trying to contact him or her. (The message box is displayed, even if the person is running another application.) If the other user decides to reply, their login name is displayed in the top border of the top window shown in Figure 15-8, and your login name is displayed in the bottom of the bottom window. At that point, you can begin "talking" to each other.

You can use Intercom at any time, even when you or the person you are contacting is in the middle of running an application. When you leave Intercom, you are returned to the application that you were running before you started Intercom.

To disable Intercom, you can select the Disable menu option. That way, no one can contact you via Intercom and interrupt what you are doing.

User Directory

The user directory shows the login names, actual names, company names, and phone numbers of each user on the system. To access this list, select Application from Manager's main menu, and then select User Directory. Manager displays the User Directory screen, which includes a menu that allows you to manage the user directory listing.

SCO Professional

SCO Professional combines three powerful programs—spreadsheet, graphics, and data management—into a single application. The cornerstone of Professional is the spreadsheet, which takes the concept of an accountant's columnar notepad and transforms it into a versatile electronic worksheet that can be used in a variety of business, scientific, and engineering applications.

SCO Professional is modeled after the popular Lotus 1-2-3 spreadsheet program that runs under the DOS operating system. In fact, SCO Professional reads and writes DOS files that are compatible with Lotus 1-2-3, and its menus are substantially the same as the Lotus menus. If you are familiar with 1-2-3, you'll feel immediately at ease in Professional.

You can start Professional in one of three ways. First, if you have installed SCO Manager, you can select Application from the main menu, and then select Professional. Second, type **pro** at the XENIX or UNIX operating system prompt, and then press RETURN. The SCO Professional Manager menu system will appear on your screen, and you can then select Professional from the menu. Third, you can go directly to Professional by typing **procalc** at the system prompt. Whichever method you use, you will see a Professional screen similar to the one shown in Figure 15-9.

 NOTE   The features of the SCO Professional program are far too diverse to cover comprehensively in this section. Instead, we will give you a brief tour of Professional, highlighting some of its major commands and features along the way.

Figure 15-9.

```
C12: (C0) [W10] @SUM(C5..C10)                                              READY


        A      B        C         D         E         F         G
1                           ABC Company, Inc.
2
3    Sales By SBU      Qtr-1     Qtr-2     Qtr-3     Qtr-4     Total
4
5    Colors         $100,000  $120,000  $144,000  $172,800  $536,800
6    Inks            $50,000   $60,000   $72,000   $86,400  $268,400
7    Paints          $75,000   $90,000  $108,000  $129,600  $402,600
8    Plastics        $30,000   $36,000   $43,200   $51,840  $161,040
9    Dyes           $200,000  $240,000  $288,000  $345,600  $1,073,600
10   Brightener     $150,000  $180,000  $216,000  $259,200  $805,200
11
12   Total          $605,000  $726,000  $871,200 $1,045,440 $3,247,640
13
14
15
16
17
18
19
21-Jun-90  12:33 PM              sales.wk1
```

A Sample SCO Professional Worksheet.

The Professional Worksheet

The first thing you will see when you start Professional is a blank worksheet. (Figure 15-9 shows an example of what a worksheet looks like after data has been entered.) Worksheets are composed of columns and rows. Each column is identified by a letter, and each row by a number. A Professional worksheet contains 1024 columns and 8192 rows (768 more columns than a 1-2-3 worksheet). This is far too many columns and rows for your screen to display; therefore, your screen acts as a window onto a much larger work surface.

The intersection of each column and row is a *cell*. Cells are used to store data (labels or numbers) and formulas. To identify a cell's location in the worksheet, you use its column and row coordinates. For example, the first cell in the worksheet (in the upper-left corner) is cell A1, because it resides in column A, row 1. The cell immediately to the right of cell A1 is cell B1, because it resides in column B, row 1, and so on.

You can identify a rectangular group of adjacent cells that will be affected by a command or formula by specifying a *range*. You specify a range by defining its upper-left and lower-right corner cells. For example, to specify the range that includes the cells in columns A through H and rows 1 through 10, you would use the range A1..H10. You can also assign a name to a range and refer to it by that name in commands and formulas.

To enter data or formulas into worksheet cells, use the arrow keys to move the *cell pointer* (the reverse-video block) to the cell in which you want to enter the data. Then, type the data—either a label, a number, or a formula—and press RETURN. Professional enters the data in the current cell.

To maneuver around the worksheet, simply move the cell pointer. When you move the cell pointer beyond the edge of the window that is displayed on your screen, Professional updates the screen to show a new set of columns and rows. There are a multitude of ways to move the cell pointer quickly around the worksheet.

Formulas

The real power of Professional comes not from its ability to store raw data in worksheet cells, but from its ability to manipulate and analyze that data. One way to manipulate and analyze data is through the use of formulas.

Formulas allow you to relate the contents of worksheet cells to one another. For example, you can create a formula that adds the values in a range of worksheet cells together. With this capability alone, you can create a worksheet like the one in Figure 15-9. In this figure the special @SUM function has been used in row 12 and in column G to add values in the table of data that occupies the range C5..F10. For example, the formula @SUM(C5..C10) in cell C12 adds the values in cells C5, C6, C7, C8, C9, and C10, and records the total in cell C12. Similar formulas in row 12 add the values in columns D, E, and F of the table. The @SUM function is also used in column G to add the values in each row of the table.

Formulas are dynamic: When you change a value in one of the cells to which a formula refers, the worksheet is recalculated and the formula is updated to reflect the change. For example, suppose you changed the value in cell C5 of Figure 15-9. The @SUM formulas in cells C12 and G5 would be updated automatically to incorporate the new value. This feature allows you to perform *what-if* analysis in a worksheet. By changing the values in one or more cells, you can see what effect those changes have on other cells in the worksheet.

The example presented in this section is only one among thousands, perhaps millions, of possible applications for formulas in an SCO Professional worksheet. Nonetheless, it should give you a hint of the power you have at your fingertips when you use formulas with SCO Professional.

Commands

Commands allow you to control the operation of Professional as well as to manipulate and analyze data. To use a command, simply press the / (slash)

Figure 15-10.

```
C12: (C0) [W10] @SUM(C5..C10)                                           MENU
Worksheet Range Copy Move File Print Graph Data System Learn Transfer Quit
Global, Insert, Delete, Column-Width, Erase, Titles, Window, Status, Page
      A       B       C        D        E        F        G
1                        ABC Company, Inc.
2
3  Sales By SBU      Qtr-1    Qtr-2    Qtr-3    Qtr-4     Total
4
5  Colors         $100,000 $120,000 $144,000 $172,800   $536,800
6  Inks            $50,000  $60,000  $72,000  $86,400   $268,400
7  Paints          $75,000  $90,000 $108,000 $129,600   $402,600
8  Plastics        $30,000  $36,000  $43,200  $51,840   $161,040
9  Dyes           $200,000 $240,000 $288,000 $345,600 $1,073,600
10 Brightener     $150,000 $180,000 $216,000 $259,200   $805,200
11
12 Total          $605,000 $726,000 $871,200 $1,045,440 $3,247,640
13
14
15
16
17
18
19
21-Jun-90  12:33 PM           sales.wk1
```

The SCO Professional Menu.

key. When you press this key, the Professional command menu appears near the top of your screen, as shown in Figure 15-10. The options on Professional's main menu are discussed briefly in the following sections.

/Worksheet   The /Worksheet command performs a variety of functions in Professional. It includes these options:

Global	Sets the defaults for the display of data in a Professional worksheet. Also sets the width of columns for the worksheet and protects the worksheet from data entry.
Insert	Inserts new columns and rows into the worksheet.
Delete	Deletes columns and rows from the worksheet.
Column-Width	Changes the width of the columns in the worksheet.
Erase	Removes the current worksheet from memory.

Titles	Specifies columns and rows that will remain on your screen, regardless of where you move the cell pointer.
Window	Splits the worksheet into two windows so you can view divergent portions of the same worksheet on your screen. You can also use this feature to view two entirely different worksheets at the same time.
Status	Displays a settings sheet that lists Professional's current default settings.
Page	Inserts a page-break symbol into the worksheet. When you print a range that contains a page-break symbol, Professional ends the current page and starts the next one when it encounters the page-break symbol.

/Range   The /Range command is used primarily to change the displayed appearance of your data; however, its capabilities go far beyond that. The Range command includes the following options:

Format	Formats a range of cells to display data in a certain way. You can choose from a variety of available formats. For example, you might format a range as Currency 2, which causes a leading dollar sign to appear in front of a number, separates thousands with commas, and displays two places after the decimal; thus, the number 10000 would become $10,000.00.
Layout	Affects the alignment of labels in cells. You can choose from left-aligned (the default), centered, or right-aligned.
Erase	Erases the contents of the cells you specify.
Name	Lets you assign a name to a range of cells. You can then use that name to refer to the range in commands and formulas.

Justify	Justifies a range of labels to fit within a specified width.
Protect	Reprotects a range of cells to prohibit data entry to those cells.
Unprotect	When you protect an entire worksheet with the Worksheet Global Protection command, this command allows you to unprotect specific cells so that data entry is allowed in those cells. If you change your mind, you can reprotect the cells with the Range Protect command.
Input	Presents a custom data-entry form that you have previously prepared. This command is often used in an interactive macro to present a custom form for data entry to a Professional database.

/Copy and /Move   The /Copy command allows you to replicate data in the worksheet, and the /Move command allows you to move data from one location to another. The /Copy command saves you time by allowing you to quickly replicate existing data and formulas in another area of the worksheet, rather than retyping the information manually. The /Move command is useful when you want to change the organization of a worksheet or make room for new data.

/File   The /File command lets you manage your Professional files. For example, you can save a worksheet that you've created in Professional to disk in the form of a file. The /File command is used primarily to save worksheet files to disk and to load existing files into Professional; however, you can also use the /File command to perform a number of other functions. The /File command offers the following options:

Retrieve	Loads an existing worksheet file into Professional.
Save	Saves a worksheet file to disk under a name you specify.
Combine	Combines two worksheet files.
Extract	Extracts all or part of the worksheet file in memory to a file on disk under a name that you specify.

List	Displays a list of Professional files that are currently on disk.
Import	Imports the contents of ASCII text files into the worksheet.
Directory	Changes the current directory in which Professional looks for its files and in which it saves your files.
Type	Lets you specify the file format in which Professional saves its files (/File Save). You can also use this option to load a file whose format differs from that of Professional (/File Retrieve). The following formats are available: SCO Professional/Lotus 1-2-3 Release 2 format (.WK1); Multiplan format (.SLK); Data interchange format (.DIF); dBASE II or dBASE III format (.DBF); and SCO Professional Release 1/Lotus 1-2-3 Release 1A format (.WKS).

/Print   The /Print command is used to print the data in your worksheets. You can send the printed output either to your printer or to a text file. To send data to your printer, use the /Print Printer command. To send data to a file, use the /Print File command. Both commands offer the following menu options:

Range	Lets you select a range to print.
Line	Advances the printer by one line. Use this option to leave a blank line between print ranges.
Page	Advances the printer to the beginning of the next page.
Options	Lets you specify various formatting options for the print job such as headers, footers, margins, borders, and page length. You can also use this option to send a printer control code (setup string) to your printer. For example, you might send a printer control code to your laser printer that causes it to print in landscape mode (sideways).
Clear	Deletes various print settings.
Align	Starts a new page.
Go	Readies the print job.

Select   Lets you select a new default printer.

Quit   Removes the /Print menu and sends the data to your printer or to a file.

/Graph   The /Graph command allows you to create a graphics image that represents the data in your worksheet. For example, Figure 15-11 shows a sample SCO Professional graph that was produced using the data shown earlier in Figure 15-10. The Graph command includes the following options:

Type   Allows you to choose the type of graph you want to produce. You can choose from bar, stacked bar, line, pie (or rectilinear pie), and XY. Figure 15-11 shows an example of a bar graph.

X and A - F   These letters allow you to choose different ranges of data from the worksheet to be plotted in the graph. X is usually used to select a range containing data that will appear along the X-axis, and A through F are usually used to select data ranges that will be plotted along the Y-axis.

Reset   Clears the current /Graph settings.

View   Displays the current graph on screen.

Save   Saves the current graph to a file with a .GPH extension so you can print the graph at a later time or with another program.

Options   Lets you specify various enhancement options for the graph. For example, you can specify titles, legends, data labels, grid lines, scaling, data format, and more.

Name   Lets you assign a name to the current graph settings so you can recall them easily.

Print   Prints your graph. This command accesses a printing facility that lets you further enhance your graph, as well as position it on the page.

Graph-Transfer   Copies or retrieves graphs from the clipboard.

Figure 15-11.

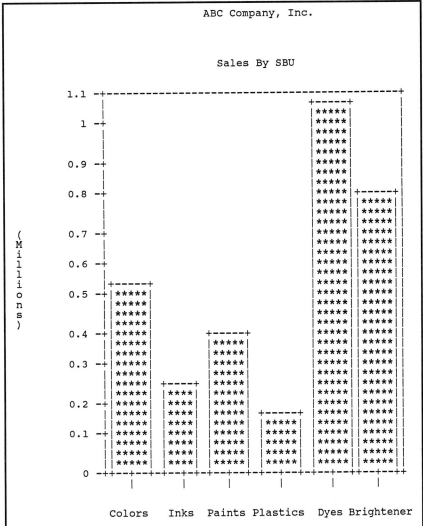

A Sample Professional Graph.

The graphics images created by Professional on most equipment are rather poor compared to those created by many standard graphics packages. You can improve these images dramatically by using one of the few graphics terminals or printers Professional supports, but be sure the device has been properly installed and configured. Alternatively, you can import SCO Professional data directly into SCO ImageBuilder, a graphics presentation product available from SCO that is covered later in this chapter.

/Data   You can use the /Data command both to manage data in an SCO Professional database and to manipulate and analyze data in the worksheet. Although SCO Professional is not a database package per se, you can create and maintain a small database in the worksheet. Once the database is created, you can use the /Data command both to sort and to query the records it contains.

In addition to managing a database with the /Data command, you can use it to manipulate and analyze data. For example, you can quickly fill a range with numbers, dates, or times, or you can use it to parse words and numbers in long labels into individual cells. You can also use /Data to create data tables that evaluate the effect of changing one or two variables in a formula. Furthermore, /Data allows you to perform matrix arithmetic or regression analysis and to calculate frequency distributions.

The /Data command offers the following menu options:

Fill	Fills a range with consecutive numbers
Table	Creates data tables that show the effect of changing one or two variables in one or two equations
Sort	Sorts a range of data in alphanumeric order
Query	Lets you query the records in a Professional database
Distribution	Performs a frequency distribution
Matrix	Performs matrix arithmetic in the worksheet
Regression	Performs regression analysis
Parse	Parses long labels into individual cells

Macros

SCO Professional also offers a comprehensive macro facility. Macros allow you to automate the use of SCO Professional. You can use macros to mimic keystrokes that you might enter from the keyboard, which helps you perform repetitive operations quickly. In addition, SCO Professional offers an extensive macro programming language that includes commands you would usually find in a higher-level language. Using this language, you can create sophisticated applications that perform specialized data management tasks. For example, you might create a menu-driven application that displays a custom fill-in-the-blank form for data entry. Once you've filled in the form, your macro can add that information to an SCO Professional database.

@Functions

SCO Professional includes a number of @functions that perform specialized calculations. These functions are grouped into eight categories: date, database, financial, mathematical, statistical, string, logical, and special. For example, you can use the financial @functions to calculate net present value (@NPV) or mortgage payments (@PMT).

Using Multiple Worksheets

With SCO Professional you can display two worksheet files on your screen at the same time. This can be tremendously helpful when you want to combine two files or create a link between two files, or when you simply need to compare the contents of one file with another.

You can also link one Professional worksheet file to another. Links allow you to refer to a range of data in another file from the current file. The worksheet file that contains the link is the *dependent* file. The worksheet file to which the link refers is the *principal* file. When you create the link, the data referenced in the principal file is copied to the dependent file. If you later change the linked range in the principal file, the dependent file is automatically updated to reflect the change.

SQL Queries

You can query an SCO Integra database table from within an SCO Professional worksheet. To do this, you must enter a SQL statement in an SCO
Professional worksheet cell. The statement must use the SQL Select command to reference a specific SQL table and select records from that table.
The appropriate records are then copied into the worksheet. The original
SQL table is not affected. Once the records have been copied to the
worksheet, you can manipulate the data in those records, just as you can any
other worksheet data.

Compatibility with 1-2-3

As mentioned, SCO Professional is modeled after the popular Lotus 1-2-3
spreadsheet program that runs under the DOS operating system. In fact, the
similarities between the two are striking. Both use the same menus, @func-
tions, and macro commands, and save files in the same format. Thus, you
can load a Lotus 1-2-3 worksheet file directly into SCO Professional and
vice versa. However, if you are using Professional Version 2, keep in mind
that the Professional spreadsheet contains 1024 columns versus 1-2-3's 256;
therefore, when you load a Professional worksheet file into Lotus 1-2-3,
those extra 768 columns will be truncated.

 NOTE   Since the similarities between SCO Professional and Lotus 1-2-3
are so great, you may find books on 1-2-3 useful as you learn SCO
Professional.

SCO Lyrix

SCO Lyrix is a word processing package that includes a number of useful
features. It offers many standard features that you would expect from a word

processor, such as automatic word wrap, automatic formatting, copy, move, delete, and so on; however, Lyrix also offers some features you might not expect. For example, you can insert multiple rulers in a document to change the margins and tab stops in different areas. You can also enhance your text with boldface, underlining, italics, and so forth. Lyrix also offers search and replace, a spelling checker and thesaurus, mail merge, section numbering, headers and footers, page numbering, footnotes, indexing, forms, four-function math for columns of numbers, and even rudimentary line drawing, so you can draw boxes around your text.

You can start Lyrix in two ways: If you are using SCO Manager, select Application from the main menu, and then select Lyrix, or, simply type **lyrix** at the system prompt and then press RETURN.

 NOTE   Although Lyrix has been SCO's flagship word processor for some time, most new customers are turning to SCO's version of Microsoft Word for their word processing needs. Although some of the features Lyrix offers are quite powerful, its screens are less appealing and more difficult to use than Word's screens are.

The Lyrix Manager Menu

The first thing you see when you start Lyrix is the Lyrix Manager menu shown in Figure 15-12. This menu gives you access to the various modules that make up the Lyrix package. The options on the Manager menu perform the following functions:

Edit	Starts the Lyrix editor
View	Shows you roughly what a document will look like when you print it
Print	Takes you to the Printing and Mail Merge menus
File	Takes you to the File management menu, which includes options to copy, rename, and delete files; and perform other file-related tasks

Mail	Lets you send and read electronic mail
Options	Lets you modify many of the default settings for Lyrix and customize the program to meet your specific needs
Transfer	Copies documents to the clipboard and pastes data from the clipboard into your document
Xtra	Lets you add, delete, and list words in your personal spelling library
System	Takes you to the UNIX or XENIX system prompt

The Lyrix Editor

To access the Lyrix editor, select Edit from the Lyrix Manager menu. When you select this option, Lyrix prompts you for a file name and displays a list

Figure 15-12.

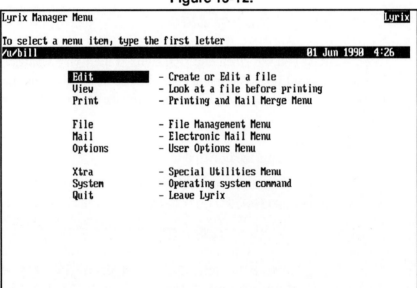

The Lyrix Manager Menu.

of files and subdirectories in the current directory. To create a new file, type a name for the file and press RETURN. To edit an existing file, either type the file name or select it from the list. Whichever method you use, the Lyrix editor will appear. Figure 15-13 shows an example of what the editor looks like.

Once the editor is on your screen, you can start typing your document. You do not need to press RETURN when you reach the end of a line. Lyrix automatically wraps the text to the next line for you.

Immediately above the document display area is the ruler. On most computers, this is a reverse video bar. The ruler defines the left and right margins for the document, as well as the tab stops. You can have more than one ruler in a document, which allows you to change the margins and tab stops for selected areas of the document. A ruler remains in effect until Lyrix encounters the next ruler or reaches the end of the document.

At the top of the Lyrix screen is a series of menu options that allow you to perform a number of specialized tasks. To access this menu, press ESC.

Figure 15-13.

```
corres1                        [I/F/D] #1        1:1          Edit
 Block  Copy  Delete  Effects  File  Goto  Help  Layout  Menu  Quit
 Options  Paste  Reference  Search  Transfer  Undo  Window  Xtra
Press <ESC> to use Lyrix Command Menu
L........T........T........T........T........T........T........T........T....R
June 1, 1990♦
♦
♦
John Roberts♦
Generic Systems♦
200 Technology Way♦
Houston, TX 90123♦
♦
♦
Dear John:♦
♦
We took your recommendation and bought the Office Portfolio Suite from SCO.
In fact, I'm writing you this letter with a word-processing package called
Lyrix.  I haven't had time to explore all of its features yet, but "it looks
like the beginning of beautiful relationship."♦
♦
By the way, I'm also learning how to use electronic mail.  Maybe we can save
ourselves some correspondence time by using Mail instead of writing all those
darn letters and playing phone tag all the time.  It looks to me like Mail is
```

The Lyrix Editor.

The options on the menu perform the following functions:

Block   Lets you copy or move a block of text to the paste buffer, an area of memory that is used to store text temporarily. You can then paste the text from the buffer into another part of the document using the Paste command. The Block option can also be used to delete a block of text.

Copy   Copies a block of text to the paste buffer.

Delete   Deletes a block of text.

Effects   Lets you format a block of text as boldface, underlined, italic, double-strike, overstrike, subscripted, or super-scripted. Although these effects do not show on your screen, they will appear when the document is printed, providing your printer supports these features.

File   Lets you save the current file, import text from a file into the current document, export text from the current document to an external file, or print the current document.

Goto   Lets you jump to different places in a document. You can go to the top or bottom of the document, to the left or right margin, or one full screen up or down.

Help   Accesses the Lyrix on-line help system.

Layout   Inserts formatting codes into a document. These codes allow you to specify page breaks, new rulers, page length, line spacing, widow and orphan control, fixed or propor-tional fonts, and footnotes and endnotes. They also let you keep sections of text on the same page, stop auto-format-ting for a block of text, change the language for spell checking, join two lines, or split two lines.

Menu   Accesses the Lyrix editor portion of the Lyrix Manager menu.

Options   Toggles the following on or off: insert versus overstrike mode, auto-formatting, display of formatting characters, and display of the Lyrix Edit menu.

Paste	Pastes the contents of the paste buffer into the current document.
Reference	Allows you to create or edit headers, footers, and footnotes; to edit, delete, reset, or format an automatically numbered list; and to enter text for indexed entries.
Search	Searches and optionally replaces text entries.
Transfer	Transfers information to and from the clipboard.
Undo	Undoes the last command.
Window	Opens another window to edit or view a different file, closes a window, or switches back and forth between two open windows.
Xtra	Allows you to spell check a document, use the thesaurus, reformat a block of text, turn on hyphenation for a block of text, draw lines or boxes in a document, define or run a custom entry form, activate the four-function math calculator, or change a block of text from lower- to uppercase.

You can use the Lyrix editor to edit flat (ASCII) text files such as shell scripts, electronic mail messages, and application configuration files. When you load a flat text file into Lyrix, the program detects the absence of a header and other formatting codes (hard returns and so on). Lyrix then allows you to choose from a two option menu that includes Document or Text. If you choose Document, Lyrix places a header at the start of the file and hard returns at the end of each paragraph and blank line. The text is also formatted, as defined by the current left and right margins. If you choose Text, Lyrix loads the file, but does not format it. Hard-return symbols are displayed at the end of each line of text, but these are only temporary; they are omitted when you save the edited file to disk.

 NOTE For Lyrix to print text enhancements such as boldface, underlining, italics and so on, your XENIX or UNIX system must be properly configured to access these features on your printer. To configure the printer, you must select or create the appropriate **pcap** file. A **pcap** file contains certain control code information that Lyrix needs to get the most from your printer. When you install Lyrix, a series of **pcap** files are copied to the

/usr/lib/wp6/pcap directory. These files contain the control codes that are required to take full advantage of certain printers from several major manufacturers, including HP (Hewlett-Packard), Epson, and Diablo. You must specify the appropriate **pcap** file by logging on to the system as the root and using the **sysadmsh** program to add to or edit the installed printers on the system. Unfortunately, you'll find the number of available **pcap** files is rather limited; if your printer does not correspond to a particular **pcap** file, it may emulate a supported printer.

The Lyrix Mail Merge Feature

Lyrix includes a Mail Merge feature. To access this feature, select the Print option from the Lyrix Manager menu. The Mail Merge feature allows you to create custom form letters, but it also has other uses. Using the Mail Merge feature involves the following steps:

1. Create a mail-merge text file. This file contains a custom form that you design. In this form, you define *variables,* which determine what type of information will be merged in the document and where it will be merged. These variables reference the contents of another file known as the mail-merge data file.

2. Create a mail-merge data file. This file contains the data that will eventually be merged into the mail-merge text file. The data in this file is organized as a database composed of records and fields. Each record contains all the information for a particular item in the database, such as an employee's name and address. Every record contains the same fields of information, for example, first name, last name, address, city, state, and zip. These fields are matched with the variables that you defined in the mail-merge text file.

3. Invoke the Mail Merge Viewscreen and fill in the appropriate entries. This screen allows you to define the name of the mail-merge text file and mail-merge data files you want to use. (You can also choose whether you want the merged output sent to the printer or to a file.) When you're ready, you can begin the mail-merge process.

Once the process is started, Lyrix matches the variables that you defined in the mail-merge text file with the fields of data in the mail-merge data file. Using the text file as a guide, Lyrix prints one document for each record in the data file. The mail-merge process is completed when no more records remain in the data file.

SCO Integra

SCO Integra is a SQL-based relational database management system. A database provides a structured environment for the storage of information. A database management system provides a means to create a database, add new information to it, edit the information, and delete outdated information. It also provides the means to query the database, that is, to search for certain types of information in the database and make that information available for viewing and reports.

Integra lets you create and manage a database in two ways. First, Integra provides an extensive menu system as well as default forms and reports that help you to create, manage, and query a database. Second, Integra gives you access to the SQL language (Structured Query Language). SQL is composed of a series of commands. You can enter these commands individually or place them in a command file and batch process them. The SQL language provides all the functionality of the Integra menu system, and much more.

There are two says to start Integra: If you have SCO Manager, select Application from the main menu and then select Integra; otherwise, type **integra** at the operating system prompt and press RETURN. Whichever method you use, you'll see the screen shown in Figure 15-14.

What Is an Integra Database?

An Integra database is composed of one or more tables of related information. For example, imagine you want to create a database that stores information about your company's inventory. This database might be

Figure 15-14.

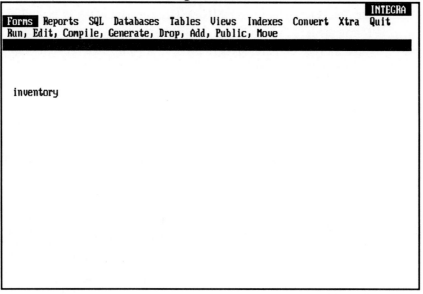

The Integra Main Menu Screen.

comprised of two tables: one for part numbers and descriptions; and a second for information about quantity on hand and on order, reorder point, reserved amount, and due-date information for each part number. The database itself and the tables within it would be defined by names. For example, the name of the database might be INVENTORY, the first table might be named PART, and the second QUANTITY.

Database tables store information in rows and columns. Each row contains a record. A record contains all the information about a particular item in the database. Each column in the database table is called a field. Fields contain the individual pieces of information that make up each record. At the top of each column (field) is a field name. Field names are used to reference a specific column when you query the table. For example, here is a small database table named QUANTITY.

PART_NO	ON_HAND	RESERVED	RE_ORDER	ON_ORDER	DUE_IN
00123	2500	2000	500	3000	05/03/90
00124	550	250	250	1000	05/09/90
00125	10000	8000	2000	10000	05/27/90

The first record in this table is for part number 00123. There are 2500 units on hand, and 2000 of these are reserved. The reorder point is 500; 3000 units are on order and due to arrive on 05/03/90. Each record has six fields which are defined by the following field names: PART_NO, ON_HAND, RESERVED, RE_ORDER, ON_ORDER, and DUE_IN. Each field contains only one type of data. For example, the first field, PART_NO, contains all text strings (00123 looks like a number, but it is actually a text entry). The second field, ON_HAND, contains all numbers, as do the third, fourth, and fifth fields; and the last field, DUE_IN, contains all dates. Thus, each field in each record contains the same type of data, and the result is a uniform block of information.

NOTE   Integra is case-sensitive in terms of database names, table names, field names, and information contained within fields. In the example above, all names are in uppercase letters. This makes them easier to read when you are querying the database.

SCO Integra supports the following data types for database fields: character, currency, smallint, integer, numeric, float, date, time, and serial. When you create a database, you must define the data type for each of its fields. Creating a database with the Integra menu system is discussed later.

You can use Integra to create and manage multiple databases on your system. However, you can only use one of those databases at a time.

Relating Database Tables

When you create tables within a database, you will often relate the tables to each other by using a common field. For example, building on the INVEN-

TORY database discussed earlier, you might create the following tables named PART and QUANTITY, respectively:

The PART table

PART_NO	DESCRIPT
00123	Part 123
00124	Part 124
00125	Part 125

The QUANTITY table

PART_NO	ON_HAND	RESERVED	RE_ORDER	ON_ORDER	DUE_IN
00123	2500	2000	500	3000	05/03/90
00124	550	250	250	1000	05/09/90
00125	10000	8000	2000	10000	05/27/90

These tables have a field in common named PART_NO. It contains a unique part number for each inventory item. Notice that the PART_NO field in each table contains the same information. By using the contents of these two fields, Integra can match two records from different database tables. For example, it can match the first field in the PART table to the first field in the QUANTITY table by using the 00123 part number. In this way, you can relate the contents of one table to the contents of another. In database parlance, a common field in a table is referred to as a *key* field.

 NOTE   In the previous example, both tables have the same name for the key field, but this is not necessary. You can relate two tables whose key fields have different names, providing they contain the same information.

How Does Integra Work?

To get started with Integra, you must first create a database. Once the database is established, you must create the table or tables that make up that database. Once the tables have been created, you can add, edit, and delete information. You can also query the tables to obtain specific information.

Forms   To add information to a database or to edit information, you must use a *form*. Forms simply display a single record in a database. If the record is blank (contains no data), you can use the form to fill in the information for each field in the record. On the other hand, if the record already contains information, you can use a form to edit the information. Figure 15-15 shows a sample form for the QUANTITY table, shown earlier. Notice that the field names for the table are displayed along with blank areas enclosed by square brackets ([ ]), in which you can enter or view information.

The form shown in Figure 15-15 is a default form provided by Integra, but you can also create your own custom forms for displaying records. When you get behind the scenes in Integra, you'll find that forms are contained in files with an .FMS extension. You can create you own .FMS files to display forms that are far more attractive that the one shown in Figure 15-15.

Figure 15-15.

```
┌──────────────────────────────────────────────────────────────────────┐
│ Query  Add  Del  Update  Next Back  Jump  Screen  Table  Parent  Child  More │
│ Query the database using this form                                     │
│                                                            quantity     │
│                                           Screen : 1                    │
│          _____      │
│                                                                        │
│ part_no [         ]                                                    │
│ on_hand [          ]                                                   │
│ reserve [          ]                                                   │
│ re_orde [          ]                                                   │
│ on_orde [          ]                                                   │
│ due_in  [          ]                                                   │
│                                                                        │
│                                                                        │
│                                                                        │
│                                                                        │
│                                                                        │
│                                                                        │
│                                                                        │
│                                                                        │
└──────────────────────────────────────────────────────────────────────┘
```

A Default Integra Form.

Views   A SQL database can be very complex, with many related tables and lots of rows in each table. Consider a SQL database that has nine tables of information, all related in some way. Say you want to look at a name from TABLE 2, a date from TABLE 5, and an amount from TABLE 7. Rather than sorting through all the tables to find these bits of information, you can define an alternate way of looking at information called a *view*. The view determines what column to include from each table, and the order in which the columns appear. Views differ from tables in that they don't actually contain any data; a view simply borrows what it needs from the appropriate database tables.

Views are simply another way of arranging the information contained in tables that lets you look at information from more than one table at a time. For example, let's return to the INVENTORY database with its two tables, PART and QUANTITY, which are shown again here:

The PART table

PART_NO	DESCRIPT
00123	Part 123
00124	Part 124
00125	Part 125

The QUANTITY table

PART_NO	ON_HAND	RESERVED	RE_ORDER	ON_ORDER	DUE_IN
00123	2500	2000	500	3000	05/03/90
00124	550	250	250	1000	05/09/90
00125	10000	8000	2000	10000	05/27/90

You can create a view that incorporates information from both of these tables. For example, Figure 15-16 shows a form that displays a view of the first record from both the PART and QUANTITY database tables. Notice that this view includes fields from both tables.

You can also use a view to display information that is not directly available from a table. For example, you might create a field in a view that contains the result of an arithmetic calculation. This field might show the result of multiplying the contents of a field in one table by the contents of a field in another table. Thus, views also allow you to manipulate information for display purposes.

Views are saved as files, so once you've created a view, you can easily activate it at a later time to organize the way information is displayed.

 NOTE Views can only by used to display the information in database tables; you cannot edit information in a view.

Reports Reports are simply a way of presenting information in a database. You can send a report to your screen, to your system printer, or to a file. As you might imagine, reports are used solely to present information, not to modify it.

Reports can be used to display information in a database in different ways. For example, the data in a report can come from a single table, from a view, or from specific fields in different tables. You can also create a report that shows the results of an arithmetic calculation, such as multiplying the contents of a field in one table by the contents of a field in another table.

Figure 15-16.

```
┌──────────────────────────────────────────────────────────────────┐
│ Query Add  Del  Update  Next Back  Jump  Screen  Table  Parent  Child  More │
│ Query the database using this form                                 │
│ ──────────────────────────────────────────────────────────────────│
│                                                        iven_view   │
│                                              Screen : 1            │
│        ─────────────────────────────────────────────────────────  │
│                                                                    │
│ part_no  [00123    ]                                               │
│ descript [Part 123    ]                                            │
│ on_hand  [    2500]                                                │
│ reserved [    2000]                                                │
│ re_order [     500]                                                │
│ on_order [    3000]                                                │
│ due_in   [05/03/90]                                                │
│                                                                    │
│                                                                    │
│                                                                    │
│                                                                    │
│                                                                    │
│                                                                    │
│                                                                    │
│                                                                    │
│ Number of records selected = 3                                     │
└──────────────────────────────────────────────────────────────────┘
```

A Form Displaying a View.

Integra provides a default report format, but you can also create your own custom reports. Like forms, reports are saved as files, so you can reuse them at a later time. Report files have an .RPS extension.

Indexes   To help you quickly locate information in a database, Integra creates an *index* for each table. Integra uses an index for a database table much as you use the index for a book to look up a particular topic. Rather than searching page by page through the entire book, you can go to the index where information is arranged in alphabetical order, and quickly find the page number for a particular topic.

Indexes sort the information for specific database fields in ascending or descending order. Because the information in the index is already sorted, Integra can quickly find a particular item in a field and then jump to the record that contains that item.

The Integra Menu System

When you start Integra, the Integra main menu is displayed at the top of your screen, as shown earlier in Figure 15-14. The main menu options are briefly covered in the sections that follow. They are not presented in exactly the order in which they appear on the Integra screen. Instead, they are presented in the order in which you are most likely to use them.

 NOTE   The SQL option, which lets you use the SQL language to create and manage Integra databases, is not covered in this section. It is discussed under a separate heading later in this chapter.

Databases   The Databases menu option allows you to create a database and select a database for use. It offers the following suboptions:

Select   Activates a database that has already been created.

Finish   Closes a database so that you can select (open) another.

Create   Creates a database. When you select this option, Integra prompts you for a name for the database, and then creates it.

Drop   Deletes a database and the tables it contains.

Print   Prints the contents of the currently selected database. A submenu lets you define specific tables or views to use when printing.

Tables   The Tables option lets you create, alter, or delete the tables for a particular database. Before you use this option, use the Databases option to select an existing database. When you create or alter a table, Integra displays a form similar to the one shown in Figure 15-17 that assists you in defining the table. The Tables option gives you access to the following submenu options:

List   Lists the tables in the currently selected database.

Create   Presents a form that allows you to name a table and define its fields. You are prompted to enter a field name; a field data type (character, currency, smallint, integer, numeric, float, date, time, or serial); a width for the field; and a brief description. If the field is a numeric field, you are prompted for the number of digits before the decimal and the number of places after the decimal.

Alter   Lets you alter an existing table definition. If you delete a field from a table, Integra warns you that data may be lost before it actually removes the field.

Drop   Deletes a table.

Generate   Creates a SQL *make table* statement that re-creates the table you subsequently specify. The statement is saved to a file under a name of your choosing. You can then use this file to re-create the table on any computer that is running SQL.

Verify   Checks the table you specify against its indexes to verify that they correspond. If the data files have been corrupted, this option helps you identify the problem so you can correct it.

SQL   Lets you use the SQL language.

Forms   The Forms menu is very powerful. It not only lets you create custom forms, it also lets you use forms to add information to a database, edit information, and query a database.

Running Forms   The first option on the Forms menu is Run. This option lets you run a form that currently exists. When you create or modify a table or view, Integra automatically creates a default form file for that table or view and compiles it. You can use the Run command to activate any of these default forms, or to activate custom form files that you create. When you run a form file, the form created by that file is displayed on screen for your use.

When you select a custom form to run, you are automatically taken to a submenu. This menu includes options that let you add records to the database, edit records, and delete records. All of these operations are conducted using the form that you selected. You can also query the database to select records that meet specific conditions. You can then move among

Figure 15-17.

```
┌──────────────────────────────────────────────────────────────┐
│                                                    ▐ALTER TABLE│
│ ▐Insert▌ Delete  PrevPage  NextPage                            │
│ Insert a field                                                 │
│ ▬▬▬▬▬▬▬▬▬▬▬▬▬▬▬▬▬▬▬▬▬▬▬▬▬▬▬▬▬▬▬▬▬▬▬▬▬▬▬▬▬▬▬ Database: inventory │
│                                                                │
│                                                                │
│ Table      :quantity                                           │
│ Comments   :quantity information                               │
│                                                                │
│ Field                    Type       Length   Decimals  Description │
│ ─────                    ────       ───────   ────────  ─────────── │
│ ▐part_no          ▌      Character     8         0         *    │
│ on_hand                  Numeric       8         0         *    │
│ reserved                 Numeric       8         0         *    │
│ re_order                 Numeric       8         0         *    │
│ on_order                 Numeric       8         0         *    │
│ due_in                   Date1         8         0         *    │
│                                                                │
│                                                                │
│                                                                │
│                                                                │
│                                                                │
│ Enter a name up to 30 characters starting with a letter        │
└──────────────────────────────────────────────────────────────┘
```

The Table Definition Screen.

the selected records, viewing and editing information. Additional options on this menu let you perform sophisticated data management tasks such as Begin Transaction, Commit, and Rollback, but these are beyond the scope of this brief product overview.

 NOTE   You can also access forms directly from the operating system prompt by using the **formrun** command. For example, to access a form named quantity in the current directory, you would type **formrun quantity** and press RETURN.

Editing Forms   As mentioned, when you create a table or view, Integra automatically creates a default form file for that table or view and compiles it. Actually, two files are created: a text file with an .FMS extension and a compiled file with an .FMC extension. The source (.FMS) file is a text file that contains the raw coding required to display the form. The compiled (.FMC) file is the machine-readable version.

Integra also allows you to create your own custom form files and compile them. To do this, you can use an existing default form file, or you can create a new one from scratch. To use an existing default form file, select the Generate option from the Forms menu. This option lets you create a new source (.FMS) file under a different name. You can then load that file into a text editor, or you can select the Edit option from the Forms menu to edit the file. The Edit option takes you to the **vi** editor, covered in Chapter 7, and displays the form file for editing. After you have finished editing the file and saved it, you can use the Compile command to compile the source file into an executable (.FMC) file. You can then run the form in the usual way.

 NOTE   The conventions for coding form files go beyond the scope of this brief overview.

The Other Forms Options   The remaining options on the Forms menu perform the following functions:

Drop   Deletes a form

Add   Registers the current form in a dictionary of forms maintained by Integra

Public   Makes a compiled form available for use by others

Move   Moves a compiled form to a different directory

Views   The Views menu option allows you to create views that can be used to organize forms and reports. You can also list the contents of a particular view or delete a view.

Creating a view is somewhat like creating a table definition; however, the fields you define for a view must already exist in a table. You can include fields from more than one table in a view. In this way, you can use a view to display information from more than one table at the same time. Finally, when you create a view, you can specify either a field name from an existing table or an arithmetic expression that involves more than one field. You can use addition, subtraction, multiplication, and division in an expression, as follows:

tablename.fieldname+tablename.fieldname.

Thus, you can create the equivalent of calculated fields in views.

When you create a view, Integra prompts you for a name, and saves the view under that name, so you can easily activate a view at a later time.

When you select the Views option from Integra's main menu, the following options are displayed:

List   Lists the tables and fields included in a view.

Create   Allows you to create a view. When you select this option, Integra displays the screen shown in Figure 15-18. You use this screen to name the view and define its fields. For each field in the view, you must supply a table name, a field name or expression, and a name for the view field. If you use fields from more than one table, Integra prompts you to relate the two tables on a common key field. This is done by means of a formula, for example: *QUANTITY.PART_NO= PART.PART_NO.*

Drop   Permanently deletes a view.

Figure 15-18.

```
                                                         ┌──────────────┐
                                                         │  CREATE VIEW │
 ▐Insert▌ Delete   Alias Table-List  Field-List          └──────────────┘
 Insert a field
                                                      Database: inventory

 View Name: ▐▬▬▬▬▬▬▬▬▬▬▬▬▬▬▌
 Comments :

 Table Name    Table Field/expression   View Field
 ----------    ----------------------   ----------










 Enter View Name up to 18 characters starting with a letter
```

Creating a View.

 NOTE Keep in mind when defining table and field names in a view that Integra is case-sensitive. If you spell a table or field name correctly, but the capitalization is wrong, Integra will display an error message informing you that the table or field does not exist.

Reports The Reports menu option lets you run existing reports and create custom reports. The use of the Reports menu is very similar to that of the Forms menu. In fact, the two menus include the same options.

When you create a table or view, Integra does not automatically create a default report for that table or view. However, you can use a default form to create a report. You can also create a custom report that includes fields from more than one table.

To create reports, you must first create a report source file. This file contains commands that tell Integra which fields from which tables are to be included in the report, and how the data is to be formatted. Report source files have an .RPS extension. The commands used in report source files are beyond the scope of this brief overview.

Once the source file is prepared, you can compile it into machine-readable form. Compiled report files have an .RPC extension. Once the compiled report file has been prepared, you can run it either by using Integra's Reports Run command or by issuing the **rptrun** command at the operating system prompt.

 NOTE You can generate a default report from either an existing form, an existing custom report, or from a view. If the default report meets your needs, you do not have to prepare a report source file and compile it.

When you select the Report command from Integra's main menu, the following submenu options are displayed:

Run   Runs an existing compiled report file.

Edit   Takes you to the **vi** editor so you can edit a report source file. (Chapter 7 discusses the **vi** editor in detail.)

Compile   Compiles a report source file (.RPS) into a machine-readable file (.RPC).

Generate Generates a report source file using an existing form or view as a model. You can then edit the source file if necessary, and use the Compile option to compile the source file into a machine-readable file.

Add   Adds a compiled report to the reports dictionary.

Public   Makes a report available for use by others.

Move   Moves a report to another directory.

Indexes   As mentioned, you can create indexes for fields in database tables. Indexes sort the contents of a field in ascending or descending order. When field contents are presorted in this way, Integra can find selected information in a field much faster, and respond to your queries more efficiently.

To list, create, maintain, and delete indexes, you use the Indexes option from Integra's main menu. When you select this option, Integra prompts you for the name of a particular table. The following submenu options are then displayed:

List   Lists the indexes that currently exist for a table

Create   Creates an index for a specific field

Reindex   Rebuilds an index that has been corrupted

Drop   Deletes an index

Xtra   The Xtra menu includes a number of features you may find useful. For example, it allows you to translate the table definition for an Integra database into other popular programming languages. You can also back up a journal file for a SQL database. In addition, you can assign a name to a SQL statement. You can then use that name to execute the statement, rather than typing the whole statement again. When you save a SQL statement under a name, it is referred to as a macro. You can also use the Xtra menu to assign synonyms (alternate names) to database tables. When you select the Xtra menu, the following submenu options are displayed:

Fielddefs   Creates an ASCII text file that contains the field definition for an Integra table translated into the source code language that you specify. You can choose from BASIC, C, COBOL, Fortran, or Pascal.

Journal   When you create a database, Integra asks whether you also want to create a journal file for that database. A journal file contains a list of transactions to a database, and is useful in rollback operations. You can back up a journal file either to disk or to an alternate storage device, such as a tape.

Macros   Saves a SQL statement under a name. When you select this option, Integra displays a submenu. To create the macro, select Edit from this menu. Integra prompts you for a macro name and then takes you to the **vi** editor (or to the editor defined by your **SQLEDITOR** environment variable), where you can type the SQL statement and save it.

Then you can run the macro using the SQL run macro command.

Synonyms   Assigns an alternate name to a database table.

Convert   The Convert menu option allows you to convert data files from other software products to Integra format. You can also use this option to save an Integra database table to a file format that is usable by another software product. The following file formats are available:

- .DBF format for dBASE II and FoxBASE

- .WKS format for Lotus 1-2-3 Release 1A and SCO Professional Version 1

- Delimited ASCII files

- INFORMIX Relational Database Management System

Using SQL

You can access the SQL command language from almost any menu in Integra. SQL (pronounced "sequel") is an advanced relational database language with powerful selection capabilities. It is primarily used to define sets of information or tables and study relationships found in and among them by means of queries. The SQL language includes a rich assortment of commands that allow you to perform virtually all the functions offered by Integra's menus plus many more. The version of SQL Integra offers is based on the Structured Query Language developed by IBM and standardized by the ANSI committee.

SQL is a language in that it has commands that cause some action to occur, follows strict entry rules, and is statement-based. It can work in an interactive mode, in which you type commands and Integra responds to them, or you can include SQL commands in a file and batch process them.

SQL is a nonprocedural language in that it does not include constructs such as FOR statements or looping commands to control program flow. These constructs, as well as commands to build a clean user interface must be borrowed from another source, such as SCO ACCELL, which is discussed in the next section.

To enter a SQL statement, select the SQL menu option from Integra's main menu or from one of its submenus. A window appears that allows you to enter a SQL statement. The statement is executed as soon as you press CTRL-x. For example, one of the more common and powerful SQL commands is Select. You might use the Select command in the following statement:

```
select all from quantity
```

This statement calls for a listing of all the records from the quantity table. When you press CTRL-x to execute the statement, the records from the quantity table will be displayed on your screen.

If you have a question about a particular command's entry rules, or *syntax*, you can request help. For general help, enter **help**; for specific help with a command, enter **help** followed by a space and the name of the command. Because most SQL commands act the same at the SQL prompt as they do in a program, you can test a command to see how it works at the command line before using it in a program.

As an alternative to selecting SQL from an Integra menu, you can type **sql** at the operating system prompt and press RETURN. You will then be in SQL. Once you are in SQL you can enter a statement and press RETURN to execute it. Each statement must end with a semicolon (;). To leave SQL, type a semicolon and press RETURN.

If you make an error while typing a command, SQL tells you about the error by displaying an error message that applies to your situation. The help facility is also context-sensitive; it displays the help screen that provides information most relevant to your particular error.

Although there are relatively few commands in the SQL language by comparison with commands available in other programming languages, these commands are quite powerful. What's more, statements for SQL commands can become quite complex. A discussion of the commands available, what those commands do, and how you use them is beyond the scope of this brief overview.

Customizing Integra with ACCELL

Although Integra provides a complete menu system for creating and managing databases, it is still basically a raw database engine. Commands for controlling program flow are not provided. These constructs, as well as other commands required to build a clean user interface must come from another source. To meet this need, SCO offers a product called ACCELL, which lets you customize the Integra environment.

ACCELL is an integrated development system designed specifically to complement SCO Integra. It includes a fourth-generation programming language, as well as a powerful screen-painting tool.

ACCELL's programming language is an event-driven language composed of a series of English-like commands. Within this language you can incorporate nonprocedural SQL calls to an Integra database. You can also incorporate calls to C programs, which brings an added degree of flexibility to your development efforts. ACCELL also allows you to develop applications that exchange information with other products in the SCO Office Portfolio.

In addition, ACCELL includes a Generator facility. The Generator allows you to "paint" application forms as they will actually appear to the end user. You can then define screen characteristics and field attributes by means of pop-up specification windows. This entire process is accomplished through menus. When you are finished creating a form, the code describing that form is saved to a file. You can use this code directly in your application, or you can further customize it using ACCELL's fourth-generation programming language.

SCO Statistician

SCO Statistician is a statistical analysis package that offers a variety of statistical functions. It also includes data management, and can present its analyses in the form of various tables, reports, and graphs. The statistical analysis functions offered by SCO Statistician include the following:

- Descriptive analysis

- Analysis of variance

- Correlation analysis

- Regression analysis

- Time series analysis

- Nonparametric analysis

- Distribution functions

SCO Statistician attempts to simplify the process of statistical analysis through pull-down menus and a "see and select" interface. Instead of programming commands, SCO Statistician lets you select variables, files, directories, parameters, and so on.

SCO Statistician also includes an output manager that can convert numeric output into different graphic presentation formats.

You can exchange data from SCO Statistician with other applications in the SCO Office Portfolio that support the SCO clipboard format, such as SCO Lyrix and SCO Professional. SCO Statistician can also read data directly from FoxBASE and FoxBASE+. Further, SCO Statistician includes import and export functions that let you import and export data in the form of flat text files.

SCO Masterplan

SCO Masterplan is an interactive project management package that is based on the Critical Path method of resource management. You can use it to plan, schedule, coordinate, and monitor one or more projects. In fact, you can schedule up to 10,000 resources, making SCO Masterplan suitable for coordinating even your most ambitious projects.

SCO Masterplan allows you to track a project in both forecast-versus-actual and percent-complete formats. It also allows you to generate various reports showing start-to-start, finish-to-finish, and percentage relationships.

SCO Masterplan provides several views of a project and supports interactive data input and tracking. It includes network, activity, calendar, and forecast screens. You can modify SCO Manager's Calendar screen for different work schedules and create individual calendars for each resource. The forecast screen shows dual Gantt charts that compare the original schedule for a project to its current schedule. This allows you to identify visually which activities are behind schedule and which are on schedule.

There is also an optional CGI graphics package for SCO Masterplan that uses the **termcap** and **terminfo** databases. Thus, you can configure SCO Masterplan to run on a variety of terminals. You can also create graphics output by using plotters and laser printers that are supported by CGI graphics.

As you might have imagined, you can also exchange data with other applications in the SCO Office Portfolio that support the SCO clipboard format, such as SCO Lyrix and SCO Professional.

SCO ImageBuilder

SCO ImageBuilder is a graphics presentation package. You can use it to create and edit graphics pictures and charts.

Graphics pictures can be as simple as text charts that are enhanced with various fonts (type styles and sizes). You can also add objects such as lines, circles, or boxes of various sizes. You can even create a free-form drawing and include symbols (clip-art) from ImageBuilder's symbol library.

In addition to pictures, you can create data charts (graphs) based on numeric data. You can enter the data yourself, or you can import it from SCO Professional. You can choose from various types of data charts including vertical bar, line, scatter plot (XY), area, mixed, horizontal bar, or pie (including exploded pie).

You can also combine a text chart and a data chart. For example, you can create a picture and then add the current data chart to it.

To start ImageBuilder, simply type **image** at the system prompt. The main ImageBuilder screen will be displayed on your terminal.

 NOTE   You must have a graphics terminal (CGA or EGA) to run SCO ImageBuilder. Without one, the product simply will not run. When you install ImageBuilder, special CGI drivers are installed on your system that will drive either a CGA or an EGA terminal. In addition, if you want to print, you must have a graphics printer or plotter. CGI drivers are also automatically installed for this purpose. Finally, you must configure the operating system to recognize these display and output devices. For example, if you are using an EGA terminal rather than the default CGA, and your login shell is the C shell, you must use the command **setenv DISPLAY ega**. Further, if you are using an HP LaserJet printer, you must use the command **setenv OUTPUT "laserjet | lp</dev/null"**. You can type these commands at the operating system prompt, add them to your **.login** file, or place them in the shell script **/usr/bin/image**.

ImageBuilder's Main Menu

ImageBuilder's main menu includes the following options:

Draw
: Provides access to the Draw module, which lets you create and edit graphics pictures. Graphics pictures are composed of various *objects* that you place on the screen, including text in various fonts, boxes, circles, clip-art, and so on. Using these objects, you can create text charts, diagrams, and even free-form drawings.

Chart
: Gives you access to the Chart (graph) module, which lets you create and edit data charts. This module provides a means for you to enter data, and then create various types of graphs to present that data visually. You can choose from vertical bar, line, scatter plot (XY), area, mixed, horizontal bar, or pie (including exploded pie).

Background Lets you choose either a solid or a gradated background for a picture or data chart.

Palette Lets you create or change color palettes.

Makeslide Lets you transmit text and data chart files to the MAGICorp slide service for processing 35mm slides, transparencies, color prints, or black-and-white copies.

The Draw Module

To activate the Draw module, select the Draw command from ImageBuilder's main menu. When you select this command, ImageBuilder displays a submenu that offers the following options:

Create Lets you create text in various type styles and sizes (fonts) for display in a picture. You can also draw lines, build boxes or circles in various sizes, and create polygons of your own design. For example, you might make arrows that point to key items in a picture. You can also use this option to change the default display of text, lines, and shapes.

Modify Lets you alter objects or words in a picture. You can also delete objects, copy objects from one location to another, rotate objects, move objects, compress or stretch objects, group objects for commands, and change the order in which objects are drawn on the screen.

Erase Clears the screen.

Transfer Transfers text to and from the clipboard.

Print Previews or prints a text chart.

File Lets you save the current picture to a file and load existing picture files into memory. You can also add a saved picture file to the current picture or add a symbol from the symbol library to the current picture. In addition, you can change the current directory and delete picture files.

Zoom   Allows you to select a section of the current picture to
                zoom in on (increase its displayed size). This lets you do
                fine detail work on a specific area.

AddChart   Adds the current data chart to the current picture.

You can use the Draw menu to create graphics such as the text chart
shown in Figure 15-19. The first entry in that graphic, "ABC Toy Company"
is in large boldface type. The underline beneath these words is actually an
elongated box. The bullets that mark the remaining text entries are actually
small boxes with a solid background, but, if you wanted to, you could just
as easily use circles with a patterned background. The remaining text entries
are the same boldface font as the first text entry, but in a smaller size.

As mentioned earlier, you can add images from the symbol (clip-art)
library with the Draw command. To do this, simply select Draw File

Figure 15-19.

ABC Toy Company

- ■ Leading manufacturers
  of safe children's toys

- ■ Preferred by mothers
  worldwide

- ■ Developers of the first
  fireproof toy

A Sample Text Chart.

Library, and then select the file name that describes the symbol you want. The symbol is automatically added to the current picture file. Figure 15-20 shows an example of a symbol with some text added.

The Chart Module

The Chart module lets you build data charts to graphically depict data that you enter. Figure 15-21 shows a sample data chart. To access the Chart module, select Chart from ImageBuilder's main menu. When you select this option the following menu items are displayed:

Data
: Lets you enter X-axis labels and data for ImageBuilder to plot. You can specify up to 5 data sets with as many as 50 items in each set.

ChartType
: Lets you choose the type of data chart you want to create. You can select from vertical bar (the default), line, scatter plot (XY), area, mixed, horizontal bar, or pie (including exploded pie).

Options
: Allows you to specify various options for the display of a data chart. For example, you can change the color of bars or areas in charts for each data set. You can also specify a background pattern for bars and areas. In addition, you can prevent a selected data set from being displayed in the data chart.

Layout
: Lets you specify various options for the layout of the graph. For example, you can specify both a main title and a subtitle for a data chart, and also choose the color and font in which these are displayed. You can specify certain options for the X- and Y-axes, including scaling and grid lines. You can also alter the display of bar and area stacking to produce stacked bar and stacked area charts.

Erase
: Erases the current data chart and all of its data.

Transfer
: Transfers data charts to and from the clipboard.

Print   Prints the current data chart.

File   Lets you save the current data chart to a file on disk and
                     load existing data chart files into memory. You can also
                     use this option to import SCO Professional Version 1
                     (.WKS) worksheet file data into ImageBuilder. Finally,
                     this option allows you to change the current directory, and
                     delete data chart files.

 NOTE   ImageBuilder requires a great deal of printer memory to print even
the most rudimentary data chart. If your graphics printer has a half megabyte
of memory or less, it is highly unlikely that you will be able to print a data
chart.

Figure 15-20.

A Symbol with Text Added.

Figure 15-21.

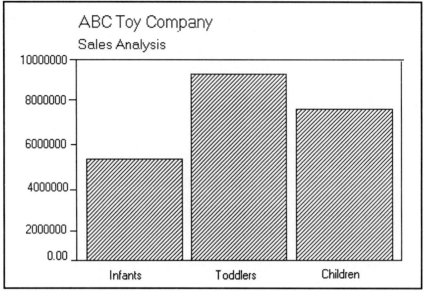

A Sample Data Chart.

Microsoft Word

Microsoft Word is a full-featured word processing package licensed from Microsoft. The newest version, Version 5.0, which is discussed here, includes a wealth of text formatting and page layout features. In addition, Microsoft Word comes to you with a healthy complement of available printer drivers that let you take full advantage of your printer.

To start Microsoft Word, simply type **word** at the system prompt and press RETURN. After a moment, the main Microsoft Word screen shown in Figure 15-22 will appear. You can then start typing the text for your document. As you type, your text is displayed on the screen. If you make a mistake, simply press BACKSPACE to delete the errant text. When you reach the end of a line, you do not need to press RETURN; Microsoft Word automatically wraps your text to the next line.

Figure 15-22.

```
┌────────────────────────────────────────────────────────────────┐
│┌──────────────────────────────────────────────────────────────┐│
││ ********************Paper Recycling Plan********************   ││
││                                                                ││
││ Recycling all of our paper is an easy task that requires an    ││
││ initial effort and a continued effort. The initial effort:     ││
││ put a box  designated for discarded paper next to every        ││
││ garbage can where paper is thrown away. The continued          ││
││ effort: when a box gets full, empty the paper into a yellow     ││
││ recycling bin. It won't take any extra effort to put paper      ││
││ in a Recycling Box instead of a garbage can because the        ││
││ Recycling Box will be right next to the garbage can.           ││
││                                                                ││
││ Why use a Recycling Box as a middle man? Why not deposit        ││
││ paper directly into a yellow recycling bin? Let the            ││
││ photocopier upstairs near the elevator serve as an example.    ││
││ The garbage cans next to that photocopier are often full of    ││
││ paper because there is  no yellow bin nearby. It takes time     ││
││ and effort to walk to the  yellow recycling bin to discard      ││
││ one piece of paper. Multiply that times the number of pieces   ││
│└─────────────────────────────────────────────────────recycling─┘│
│COMMAND: Copy Delete Format Gallery Help Insert Jump Library      │
│         Options Print Quit Replace Search Transfer Undo Window   │
│4607 characters                                                   │
│Pg1 Col          {}                              Microsoft Word   │
└────────────────────────────────────────────────────────────────┘
```

A Microsoft Word Screen.

The Microsoft Word screen is divided into two parts: the *window* that displays the text you type, and the *command area* below. The main function of the window is to display your documents. You can split the window into as many as eight smaller windows, each containing a different document. In addition, when you are working with multiple windows, you can easily zoom any given window to full screen size. The command area contains the main menu for Microsoft Word, and is composed of four lines. The first two lines are used for menu items, the third displays messages, and the fourth conveys status information.

The Word Menu

To access the text formatting, page layout, and file handling features of Microsoft Word, you must use its menu system. To access the menu system, simply press ESC to activate the main menu in the command area.

Many of the commands in Microsoft Word's main menu allow you to manipulate blocks of text. Before you use a block-oriented command, you must select the block of text the command will affect. Although there are a number of ways you can select text, the simplest way is to press the SHIFT key to anchor the cursor and then use the arrow keys. As you press an arrow key, Word begins highlighting text in the direction of the arrow. When you are ready, you can press ESC to access the main menu, and select a command that will affect the highlighted text.

To select a menu option from Microsoft Word's main menu, you can use one of two methods: you can use the arrow keys to highlight a menu choice and then press RETURN, or, you can simply type the first letter of a menu option.

Briefly, the menu options in Microsoft Word's main menu perform the following functions:

Copy   Lets you copy a single word or a block of text from one area of the document to another.

Delete   Lets you delete individual words or blocks of text from your document. When you delete text with this option, the text is not lost; it is saved in a *scrap buffer*. If you want to use the text again, you can use the Insert command to insert it elsewhere in the document. (You can also delete text permanently and insert new text without affecting the contents of the scrap buffer.)

Format   This menu option gives you access to a host of text formatting, page layout, and document management options. For example, you can select text enhancements such as boldface, underlining, or italics, and you can select different fonts (type sizes and styles). You can also reformat paragraphs, set tab stops, draw lines or boxes around selected paragraphs, and create footnotes. In addition, you can set margins, page numbers, and line numbers, create running heads, and attach style sheets for the formatting of documents. This menu option also gives you access to search and replace for formats and applied styles, and lets you check revision marks, annotate a document, and create bookmarks. Many of these options are explained in the following sections.

Gallery   Offers commands for creating and editing style sheets.

Insert   Inserts text from the scrap buffer or a glossary file, and lets you run macros stored in glossary files.

Jump   Lets you quickly jump to specific points in a document. You can choose a specific page or you can jump back and forth between a bookmark, footnote, or annotation and its associated text.

Library   Provides access to a number of features including sorting, hyphenation, indexing, spell checking, and the thesaurus. You can also use this option to import data from a spreadsheet program, import a graphics image, or import information from another document. In addition, you can number headings in outlines or paragraphs in documents, and you can create a table of contents. You can even run a XENIX or UNIX command without quitting Word.

Options   Lets you configure the display and operation of many Word features.

Print   Lets you print your work and set printing options, as well as perform mail-merge operations.

Replace   Lets you replace a word or phrase with a new word or phrase throughout a document.

Search   Searches forward or backward for text.

Transfer   Allows you to manage file operations and use the clipboard. For example, this option is used to save and load files, as well as to delete a file, merge two files, and set the default directory in which Word searches for and saves its files. You can also use this option to copy and paste information to and from the clipboard.

Undo   Undoes the last edit or command.

Window   Lets you open, close, move, and resize windows.

The Word Feature Set

Microsoft Word includes all the standard word processing features you might expect from a top-level word processor, and some you might not expect. The sections that follow provide a brief overview of some of Microsoft Word's major features.

Help   The Word Help menu contains detailed information about almost every Word feature, and you can easily find information about a particular topic. You access the Help menu by selecting Help from the Word main menu, or by pressing ALT-h (or CTRL-a h) while using any of the other menus. If you start Help from the main menu, it displays basic information about Word and tells you how to find the topic of your choice. If you start Help by pressing ALT-h while using a different menu option, Help displays information about the task you are currently doing. For example, if you are in the Format menu, Help displays information about formatting. To get help on a particular topic, select Index from the Help menu, and then select the topic of your choice.

Automatic Numbering   Word automatically keeps track of the numbers of pages, lines, footnotes, annotations, and any other elements you might want to count. These numbers are not usually displayed in the document, but you can request Word to display them and even include them in the file. For example, line numbers do not appear in the document as you type them, but you can instruct word to place them on every line or at regular intervals when the document is printed.

Boldface, Italic, and Other Character Formats   The following character formats become available when you select Format Character from Word's main menu:

- Bold
- Italic
- Single or double underline
- Uppercase

- Small capitals

- Superscript

- Subscript

- Strikethrough

- Hidden text (You can choose whether or not to display this text.)

Cross-References   Word's bookmark feature allows you to name particular blocks of text. You can then use this name either to move to that block in the document, or to refer to that block in your text. Word can keep track of your references to pages, illustrations, chapters, sections, and so on, and correctly fill in the numbers, even when you make changes to the document that affect the objects you are referring to. For example, if you refer to a paragraph on page 5, and that paragraph is later moved to page 6, the cross-reference automatically reflects that change. To create a cross-reference, you mark the text to be referenced with a bookmark, and then use a special code to refer to that bookmark in the text.

Forms   You can use Word to create your own forms. A form letter can contain your address, a salutation, or even text, which you can customize for multiple mailings. You can also use Word to fill out preprinted forms, create your own forms, or create multiple mailing labels on a single page. When you create and fill out a form, the form is stored in one file and the information you entered to fill it out in another. With this arrangement, you don't have to type the form again each time you want to use it. You can use the Print Merge feature to merge data with the form it belongs in.

Paragraph Formats   You can control many aspects of a paragraph's format, including whether it is aligned at the left, aligned at the right, or centered; how far it is indented from both the left and the right margin; and the amount of line spacing within and around the paragraph. You can also elect to print paragraphs side by side on a page. This is helpful for comparing paragraphs that relate to the same subject. Paragraphs can be enclosed in borders or shaded for emphasis. Word's line drawing feature also allows you to set off paragraphs or sections with lines.

Indexes   Word can automatically create an index from items that you mark in the text. The program is capable of sophisticated index formatting techniques that include:

- Multiple column indexes
- Capitalized entries
- Hyphenated page numbers for continuous references
- Indented subentries

Page Layout   Word offers a number of multiple column formats. You can use three kinds of columns in Word.

- In newspaper-style columns, a column ends at the bottom of the page and continues at the top of the next column.
- In side-by-side paragraphs, each column can continue over several pages. Paragraphs are matched one-for-one across the page.
- You can produce tables that have numerous columns for inclusion in a document.

When you change the format of a document, the new format will not be displayed on the screen unless you specify that it should be.

You can add running headers or footers to all pages or just to even or odd pages in a document. Headers and footers can include the page number, the date, the name of the document, or any other text you choose. While running heads usually appear either at the top or bottom of a page, Word allows you to place them anywhere on the page. You can even print a running head vertically in the right or left margin.

Tables of Contents   Word can automatically assemble a table of contents from special entries in your document. If you create an outline, Word can use the headings in the outline to produce multilevel tables of contents. If you do not create an outline, you can insert a special table code in the text that does not appear when the text is printed, but is used by Word to create a table of contents. If you want the entries in your table of contents to be different from the headings in your text, you can create hidden table of contents entries that do not appear in the text, but only in the table of contents. A macro supplied by Word makes it easy to designate entries for the table of contents.

Windows   Word allows you to maintain up to eight separate windows on a single screen. Windows can contain separate parts of the same document, separate documents, or differently formatted text such as footnotes and headers. You can make a window any size you want, including the size of the full screen, and you can easily toggle between windows. This allows you to edit a number of documents simultaneously, edit different parts of a document, or view both a footnote and the text to which it refers.

Footnotes and Annotations   Footnotes can be printed either at the bottom of the page where the footnote is referenced, or at the end of the chapter or document. Footnotes are numbered automatically; if you delete or add footnotes later, the numbers are changed accordingly. This makes it very convenient to create and use footnotes with your text. When you first create a footnote, it is displayed in a separate window below the text where the footnote reference occurs. You can open and close this window by selecting Window from Word's main menu. Whenever the footnote window is open, it contains the footnotes referenced in the text displayed on the screen.

In addition to footnotes, you can annotate your text with comments that can be deleted later. If several people comment on the same document, Word can keep track of each person's contributions. Like footnotes, annotations appear in a separate window that you can open and close. If you do not delete annotations before printing the document, they appear at the bottom of the page much like footnotes, and corresponding marks appear in the document to indicate where each comment belongs.

Macros   A macro is a special feature, similar to the redial feature on a telephone that lets you record keystrokes in a glossary file, and then replay those keystrokes over and over again. The macro can be assigned to a name or to a key sequence (for example, CTRL-c ch). Then, when you select the name from the glossary file or press the key sequence, the macro replays the keystrokes exactly as they were entered.

Besides recording macros, you can also enter your own keystroke representations in a document, and then save them in a glossary file. For example, the following sequence formats the current word as underlined:

```
<F8><Esc>fc<Tab2>y<Enter><<Macro to underline the current word>>
```

The entry presses the F8 key to select the current word. Next, the <Esc> entry presses the ESC key to active Word's menu. The F key chooses the Format command from the menu, and C chooses the Character option from the Format menu. The <Tab 2> entry presses the TAB key twice to move to the underline field, and Y chooses Yes in that field. The <Enter> entry presses RETURN to carry out the command. The text between the double angle brackets is a comment, and does not execute.

 NOTE If you want to get started with macros right away, you can use the **macros.glx** glossary file in **usr/lib/word/examples**. This file contains several examples of macros that you can use as is or modify to suit your own needs. Use the Transfer Glossary Load command to load the file into memory. Then, to see the list of available macros in the glossary file, select the Insert command and press F1. To choose a macro from the list, simply highlight the macro you want and press RETURN. Word executes the macro beginning at the current cursor location.

The previous example showed how you can use a macro to represent simple keystrokes. If that were all you could do with it, Word's macro feature would be severely limited; however, Word also offers several special macro instructions that let you change the flow of control in a macro or perform other special functions. For example, the IF...ELSE...ENDIF sequence lets you perform a conditional test in a macro and branch to a particular location within the macro based on the results of the test. Another example is the PAUSE command, which lets you interrupt a macro temporarily to enter text in the current command field or at the highlight in a document. Using these special instructions, you can create very sophisticated macros that let you stretch Word's power to the limit.

Glossaries   Glossaries are areas where you can store pieces of text that you want to use again. Text that you type often or specially formatted text is easily placed in a glossary entry for later retrieval. Macros are also saved as glossary entries. As you enter each piece of text or macro, you give it a name. When you want to retrieve the text or execute the macro, simply choose Insert from the main Word menu, press F1 to display a list of available glossary entries, and select the item of your choice. If the item is a glossary entry that contains text, the text will be inserted; if it is a macro, the macro will be executed.

Math   Word's math feature lets you perform simple math operations in normal text or in tables. For example, you can add, subtract, multiply, and divide numbers as well as calculate percentages. To activate Word's math feature anywhere in a document, enter two (or more) numbers separated by one or more mathematical symbols (for example, 300/20 or 15*40). Then, simply select the expression you want to evaluate to have Word calculate the answer. You can include both numbers and text in an expression. You can also enter the numbers included in an expression down or across columns.

When Word finishes calculating an answer, it places that answer in the scrap, the temporary buffer that normally holds text you have deleted from a document. The contents of the scrap appear within curly braces at the foot of the screen. You can copy the result of an expression from the scrap to any location in a document.

Outlining   Word is well known for its built-in outlining feature. As you know, an outline is a list of related ideas arranged in logical order of presentation. An outline is usually separate from the document that you produce with it, but unlike a typical outline, a Word outline is not a separate document; it is simply another view of the same document. You can flip back and forth between the full version of a document and the document outline with a single keystroke.

The main advantage of having the document and the outline connected is that it allows you to edit documents at the outline level. For example, if you move a heading to a new location, all the text associated with that heading moves too. Also, you can easily jump to a particular location in your document by moving within the outline.

Redlining As you revise a document in Word, it keeps track of all the changes you have made. To see the changes, you can turn Word's revision marks on. When revision marks are on, any text that you have deleted, inserted, moved, or replaced shows in the document, a feature known as *redlining*. Redlining makes it easy for you to compare the original version of your document with the edited version.

Spreadsheet Linking With Word, you can link all or part of an SCO Professional or Microsoft Multiplan file that is stored on disk to a specific location in your document. Then, if you later update the data in the spreadsheet file, the data in your document will be updated automatically the next time you load the document.

Style Sheets Word was the first word processor to incorporate style sheets. A *style sheet* is simply a way of storing the formatting characteristics of a document. Once you've saved a style sheet, you can apply it to other documents and those documents will automatically take on the same formatting as the original. Style sheets save you a lot of time, because they let you copy the formatting of one document to another without reentering individual settings.

Think of a style sheet as the overall design of a document. Within each style sheet is a collection of styles that you can apply to sections of text within your documents. As you can imagine, changing the style sheet attached to a document can dramatically alter the document's appearance.

Styles are integral to the way Word formats documents; in fact, Word uses a default set of styles unless you take steps to apply styles of your own choosing. Word comes with a variety of style sheets that you can use to format your documents. To access some samples, use the Format Stylesheet Attach command to attach one of the style sheet files in the **/usr/lib/word/examples** directory.

Autosave Word can automatically save all changes to your document at an interval you specify. This ensures that your changes will be saved even if the system crashes or shuts down unexpectedly.

File Formats   You can load files into Word whether they are in UNIX Word format, DOS Word format, or ASCII format. You can also save files in any of these three formats for use with other UNIX programs that cannot handle Word files.

SCO FoxBASE+

SCO FoxBASE+ is a fully functional relational database management system. It includes a comprehensive procedural programming language composed of English-like commands. You can use this language in two ways to create and manage multiple databases: you can enter commands and have FoxBASE+ respond to them interactively, or, you can create command files that contains multiple commands and have FoxBASE+ batch process them.

The command file approach allows you to create sophisticated applications that can guide other users through the process of editing information in one or more FoxBASE+ databases. In fact, your application can include custom forms and reports accessed by both text and pop-up menus, so that users can manage the database in a "see and select" environment.

SCO FoxBASE+ offers complete source and data file compatibility with the DOS version of FoxBASE+. In fact, it is basically the same product ported to the XENIX or UNIX environment. In addition, SCO FoxBASE+ is fully compatible with the source and data files generated by Ashton-Tate's popular dBASE III and dBASE III PLUS products, which run under DOS. If you have developed DOS applications under either FoxBASE+ or dBASE III, you should be able to use both the source code and the database files for those applications in SCO FoxBASE+ without modification.

 NOTE   FoxBASE+ resembles dBASE III PLUS very closely; so closely in fact, that the first page of the SCO FoxBASE+ manual recommends you find and read a text or manual on dBASE III before you attempt to use FoxBASE+. Obviously, if you are familiar with dBASE III, you'll feel right at home in FoxBASE+.

Once you've installed FoxBASE+, you start it by typing **foxplus** at the operating system prompt and pressing RETURN, which displays the screen shown in Figure 15-23. At the lower-left of the screen, just above the reverse video bar, is a dot, referred to as the *dot prompt*. This is the FoxBASE equivalent of the UNIX or XENIX system prompt. You type commands at this prompt to access the features of FoxBASE+ and to create and manage databases. Entering commands at the dot prompt is covered later in this chapter.

Creating a FoxBASE+ Database

Unlike SCO Integra, a FoxBASE database contains a single table. This table is simply called a database. A FoxBASE+ database is organized in rows and columns. Each row contains a record. A record contains all the information

Figure 15-23.

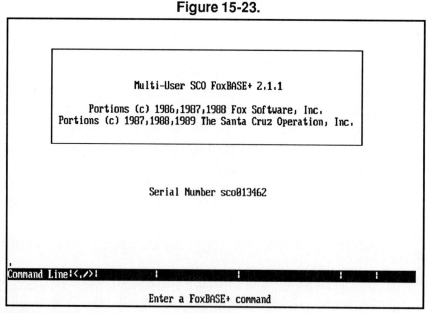

The FoxBASE+ Screen.

about a particular item in the database. Each column in the database table is called a *field*. Fields contain the individual pieces of information that make up each record. At the top of each column, or field, is a field name. Field names are used to reference information in specific columns when you query the database.

To create a database simply type **create** followed by a file name. For example, to create a database file named DONORS, you would type **create donors** at the dot prompt. FoxBASE+ then takes you to a special database design screen where you define the fields that will be included in the database. For each field you create you are prompted for a field name, a data type for the field, and its width in characters. You can choose from various field types, including character, numeric, date, logical, and memo fields. Character fields contain text, numeric fields contain numbers, date fields contain dates, and logical fields contain logical (true/false) data. Memo fields contain brief notes associated with a record. When you finish defining the fields in the database you press CTRL-w to exit the database design screen. FoxBASE+ then creates a database file under the name you specified and adds a .DBF extension, for example, DONORS.DBF.

The FoxBASE Dot Prompt

As mentioned, you can enter commands at the dot prompt that let you access the features of FoxBASE+, as well as create and manage databases. For example, imagine you have created a database entitled DONORS.DBF and you want to see its structure. To do this, you could type the following commands at the dot prompt, pressing RETURN after each one:

Command	Function
use donors	Opens the DONORS.DBF database
display structure	Combines the STRUCTURE phrase with the DISPLAY command to list the structure of the currently open database

The result of entering these commands is shown in Figure 15-24. Notice how FoxBASE+ responds interactively to commands as you enter them.

Now suppose you want to add records to the DONORS.DBF database, which is already open. To do this, type **edit** at the dot prompt and press RETURN. FoxBASE+ displays a default data entry form for the currently active database, similar to that shown in Figure 15-25. Initially, the field names for the database appear with blank data entry spaces next to them so that you can enter the information for the first record in the database. When you finish entering the data for the first record, FoxBASE+ automatically jumps to the next record, and so on. When you have finished adding records, press CTRL-w.

In addition to using the default form in Figure 15-25 to add records to a database, you can also use it to view and edit existing records. Alternatively, you can create a command file that displays a custom form of your own

Figure 15-24.

```
. use donors
. display stru
Structure for database: /u/bill/donors.dbf
Number of data records:      14
Date of last update   : 06/07/90
Field  Field Name  Type        Width    Dec
    1  FIRST_NAME  Character      10
    2  LAST_NAME   Character      15
    3  ADDRESS     Character      25
    4  CITY        Character      15
    5  STATE       Character       2
    6  ZIP         Numeric         5
    7  PHONE       Character      12
    8  DATE_GAVE   Date            8
    9  NO_UNITS    Numeric         3
   10  B_TYPE      Character       3
** Total **                      99
.
Command Line!<,/>!DONORS      !            !Rec: 1/14      !       !
                    Enter a FoxBASE+ command
```

Sample Commands Entered at the Dot Prompt.

Figure 15-25.

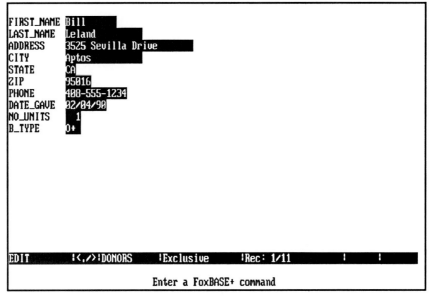

```
FIRST_NAME Bill
LAST_NAME  Leland
ADDRESS    3525 Sevilla Drive
CITY       Aptos
STATE      CA
ZIP        95016
PHONE      408-555-1234
DATE_GAVE  02/04/90
NO_UNITS        1
B_TYPE     0+



EDIT          |<,/>|DONORS     |Exclusive     |Rec: 1/11        |         |
                        Enter a FoxBASE+ command
```

A Default Form for Adding or Editing Records.

design for editing and viewing records. See "Creating a Command File Program" later in this chapter for details.

You can also enter commands at the dot prompt to query the database. For example, imagine you want to view the contents of selected fields in the DONORS.DBF database, which is already open. To do this, you can use the DISPLAY command followed by a fields list, as shown in Figure 15-26.

Notice in each of the preceding examples that a database must be open in order to apply commands to it. FoxBASE+ allows you to have up to ten databases open at any time, but only one of those databases can be the active database; thus, you can apply commands to only one database at a time.

There are many more commands you can enter at the dot prompt to manage information in a FoxBASE+ database. In fact, the examples in this section don't even scratch the surface, but they do give you a hint of the dot prompt's interactive power.

Figure 15-26.

```
. use donors
. display all first_name,last_name,date_gave
Record#  FIRST_NAME LAST_NAME      DATE_GAVE
      1  Bill       Leland         02/04/90
      2  Sharon     Smith          04/06/90
      3  Ed         Hambrick       09/13/90
      4  Ross       Gates          04/05/90
      5  Bob        Greensberg     08/09/90
      6  Martin     Yein           03/02/90
      7  Eric       Michels        09/16/90
      8  Jane       Thomas         02/03/90
      9  Grace      Jamsa          03/15/90
     10  Amy        Mathers        05/15/90
     11  Pamela     Adams          04/07/90

.
Command Line!<,/>!DONORS      !              !Rec: EOF/11      !      !

              Enter a FoxBASE+ command
```

Using the DISPLAY Command to Query a Database.

Creating a Command File Program

After you've used FoxBASE+ for even a short time, you'll want to leave the dot prompt behind and do some command file programming. Command files are simply text files that contain a series of FoxBASE+ commands. Once a command file is prepared, you can run it and FoxBASE+ will process the commands it contains.

To create a command file, enter **modify command** at the dot prompt followed by a name for the file. For example, to create a command file named DONOR, type **modify command donor** at the dot prompt and press RETURN. When you press RETURN, FoxBASE+ takes you to its on-board text editor. You can then begin typing the commands that will make up your command file. For example, Figure 15-27 shows the FoxBASE+ text editor with a command file already underway. When you have finished creating the command file, press CTRL-W to save it. FoxBASE+ saves the file under

Figure 15-27.

```
Edit: /u/bill/donor.prg

 CURSOR  <— —>            UP   DOWN     DELETE        Insert Mode:  ^V
  Char:  ^S  ^L   Field:  ^E   ^X   Char:    ^G       Insert line:  ^N
  Word:  ^A  ^F   Page:   ^R   ^C   Word:    ^T       Save: ^W Abort: ^Q
  Line:  ^Z  ^B   Find:   ^KF  Line:    ^Y            Readfile:     ^KR
  Reformat: ^KB   Refind: ^KL                         Writefile:    ^KW


CLEAR                       &&Clear the Screen                      <
STORE " " TO Menu           &&Create two variables                 <
STORE 0 to Number                                                  <
USE Donors                  &&Activate the Donors database          <
APPEND BLANK                &&Append a blank record                 <
                                                                   <
* Start a DO WHILE--ENDO loop                                       <
                                                                   <
DO WHILE Menu<>"q"                                                  <
                                                                   <
* Display a custom form for data entry                             <
                                                                   <
@1,20 SAY"Donor Data Entry Screen"                                 <
@2,20 SAY"==========================="                             <
@4,10 SAY " Firstname: " GET FIRST_NAME                            <
```

The FoxBASE+ Text Editor.

the name you've specified, this time adding a .PRG extension, for example DONOR.PRG. To run the program, use the DO command at the dot prompt followed by the name of the command file. For example, to run the DONOR.PRG file, you would type **do donor** and press RETURN.

Figure 15-28 shows an example command file that is used to display the custom form and menu shown in Figure 15-29. Briefly, the command file in Figure 15-28 works as follows: The CLEAR command in the first line of the command file blanks the screen. Next, the STORE command creates two variables named Menu and Number, respectively. Variables allow you to store information temporarily. Later in the program, these variables will be used to capture user input. Next, the command USE Donors activates the DONORS.DBF database. The command APPEND BLANK adds a new blank record to the DONORS.DBF database. Next, a DO WHILE...ENDDO loop begins.

The DO WHILE...ENDDO command sequence causes the program to run in a continuous loop. The DO WHILE command defines the beginning

Figure 15-28.

```
CLEAR                           &&Clear the Screen
STORE " " TO Menu               &&Create two variables
STORE 0 to Number
USE Donors                      &&Activate the Donors database
APPEND BLANK                    &&Append a blank record

* Start a DO WHILE—ENDO loop

DO WHILE Menu<>"q"

* Display a custom form for data entry

@1,20 SAY"Donor Data Entry Screen"
@2,20 SAY"========================="
@4,10 SAY " Firstname: " GET FIRST_NAME
@6,10 SAY "  Lastname: " GET LAST_NAME
@8,10 SAY "    Address: " GET ADDRESS
@10,10 SAY "        City: " GET CITY
@10,40 SAY "  State: " GET STATE
@10,55 SAY "Zip: " GET ZIP
@12,10 SAY "        Date: " GET DATE_GAVE
@14,10 SAY "       Units: " GET NO_UNITS
@16,10 SAY"        Type: " GET B_TYPE
READ

* Present a menu
STORE " " to Menu
@18,10 SAY"(A)dd record, (E)dit record, (G)oto record,
(Q)uit: " GET Menu
READ

* Respond to the menu

DO CASE
    CASE UPPER(Menu)="A"
        APPEND BLANK
        LOOP
    CASE UPPER(Menu)="E"
        CLEAR
        LOOP
    CASE UPPER(Menu)="G"
        @19,10 SAY"Enter the record number: " GET Number
        READ
        GOTO Number
```

A Sample Command File.

Figure 15-28.

```
        CLEAR
        LOOP
     CASE  UPPER(Menu)="Q"
        CLEAR
        RETURN
     OTHERWISE
        CLEAR
        LOOP
  ENDCASE
  ENDDO
  RETURN
```

A Sample Command File (continued)

of the loop and the ENDDO command marks the end of the loop. (Notice that the ENDDO command appears in the second-to-last line of the program.) The DO WHILE command also states a condition. As long as this condition remains true, the program will continue looping. In this case the condition is, DO WHILE Menu <>"q". As long as the Menu variable is not equal to "q", FoxBASE+ will continue to process the loop.

The code within the DO WHILE...ENDDO loop commands is used to display the custom form and menu in Figure 15-29. To display the form, a series of @...SAY...GET commands are used. The @...SAY portion of the command allows you to position text on the screen, and the GET portion allows you to display a field from a database for data entry. The user can then enter the information for each field of the new record.

You can also use the @...SAY...GET command to display a text message and to present a variable for data entry. For example, in the command file in Figure 15-28, the line

```
@18,10 SAY"(A)dd record, (E)dit record, (G)oto record, (Q)uit: "
Get Menu
```

displays the menu shown at the bottom of Figure 15-29. When the user types a response, the keystroke is captured in the Menu memory variable. The program then assesses the user's response by evaluating the contents of the Menu memory variable.

Figure 15-29.

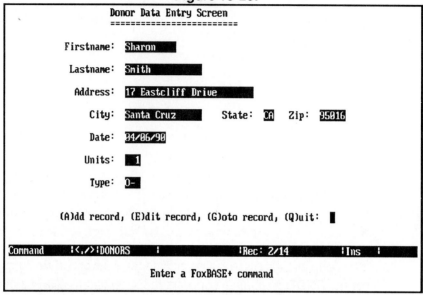

A Custom Form and Menu Created by the Command File in Figure 15-28.

To evaluate the contents of the Menu memory variable, the DO CASE...OTHERWISE...ENDCASE command sequence is used. This command sequence allows you to evaluate several possible events and respond differently to each one. For example, if the user presses A to select (A)dd record from the menu, the letter *a* is stored in the Menu memory variable. The first CASE statement in the DO CASE...ENDCASE command sequence anticipates this event. The commands following the first CASE statement are then executed. For example, the APPEND BLANK command is used to add a new blank record to the database, and the LOOP command then loops back to the beginning of the DO WHILE...ENDDO loop and again displays the custom form for data entry. Similar CASE statements are used to set traps for the E, G, and Q keystrokes. Pressing E allows the user to edit the same record, pressing G allows the user to jump to a specific record number, and pressing Q ends the program.

The command file in Figure 15-28 is relatively short and performs a fairly simple task, using only a handful of the hundreds of commands available in the FoxBASE+ language. In practice, FoxBASE+ command files can be quite lengthy and perform functions that are extremely sophisticated. You can even create multiple command files for a given application.

Using Multiple Databases

As mentioned, FoxBASE+ allows you to have up to ten databases open at once. Each database you open is stored in a separate work area. Although you can easily switch back and forth between open databases, only one database at a time can be the active database—the database to which you apply commands.

You can also relate one database to another using the SET RELATION TO command. This command allows you to use the contents of a field that is common to both databases (often called a *key* field) to match records across databases. The key field contains a text string or number that uniquely identifies each record in the database. For example, if you were creating a database system to maintain employee records, you might assign each employee a unique employee number. The key fields in both databases must contain the same information. Once the relationship is established, FoxBASE+ can match a record in one database to the associated record in another database by using the unique information in the key field. Thus, in the previous example, you could simultaneously access records for a given employee in two or more databases.

Indexes

FoxBASE+ also supports the use of index files. Index files allow you to sort the information in a database based on the contents of one or more of its fields so that FoxBASE+ can search the database more rapidly.

FoxBASE+ uses index files much as you use an index in a book. Rather then leafing through page-by-page to find a specific topic, you go directly to the index to find the topic quickly. In the same way, FoxBASE+ accesses an index file to locate information quickly in a database.

Format Files

Once you begin command file programming you'll inevitably start looking for shortcuts to make your job easier. One shortcut you might want to consider is the use of format files. Format files, which have an .FMT extension, allow you to create a custom form for display. Once you've created a format file, you can call it from any program at any time. Thus, you can create a form only once, and reuse it whenever you need to.

Labels

FoxBASE+ also allows you to create custom labels for mailings. In fact, a special utility is provided just for this purpose. The label utility allows you to create label files that are associated with a particular database. Label files, which have an .LBL extension, let you describe the label you want to create in great detail. You can indicate what fields from the database you want included in the label, and you can also specify different sizes for labels, margins, lines between labels, and so on. You can even print labels up to four across.

To access the label utility, enter the CREATE LABEL command at the dot prompt followed by a name for the label file. For example, to create a label file name DONOR.LBL, type **create label donor** at the dot prompt. The label utility screen will then appear, and you can define the attributes for the label you want to create.

As mentioned, you can call a label file into use from any program. For example, you might create a program that indexes the database, initializes the printer, and prints selected records in the database using your custom label as a guide.

Reports

FoxBASE+ provides a powerful report design utility. This utility lets you design a custom report and save it to a file with an .FRM extension. Report files are always associated with a particular database file.

To access the report utility, enter the CREATE REPORT command at the dot prompt followed by the name you want to use for the report file. For example, to create a report named DONOR.FRM, type **create report donor** and press RETURN.

The report utility allows you to specify various layout and formatting options for reports. For example, you can specify a title for the report, the default left and right margins, the page width, and the number of lines per page.

Reports are composed of up to 24 columns. The report utility lets you specify a header for each column, as well as the field or fields from the database you want to use for that column. You can build an expression for a column that incorporates more than one field in the database. In addition, you can specify subtotals at both the group and subgroup levels, as well as a grand total for the entire report.

As with label files, you can call a report file into use from any program. Here again, you might create a program that indexes the database, initializes the printer, and prints selected records in the database, this time using your custom report as a guide.

Compiling FoxBASE+ Programs

You can also compile FoxBASE+ command files. In FoxBASE+, standard command files and compiled files run at the same speed. However, compiled files are loaded into memory much faster than standard command files; therefore, if you are developing a multiple-file application, you gain a distinct speed advantage by compiling your command files.

Installing the SCO Business Series Software

To install the products in the SCO business software series, you use the **custom** program. This versatile program provides a menu-driven interface for installing all of the products in the SCO Office Portfolio as well as standalone products, such as Microsoft Word or FoxBASE+.

To run the custom program, you must log in as root and give the root password. You can then type **custom** and press RETURN. The custom program starts and the following menu choices appear on your screen:

1. Operating System

2. Development System

3. Text Processing System

4. Add a Supported Product

Select a set to customize or enter q to quit:

To add a business series product, select 2, Add a Supported Product. The custom program will display a message similar to this:

Installing custom data files...

Insert distribution volume 1

and then press RETURN or q to quit:

Insert volume 1 of the product you want to install in drive A, and then press RETURN. You'll see the following menu choices:

1. Install one or more packages

2. Remove one or more packages

3. List the available packages

4. List the files in a package

5. Install a single file

6. Select a new set to customize

7. Display current disk usage

8. Help

Select an option or enter q to quit:

Select 1, Install one or more packages, and press RETURN. The various packages in the product you are installing will be displayed on your screen. You can elect to install all the packages associated with a particular product, or just selected packages. Initially, it is recommended that you install all the packages; if you find that you do not need a particular package, you can always remove it later. To install all the packages, type **all** and press RETURN. You will then be prompted to insert each of the distribution disks associated with the product you are installing, and the appropriate files will be copied to your hard disk.

Once the files have been copied, you will be prompted for a serial number and an activation key code. These should be on a separate, brightly colored card that came with the software. Type the serial number and activation key code when you are requested to do so, and the custom program will complete the installation. During this process you may be requested to respond to information specific to the product you are installing. For example, you may be asked whether you want to relink the kernel or choose drivers for your specific equipment set.

When you are finished installing a product, put the activation card in a safe place where you can find it again. If you ever have to remove the installed product for some reason, you'll need the activation key card to reinstall it.

You can also use the custom program to remove a product from the system. In fact, this is very easy to do. For example, imagine you've installed SCO Lyrix and need to remove it for some reason. Simply start the custom program in the usual way. You'll see the following menu:

1. Operating System

2. Development System

3. Text Processing System

4. Add a Supported Product

5. SCO Lyrix

Select a set to customize or enter q to quit:

Select 5 and press RETURN. The following menu will appear:

1. Install one or more packages

2. Remove one or more packages

3. List the available packages

4. List the files in a package

5. Install a single file

6. Select a new set to customize

7. Display current disk usage

8. Help

Select an option or enter q to quit:

Select 2 and press RETURN. The custom program then allows you to indicate which packages associated with SCO Lyrix you want to remove. You can remove all of the packages or just selected ones.

Disk space is always an issue when you are installing the products in the SCO business series, but this is especially true if you are installing on the SCO UNIX/386 operating system. You can check the documentation for each product to see approximately how much disk space it requires, or see Appendix B of this book, which contains a summary of product sizes. This appendix will show you at a glance the approximate amount of disk space required to install one or more products.

This chapter has provided a brief overview of the products in SCO's business software series. To learn more about these packages, consult the individual manuals that accompany each product.

A P P E N D I X

Command Reference

This appendix briefly explains the functions of many SCO UNIX commands. Related commands are grouped together, and you'll find the chapter or chapters in which each command is discussed listed after each description, so you can refer to the appropriate chapter for details. You can also refer to the *SCO UNIX User's Reference* or to the on-line **man** pages for more information about these commands.

XENIX   On XENIX, you can also use **help** to get a brief explanation of any command. Type

   help *command*

where *command* is the name of the command that you want information about.

Communication

mail	Allows you to send and receive electronic mail (see Chapters 2 and 9).
mesg	Allows or denies messages sent to your terminal (see Chapter 2).
who	Lists the users currently logged on to the system (see Chapter 2).
hello	Writes directly to another user's terminal (see Chapter 2).
write	Writes directly to another user's terminal (see Chapter 2).
cu	Calls another UNIX system (see Chapter 13).
uucp	Transfers files between UNIX systems (see Chapter 13).

Text Processing

nroff	Formats text for printing on a line printer or letter-quality printer (see Chapter 7).
pr	Divides files into pages (see Chapters 6 and 8).
sed	Edits files noninteractively (see Chapter 6).
vi	Invokes the visual text editor (see Chapter 7).
lyrix	Invokes Lyrix, the word processor supplied with the SCO UNIX Office Portfolio Suite (see Chapter 15).
word	Invokes Word, the Microsoft word processor available for both SCO UNIX and XENIX (see Chapter 15).

File and Directory Management

cat	Creates, joins, and displays files or standard input (see Chapters 4 and 6).
cd	Changes the user's current directory (see Chapter 4).
chgrp	Changes the group ID of a file (see Chapter 4).
chmod	Changes the read, write, and execute permissions on files and directories (see Chapter 4).
chown	Changes the ownership of a file or directory (see Chapter 4).
cp	Makes copies of files (see Chapter 4).
cpio	Copies files into and out of archives for storage, moving, or backups (see Chapter 12).
file	Examines a file or directory and reports what type of file it is (see Chapter 4).
find	Recursively searches directories for files that meet certain criteria (see Chapter 4).
grep, egrep, fgrep	Search standard input for specified regular expressions (see Chapter 6).
ls	Lists the contents of directories (see Chapter 4).
mkdir	Creates a directory (see Chapter 4).
mv	Moves and renames files, and renames directories (see Chapter 4).
pwd	Prints the full pathname of the current directory (see Chapter 4).
rm	Removes files and directories (see Chapter 4).
rmdir	Removes directories (see Chapter 4).

split	Splits a file into pieces of equal length (see Chapter 6).
tar	Saves and restores files to and from archive media (see Chapter 12).
umask	Sets the file creation mode mask (see Chapter 4).
uucp	Transfers files between UNIX systems (see Chapter 13).

System Information

cal	Prints a calendar (see Chapter 3).
date	Prints or sets the current time and date (see Chapter 3).
id	Prints your user and group ID names and numbers (see Chapter 3).
news	Displays system news items (see Chapter 3).
ps	Reports the processes a user has running (see Chapter 5).
tty	Prints the pathname of a terminal's device file (see Chapter 3).

Data Manipulation

awk	Scans for patterns and performs actions on lines of input (see Chapter 6).
echo	Reads arguments and displays them on the standard output (see Chapters 10 and 11).
head	Gives the first few lines of input as output (see Chapter 6).
more	Displays files one screenful at a time (see Chapter 6).
pg	Displays files for reading one screenful at a time (see Chapter 6).

pr   Divides files into pages (see Chapters 6 and 8).

sed   Edits files noninteractively (see Chapter 6).

sort   Alphabetizes lines according to the ASCII collating sequence and merges files (see Chapter 6).

split   Splits a file into pieces of equal length (see Chapter 6).

tail   Gives the last few lines of input as output (see Chapter 6).

tee   Pipes the standard input to both the standard output and to specified files (see Chapter 5).

uniq   Prints one occurrence of each input line, even if that line is duplicated (see Chapter 6).

Process Control

at, batch, crontab   Executes commands at a later time (see Chapter 12).

kill   Terminates a process (see Chapter 5).

ps   Reports process status (see Chapter 5).

Terminal Control

clear   Clears the user's terminal screen (see Chapter 3).

lock   Locks a user terminal (see Chapter 3).

mesg   Allows or denies messages sent to your terminal (see Chapter 3).

stty   Displays and sets terminal parameters (see Chapter 3).

tty   Prints the pathname of a terminal's device file (see Chapter 3).

Printing

lp	Sends and cancels requests to a line printer (see Chapter 8).
lpstat	Reports the status of the **lp** printing service (see Chapter 8).
pr	Divides files into pages (see Chapter 8).

Shell Management

csh	Invokes the C shell command interpreter (see Chapter 10).
sh	Invokes the Bourne shell command interpreter (see Chapter 11).
su	Temporarily switches your effective user ID to that of another user (see Chapter 12).

Business Applications

foxplus	Invokes SCO FoxBASE+, a relational database management system offering source language and data file compatibility with dBASE 3PLUS (see Chapter 15).
image	Invokes SCO ImageBuilder, a graphics presentation package that allows you to create graphics, charts, diagrams, and slides (see Chapter 15).
integra	Invokes SCO Integra, a SQL-based relational database management system (see Chapter 15).
lyrix	Invokes SCO Lyrix, the word processor included in the Office Portfolio Suite (see Chapter 15).

op   Invokes the Office Portfolio Manager, a menu interface that gives you access to the products in the SCO Office Portfolio Suite (see Chapter 15).

pro, procalc   Invokes SCO Professional, the spreadsheet program included in the SCO Office Portfolio Suite (see Chapter 15).

Software Reference

This appendix lists the sizes of most SCO UNIX and SCO XENIX software packages. Use this table to determine the size of the hard disk you will need to install all the software you want. Sizes are given in both blocks (as listed in the release notes for each product) and in approximate megabytes. To get the exact size in megabytes, divide the number of blocks by 2000. Packages under 0.1MB are not listed.

XENIX and UNIX Operating Systems

Package	Size in Blocks	Approximate Megabytes	Name
SCO UNIX Operating System Packages			
ALL	52844	26	Entire operating system set
RTS	24366	12 '	UNIX run-time system
LINK	4720	2	System V link kit files
BACKUP	314	0.2	System backup and recovery tools
BASE	2162	1	Basic extended utility set
DOS	504	0.3	DOS utilities
EX	494	0.3	The **ex** and **vi** editors
FILE	1122	0.6	File manipulation tools
LAYERS	372	0.2	System V layers
LPR	3824	2	Multiple line-printer spooler
MAIL	5350	2.7	Electronic mail and Micnet
MAN	3450	1.7	Operating system manual pages
MAPCHAN	238	0.1	International character-set mapping
SYSADM	1290	0.6	Additional system administration tools
TPLOT	610	0.3	Tplot, Graph, and Spline
UUCP	2280	1	**uucp** and **cu** communications utilities
UPD.UFA	3578	1.8	V/386 Maintenance Release Update A
SCO XENIX Operating System Packages			
ALL	16344	8	Entire operating system set
LINK	2112	1	The link kit

Package	Size in Blocks	Approximate Megabytes	Name
RTS	4742	2	XENIX run-time system
BASE	1242	0.6	Basic extended utility set
BACKUP	306	0.2	System backup and recovery tools
SYSADM	1496	0.7	System administration tools
FILE	528	0.3	File manipulation tools
LPR	552	0.3	Multiple line-printer spooler
IMAGEN	228	0.1	Imagen laser printer support
MAIL	648	0.3	Electronic mail and Micnet
DOS	364	0.2	DOS utilities
VSH	266	0.1	The visual shell
EX	332	0.2	The **ex** and **vi** editors
UUCP	2008	1	**uucp** and **cu** communications utilities
TERMINF	500	0.3	Terminfo database
HELP	520	0.3	Help utility and related files

SCO XENIX Manual (man) Pages

Package	Size in Blocks	Approximate Megabytes	Name
ALL	3218	1.6	Entire set of on-line manual pages and utilities.

Business Applications

Package	Size in Blocks	Approximate Megabytes	Name

SCO XENIX and UNIX Manager

Package	Size in Blocks	Approximate Megabytes	Name
ALL	11598	6	All available packages

Package	Size in Blocks	Approximate Megabytes	Name
MGR	7026	3.5	SCO Manager
CGI	2390	1	SCO CGI drivers
EGA	414	0.2	SCO CGI EGA drivers
TRANS	1648	0.8	SCO translators

SCO XENIX and UNIX Integra

ALL	4852	2	Integra

SCO XENIX and UNIX Lyrix

ALL	5184	2.5	All available packages

SCO XENIX and UNIX Professional Spreadsheet

ALL	4572	2.3	SCO Professional—all available packages

SCO XENIX and UNIX FoxBASE

ALL	2036	1	All FoxBASE+ packages
FOX	1962	1	FoxBASE+ database management system

Microsoft Word

ALL	7676	3.8	All Microsoft Word packages
WORD	3170	1.6	Microsoft Word
DICT	1168	0.6	Microsoft Word dictionaries
TOOLS	512	0.3	Microsoft Word tools
PRINT	2706	1.4	Microsoft Word printers

SCO XENIX and UNIX Multiview Run-time System

ALL	852	0.4	All available packages
MVWRTS	750	0.4	SCO Multiview run-time system

Software Development

Package	Size in Blocks	Approximate Megabytes	Name
SCO UNIX Software Development System			
ALL	31774	16	Entire Development System set
SOFT	14796	7	Basic software development tools
386XDEV	1442	0.7	XENIX 386 cross development libraries
286XDEV	4244	2	XENIX 286 cross development libraries
DOSDEV	2274	1	DOS cross development utilities and libraries
OS2DEV	3838	2	OS/2 cross development libraries and utilities
MAN	2740	1.4	Development System manual pages
LINT	566	0.3	Syntax and usage check files and tools
SBS	896	0.4	Source code control system
SAMPLE	230	0.1	Sample device drivers
SCO UNIX cgi Drivers Packages			
ALL	7994	4	SCO CGI extended package
286	620	0.3	SCO CGI 286 libraries
386	412	0.2	SCO CGI 386 libraries
DRIVER	5358	2.7	SCO CGI drivers
TEST	1124	0.6	SCO CGI test files
EGA	378	0.2	SCO CGI EGA driver

Package	Size in Blocks	Approximate Megabytes	Name
SCO XENIX Software Development Packages			
ALL	14922	7	Entire Development System set
SOFT	8428	4	Basic software development tools
CREF	466	0.2	Cross reference programs
CFLOW	114	0.1	Generates C flow graphs
LINT	418	0.2	Syntax and usage check files and tools
SMALL	508	0.3	Small model 8086/286 library routines
MEDIUM	530	0.3	Medium model 8086/286 library routines
COMPACT	544	0.3	Compact Model 8086/286 library routines
LARGE	564	0.3	Large model 8086/286 library routines
SBS	664	0.3	Source code control system
DOSDEV	2272	1	DOS cross development libraries and utilities
HELP	138	0.1	Help utility and related files

Communications

Package	Size in Blocks	Approximate Megabytes	Name
SCO XENIX tcp/ip Packages			
ALL	4904	2	SCO TCP/IP run-time

Package	Size in Blocks	Approximate Megabytes	Name
TCPRT	4568	2	SCO TCP/IP run-time utilities and drivers
MAILCF	266	0.1	Sample sendmail configuration files
UPD.UFA	216	0.1	SCO TCP/IP run-time maintenance
RUNTIME	282	0.1	Streams run-time

SCO XENIX uunet Packages

Package	Size in Blocks	Approximate Megabytes	Name
ALL	2962	1.5	Entire UUNET/USENET news set
NEWS	1486	0.7	The basic news utilities
RN	276	0.1	The **rn** program for reading news
NEWSMAN	400	0.2	On-line manual pages for news and **rn**
NEWSDOC	710	0.4	Documentation for news
ALL	5304	2.7	SCO CGI Extended package
286	720	0.4	SCO CGI 286 libraries
386	240	0.1	SCO CGI 386 libraries
DRIVER	3830	2	SCO CGI drivers
EGA	346	0.2	SCO CGI EGA driver

Text Processing

Package	Size in Blocks	Approximate Megabytes	Name

SCO XENIX Text Processing System

Package	Size in Blocks	Approximate Megabytes	Name
ALL	2794	1	Entire text processing set
TEXT	828	0.4	Basic text processing commands

Package	Size in Blocks	Approximate Megabytes	Name
EQN	154	0.1	Math equation formatter
MANMAC	172	0.1	Man macro package
SPELL	372	0.2	Spelling checker
NROFF	206	0.1	**nroff** formatting tools and tables
TROFF	232	0.1	**troff** formatting tools, tables, and fonts

INDEX

The manuscript for this book was prepared and
submitted to Osborne/McGraw-Hill in electronic
form. The acquisitions editor for this project was
Elizabeth Fisher, the technical reviewer was
Jeff Lieberman, and the project editor
was Madhu Prasher.

This book was designed by Marcela Hancik,
using Times Roman for text body and Swiss
boldface for display.

Typesetting, screen dumps, and technical illustrations
were done by Peter Hancik - EuroDesign.

Cover art is by Bay Graphics Design Associates, Inc.
The Color separation and cover supplier was
Phoenix Color Corporation. Screens were produced
with Inset, from InSet Systems, Inc.
This book was printed and bound by R.R. Donnelley
& Sons Company, Crawfordsville, Indiana.